In this innovative volume, Jerry D. Moore discusses public architecture in the context of the cultural, political, and religious life of the prehispanic Andes. Archaeologists have invested enormous effort in excavating and documenting prehistoric buildings, but analytical approaches to architecture remain as yet underdeveloped. *Architecture and Power in the Ancient Andes* uses new analytical methods to approach architecture and its relationship to Andean society, exploring three themes in particular: the architecture of monuments, the architecture of ritual, and the architecture of social control. It provides both a methodology for the study of public architecture and an example of how that methodology can be applied. The author's clear and richly illustrated discussion represents an original perspective on architecture and its role in ritual, ideology, and power in the ancient world.

NEW STUDIES IN ARCHAEOLOGY

Architecture and power in the Ancient Andes

The archaeology of public buildings

NEW STUDIES IN ARCHAEOLOGY

Series editors
Clive Gamble, *University of Southampton*
Colin Renfrew, *University of Cambridge*
Jeremy Sabloff, *University of Pennsylvania Museum of Anthropology and Archaeology*

Archaeology has made enormous advances recently, both in the volume of discoveries and in its character as an intellectual discipline: new techniques have helped to further the range and rigour of inquiry, and encouraged inter-disciplinary communication.

The aim of this series is to make available to a wider audience the results of these developments. The coverage is worldwide and extends from the earliest hunting and gathering societies to historical archaeology.

For a list of titles in the series please see the end of the book.

JERRY D. MOORE

California State University, Dominguez Hills

Architecture and power in the Ancient Andes

The archaeology of public buildings

Published by the Press Syndicate of the University of Cambridge
The Pitt Building, Trumpington Street, Cambridge CB2 1RP
40 West 20th Street, New York, NY 10011–4211, USA
10 Stamford Road, Oakleigh, Melbourne 3166, Australia

First published 1996

Printed in Great Britain at the University Press, Cambridge

A catalogue record for this book is available from the British Library

Library of Congress cataloguing in publication data

Moore, Jerry D.
    Architecture and power in the ancient Andes: the archaeology of
public buildings / Jerry D. Moore
        p.   cm. – (New studies in archaeology)
    Includes bibliographical references and index.
    ISBN 0 521 55363 6 (hc)
        1. Indian architecture – Andes Region.   2. Indians of South
America – Andes Region – Politics and government.   3. Indians of South
America – Andes Region – Rites and ceremonies.   4. Andes Region –
Antiquities.   I. Title.   II. Series.
    F2230.1.A5M66   1996
    720'.98 – dc20   95-44357   CIP

ISBN 0 521 55363 6 hardback

CONTENTS

FIGURES

TABLES

ACKNOWLEDGMENTS

This book was written during a 1992–93 fellowship in Precolumbian Studies at the Dumbarton Oaks Research Library and Collection in Washington DC. Simply, this study would not have been written without the support, superb resources, and most of all the *time* which the Dumbarton Oaks fellowship made available. I wish to thank Dr. Angeliki Laiou, Director, for preserving and enriching the stimulating intellectual environment at Dumbarton Oaks. I am deeply indebted to Dr. Elizabeth Boone, then Director of Precolumbian Studies, for her interest, critical readings, and continuous encouragement of my research. I would like to acknowledge the support of the Senior Fellows in Precolumbian Studies: Dr. Barbara Voorhies, Dr. Heather Lechtman, Dr. Jeremy Sabloff, Dr. Richard Burger, and Dr. Cecelia Klein. Mrs. Brigit Toledo was an enormously helpful guide to the fine Precolumbian studies library at Dumbarton Oaks, and Dr. Carol Callaway and Ms. Janice Williams helped me in numerous ways throughout my stay.

The ideas in this book were developed in conversations with the other fellows in Precolumbian Studies at Dumbarton Oaks. Ruth Shady Solís was a source of valuable insights into Peruvian archaeology, particularly on the Formative period. I also appreciate Ruth's insistence on rigor in argument and evidence, and I was saved from several false steps by her penetrating critiques. Brian Billman shared unpublished survey from the Moche Valley and his knowledge of North Coast archaeology. Mary Pye drew on her knowledge of Mesoamerican archaeology to offer valuable critiques of my ideas. I also learned a great deal from other fellows and staff associated with Dumbarton Oaks, particularly Timothy Davis, who introduced me to the literature on the phenomenology of landscape.

I also have benefited from the ideas and comments of a number of fellow Andeanists, including Richard Burger, Christine Hastorf, Ulana Klymyshyn, Carol Mackey, Joanne Pillsbury, Thomas Pozorski, and Shelia Pozorski.

I would like to acknowledge the administrators and faculty at California State University, Dominguez Hills, who approved my leave from teaching responsibilities and supported this project, particularly Dr. Yolanda Moses and Dr. Richard Palmer. I also thank my colleagues, Sandra Orellana and Robert Franklin, for their interest and support.

I particularly appreciate Christopher Donnan for providing me with photographs of a Chimu architectural model and permission to reprint the photograph, and for reading the section on Pacatnamú. I also want to thank Alan Kolata for allowing me to reproduce his illustration of the formal typology of U-shaped rooms.

I was very fortunate to have Jessica Kuper as my editor at Cambridge University Press; her judgment and interest improved this book. I am also grateful to Margaret Deith, whose careful copy-editing winnowed errors of typography, style and logic; I deeply appreciate the care Dr. Deith has given my book.

I also very much appreciated the comments on early drafts made by Garth Bawden and two anonymous reviewers for Cambridge University Press. Of course, any errors of fact or omission are my own.

I am most indebted to Janine Gasco, who patiently supported this project and tolerated me during the writing of this book. As this project developed, so has our young son, Nathan, and I dedicate this book to Jan and Nathan as a small gesture of my deep thanks and love.

I

The contemplation of ruins: archaeological approaches to architecture

At this time the fortress serves only as a witness of what it once was.
Cieza de Leon, 1550–52, on the site of Paramonga

Ancient traces of stone suggest humans have lived in buildings for at least 350,000 years. If the features and dates from the Paleolithic site of Terra Amata, France, are interpreted correctly (de Lumley 1969; cf. Villa 1983), early humans built small, temporary huts of saplings, cobbles, and brush on the edge of the Mediterranean during the Holstein interglacial. More permanent dwellings date from ca. 12,000–10,000 bp, as proto-agricultural Natufian peoples crowded around permanent springs in the post-Pleistocene Levant (Henry 1989) and sedentary hunters and gatherers using Jomon pottery settled the forested river valleys of the Japanese islands (Aikens and Higuchi 1982; Pearson 1986; Watanabe 1986). An unbroken legacy of human buildings stretches from the massive walls and tower built 9,350 years ago at Jericho, perhaps the oldest example of communal construction (Kenyon 1952, 1972; cf. Mellaart 1975; Bar-Yosef 1986), to the Louisiana Superdome, the world's largest arena with seats for 95,000. And with an apparent inevitability which is simply an artifact of hindsight, humans translated early dwellings into other architectural forms as rooms served as burial crypts, pithouses became kivas (Cordell 1979: 134; Scully 1975), and houses of men were transformed into dwellings of gods (Bukert 1988; Fox 1988). Over the last 10,000 years, the built environment has become coterminous with the human environment, as people have raised artificial boundaries defining private and public, secular and sacred spaces.

As we move through this constructed reality, it is rare to consider architecture except in a personal manner, as series of ugly strip malls, imposing skyscrapers, or comforting homes that we use, view, or live in but rarely think much about. When some commentary is required, a historic building may be dubbed "interesting," a national monument described by the patriotic feelings it elicits, or a home characterized as spacious, tiny, or comfy. Simply, these buildings have become such an integral part of our cultural existence that it is hard to think of them as something separate from our Self. We are usually, to use Edward Relph's (1976) apt phrase, "existential insiders."

Yet, the patterns and meanings of architecture stand separate from personal experience. How could I or any other outsider correctly intuit that an Ainu house on Sakhalin Island was oriented to the dwelling place of the forest deities

(Ohnuki-Tierney 1972) or that the longhouses of the Pirá-paraná of lowland Colombia (Hugh-Jones 1979: 238–251) are alternately thought of as a model of the universe, a womb, and an enormous bird with the head of a tapir? Would it be possible to identify the significance of Navaho hogans in the Blessingway ceremonies (Jett and Spencer 1981: 14)? How could any foreigner recognize that the small hole in the dirt floor of a Hopi kiva was an opening into the underworld, the navel of original emergence (Frigout 1979: 568)? Is it true (Griaule and Dieterlen 1954) or false (Van Beek 1991) that the organization of the Dogon house is based on body symbolism, and how could an outsider's ethnographically uninformed architectural experience lead to either conclusion? And specifically, how could an archaeologist learn such emic knowledge?

These examples are more than ethnographic exotica, not merely the "spoilers" which archaeologists find so frustrating. The patterns and meanings associated with the built environment reflect fundamental cultural concepts uniquely shaped by particular societies at specific times (see Wilson 1988: 57–78). Does this imply that architecture falls outside the limits of archaeological inquiry? Hopefully not, or this book would be very brief. But such concerns do lead to questions about how to think about buildings, and, more specifically, how we can think about constructions from another time built by another culture. How is it, as Cieza de Leon remarked, that a building can be a witness of what it once was?

In this book I attempt to address some of these questions by developing a small body of theory and a handful of analytical methods, and applying them to a corpus of architectural data from the prehistoric Andes. This study intentionally balances generalizing theory and specific substantive results in a manner I hope will be relevant to Andeanists and archaeologists working in other regions. I hope to provide useful analytical examples and provoke new lines of inquiry. My goal is to illustrate the directions a well-developed archaeology of architecture might take, exemplified in a study of prehistoric public architecture.

Public architecture and political power

Architecture may reflect a variety of cultural behaviors, from artistic styles to planning for seismic stresses, but I am interested in the ways public architecture reflects larger dimensions of social order; loosely stated, I am interested in buildings and politics. Following Swartz, Turner, and Tuden (1966: 7), "The study of politics . . . is the study of *processes* involved in determining and implementing public goals and in the differential achievement and use of power by the members of the group concerned with those goals" (original emphasis). Such a definition negates a sharp, a priori division between religious ceremony and public spectacle (Adams 1977: 28); the social separation of church and state is an empirical matter. Instead, I am interested in understanding the bases of public actions in ancient Andean societies, and I assume that public buildings – whether impermanent ritual structures or massive royal compounds – are evidence of differing public orders and social motives. Public buildings are physical testimonies of the use of power.

If, as a rough agreement in the anthropological literature suggests (e.g. Adams

1970: 117, 1977: 388; Balandier 1970: 37–39; Haas 1982: 156–158), power involves a dissymmetry in social relations – even if only temporarily – then it seems equally clear that power rests on the twin foundations of legitimacy and force, consensus and coercion (Swartz et al. 1966: 14–16). It also seems certain that different social entities – from hunting bands to complex bureaucracies – vary in their relative reliance on consensus and coercion. And finally if one expression of power is the direction of social effort, then public constructions may reflect the exercise of power in concrete form.

This is familiar ground: archaeologists have discussed public architecture as the material expression of power since at least the time of V. Gordon Childe (1974 [1950]: 11), citing "[t]ruly monumental public buildings . . . [that] symbolize the social surplus." This approach to architecture as the physical index of social effort is discussed in Chapter 3. But architecture is more than a passive product of potential labor investment; it reflects other dimensions of public life and, in turn, helps shape the nature of social interaction. It is this larger arena of inquiry that concerns me.

Those concerns are shared with scholars of landscape, particularly those who consider the cultural modification and interpretation of the environment, built and natural. For example, Denis Cosgrove (1984: 15) defines landscape as an explicitly ideological concept, representing the "way in which certain classes of people have signified themselves and their world through their imagined relationship with nature, and through which they have underlined and communicated their own social role and that of others with respect to external nature." Given the subject of this book, I focus on the built environment rather than on Cosgrove's broader "external nature," but his emphasis on the communicative nature and social context directly parallels my approach to prehistoric Andean architecture. Public architecture as a medium contains information about social relations associated with power; as Tuan (1974: 151) noted, "Power is seldom expressed directly as a physical force even in the animal world. In the human world it is exercised through the recognition and acceptance of the symbols of legitimacy."

Archaeologists accept the notion that architecture may reflect the exercise of power; the theory linking settlement hierarchies to administrative states is an example (Wright and Johnson 1975; Isbell and Schreiber 1978). But such approaches treat architecture as a passive, though concrete, reflection of political structure often expressed in levels of socio-political complexity. Rather than wonder if a particular society "was" a chiefdom or a state, I am interested in the varying modes of political process which produced and were reproduced by public architecture. I assume it is at least *conceivable* that specific Andean societies – like the Balinese supralocal polities described by Geertz (1973: 336):

> did not consist of a neat set of hierarchically organized sovereign states . . .
> [nor] . . . did it consist of any overall domination by a "single-centered
> apparatus state" under an absolute despot, "hydraulic" or otherwise. What it
> consisted in was an extended field of highly dissimilar political ties,
> thickening into nodes of varying size and solidity at strategic points on the
> landscape and then thinning out again to connect, in a marvelously
> convolute way, virtually everything with everything else.

Equally, I recognize there were periods of Andean prehistory – most notably under the Inca Empire – when strong centralized states did reshape the nature of social existence. The architecture discussed in this book was the creation of social units ranging from families to empires, but the political process was common to all of them once they decided to build public constructions. Hilda Kuper (1972: 421) has written:

> The process of political interaction may be expressed empirically through disputes over or manipulations of sites, and symbolicallly in the language of sites. It does not matter whether the site be a cattle byre, a house of parliament, a public hall, or even a university! Though the process is similar, the range of people and groups affected may vary from a few individuals to an entire nation.

Thus the political process cross-cuts social units of different scales, although different political concerns and configurations are associated with different groups. The problem is how to discover architectural evidence for such different configurations of power.

Public architecture is a particularly useful body of evidence because it so multidimensional. Public buildings may serve as monuments, commemorative constructions to be viewed (Chapter 3). Public architecture also may be used, in a very tangible way, as stages on which social dramas occur (Chapter 4). Not all public constructions are involved in similar social dramas; some constructions may serve as the visual focus of large numbers of people, while others may be restricted to a handful of initiates. Not all public structures are catalysts for social coalescence; buildings may be designed to define, separate, or exclude (Chapter 5). Yet it is the multiplicity of uses for public architecture which makes its analysis so interesting, because different types of buildings reflect and shape different configurations of social life. In this study, I attempt to illuminate the prehistoric configurations of power by an examination of ancient Andean architecture. And that attempt requires a perspective distinct from traditional archaeological approaches to architecture.

Traditional archaeological approaches to architecture
Traditionally, archaeologists have pursued two lines of inquiry when considering architecture, which I will call "art historical" and "art critical." The first approach views architecture from the classic perspectives of traditional art history: architecture embodies a large set of stylistic features and construction techniques that represent shared knowledge, and a taxonomy of buildings based on their similarities allows for the delineation of tradition and the recognition of genius. Derived from a tradition that considers architecture one of the fine arts, the scope of inquiry is centered on objects that exhibit "an artistic-aesthetic intention" even if the architectural expression of intent includes "space-configurations and organization of mass, planning of roads and squares, and, in the higher cultures, town-planning" (Haselberger 1961: 342). This approach, emphasizing the formal properties of art and the aesthetic responses they evoke, has a long history in Western culture, and it shaped initial anthropological approaches to art (Layton 1981: 4–5).

A classic example is Franz Boas' *Primitive Art* (1951 orig. 1927), which demonstrated the aesthetic intent of traditional artists by citing their mastery of technique, variation of motif, and use of symmetry and rhythm in media ranging from birchbark buckets to face painting. Boas' view of human societies in "constant flux" – so inconstant that "the cultural form may become a kaleidoscopic picture of miscellaneous traits" – led him to emphasize the role of diffusion in the spread of isolated traits. Boas sharply criticized attempts by Clark Wissler and Alfred Kroeber to order traits chronologically based on the age–area hypothesis (Boas 1951: 6–7). That debate turned on the extent to which complexes of traits were adopted en masse. Wissler, for example (1914: 491), argued that material traits diffused "as to take over whole complexes with all their concepts." The debate was not over whether cultural complexes could or should be viewed as sets of traits; that was given.

Alfred Kroeber's (1931) resilient analogy between culture change and organic growth led to the conclusion that "one may compare species to culture traits or elements, and genera or families to culture trait complexes." Via his early researches in Peruvian archaeology, Kroeber's general view of culture and traits specifically shaped archaeological approaches in the Andes. In his work on ceramics (e.g. Kroeber 1925; Gayton and Krober 1927) and textiles (O'Neale and Kroeber 1930), Alfred Kroeber expanded on Max Uhle's work (Rowe 1954a) and outlined an approach to the study of stylistic change and cultural processes that was absolutely fundamental to Peruvian prehistory. Kroeber's research shaped the "Berkeley school" of Andean archaeology, whose preminent practitioners were John Rowe (e.g., 1946, 1962b) and Dorothy Menzel (1977; Menzel et al. 1964), among others. Kroeber's conceptual contribution was the recognition of horizon styles vs. local styles; more broadly, his consideration of artistic style was influential among anthropologically inclined art historians. Kroeber's significance, for example, has been acknowledged explicitly by George Kubler (1962: 2; Rowe 1963a; however, *vide* Kubler 1991: 176–178 for a sharp retrospective). Although Kroeber's (1952) "Great Art Styles of Ancient South America" focused primarily on ceramic and sculptural traditions, architecture was subsumed in this scheme in brief references to Inca masonry and the "'Arabesques' of more or less geometrically patterned adobes" found in Chimu architecture. But such a scheme introduced the concept of horizons and periods so influential in Andean archaeology (Rowe 1962a), viewing architectural patterns as one class of archaeological traits which could be used to plot the growth, expansion, and decline of pan-Andean traditions or more restricted, regional styles.

This approach to Andean architecture has a rich literature. Given the interest in Inca society and empire, the distinctive Inca masonry architecture has received extensive study (Agorto Calvo 1987; Gasparini and Margolies 1980; Kendall 1985; MacLean 1986). In some cases the rich ethnohistoric record allows for identification of specific Inca settlements and installations (Morris 1967, 1972; Niles 1987), but more importantly the ethnohistoric record of Inca conquest and domination of the Andes can be traced by the imposition of architectural forms such as storehouses (Morris 1967; D'Altroy and Hastorf 1984), roads (Hyslop 1984), or provincial capitals (Morris and Thompson 1985; Hyslop 1985). Thus, in the Inca case, the spread of architectural traits marks the expansion of empire, a point made more than three decades ago by Dorothy Menzel (1959: 127–131).

Thus, studies of the temporal and spatial distributions of architectural traits have been associated with the spread of specific prehistoric cultures and usually with the expansion of Andean states. For example, discussions of the territorial growth of the Chimu state – which is the subject of much of Chapter 5 – are based partially on the recognition of certain architectural traits as being distinctively Chimu (e.g. Keatinge and Conrad 1983; Mackey 1987). Similarly, supposed shifts in the center and peripheries of the Moche state are associated with changes in the location and scale of large pyramidal mounds (e.g. Moseley 1992: 166, 212–214). Yet arguably, it is with the study of the Middle Horizon and the spread of Huari culture that architecture has been most consistently used to trace the expansion of an Andean state. This concern begins with Rowe's (1963b: 14–15) statements about the distinctiveness of Huari architecture, its widespread distribution, and his inference that Huari was an administrative empire which expanded through military conquest. With William Isbell's work at the site of Huari (1978a, 1991) and subsequent investigations of Huari provincial centers by Martha Anders (1981, 1991), Gordon McEwan (1984) and Katharina Schreiber (1978, 1987a, 1987b, 1992), issues about architectural traits and imperial expansion become central to a major debate in Andean archaeology: what was the nature of Huari? An answer to this question is beyond the scope of this chapter and its author's expertise (for discussions, see Isbell 1987; Isbell and McEwan 1991; Isbell and Schreiber 1978; cf. Shady Solís 1982). But it is important to note that the analytical treatment of architecture employed by these studies is almost identical to that outlined by Kroeber: architecture consists of traits and the spread of those traits forms the basis of historical reconstruction. The mechanisms of diffusion or the causes behind the spatio-temporal distribution may be different; the theoretical reasons which prompt modern scholars to look at the distribution of Huari architectural traits are different from those envisioned by Kroeber. But the basic architectural approach is the same: the delineation of an architectural tradition and the explanation of its spread through space and time.

The second traditional approach to architecture is borrowed from architectural criticism. Minimally, architectural criticism conveys a critic's informed aesthetic response to a larger audience. Architectural criticism, as Witold Rybcsynski (1992) recently noted, has a long tradition dating back to Vitruvius, but it is a genre that, for better or worse, has seen major growth in the twentieth century. Architectural criticism may rival other forms of art criticism, or it may serve as a camouflaged polemic of normative dicta or even decline into a murky hucksterism, touting an architect's unique vision to justify the award of a contract (for examples by Frank Lloyd Wright, see Gill 1987). Of course, critical statements about Andean architecture are never so malign; their sole intention is to draw attention to specific elements of prehispanic constructions.

The cross-fertilization of precolumbian anthropology and art history has been alluded to above, and in the work of George Kubler (1984; Reese 1985) one finds well-defined examples of critical statements about Andean architecture. Kubler's panoramic view of native American art encompassed a wide range of media and regions (Klein 1982; Kubler 1984), but though he mastered diverse data and developments in American archaeology, Kubler's approach was almost vehemently non-anthropological:

> Archaeology is a scientific technique rather than a fully autonomous discipline. It is important whenever documents fail to yield direct evidence of the past. In the hands of the anthropologists, it is applied to the recovery of information about social structure and economic life. In this context works of art are used as sources of information rather than as expressive realities.
> (Kubler 1984: 33)

A case can be made that Kubler's assessment of archaeology as practiced in the 1930s was essentially accurate, though not true of research fifty years later when the third edition of *The Art and Architecture of Ancient America* was issued. But more importantly, Kubler's work is an explicitly critical piece of writing, emphasizing – as Boas had – aesthetic intention and evocative response. Writing for Western art historians, Kubler attempted to show that precolumbian art was art and not merely ethnographic curio. Kubler (1984: 39) wrote:

> When a building or an object is discussed and illustrated here, it is because of a peculiar perceptual quality. Unlike physical or chemical properties, this perceptual quality cannot be measured. Its presence is unmistakable. It is altogether absent from no artifact. Works of art display it more than utilitarian objects. It is present in nature wherever humans have been active, as in pure-bred animals[!], and in some landscapes. It appears in scenes and things called beautiful as well as in those that arouse disgust.

Kubler went on to outline three properties serving to distinguish art from artifact: a work of art is the product of a cumulative technical tradition, it is imbued with complexity of meaning, and it exhibits its maker's sensibility. And finally, Kubler constructed a conceptual barricade to defend aesthetic recognition – kept intrinsic and pure – from evolutionary, neo-Marxian, or "configurationism," the latter having its roots in structuralism and Gestalt psychology (1984: 41–42).

If this is a fair sketch of Kubler's position, and I hope it is, then how is this characterized by his assessments of Andean architecture? A few examples should make the point:

> Building in the Andes lacks the spatial complexity of Maya and Mexican architecture.
> (Kubler 1984: 359)

> Huaca de los Reyes in the Moche Valley exhibits a symmetry of plan more rigorous than anything else in ancient America. Only La Venta in Mesoamerica is comparable.
> (Kubler 1984: 360)

> The architectural forms [associated with Chavín] are grandiose terraced platforms.
> (Kubler 1984: 363)

> The relation of the masses [of the *castillo* at Chavín de Huantar] to enclosed volumes is like that of a mountain range, where geological formations enfold caves and vents of bewildering complexity.
> (Kubler 1984: 369)

> The Chimu tradition of imperial rule, manipulated by aggressive expansion and by economic regulation, must surely have become the heritage of the Inca dynasty in the fifteenth century. One of the prices paid for this imperial political organization seems to have been the progressive loss of aesthetic vigour and inventiveness.
> (Kubler 1984: 408)

These statements are extracted from their context, and most of Kubler's text is concerned with location, chronology, and description (e.g., his 1984: 383–387 excellent summary of Moche architecture). Yet such passages capture his critical approach to precolumbian architecture, in which aesthetic judgment is seldom distant, as in his repeated references to prehistoric builders' "slovenliness." Kubler rarely considers the significance of a work of art in the context of a specific, prehispanic culture because that was never his critical aim. Simply, Kubler's goal was not anthropological.

One might reasonably include several of Terence Grieder's (1978, 1982, 1988c) discussions of Andean architecture within this critical tradition, although Grieder is more concerned with the aesthetic significance of art to its prehispanic makers than Kubler is. For example, *Art and Archaeology of Pashash* (1978) links the magnificent ceramic and metal artifacts associated with a burial chamber to a symbolism intertwined with shamanism. In a free-ranging appeal to disparate ethnographic examples of art and shamanic cosmology, Grieder (1978: 189) concludes:

> Perched on its high ridge behind its massive walls, Pashash is a dramatic image of insecurity. The militaristic foreign elite who ruled there asserted their right by an art style which manifested their alliance with the divine powers that rule the cosmos. Mortality, the ultimate insecurity, inspired the greatest outpouring of ritual power to maintain the stability of earthly order by an access of divine energy.

This is evocative critical writing; it is, also, unverifiable. This does not mean that Grieder comes to such conclusions with no evidence. Rather, like all critical statements, these phrases are designed to draw our attention to the previously unnoticed, to mimic an aesthetic response, or to weigh merit. They are not necessarily designed to be proved.

William Conklin's critical writings (1990; Conklin and Moseley 1987) on ancient Andean architecture are particularly important. A practicing architect and expert on ancient Andean textiles and architecture, Conklin's work is filled with insight. When compared with other Andeanists, Conklin's unique combination of training and interests leads him to a unique view of Andean architecture. His writings also are the best examples of architectural criticism in Andean studies, and in them the limitations of this approach are bared:

> The U-shaped mound [at Los Chinos in the Moche Valley] faces directly toward a symmetrical three-part mountaintop to the north. The visual conversation and implied relationship between the man-made mountain and the actual mountain perhaps invoked the transfer of power to the *huaca*.
> (Conklin 1990: 48)

Well, perhaps – but how can we ever know? Conklin's critical statement draws our attention to the relationship between mountain and mound, yet the inferred relation is intriguing but unverifiable. And thus his work frequently falls within the tradition of architectural criticism, a tradition with specific but limited utility to the archaeologist.

Critical comments are often problematic. Critical statements can be misleading because they can masquerade as descriptive observations. An example makes the point. Archaeologists blithely cite Louis Sullivan's famous rule, "Form follows function." Archaeologists are comfortable with notions like form and function and, equipped with a utilitarian view of culture, we can accept that function would have a certain causal priority; the fact that jars are hollow, taller than they are wide, and have an opening at the top rather than the bottom is because they function as containers. Yet, such an interpretation misses a very important element of Sullivan's statement: his was a prescriptive statement, literally "Form [should or ought to] follow function," an architectural battle-cry which was a reaction to the functionally irrelevant gingerbread and filigree of late Victorian architecture. Sullivan's statement was not descriptive; it was critical.

Like other critical genres, architectural criticism may assume a metaphorical property, using vivid language to highlight (but not necessarily explain or measure or define) specific features of buildings. This may lead to a certain impressionism in language, as the architect Bruno Zevi complained over three decades ago:

> The average reader, leafing through books on the aesthetics and criticism of architecture, is horrified by the vagueness of the terms: *truth, movement, force, vitality, sense of outline, harmony, grace, breadth, scale, balance, proportion, light and shade, eurhythmics, solids and voids, symmetry, rhythm, mass, volume, emphasis, character, contrast, personality, analogy.* These are attributes of architecture which various authors use as classifications without specifying what they refer to.
> (Zevi 1957: 21, emphasis in the original)

While some of these terms (e.g., mass, volume, scale) could be reduced to measurable dimensions, most cannot be and none were meant to be, as they are value-laden terms of an implied aesthetic code. In short, the principal difference between architectural criticism and archaeological inquiry is that in the former we are interested in the critical response as communicated to a contemporary audience and in the latter we are not.

At its best, architectural criticism is instructive, pointing out unnoticed elements and unseen patterns and sharing the informed observations and insights of the critic with an audience. We applaud critics who, writing with knowledge and brio, allow us to see buildings in new ways by sharing with us their critical response. But archaeological inquiry has a different goal: we want to know about the people who constructed, inhabited, and lived in a built environment. Ideally, we want to know what *they* thought about their architecture, and no number of intriguing observations by a modern observer is a substitute for that. And thus architectural criticism and archaeological analyses of architecture have quite different obligations and goals, and to confuse them is an error.

As anthropologists of the past, archaeologists attempt to understand the cultural construction of built space, the ways humans create and conceive of architecture. This approach has many difficulties, and there are undoubted limits to what we can retrieve from prehistory. And yet, the archaeological enterprise has distinct, unrealized potential for which architectural criticism is no substitute. For that reason, I argue that archaeological approaches to architecture should be grounded in that worn, but useful, anthropological concept – holism.

Anthropological holism and approaches to architecture

The archaeologiocal analysis of architecture, I believe, must be derived from basic anthropological concerns and perspectives. First, the built environment is a culturally constructed landscape which, like other cultural dimensions, includes utilitarian and non-adaptive, innovative and conservative elements. Humans both shape and are shaped by the built environment, a point of view captured in Clifford Geertz' phrase, "man is the only animal suspended in webs of meaning which he himself has spun" (Geertz 1973: 5). And thus while architecture and landscape are created by humans, they are not passive creations; rather those creations, reified by society, in turn may mold subsequent human action. So at a basic level, an anthropological perspective on architecture focuses on how human societies create, conceptualize, and are influenced by cultural modifications – physical and symbolic – of the environment.

A second element is the importance of a truly holistic approach to architecture. A single building may embody a wide range of cultural decisions (e.g., retention of heat, expression of social status, or orientation with cosmic forces; see Wilk 1990: 34–35 for discussion). No single scholar gives equal attention to every dimension of the built environment, which is one reason why there are such diverse approaches to architecture (Lawrence and Low 1990). This study is no exception; in the following chapters I explore how one class of architecture (public constructions) may have functioned in religion and politics in prehispanic Peruvian societies. Yet, my choice to explore that question does not imply that I discount other factors such as the availability of materials, engineering constraints, the relationship between construction costs and social systems, or the possible significance of astral alignments in shaping Andean architecture. Although we select certain factors and ignore others for purposes of study, it is important to remember such different dimensions comfortably co-exist in the minds of builders and users of space. Thus, the masonry pueblos of the Hopi are shaped by the availability of stone, insolation in an environment of temperature extremes, intramural storage and facilities, the size of the residence unit, the existence of sodalities anchored by ceremonial structures, and basic elements of world view (Nabokov and Easton 1989; Ortiz 1969). An anthropologist may examine a single causal thread, but should not mistake it for the entire cultural fabric. The anthropological approach to architecture may result only from collective effort, but it is an important shared goal.

This holistic, collective enterprise already exists, and it is documented in Denise Lawrence and Setha Low's (1990) impressive review of the literature on anthropological and related approaches to the built environment. With their backgrounds in anthropology and environmental studies, Lawrence and Low present architecture as tangent to multiple spheres of human behavior. After summarizing early ethnographic approaches to architecture – such as Lewis Henry Morgan's 1881 *Houses and House-Life of the American Aborigine* – Lawrence and Low organize the anthropological literature into four theoretical sets: (1) social organization, (2) symbolic approaches, (3) psychological, and (4) social production and reproduction. As Lawrence and Low (1990: 455) note, these theoretical arenas center on four sets of questions:

> (1) In what ways do built forms accommodate human behavior and adapt to human needs? How does the social group "fit" the form it occupies?
> (2) What is the meaning of the form? How do built forms express and represent aspects of culture?
> (3) How is the built form an extension of the individual? How is the spatial dimension of human behavior related to mental processes and conceptions of the self?
> (4) How does society produce forms and forms reproduce society? What roles do history and social institutions play in generating the built environment? What is the relationship between space and power?

Of these four areas, archaeologists are most familiar with the first, which concerns the relationship between social organization and built form, particularly as it relates to household and dwelling. For example, a well-established literature considers the ways that domestic architecture reflects changes in familial and suprafamilial social organizations (see Rapoport 1969; Kent 1990c; Wilk and Ashmore 1988; Wilk and Rathje 1982). One cluster in this literature involves the relationship between house size and residence group size (Naroll 1962; LeBlanc 1971; Kramer 1982), and between house form and patterns of social interaction (e.g. Bawden 1990; Ember 1973; Rodman 1985). Another set of archaeological studies of the household draws on Goody's (1971) model of the developmental cycle of the household (see Wilk and Ashmore 1988), in which variations in domestic architecture are viewed as reflecting the founding, growth, fission, and decline of specific residence groups. Other approaches to house form consider the shape, size, and permanence of structures as reflecting broader patterns in economy and society, such as the development of sedentary village life based on intensive food collection or early agriculture (Flannery 1972; Glassow 1972). Another set of studies considers the household as a minimal social unit which is incorporated into larger social and political entities. Thus the authors in *The Early Mesoamerican Village* (Flannery 1976) treat the Formative household in Mesoamerica as a component organized into household groups, which are grouped into villages, barrios, towns, and regional systems like a nested set of Chinese boxes. Alternatively, dwellings may reflect intra-community social differences such as distinct kin-based corporate groups (e.g., Aldenderfer 1993b; Stanish 1989, 1992) or social classes based on access to wealth, power, or prestige (e.g., Arnold and Ford 1980; cf. Folan et al. 1982; Haviland 1982). Another archaeological approach to dwellings is essentially non-architectural, emphasizing the way in which activities structure space (Kent 1984). In extreme cases (e.g., Moore 1985), activity area studies may virtually ignore the architectural setting, instead relying on other artifactual data which happen to be contained within walls. But archaeologists generally recognize the relationship between architecture and social organization, particularly as exemplified by house and household.

With the development of post-processual approaches in archaeology (Hodder 1982a, 1986; Preucel 1991), more attention has been given to symbolic content in prehistoric architecture. As Lawrence and Low (1990: 466) note, symbolic approaches to the built environment may take a number of forms, although archaeologists have pursued only a few. Archaeologists more willingly engage in symbolic interpretations when either written records or iconography provide a basis for interpretation or when the direct historical approach allows the documentary record to illuminate the twilight of prehistory. Another approach used by archaeologists is what Lawrence and Low (1990: 467) term "social symbolic." Such approaches posit that, "Built forms and site plans act as communicative or mnemonic devices expressing or reaffirming . . . relationships between groups, or positions held by individuals within a culture's framework." Thus Renfrew (1984: 165–199) argues that megaliths served to communicate territorial boundaries between different segmentary societies during the European Neolithic. In a different approach, Hodder (1984) interprets formal parallels and symbolic connections between Banderkeramik longhouses and Atlantic European long barrows as reflecting changes in male–female relationships which, in turn, were restructured by competition over the control of labor. It is worth noting that although Hodder (1984: 52) proposes his analysis as an alternative to Renfrew's hypothesis, neither archaeologist questions the social-symbolic role of architecture. Their interpretations are different, although their basic assumptions are similar.

A second symbolic approach that archaeologists have used could be loosely termed "structural" (Lawrence and Low 1990: 467). Such studies share with Lévi-Strauss' classic approaches an interest in searching for shared structure and a reliance upon a linguistic metaphor, although most studies interpret shared structures as reflecting learned cultural patterns rather than unconscious collectivities.

Such studies have been most fully developed – not surprisingly – in ethnographic studies of material culture. Thus in his analysis of Chamula ritual symbolism, Gossen (1972: 149) links the spatial patterns within homes and in processions as reflecting "the cosmogonic moment of the sun's ascent into the heavens" which "provided the necessary spatial and temporal categories for an orderly social existence." Alfonso Ortiz' (1969) study of Tewa pueblo showed how the placement of dance squares, the spatial division of the village, and conceptual framework of the natural environment all reflect fundamental cultural structures.

Other analyses employ a linguistic model in which architectural patterns are "morphemes" in a spatial syntax (Lawrence and Low 1990: 470–471). Sutro and Downing (1988) analyzed the organization of modern Zapotec households in this manner, identifying repetitive patterns of roofed and unroofed areas. In a rare archaeological application, a structuralist approach to monumental Andean architecture has been attempted by Czwarno (1988, 1989), using a symbolic notation to discover repetitive features of Huari architecture. In a stimulating series of articles, David Small (1987, 1991) has combined historical texts and architectural analyses to examine the ideational structures associated with gender differences and female seclusion in a variety of cultures.

The ethnographic richness of symbolic approaches is so fascinating, there is every reason why prehistoric archaeologists would want to emulate such inquiries. But there is a basic problem – linguistic approaches to prehistoric architecture stumble on the issue of meaning. This stumbling block exists whether the approaches are based on structure, semiotics, or metaphor (see Lawrence and Low 1990: 471–474). One may find repetitive combinations of architectural traits and/or spaces and conclude that they represent patterned units of cultural behavior, and yet never be able to decide what such patterns mean. It is like recognizing that "ly" is found repeatedly in English, yet not knowing that it denotes an adverb because one cannot distinguish between nouns or verbs, adjectives or prepositions. Even if we correctly guess the meanings we cannot know we are correct, simply because there are no native "speakers" to tell us we are making sense.

Such concerns should not eliminate symbolic approaches to prehistoric architecture, but we should be clear that at least two steps are involved – first, the recognition of pattern; second, the determination of meaning. Studies of symbolic patterns could be interesting without the meaning of those patterns ever being known; for example if the spatial syntax discovered by Sutro and Downing (1988) in modern Zapotec houses showed continuities with the houses of prehispanic Oaxaca, then that would be interesting even if we did not know what those patterns meant. But the point remains – pattern and meaning are two different aspects of symbolic behavior with different epistemological demands.

Perhaps the theoretical arena least explored by archaeologists relates to psychological aspects of the built environment; this is not surprising given archaeologists' traditional avoidance of "mental" explanations and denial of the individual in prehistory (for a non-idealist approach to the individual see Hill and Gunn 1977: 4–5). The only psychological approach that percolated into the archaeological literature is the work of Edward T. Hall (1959, 1966) on proxemics. Archaeological references to proxemics are rare and brief, usually distilled into the concept that cultures have different notions of personal space.

In contrast, archaeologists are quite familiar with theories of the social production of built form, theories which "focus on the social, political, and economic forces that produce the built environment, and conversely, the impact of the socially produced built environment on social action" (Low and Lawrence 1990: 482). Archaeologists, however, have taken a unidirectional view of this problem, emphasizing the role of society, polity, and economy in shaping architecture, but not the reverse. The best developed subset within this body of theory is the "energetics approach" to architecture (Abrams 1989). This approach views the scale of public architecture as an index of socio-political complexity; it is an approach with an archaeological pedigree dating from V. Gordon Childe (1974 [1936]) and a common theme in Western intellectual traditions. As evolutionary approaches in archaeology were stimulated by Leslie White's (1959) *Evolution of Culture*, monumental architecture became a central subject of archaeological analysis because it is social energy in fossil form. Archaeologists could use the kind and scale of public architecture to create site typologies (e.g., Willey 1953), to rank those sites (e.g., Sanders and Price 1968; Wright and Johnson 1975), and then assess the overall complexity – in a Durkheimian sense – of particular prehistoric societies (e.g., Isbell and Schreiber 1978). The energetics approach is the most common class of analysis of New World architecture since the advent of New Archaeology in the 1960s. The energetics approach is discussed in more detail in Chapter 3, but for the moment we should note this approach emphasizes the passivity of architecture. Architecture reflects or exemplifies or indicates, but it does not shape or structure or limit.

Archaeologists have examined the social, political, and economic forces that shape prehistoric architecture, but usually not the inverse, examining social production but not social reproduction. For example, José Canziani Amico (1989) has written a valuable study summarizing North Coast archaeological data from sites dating from PaleoIndian to Moche V periods. The basic thrust of his work is: "that human settlement in the [North Coast] territory is present as the fundamental material base for a determined mode of production and that there exists a dialectical relationship between the way of life of a specific society and the established settlement model" (Canziani Amico 1989: 25; translation mine).

Following Lumbreras' (1969) evolutionary framework, Canziani divides sites into Archaic, Formative, and Regional Development periods, each characterized by a distinct mode of production. Rather than classic Marxist modes of production, the categories refer to the specific articulations of labor, resources, and control inferred from archaeological data, particularly (a) the development of irrigation agriculture (e.g. Canziani Amico 1989: 52–59), (b) the emergence of craft specialists and the development of status differences such as priesthoods (Canziani Amico 1989: 92–97), and (c) the asymmetric relationships between centers and hamlets (Canziani Amico 1989: 98–99) and, by extension, the existence of exploitative class differences. In addition to this discussion – with its antecedents in Childe, Engels, and most of all Lumbreras

– Canziani Amico has provided one of the clearest efforts to link settlement patterns to large socio-political processes using a deep, diachronic perspective, but the study falters on its lack of specificity. How is it that theocratic government was expressed in the Moche pyramids rather than some other architectural form? What distinguishes such governments from earlier forms, also founded on religious authority, but which raised more modest public constructions? How do similarities in architectural forms – such as the Formative Period's U-shaped ceremonial centers or circular sunken courtyards – reflect analogous social or political or religious forms? Canziani Amico's theory posits a dialectic, but the analysis leaves ambiguous the relationship between architecture and social reproduction. Thus Canziani Amico's study, for all its strengths, exemplifies the unidirectional approach within which archaeologists have viewed the relationships between social forms and built forms.

The present study is an attempt to look at prehistoric Andean architecture from both directions. I am interested in how architecture reflects the development of different social forms in Andean prehistory, and I am also concerned with the ways in which Andean architecture may have communicated those social forms to members of prehispanic societies. For that reason, the study only considers *public* architecture. As a product of social effort, patterns of public architecture may communicate the nature and scale of social order. And thus my goal is to understand the changing nature of Andean social complexity, so impressively realized during the sixteenth century by the Inca empire, the largest New World state. But before the Inca achievement, numerous social forms developed which were based on different structural and ideological principles. Some of those were expressed in and communicated by ancient Andean architecture, and they are the subject of this book.

Power and place: architecture, social production and reproduction

My basic argument can be summarized in four statements: (1) buildings as cultural constructs are imbued with symbols; (2) public buildings often contain public symbols; (3) the nature of the symbols informed prehistoric societies about the basis of social order; and (4) it is possible for archaeologists to make limited, but significant, inferences about the composition of the social group and basis of social order from analyses of prehistoric architecture.

Of course, it is easier to state an argument than to implement its logic or prove its veracity, as the following pages prove. But the argument leads directly to some simple questions about the social uses of architecture: Where is a public building located? How could it be visually perceived? How many people could fit inside of it? What was its design life? Were activities associated with the building designed to be hidden or visible? Was access within the building restricted or open? Were there diachronic changes in access among similar architectural forms? What do the above imply about the nature of the social formations which designed, built, and used public buildings in the prehistoric Andes?

As a cultural environment, the built environment is imbued with social meanings. Such meanings may range from simple instructions about the use of a building (e.g., "EXIT") to the complex symbolism of a façade, what Eco (1980) respectively refers to as primary and secondary sign functions. While our attention may be captured by fine façades or architectural adornment, there may be hidden information in more prosaic patterns. Witold Rybczynski (1989: 161) writes: "The symbolic meaning of architecture can be profound, as it is in the case with places of worship and important public buildings. But the language of buildings can also convey more mundane messages: where to go, what is important, how the building is to be used."

Such meanings may not be identically recognized by every member of a society, but they are understood by more than one person. If such meanings are associated, through enculturation, with certain behavioral responses, then we can say that the built environment "shapes" behavior – in the same way that the design of freeways, construction of off-ramps, and the placement of signs usually (but not always) shape driving behavior in the modern United States. Much in the same way, aspects of the built environment elicit behaviors because architecture is imbued with symbolic content. Again, these symbols may be relatively uncomplicated and yet shape behavior in complex ways. When we recognize a structure as a "house," we also know that behaviors acceptable in a house are different from acceptable behaviors in a church or a honky-tonk. Homes, churches, and honky-tonks not only reflect social behavior, they shape it.

One might refer to this approach as a study of architecture as discourse, but that makes me uncomfortable. I have tried to avoid the pitfall which Gould (1990) wickedly refers to as "savant du jour," and I have attempted to state what I mean rather than rely on the names of *philosophes* as icons to ward off inquiry. Yet any discussion of social uses of symbols and meaning leads to a consideration of discourse, and one particularly important archaeological example is Christopher Tilley's (1991) analysis of the rock art of Nämforsen, Norway.

Tilley adapts a coherent theory based on semiotics, hermeneutics, and discourse to an archaeological problem; his approach draws on language and conversation as models of symbolizing and truth-seeking. Following Derrida (1976), Tilley (1991: 16) argues that "practices involving spacing, differentiation, articulation and rearticulation of units or entities form a primordial part of human consciousness" which, like writing, transform human practice, communicate between people, and create meaning. Employing Saussure's distinction between *langue* and *parole*, Tilley (1991: 18) applies the concepts of language and speech to material culture, showing how one might refer to the "languages" of culinary practices, ceramic design, or funerary custom, each set of behaviors governed by fundamental rules but modified by specific practice. Clearly, the exercise of such behavioral "speech" creates variation, not because errors are made or improprieties are committed, but because the very use of symbols involves adapting old designs to new meanings (as in Lévi-Strauss' [1966: 17–18] concept of *bricolage* [Tilley 1991: 96–97]) and because the receivers of symbols themselves may create meanings.

The above implies that there are speakers and listeners, and discourse refers to their interchange. But in societies where some symbols are not available equally to all members, then discourse enters the political realm and art becomes power (an issue reconsidered in Chapter 5). As Tilley (1991: 151–152) puts it:

in pre-capitalist social formations in particular, art is not just a series of representations of the world but may act powerfully to structure and restructure socioeconomic practices in a material way. It is not a separate sphere of activity. Because it may play such a crucial role in the production and reproduction of social relations in small-scale societies, it may also be important in reproducing and sustaining relations of dominance.

This is not to say that the viewers of art or the audience of a material discourse are passive or inert, but simply that the symbolic system they are "reading" is considered sufficiently valid and its creators legitimate. "The position of those in power and authority need not be accepted as preordained or right but it nevertheless has to be regarded as legitimate in some way" (Tilley 1991: 152). Symbolic creations that maintain relations of dominance "must offer substantial incentives for ideological adherence to a particular position which legitimizes the interests of the few in the name of the many" (Tilley 1991: 152). In this sense, discourse links symbolic use to power and ideology.

Yet the difficulty facing any historical approach is the process of untangling the different threads of discourse. As an archaeologist educated during the heated exchanges of the New Archaeology, I am well aware that current intellectual paradigms limit what we ask of the past. It also seems to me that while some explanatory principles have cross-cultural validity, I am most interested in understanding the unique paths that prehistoric societies have taken and in comparing those distinct social routes to highlight the diversity of human experience. Thus, I do not rely on an all-encompassing, monolithic theory of human nature free from culture and history. But neither am I interested in a free-floating relativism in which statements cannot be subject to verification or opinions measured against evidence, and my lack of interest stems from the special requirements of the archaeological record. Simply put, as an archaeologist I do not engage in a dialogue with a site; I have a one-sided conversation. And for that reason, I am extremely uncomfortable with the metaphor of the archaeologist as interpreter simply because there is no "other" to tell me I am wrong.

In lieu of such a dialogue, I have tried to be explicit. The process of posing hypotheses, articulating their implications, and testing those implications against relevant data forces one to make intent, logic, and method transparent. This approach allows for pointed critiques from other scholars and, when the analysis pauses, an interim summary of knowledge and ignorance. In this manner I hope to move in small steps across the threshold between present and past.

Conclusion

In the following chapters, I attempt to explore the changing relationship between public architecture and religion, economy, and politics on the North Coast of Peru; central to this attempt are relations between space and power. What concerns me is the social production of built environment and the built environment's reproduction of society. Simply, I am interested in how archaeologists can study architecture and thus learn more about the prehistoric societies that built it. As a matter of personal conviction, I am certain that archaeologists have not exhausted the data contained in prehistoric architecture. Retrieving those data, however, requires using different methods to ask new questions sparked by diverse theoretical concerns.

In Chapter 2 I present a critical review of the archaeological data that will form the basis of this analysis. This review summarizes archaeological data from twenty-two sites, presenting information on the extent of research, dating, and functional interpretations in addition to basic descriptive information on the public architecture. As I discuss, the sample is a purposive one, a selection of well-reported and well-documented examples of public architecture that span Andean prehistory.

The analyses begin with a discussion of monumentalism (Chapter 3). The basic questions raised are: "What is a monument, how does it communicate meaning, and what patterns are discernible among Andean monuments?" A set of techniques borrowed from the visual analysis of landscapes is applied to examples of massive pyramidal mounds known from the North Coast. The analysis suggests that, although these mounds may appear similar at first glance, these monuments had diverse audiences and distinct social purposes for different prehispanic Andean societies.

Another arena of inquiry involves the architecture of ritual (Chapter 4). Public architecture in the Andes was ritual architecture long before it met more secular social goals. The communicative potential and the symbolic intent of ritual architecture can be inferred from answers to some very basic questions about the scale, placement, visibility, and longevity of ceremonial structures. In turn, those changes suggest the differences in basic dimensions of early Andean societies.

A third focus of inquiry concerns the architecture of social control (Chapter 5). While means of control are found in all human societies, the use of complex architecture to limit the movement of peoples was a relatively late development in the Andes. By using basic techniques from network graph analysis, it is possible to measure, characterize, and compare the changing architectural patterns, and thus identify some of the ways the built environment was used as a means of social control. Much of this discussion focuses on the architecture of the Chimu state, examining such themes as the pre-Chimu antecedents for complex monumental architecture, differences between architecture in the core and the periphery of the polity, and the possible evidence for the development of divine kingship in the Chimu state.

I have no illusions: this approach to architecture will not answer all the questions about the built environment, and this study will not exhaust all questions about the development of Andean societies. But, minimally, I hope that the analysis will stimulate archaeologists to think in new ways about the built environment because, I believe, it contains unexplored potential for understanding the past.

2

A sample of ancient Andean public architecture: a critical description

We are just as amazed by the vast number of them . . .
        Bernabe Cobo 1990 [1653] on coastal huacas

The following summarizes archaeological data from twenty-two Andean sites spanning the period of approximately 5900 BC to AD 1470. These sites are located in central and northern Peru, principally in the central highlands and Pacific coast (Figure 2.1). The sites range from relatively small structures to truly monumental constructions; some are located in the midst of residential zones and yet others lack evidence of significant habitation. Some of these sites are unique, while others fit comfortably into well-documented architectural traditions. For all their variation, these sites may not truly represent the range of prehispanic Andean constructions; the current data rarely are sufficient to reconstruct well-defined settlement patterns or to evaluate these sites' positions in regional settlement systems. Simply, our knowledge of Andean architecture is outweighed by our ignorance.

Thus, the sample is not ideal, but there are good reasons for selecting these particular sites. First, the focus was somewhat arbitrarily limited to central and northern Peru – an area familiar to me – and therefore ceremonial centers located elsewhere in the Andes, such as the Archaic site of Asana (Aldenderfer 1990, 1991), were excluded from the sample. Further, I selected sites for which detailed plans based on excavated data were available, and which had maps showing the relationship of a particular structure to the larger settlement. Thus, for example, I reluctantly did not include Bonnier's interesting investigations of early ceremonial architecture at Piruru, Huanuco (Bonnier 1983, 1988; Bonnier and Rozenberg 1988; Bonnier, Zegara, and Tello 1985), because it is not clear how the Late Preceramic shrine articulates with a given prehistoric community. Similarly, I excluded interesting data from archaeological surveys (e.g., Willey 1953; Wilson 1988) which did not present necessary architectural detail regarding construction methods, access patterns, room sizes, the locations of friezes, and so on. Additionally, I only chose sites with public architecture, assuming that if the excavator argued for the non-domestic function of the structure, then the site was a candidate for study (regardless of what other archaeologists might think about the excavator's interpretation).

But a final reason for selecting this group of sites is that they form a remarkable architectural corpus, including some of the earliest public buildings and some of the most complex constructions known from the New World. The sample partly

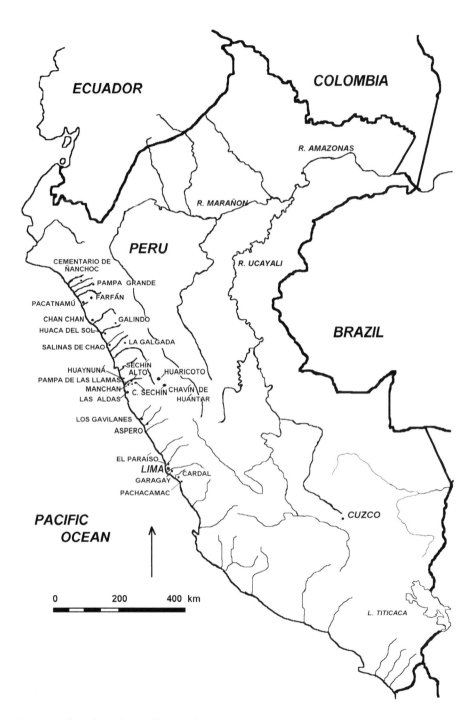

Figure 2.1 Locations of sites discussed in text

reflects the incredibly dynamic architectural developments that occurred in the Andes between 3500 and 200 BC. Andean peoples were constructing truly monumental buildings by ca. 1800 BC, and these constructions were preceded by earlier, though smaller, public structures. Early Andean public architecture incorporated a variety of forms: multi-platform terraces, sunken chambers, enormous U-shaped mounds, platform mounds, semi-subterranean circular patios. Some of these forms replaced other architectural traditions, others co-existed with starkly divergent forms. The sample also includes some very different classes of public architecture, such as the monumental walled enclosures or *ciudadelas* of Chan Chan. This sample of prehispanic Andean architecture defies easy generalization, and it was designed to do so.

Some explanation is required for a seemingly inexplicable oversight: the scanty references to Inca architecture. Given the numerous studies of Inca architecture (e.g. Gasparini and Margolies 1980; Kendall 1985; MacLean 1986; Protzen 1993) and the extraordinary skill which it represents, the exclusion of Inca buildings from a study of Andean public architecture may seem a terrible blunder. Perhaps, but I had my reasons. Inca architecture represents a distinct architectural tradition in Peru, very different from the patterns of buildings constructed on the Peruvian coast. For example, large mound construction is a common element at various periods in North Coast prehistory (see Chapter 4), but not in Inca architecture. Conversely, the basic characteristics of Inca architecture – rectangular masonry buildings without internal divisions, peaked roofs, circular buildings and curved walls, two-story structures, and trapezoidal doors and niches (Hyslop 1990: 5–10) – are rarely found in the public architecture in north central Peru until the region was incorporated into the Inca Empire and even then, only rarely (for an exception at Marca Huamachuco, see J. Topic 1991). And thus, Inca architecture appears to represent a separate architectural tradition – with elements common to other highland societies – but one outside the limits of this sample.

Another point of explanation is required by the site plans and figures used to illustrate the sample sites. In each case, the figures were redrawn from the best available plans. The original plans, however, frequently contained details which the excavator included to document fully a site or excavation, but which are not relevant for my purposes or possible to reproduce at a reduced scale. For example, the 1:500 scale drawings of Chan Chan (Moseley and Mackey 1974) cannot be reproduced at much smaller scale without loss of detail. In the drawings I have emphasized basic architectural information about public constructions, deleting information about domestic structures and non-architectural features. The figures are based on available plans, and I was not able to ground check published plans for each site.

The following chapter is a critical description, presenting archaeological data and evaluating alternative interpretations when germane. I realize that architectural descriptions seldom make for scintillating prose, but I did not hide them in an appendix because I believe the reader should understand the empirical bases of my subsequent analyses. The summaries are my best efforts to portray accurately the results of other archaeologists' work. I have tried to focus on "site-specific" issues rather than general theoretical matters, although in some cases the debated interpretations of certain sites foreshadow larger issues discussed in later chapters.

Description of sites in the sample

Cementario de Ñanchoc and CA-09–27, Zaña Valley

A rare example of Archaic architecture is discussed by Dillehay, Netherly, and Rossen (1989) who present preceramic settlement data from the upper Zaña Valley of northern Peru. Their multi-year survey and excavation program documented 52 preceramic sites and the existence of a prehistoric mixed economy based on hunting, plant collection, and limited plant cultivation. Although this suggests a relatively high degree of sedentism, it was not expressed in substantial ceremonial structures. The site of CA-09–27 contains the only architecture which might have had a ritual function – a small (1.5 × 1.0 m) elliptical stone platform with associated quartz crystals, crystalline quartz, and land snail shells (Dillehay et al. 1989: 749). Dating to 7950 ± 180 bp, the site also contains the remains of wattle and daub residences with stone and adobe foundations; based on the excavation of one such structure, measuring 2.3 × 2.0 m, it may be that the dwellings were larger than the elliptical stone platform (Dillehay et al. 1989: 749–751).

The architectural data from Zaña are scant, but they do conform to general expectations about Archaic ritual architecture: impermanent, simple, small scale structures associated with each settlement (Adler and Wilshusen 1990). A fairly obvious hypothesis is that public architecture became more formalized as sedentism increased during the Archaic; such a transformation may be hinted at by the site of Los Gavilanes.

Los Gavilanes, Huarmey

Los Gavilanes is located north of the Huarmey Valley, approximately 1 km inland from the Pacific Ocean (Bonavia 1982). Covering 1.7 ha, Los Gavilanes is best known for its rich botanical remains, particularly evidence for very early maize (Bonavia 1982; Kelly and Bonavia 1963; Grobman et al. 1982). The site is interpreted by Bonavia (1982: 24) as representing short-term encampments. The only evidence for architecture is a small (4.5 × 4.0 m), quadrangular structure which Bonavia (1982: 61–65) identifies as a "public structure" (Figure 2.2). The structure was built on an intentionally leveled hilltop. A mud plaster floor was cut by a circular hearth, 42 cm in diameter and burned brick-red (Bonavia 1982: 63–66). Two radiocarbon dates associated with the structure produced results of 3595 bp ± 140 and 3250 bp ± 155 (Bonavia 1982: 75). Bonavia (1982: 266–267) draws strong parallels between the hearth at Los Gavilanes and hearths at sites like La Galgada, Aspero and Kotosh, but from the excavator's reconstruction (Bonavia 1982: 272–273) the public building at Los Gavilanes was much less impressive than structures at those sites. The activities associated with this structure are poorly known, and Bonavia's conclusion that it is a public structure, though possible, seems to stretch the archaeological evidence.

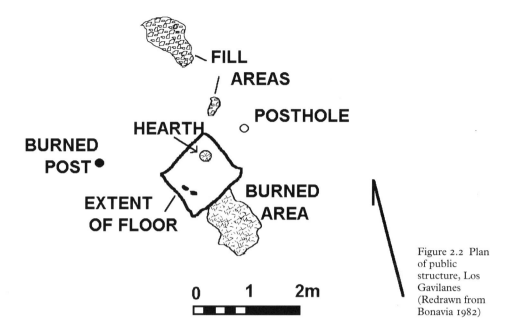

FILL
AREAS

POSTHOLE

HEARTH

BURNED
POST

BURNED
AREA

EXTENT
OF FLOOR

0   1   2m

Figure 2.2 Plan
of public
structure, Los
Gavilanes
(Redrawn from
Bonavia 1982)

Huaynuná, Casma Valley

Evidence for more permanent public architecture comes from the preceramic coastal
site of Huaynuná (Figure 2.3), located north of the Casma Valley (S. Pozorski and
T. Pozorski 1987, 1992; T. Pozorski and S. Pozorski 1990). A series of archaeological components are found around the small bay at Huaynuná, but the earliest occupations date to between 4200 bp ± 80 and 3450 bp ± 65 (T. Pozorski and S. Pozorski
1990: Table 1).

The preceramic component at Huaynuná consists of midden deposits and architectural features. A midden 1.0–1.5 m thick covers an area of 8 ha and contains cultigens (potato, sweet potato, achira, and cotton) as well as abundant evidence of the
maritime orientation of the economy (S. Pozorski and T. Pozorski 1987; T. Pozorski
and S. Pozorski 1990). At least seven cobble and mat dwellings indicate a small but
resident population at the site.

Architectural evidence of public activities takes two distinctive forms. First, a
small structure consists of an enclosure 3 × 2.5 m in area, surrounded by stone walls
40–50 cm high, and finished with a plastered floor (Figure 2.3). The structure sits
on a low (1.5 m) artificial mound 10 × 10 m in area. A centrally located, fire-reddened hearth 70 cm long, 40 cm wide, and 12 cm deep is connected to a subfloor
flue which passes outside of the wall of the stone enclosure. T. Pozorski and S.
Pozorski (1990: 20–21) consider this hearth analogous to ventilated hearths known
from highland ceremonial sites (e.g., Huaricoto and La Galgada, see below). A
radiocarbon sample from the hearth dated to 3810 ± 60 bp.

Second, there is terraced, hillside construction in the southwestern portion of the
Huaynuná (Figure 2.3). Rising 8 m in four planes, the cut and fill terraces were faced
with stone quarried from the hillside. A central stairway leads up the terraces to the

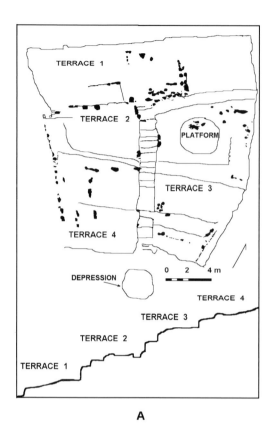

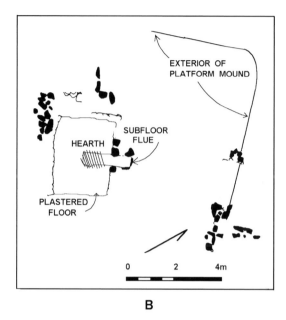

A

B

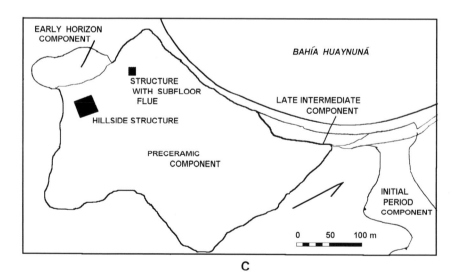

C

Figure 2.3 Huaynuná: (A) plan of hillside structure; (B) plan of structure with hearth; (C) schematic site plan (Redrawn and modified from T. Pozorski and S. Pozorski 1990)

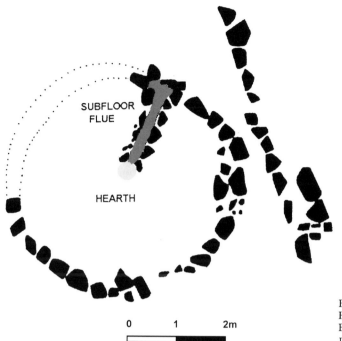

SUBFLOOR
FLUE

HEARTH

0   1   2m

Figure 2.4 Ritual chamber,
Huaricoto (Redrawn from
Burger and Salazar-Burger
1985)

hilltop and to a circular depression, 1.7 m in diameter, cut into the bedrock. On Terrace 2, a circular platform 61 cm tall was constructed from quarried stone and beach cobbles; it may have been plastered. The functions of these circular features are unknown.

T. Pozorski and S. Pozorski (1990: 23–25) cautiously suggest that two architectural traditions are represented in incipient form at Huaynuná. They note parallels between the arrangement of staircase and terraces on the hillside structure and the bilateral symmetry found in Initial Period mound constructions, such as at Pampa de las Llamas-Moxeke and Las Aldas. Secondly, the ventilated hearth at Huaynuná may be similar to hearths at Huaricoto, Galgada, and Kotosh, perhaps reflecting contacts between coastal and highland ritual traditions (T. Pozorski and S. Pozorski 1990: 23–24).

Huaricoto, Callejón de Huaylas
The highland site of Huaricoto is located at 2,750 m elevation in the Callejón de Huaylas. In excavations between 1978 and 1980, Burger and Salazar-Burger exposed thirteen superimposed, deeply buried ritual structures, dating between 2200 BC and 200 BC, with distinctive architectural features (like those illustrated in Figure 2.4) associated with the Kotosh Religious Tradition (Burger 1985b; Burger and Salazar-Burger 1980, 1985, 1986).

In these structures, offerings were burned in semi-subterranean hearths. The majority of the hearths range from 2 m to over 5 m in diameter (Burger and Salazar-Burger 1985: 120), and they are generally subfloor pits associated with plastered floors. The oldest hearths at Huaricoto date to 4210 bp ± 120 and 3970 bp ± 110, a late preceramic date (Hearths XIII, XII, XI; Burger and Salazar-Burger 1985: 121–122). The early hearths lack some of the features associated with later hearths, such as ventilator flues. The earliest Initial Period hearth (IX) is a subrectangular hearth surrounded by a low stone wall and set into a plastered floor (Burger 1985b). Based on its stratigraphic position, Hearth VIII is the oldest hearth at Huaricoto with a subfloor ventilator flue, a feature also found at Shillacoto (Izumi et al. 1972: 48–49, Figure 9), Kotosh (Izumi and Sono 1963: 68–70), and La Galgada (Grieder 1988a).

No domestic features or debris were found in the structure, suggesting their non-secular functions (Burger 1985b: 506; Burger and Salazar-Burger 1985: 115). Some of the hearths were filled with ash and charcoal, burnt bone, and clear flakes of quartz (Burger and Salazar-Burger 1980: 28), while marine shells were sprinkled on the floor around some hearths.

Two other possible ritual constructions were found at Huaricoto. First, a series of stone-lined ditches are interpreted as non-utilitarian canals associated with agricultural fertility ritual and the symbolic cleaning of irrigation systems (Burger and Salazar-Burger 1985: 129). Second, a sunken circular plaza, 16 m in diameter and dating to the Capilla phase (Burger and Salazar-Burger 1985: 131), was excavated at Huaricoto. Although there are parallels between the sunken circular plaza and architectural features at Chavín de Huántar, the ritual tradition at Huaricoto was neither an antecedent to nor replaced by the cult of Chavín; the two religious traditions coexisted (Burger and Salazar-Burger 1985: 131–132).

Burger and Salazar-Burger (1986) have discussed the social units possibly represented by the ritual constructions at Huaricoto. Pointing to the small size and limited labor invested in the Huaricoto structures, Burger and Salazar-Burger (1986) suggest the constructions were built by relatively small social units organized in a cargo-like system, not by large corporate labor units. They write:

> A dichotomy has been drawn here between early societies utilizing corporate labor and those using one possible alternative, a system of rotating ritual authority within which labor is mobilized through ties of blood marriage, ritual kinship, and friendship. These systems have been presented as two options which may have been exercised by the early societies of highland Peru during the first and second millennia BC.

Burger and Salazar-Burger (1986: 69) suggest that a more flexible social order built the ritual hearths at Huaricoto, a model quite different from that suggested by the excavators of La Galgada.

La Galgada, Tablachaca Valley
The site of La Galgada (Figure 2.5), located at 1,100 m on the Tablachaca River (Bueno Mendoza and Grieder 1988), contains an extraordinary assemblage of architectural constructions, burial data, and diverse artifacts and plant remains. The occupation spans the transition from the Preceramic to the Early Horizon with calibrated radiocarbon dates from 2662 BC to 1395 BC (Grieder 1988a). The complex

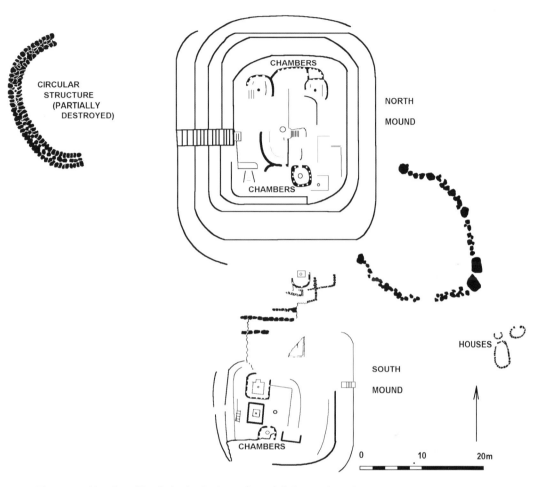

Figure 2.5 Site plan of La Galgada (Redrawn from Grieder et. al 1988)

architectural history of the site thwarts brief synopsis, and the reader is urged to consult Grieder et al. (1988) for a lucid, detailed presentation.

Architecture consists of the North and South Mounds, a ring platform built of river cobbles which ran around a circular plaza west of the North Mound, and a low circular wall apparently associated with a plaza. Five houses were defined at La Galgada, although additional residential architecture is suggested in a reconstruction (Grieder and Bueno Mendoza 1988: Figure 19) presumably based on surface remains.

Monumental construction at La Galgada primarily consists of relatively small (3–5 m in diameter), subcircular masonry chambers with plastered interiors, niches, benches, and central hearths with ventilator shafts; these chambers are located on, in, and near two large mounds at the site (Figure 2.5). Since extremely deep excavations would have destroyed the well-preserved late preceramic structures in the upper levels, little is known about the lower 13 m of unexcavated strata (Grieder and Bueno Mendoza 1988: 24). However, the upper layers consist of ritual chambers which were converted to burial places, filled in and cut by subsequent constructions. At later stages, the public architecture shifted to a singular moundtop construction (see Grieder and Bueno Mendoza 1988: 58 for a summary).

The changes in architecture at La Galgada are fascinating because of their implications for broader social changes, as public architecture shifted from ritual chambers to a moundtop U-shaped structure. As Grieder (1988c: 206) writes:

> The interior space [of the ritual chambers] was separated from the natural world by its white color, encircling wall, precision of design, and finally by the climbing and descending at the entrance, as if penetrating a barrier. Since the chambers were converted to tombs, the participants were surely aware of the chamber as a potential tomb . . . [that] the places of the living participants [would be] taken by the dead, most likely themselves transformed.

In the early phases at La Galgada, the scattered arrangement of ritual chambers may reflect a social order incompletely integrated at the suprafamilial level (Grieder et al. 1988: 195–197), while later phases indicate greater co-ordination and integration as ritual constructions were centered on the mounds. The Inital Period occupation and the development of the moundtop U-shaped structure mark significant social changes. Grieder (1988c: 212) observes:

> While the central position in a Preceramic chamber was occupied by the fire and humans could only occupy eccentric positions, in the Initial Period buildings, the center could be occupied by a human, with all non-central positions doubled symmetrically. A person could occupy the position at the top of the central stairs at La Galgada and hold the only unique and unrivaled place, a position of authority which had no antecedent in Preceramic design.

The architectural developments at La Galgada are interpreted as reflecting the important social changes from egalitarian society to emerging social distinctions, a pattern more completely exhibited among large ceremonial centers of the Peruvian coast.

Aspero, Supe Valley

Located on a rocky point north of the Rio Supe, the large (12 ha) preceramic site of Aspero has been the scene of archaeological investigations since Uhle's excavations in 1905, but an accurate assessment of the site first required seventy years of archaeological investigations in Peru. As Moseley and Willey (1973) discuss, previous interpretations of Aspero (e.g., Willey and Corbett 1954) were distorted by lack of information about the preceramic cultures of Peru and the unwarranted assumption that the people of such cultures could not have constructed large artificial mounds. The site of Aspero, according to Feldman (1980: 24), "could not be ignored, because it had too much that was of interest, but it could not be grasped because it had too little in common with other known sites."

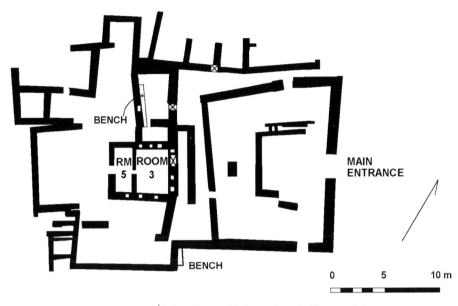

Figure 2.6 Plan of Huaca de los Ídolos, Aspero (Redrawn from Feldman 1987)

Feldman's (1980, 1985, 1987) research has resolved a number of the problems. The site consists of seven major mounds, with freestanding heights of 1 to 4 m; radio-carbon samples from two of these mounds (Huaca de los Ídolos and Huaca de los Sacrificios) date the public architecture to between 2900 and 2500 BC. The mounds represent repeated episodes of construction, fill, and subsequent construction (Feldman 1987: 10). The fieldstone walls were plastered and traces of red or yellow paint have been found. The buildings were intentionally abandoned and filled.

The uppermost structure of Huaca de los Ídolos was particularly well preserved (Figure 2.6). As Feldman (1987: 10) describes it:

> In Huaca de los Ídolos, individual rooms within the excavated levels vary considerably in size, with the largest being 11 m × 16 m. This room, or more likely open court, is the main entry area of the complex, reached by a stairway leading to a two-meter wide doorway at the top of the mound's highest or eastern face. From this first room, passages lead back to smaller rooms at the rear and sides. The central room of the rear group, measuring 5.1 m × 4.4 m [Rooms 5 and 3], is divided in half by a low wall, with a clapboard like frieze on its eastern side. This wall is broken in the middle by a narrow doorway in the shape of a double-topped T. The walls of this room, as well as those of the rooms to the north and east [Rooms 1, 2, and the courtyard], contain niches.

Feldman (1987: 11–12) emphasizes the progressively restrictive access in the structure; for example, the doorways become narrower as one moves into the structure. Particularly notable are the restrictive access and ornamentation of Rooms 3 and 5 which Feldman suggests were the ritual focus of Huaca de los Ídolos (Figure 2.6).

It is not immediately clear, however, what forms of ritual were practiced at Aspero. Huaca de los Ídolos was not designed for large congregations, highly visible public ceremonies, or burials. The repeated remodelings and filling of the rooms suggest that Huaca de los Ídolos was not a sanctified place built once and subsequently venerated, but rather was a public structure which was repeatedly reformed to meet the needs of a new social group.

Feldman (1980, 1985, 1987) argues that Aspero's corporate architecture indicates a non-egalitarian social organization associated with chiefdoms, as defined by Service (1962). Feldman contends Aspero's corporate architecture was restrictive in access, implying that a smaller social group had access to that space while others did not, a non-egalitarian society which corresponds to Service's notion of "chiefdom." And yet, "overall, the evidence for major social differentiation is not strong" (Feldman 1987: 13), leading one to wonder if other social principles are reflected in the architectural patterns of Aspero.

El Paraíso, Chillon Valley

El Paraíso is the largest known preceramic site, covering 58 ha and including as many as eleven groups of structures. Moseley (1992: 119) estimates that over 100,000 tons of rock were quarried for its construction. El Paraíso was partially reconstructed by Engel (Figure 2.7), who obtained radiocarbon dates which indicated a preceramic occupation at the site, the dates ranging from 3570 ± 150 to 3065 ± 61 bp (Engel 1966). Given the site's size and the many references to it in the archaeological literature, it is somewhat surprising that answers to basic questions awaited Jeffrey Quilter's 1983 field research (Quilter 1985).

Engel's earlier excavation of the central portion of Unit I (Figure 2.7) uncovered a multi-room complex of thick stone walls with traces of yellow and red painted clay plaster. From the main entrance, a stairway led to the largest and perhaps oldest room in Unit I (Quilter 1985: 297). A rectangular pit (4.5 × 4.25 m) in the room's floor was flanked by circular pits in each corner. Charcoal in the circular pits and the fire-reddened floor of the rectangular pit suggest the use of fire in a non-domestic, possibly ritual setting. Quilter (1985: 297) suggests a loose similarity with the Kotosh Religious Tradition, though commenting, "But the differences are greater than the similarities."

Quilter (1985: 281) obtained a series of radiocarbon dates from Unit I, Unit II, and Unit IV, that suggested a relatively short occupation at El Paraíso, lasting approximately two to four centuries (Quilter 1985: 294). Quilter's data also indicated El Paraíso was not an incipient form of the U-shaped ceremonial center as proposed by Williams León (1980). The debate over the ceremonial vs. secular nature of El Paraíso has a 25-year history (e.g., Lanning 1967; Fung Pineda 1988; Williams León 1985; vs. Moseley 1975: 96–100; Moseley and Willey 1973; Patterson and Moseley 1968, however, cf. Moseley 1992: 119–121). The argument concerns whether El Paraíso was U-shaped in plan through design or accretion, and whether it was residential or ceremonial in nature. Thus, for example, Moseley and Willey (1973: 464) wrote:

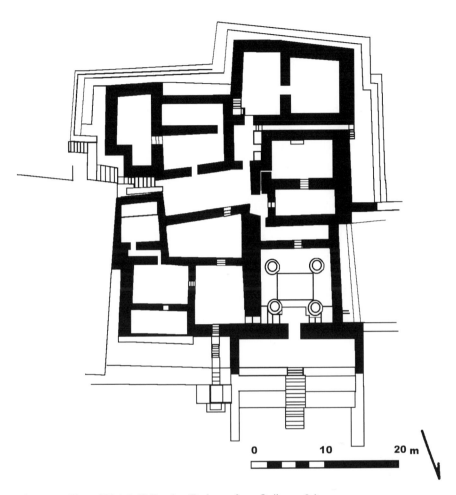

Figure 2.7 Plan of Unit I, El Paraíso (Redrawn from Quilter 1985)

In general form, El Paraíso is reminiscent of a large southwestern pueblo. The construction is massive, and walls average 1 m or more in thickness and are of double-face rubble fill form. Rooms were frequently filled over to create elevated footings for later structures, and most main buildings are presently several meters high. Lanning (1967) has labeled El Paraíso a "temple" site. Yet there is absolutely no resemblance to later buildings similarly labeled or thought of as religious in character . . . The reasoning here is that although the construction is impressive, in plan and form its closest similarities lie with later residential architecture, and the artifact content of the site is purely of a lay domestic nature with nothing anomalous that would impute a religious or ceremonial character to the material.

However, Quilter's investigations showed that, while domestic remains are present, the size and organization of the society at El Paraíso are unclear (Quilter 1985: 296). Moseley (1975a: 96–97) had concluded that the scale of the construction indicated a large population, but El Paraíso contained less midden than at much smaller sites like Aspero. Domestic debris was recovered in subfloor trash pits (Quilter 1985: 286–287), yet the residential evidence remained frustratingly thin.

Recently, Moseley (1992: 121) described El Paraíso as a precursor of U-shaped ceremonial centers, sites which he lyrically observes, "literally turn their back to the sea to face the mountains, with their great arms reaching out to the rising sun and the mountain sources of desert water." A more testable hypothesis was outlined nearly two decades ago (Moseley 1975a: 99):

> . . . later structures which archaeologists label temples are not congeries of rooms and courts but are platforms traceable to maritime antecedents . . . [T]he distinct pattern of constructing artificial platforms for presumed religious purposes was well established on the coast at the time El Paraíso was being built. The form and layout of the Aspero platforms or the Piedra Parada terrace platforms bear no resemblances to the El Paraíso architecture. Therefore, this architecture was not intended or designed to serve the same purposes as the platform mounds or terrace platforms.

Such architectural patterns are clear in the Initial Period constructions at Cardal and Garagay.

Cardal, Lurín Valley

The site of Cardal is located approximately 14 km inland in the lower Lurín Valley (Burger 1987: 366). Fieldwork directed by Richard Burger and Lucy Salazar-Burger has focused on determining the ceremonial and other activities which occurred at the site. The site covers approximately 20 ha and consists of three large platform mounds arranged in a U, eleven circular sunken courtyards, four large patio areas, and 2–3 ha of residential area consisting of household clusters (Burger and Salazar-Burger 1991). The site's population lived in dispersed domestic units; an excavated house measured 6 × 5.46 m, suggesting the residence unit was a nuclear or modified nuclear family (Burger and Salazar-Burger 1991: 278). The limited residential area at Cardal suggests a population of less than 300 people (Burger and Salazar-Burger 1991: 278).

The U-shaped ceremonial centers consist of three platform mounds made from irregular, quarried stone set into clay mortar (Figure 2.8). The central platform is 145 × 60 m and 17 m tall, the eastern platform is 300 × 90 m and 12 m tall, and the partially destroyed western platform is 120 × 55 m and 8 m tall (Burger 1987: 366). Excavations on the central platform indicate four different construction phases during the site's occupation of less than 500 years, between 1465 and 975 BC (3120–2690 bp; Burger and Salazar-Burger 1991). A steep, wide (6.5 m), well-plastered stairway led up the central platform to moundtop ceremonial structures (atria). At least two moundtop structures were uncovered at Cardal, the Late Temple, and the earlier, Middle Temple; Burger and Salazar-Burger suspect than an even earlier, though unexcavated, temple construction exists (1991: 283).

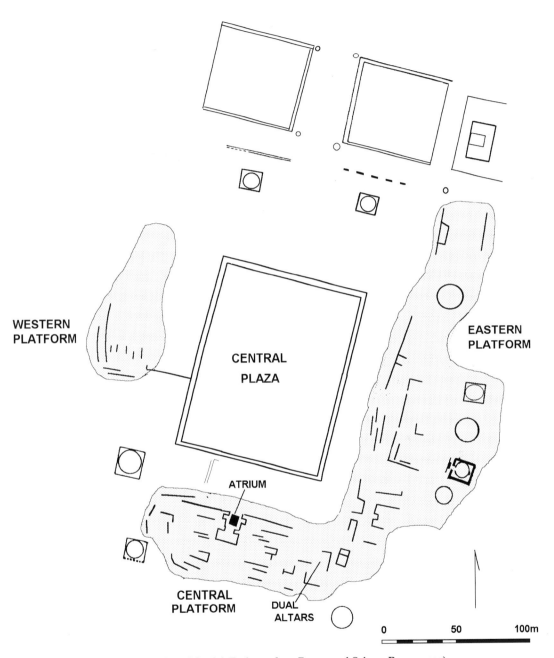

WESTERN
PLATFORM

EASTERN
PLATFORM

CENTRAL
PLAZA

ATRIUM

CENTRAL
PLATFORM

DUAL
ALTARS

0   50   100m

Figure 2.8 Site plan of Cardal (Redrawn from Burger and Salazar-Burger 1991)

The Atrium of the Middle Temple was particularly well preserved, consisting of an unroofed patio, 13.5 × 9.4 m, surrounded by 2.1 m tall walls (Burger and Salazar-Burger 1991: 285). A polychrome, bas-relief frieze on the outer atrium wall faces the large central plaza. The frieze consists of a red mouth band with overlapping yellow fangs nearly 1 m in length.

The Middle Temple Atrium was filled with carefully placed bags of shicra fill (Burger and Salazar-Burger 1991: 287). After the careful filling of the Middle Temple, a process referred to as "ritual entombment" (Burger and Salazar-Burger 1991: 287), the Late Temple was built, but following the plan and basic dimensions of the earlier construction (Burger and Salazar-Burger 1991: 288–289). Elsewhere on the mound, a complex of small rectangular rooms and passageways appear to be contemporary with the Middle Temple Atrium. These structures contain two "three-step altars" set back to back against a common wall and presumably joined by a window opening. The walls of the small room exhibit graffiti which "appear to be related to the religious ideology, rather than profane subjects" (Burger and Salazar-Burger 1991: 281).

Burger and Salazar-Burger (1991: 291) infer that Cardal had multiple ceremonial foci, designed to "accommodate public gatherings of different sizes and composition," such as the central plaza, smaller plazas, and the small, circular, sunken courts. Burger and Salazar-Burger (1991: 292) suggest that the estimated 2 million person-days of work required to build the monumental architecture of Cardal may have occurred over four centuries; in that case, the monumental construction represents the work, on average, of 100 people working two months per year. They write:

> In trying to understand the socioeconomic basis upon which Initial Period
> monumental complexes like Cardal were produced, it is critical to remember
> that they were the net result of myriad small construction episodes
> throughout centuries of occupation. In this respect, they were fundamentally
> different from the pyramids of Giza or Teotihuacán.
> (Burger and Salazar-Burger 1991: 292)

Burger and Salazar-Burger argue that the monumental constructions at Cardal do not represent the achievements of a "complex" stratified society but instead were the creations of a "rather modest egalitarian lifestyle" and motivated by religion (Burger and Salazar-Burger 1991: 293). It was a pattern, however, which was disrupted ca. 800 BC, when U-shaped ceremonial structures were abandoned along the Peruvian coast (Burger 1981: 600). These U-shaped structures, Burger and Salazar-Burger (1991: 293–294) contend, reflect regional variations on a basic shared ideology, variations reflected in differences between independent ceremonial centers like Cardal and Garagay.

Garagay, Rimac Valley
Today surrounded by metropolitan Lima, the U-shaped ceremonial structure of Garagay covers some 16 ha (Figure 2.9), most of which is a large plaza (9 ha) defined by three large platform mounds (Ravines 1979; Ravines and Isbell 1975; Ravines et al. 1982). The platform mounds were constructed from retaining walls filled with loose stone, domestic debris, or shicra fill, and then capped with clay floors. The overall construction consists a series of terraces, stairways, and open courts, conforming in a general manner to the architectural patterns described above for Cardal. A small number of radiocarbon dates (TK-178 3340 bp ± 70, CU-49 3170 bp ± 80,

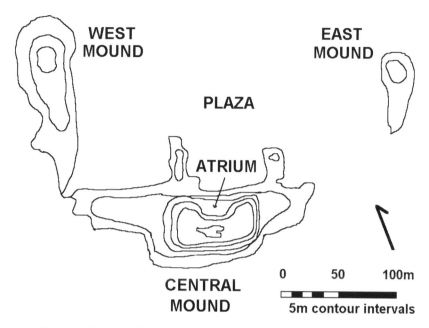

Figure 2.9 Site plan of Garagay (Redrawn from Ravines and Isbell 1975)

TK-177 3090 bp ± 70, and CU-09 2730 bp ± 70) have been published, but without provenience or information about the samples' materials (Ravines et al. 1982: 135).

Good information, however, is available for the areas and volumes of the different mounds at Garagay (Ravines et al. 1982). The central mound covers 39,550 m², is 23 m tall, and has a volume of 277,717 m³. The western platform covers 29,710 m², is 14 m tall, and contains an estimated 70,733 m³. The eastern mound is much smaller, covering only 3,440 m², rising to a maximum height of 7 m, and encompassing only 12,783 m³ (Ravines et al. 1982: 139–140). Ravines estimates that the construction volume totals 311,233 m³, but his volumes (Ravines et al. 1982: 225) total 361,233 m³, a not insignificant difference. Using his estimate of 5.3 person-days of work per 1 m³, this suggests a labor investment of 1,914,535 person-days (rather than the 1,711,781 cited in the article). Assuming an agricultural population could work full-time on monumental constructions two months of the year, a population of 100 people could build the mound in about 320 years. Alternatively, if the mound construction resulted from the steady accumulation of material over the same nine centuries as Ravines suggests (Ravines et al. 1982: 135), then a much smaller population (35 people) could have constructed the site.

Like other U-shaped ceremonial centers, Garagay has a forecourt or atrium (Ravines and Isbell 1975: 259–262). Located below the peak of the central platform mound, the atrium is 24 × 24 m and aligned on the central axis of the site. Three terrace levels rise from the floor of the atrium; large circular postholes in the terraces indicate upright roof supports. The masonry walls of the atrium were decorated with polychrome friezes, bas-reliefs modeled from fine clay and painted black, white, yellow, gray-blue, purple, and pink (Ravines and Isbell 1975: 262–266). One frieze consists of anthropomorphic heads, shown in three-quarter profile, each with a feline mouth marked by three large fangs, and surrounded by a yellow border. A second, zoomorphic figure is interpreted as a mythic insect or crustacean with four legs, a fish tail, a fangless feline head, and possibly a pair of wings, although these are poorly preserved. A third zoomorphic figure appears to have some type of feet, an eye, and a fin, but ultimately eludes interpretation. A pair of murals may have flanked the stairway leading to the eastern side of the mound. Though much destroyed, enough of the mural remains to indicate the anthropomorphic heads were similar to the first figure, exhibiting three large fangs and a stylized anthropomorphic eye. These anthropomorphic and zoomorphic figures are arranged in a procession, facing the same direction in profile, a procession which leads to the stairway and flanking murals.

Ravines and Isbell (1975: 266) discuss the stylistic similarities between the friezes of Garagay and Chavín iconography, yet suggest that sufficient differences exist – both in art and architecture – to indicate the independent religious tradition represented at Garagay. The U-shaped ceremonial centers of the central coast reflect one tradition of Formative ceremonial structures, contemporary but distinct from other early public architecture found further north at sites like Salinas de Chao.

Salinas de Chao, Chao

The archaeological complex at Salinas de Chao is located in one of the smallest and most arid coastal valleys in northern Peru. The Chao Valley contains a minuscule amount of arable land (less than 2,000 ha) and an undependable trickle of irrigation water; the number of large prehistoric sites in the valley contrasts markedly with today's dispersed, small population (Alva Alva 1986; Huaypa Manco 1977–78).

The archaeological complex of Salinas de Chao is located 8 km inland from the Pacific Ocean and 6.5 km south of currently cultivated land. A well-defined fossil embayment is located immediately north and west of the site. Based on the distribution of sites along this fossil shoreline (Alva Alva 1986: 50, 89–90), Salinas de Chao was abandoned when the bay was drastically modified by infilling. While marine resources provided the bulk of protein at the site, the presence of squash, chile, cotton, avocado, gourd, and other cultigens indicates Salinas de Chao was linked to agricultural communities in the valley (Alva Alva 1986: 76).

Monumental architecture at Salinas de Chao consists of a planned complex of platform mounds, open courtyards, terraces, residential areas, and sunken circular courtyards (Figure 2.10). The site increased through time in size and complexity, and there appear to be two major construction phases (Figure 2.11). The two phases are not tightly dated by absolute methods, although Alva Alva (1986: 54–55) notes that radiocarbon dates of 1610 BC ± 70 and 1660 BC ± 60 predate the upper constructions of one of the complexes (Unit B), while the 1330 BC ± 140 and 1360 BC ± 60 immediately postdate the uppermost constructions (Table 2.1). Thus the second phase of construction at Salinas de Chao probably dates to between 3600 and

Figure 2.10 Site plan of Salinas de Chao (Redrawn from Alva Alva 1986)

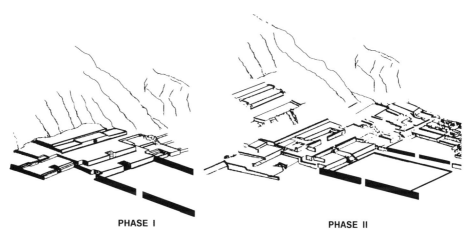

PHASE I   **PHASE II**

Figure 2.11 Hypothetical reconstruction of two building phases, Salinas de Chao (Redrawn from Alva Alva 1986)

Table 2.1. *Salinas de Chao radiocarbon dates*

	uncalibrated	material
1330 BC ± 140	3280 ± 140	cotton
1360 BC ± 60	3310 ± 60	plant carbon
1540 BC ± 80	3490 ± 80	plant carbon
1550 BC ± 70	3500 ± 70	shells
1610 BC ± 70	3560 ± 70	plant carbon
1660 BC ± 60	3510 ± 60	plant carbon
3600 BP ± 90	3600 ± 90	plant carbon
3200 BP ± 90	3200 ± 90	unburned wood

Source: From (Alva Alva 1986: 55)

3300 bp, while the first phase occurred sometime earlier. Salinas de Chao contains two complexes of monumental constructions (Units A and B) described below and eight smaller complexes of residential and minor ceremonial architecture (Units C–J) briefly summarized by Alva Alva (1986: 64–70).

The public architecture of Unit A includes a small temple (*templete*), a circular sunken court, and a large rectangular plaza. The templete measures 27 × 19 m and consists of a set of platform mounds and terraces linked by three staircases (Alva Alva 1986: 56–57). The templete rises in three levels, incorporating the natural slope, and stairways and a ramp lead to a central atrium on the uppermost level. This atrium is flanked by platform mounds and small terraces. The sunken circular court associated with Unit A is 27 m from the base of the templete. The sunken court has a maximum depth of 2 m and a maximum diameter of approximately 8 m; two opposing staircases descend into the sunken circular court. The interior is partially faced with stone walls, effectively creating narrow semicircular benches that rim the court. Alva Alva (1986: 58) suggests: "The semicircular walls could have served as benches for the participants in a hypothesized ceremonial activity which implies limited and direct visual access by individuals" (translation mine). North of the templete and sunken circular court, there is a large plaza, 8 × 20 m, but the function of the structure is unknown.

Like Unit A, Unit B also consists of a series of hillside constructions, but Unit B is much larger and more complex. Unit B was the most important architectural unit at Salinas de Chao (Alva Alva 1986: 59), and it underwent two distinct construction phases. In the earliest stage, Unit B consisted of a large rectangular plaza (1,316 m^2), from which rose three platform levels. The middle and upper levels were flanked by additional platform groups, some with terraced faces.

The lowest of the central platforms covers an area of approximately 186 m^2, placed on 180 cm of mixed fill. The second platform covers 270m^2, is 160 cm high, and is built on top of clean fill. The uppermost platform is some 2 m tall, covers 101 m^2, and is faced with a well-plastered wall. The center of this wall was decorated with a now indistinct geometric symbol, which appears to have been a pair of nested quadrangular designs with rounded corners; the exterior design was painted red, the interior black. The symbol is 1.2 m tall and its placement suggests it was meant to be viewed from the large plaza.

The second construction phase saw the addition of terraces located upslope and behind the original group, and significant remodeling of the original architectural pattern. The remodelings of earlier structures effectively reorganized the access patterns and visual domains of Unit B. Alva Alva (1986: 62) suggests that the spatial reorganization reflects changes in the functions of this sacred space, although the nature of those functions and the significance of those changes are far from clear.

In his summary of the architecture of Salinas de Chao, Alva Alva (1986: 71–74) observes that the site seems to express a coherent architectural plan. Although monumental constructions underwent two building phases, construction was along specific axes, "maintaining a coherent and recognizable spatial arrangement, achieved by alternately balancing open areas with constructed spaces" (translation mine).

Alva Alva hypothesizes that the large architectural complexes, Units A and B, were public religious constructions, but changes in these structures suggest differences in the nature of those ceremonies. In the first phase, the open plazas linked by stairways "facilitated a broad visual access." In the second phase, this visual access was interrupted by the placement of freestanding walls. "The restricted visual access of the ritual spaces," Alva Alva (1986: 91) writes, "expresses a new formal concept," a new "structuration of the monument" (Alva Alva 1986: 90). While it is not certain what this change implies for society at Salinas de Chao, Alva Alva seems to suggest that it represents the transition to more disparate social distinctions and greater social complexity. Thus the monumental constructions at Salinas de Chao presaged the social divisions which transformed coastal Formative societies.

Pampa de las Llamas-Moxeke, Casma Valley

Located 18 km inland on a dry *quebrada* north of the Casma River, Pampa de las Llamas-Moxeke was first intensively studied in 1937 by Julio C. Tello (1956). More recently, Shelia and Thomas Pozorski have conducted an extensive program of fieldwork at the site, and their articles and monograph discuss the architecture and artifacts of Pampa de las Llamas-Moxeke (S. Pozorski 1987; S. Pozorski and T. Pozorski 1986, 1987; T. Pozorski and S. Pozorski 1988, 1990).

Radiocarbon dates from Pampa de las Llamas-Moxeke indicate the Initial Period occupation at the site of ca. 3490–3070 bp (S. Pozorski 1987: 17; T. Pozorski and S. Pozorski 1988: 118; cf. Burger 1989: 479) (Table 2.2).

Pampa de las Llamas-Moxeke covers over 2 km²; its two largest mounds, Moxeke and Huaca A, sit at opposite ends of the site, precisely aligned to N 41° E (Figure 2.12). The eastern and western edges of the site contain more than a hundred small mound structures also aligned with the two gigantic mounds. The aligned structures and massive mounds border four or five huge plazas, the largest covering more than 14 hectares. Two large areas of small residential structures are interpreted as commoners' dwellings, while more substantial structures are interpreted as elite

Table 2.2. *Radiocarbon dates from Pampa de las Llamas-Moxeke*

bp	sample no.	bp	sample no.
4655 ± 95	UGA-4510	3220 ± 85	UGA-4509
3735 ± 75	UGA-4505	3175 ± 90	UGA-4511
3490 ± 75	UGA-4506	3165 ± 75	UGA-4503
3425 ± 75	UGA-4508	3070 ± 85	UGA-4504
3390 ± 150	UGA-4507	3515 ± 70	UGA-5462[1]

Note:
[1] C[14] sample UGA-5462 reported in T. Pozorski and
S. Pozorski 1988: 118; all other dates from S. Pozorski
1987: 17).

residences, containing distinctive artifacts (e.g., stone bowls, ceramic figurines, ceramic seals) and architectural features (e.g., niches and subfloor caches) (S. Pozorski and T. Pozorski 1986: 394–397). In plan, the many small mound structures seem to form either a squared U or an H shape; they vary between 10 and 50 m in length and between 2 and 5 m in height (S. Pozorski and T. Pozorski 1986: 392), but exhibit extremely uniform façades (Billman 1989). Elite residences may be attached to some of these structures, yet the absence of domestic debris or features suggests that these structures were neither residential areas nor household annexes.

The function of these smaller structures at the site is unclear, but there is no question about the monumental scale and public nature of the two principal mounds. Huaca Moxeke is 170 × 160 m at its base and 30 m tall (S. Pozorski and T. Pozorski 1986: 384). Roughly forming a truncated pyramid (Figure 2.13), the mound is built from three layered platforms crowned by a pair of additional mounds. A wide (6.7 m), red-painted, plastered staircase passes through a portico (possibly columned) to a vestibule measuring 26 × 10.3 m and decorated with figures which Tello (1956: 58)

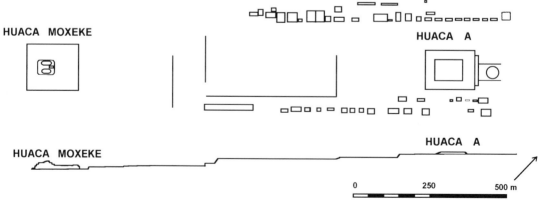

Figure 2.12 Schematic site plan of Pampa de las Llamas-Moxeke (Redrawn from S. Pozorski and T. Pozorski 1992)

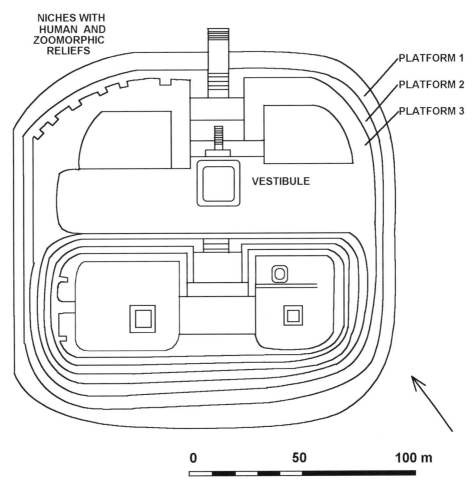

NICHES WITH
HUMAN AND
ZOOMORPHIC
RELIEFS

PLATFORM 1

PLATFORM 2

PLATFORM 3

VESTIBULE

0   50   100 m

Figure 2.13 Plan of Huaca Moxeke (Redrawn from Tello 1956)

described – with a disappointing lack of detail – as "representing many fantastic figures in high and low relief."

Fortunately, Tello (1956: 60–66, Plates 4 and 5) provided more complete documentation of two sets of magnificent reliefs that covered the north face of Huaca Moxeke. These reliefs were made from conical adobes and stone covered by thick layers of mud and then sculpted into high-relief zoomorphic and human figures. The human figures are set into niches while the zoomorphic figures are flush with the front of the terrace. Four of the human figures wear long tunics draped with some form of shawl; in one case the shawl is fringed with snakes, their forked tongues caught in mid-flick. Two figures are simply heads, a poorly preserved head which Tello interpreted as a human and a superbly executed head which Tello believed (1956: 63–64) was a jaguar. The enormous feline figure fills the niche, which is 2.4 m wide, 90 cm deep and of unknown original height. The figure was painted light red, emerald, white and black, creating a truly imposing, extremely visible figure.

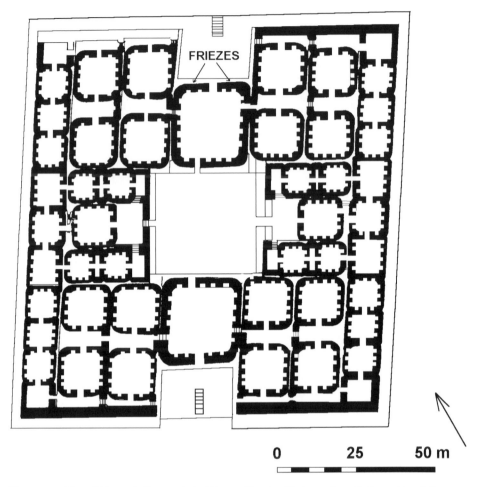

FRIEZES

0   25   50 m

Figure 2.14 Plan of Huaca A, Pampa de las Llamas-Moxeke (Redrawn from S. Pozorski and T. Pozorski 1992)

The Jaguar Idol, as Tello dubbed it, was intentionally covered up with placed fill, the faces first caked with a protective layer of mud, fragments of which retained the impressions of the modeled face (Tello 1956: 64).

The Pozorskis' excavations have focused on other structures at Pampa de las Llamas-Moxeke, particularly Huaca A. Huaca A is perfectly aligned with Moxeke; the facing stairways of the two mounds are on the same precise alignment, although 1.3 km apart. Huaca A is 140 × 140 m at its base and 9 m tall. While there is evidence of earlier construction phases at the mound (S. Pozorski and T. Pozorski 1986: 391), only limited soundings were taken to prevent extensive damage to the well-preserved architecture on top of the mound. The last construction at Huaca A differed markedly from Moxeke (Figure 2.14). Huaca A was built as a set of courts placed along the centerline of the mound; the central courts open onto smaller side rooms. The central courts progressively rise in elevation and the smaller rooms also rise from each court forming a complex set of horizontal planes.

The organization of the rooms on top of Huaca A is also complex, and this was clearly the intention of the builders. The niched walls are tall (4–7 m) constructions of mortar and stone covered with a smooth, white layer of plaster. Access to these rooms was regulated with wooden gates and bar closures (S. Pozorski and T. Pozorski 1986: 389).

The small rooms on top of Huaca A are interpreted as storage areas based on the cellular nature of the construction, the restricted access to the structures, and pollen evidence suggesting that "a variety of plant foods such as peanuts, common beans, and tubers were stored within the rooms and niches of Huaca A" (T. Pozorski and S. Pozorski 1988: 114; also S. Pozorski and T. Pozorski 1986: 390). Shelia and Thomas Pozorski suggest Huaca A was

> a repository for surplus goods and that the collection and distribution of these goods was closely monitored. Additionally, its distinct architectural configuration combined with an absence of ritual paraphernalia and friezes within the interior plazas and rooms indicate that Huaca A served as a secular counterpart to Moxeke. It was apparently the focal point for bureaucratic activities which functioned to control access to products of the site's agricultural and industrial economy.
> (S. Pozorski and T. Pozorski 1986: 390)

The opposition of sacred and secular may be indicated by the content and placement of public art at the site. Pozorski and Pozorski write:

> The location and size of each segment [of the murals at Huaca A] document clear efforts to awe the mound visitor, but with more secular power symbols. In contrast to the Moxeke friezes, where anthropomorphic depictions are dominant, the possible human figure on the Huaca [A] frieze is dwarfed by a feline and associated with what appears to be an even more secular authority symbol.
> (S. Pozorski and T. Pozorski 1986: 388)

Since most of the Huaca A mural is destroyed, its reconstruction as a large jaguar behind a smaller human is a matter of speculation, and the iconographic classification of Huaca Moxeke/anthropomorphic/sacred vs. Huaca A/feline/secular is a bit mystifying given the symbolic significance of jaguars (for a discussion, see S. Pozorski and T. Pozorski 1986; T. Pozorski 1975, 1980). There are, however, stark differences between the two largest mounds at the site. The Pozorskis outline their argument clearly:

> Huaca A and Moxeke are the two dominant mounds at Pampa de las Llamas-Moxeke. Both are clearly corporate labor constructions, and their large size suggests that they were the locus of centralized authority at the site. Close examination of the mounds reveals that each had a distinct function. Moxeke appears to have been the seat of ideological power or religion whereas Huaca A served in a more secular manner that involved the storage

and distribution of commodities that constituted the economic power base of the site elite.
(S. Pozorski and T. Pozorski 1986: 383–384)

The huge figures of Huaca Moxeke were designed to be seen from a distance, placed to be viewed from the large plaza in the site. "The public nature of the friezes and architecture suggests that rituals or ceremonies in full view of the site population were a critical aspect of religious motivation" (S. Pozorski and T. Pozorski 1986: 385).

Huaca A is obviously different; the mural – regardless of its representative content – was not placed for wide public view. Partially blocked by the atrium walls, the figures flank the entrance into the more central courts; the friezes cannot be seen from any of the residential areas at the site. The friezes probably were visible from the sunken forecourt on the north side of Huaca A, and possibly visible from the circular sunken court on the north site of the *huaca*. The Huaca A friezes were not completely hidden, but neither were they placed in an open public position like the figures of Moxeke. Such considerations lead S. Pozorski and T. Pozorski (1986: 400) to observe: "These data suggest that the Huaca A frieze may have functioned differently from the Moxeke figures, serving in a manner more in keeping with the secular nature of the mound." The possible complementary opposition of sacred and secular is an intriguing interpretation of Pampa de las Llamas-Moxeke.

Las Aldas, Casma Valley
Las Aldas is perched above a rocky coastline 30 km south of the Casma Valley and far from arable land (Engel 1970; Fung Pineda 1969; Grieder 1975; Matsuzawa 1978). Following S. Pozorski and T. Pozorski's (1987: 16–30) summary of previous research, a preceramic component and a subsequent Early Horizon component occur at the site, but most construction at Las Aldas dates to the Initial Period. Radiocarbon dates summarized by Shelia Pozorski (1987: 17) suggest an Initial Period occupation at Las Aldas between 3600 and 3100 bp (Table 2.3). Matsuzawa (1978: 666) attempted to date precisely the principal temple at the site; discrepancies in the dates, however, and a schematic presentation of the stratigraphic positions of the dates suggest that significant mixing had occurred, making the proposed, fine-scaled chronology suspect (Matsuzawa 1978: 667).

The principal constructions at Las Aldas – a large mound fronted by a series of platforms, a sunken circular court, and large open plazas (Figure 2.15) – were built during the Initial Period in a spurt of construction which was "quite brief, yet very visible" (S. Pozorski and T. Pozorski 1987: 27). The mound was built on a hilltop which was partially filled to create a building surface, and in some sections the fill is 40 m deep (Grieder 1975: 102).

The central sector of Las Aldas is a linear progression of plazas and terraces, culminating dramatically in a hilltop structure overlooking the Pacific Ocean. There are two smaller sets of rooms and platforms located north and south of the central plaza–mound group. Most archaeological investigations have focused on the central

Table 2.3. *Initial Period radiocarbon dates for Las Aldas*

bp	published source
3600 ± 95	Matsuzawa 1978
3595 ± 75	S. Pozorski 1987
3460 ± 75	S. Pozorski 1987
3430 ± 80	Grieder 1975
3400 ± 100	Berger et al. 1965
3150 ± 90	Matsuzawa 1978
3140 ± 75	S. Pozorski 1987
3140 ± 80	Matsuzawa 1978
2590 ± 80	S. Pozorski 1987

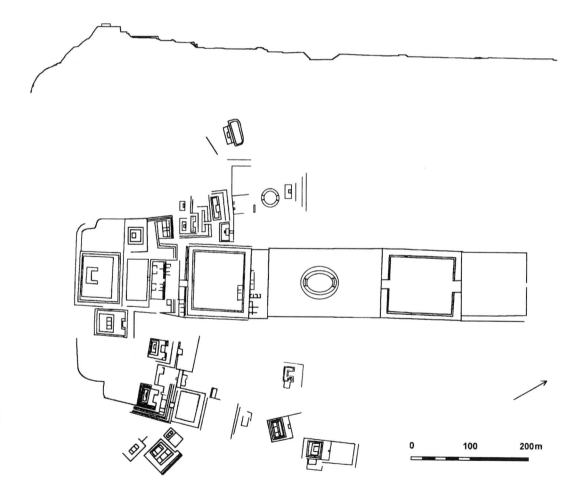

Figure 2.15 Plan and elevation of Las Aldas (Redrawn from Grieder 1975)

group of plazas and terraces to the near exclusion of the other structures and archaeological deposits, which cover an estimated 40 hectares (S. Pozorski and T. Pozorski 1987: 16; cf. Fung Pineda 1969: 30).

The central plaza and terrace group at Las Aldas covers 400 × 200 m. It is rigidly linear, with plaza entrances, the sunken circular courts, and the terrace staircases all aligned. From east to west, the eastern plaza measures 62 × 60 m, the next plaza – defined by low walls with opposing doorways – measures 76 × 65.5 m, the plaza containing the large sunken circular court is 107 × 64 m, while the westernmost plaza covers an area of 58 × 65.5 m (Grieder 1975). At this point, the site rises some 16 m in elevation in four planes which stretch across three structures (Grieder's Structures 1, 2, and 3). A chain of stairways ultimately leads to a three-sided masonry structure on top of the mound, obviously the focal point of the ceremonial complex. It is intriguing that the uppermost staircase was unfinished when the site was abandoned; Grieder (1975: 103, Figure 9) not only discovered the incomplete staircase, but also found a prehispanic mason's stake and line left *in situ*. Excavations by S. Pozorski and T. Pozorski (1987: 27) suggest that the mounds of Las Aldas may have been covered with a yellow layer of silty mud (cf. Grieder 1975: 103).

A number of excavators consider the large circular sunken patio to be the key element in the main group of structures at Las Aldas (Fung Pineda 1969; Grieder 1975; Matsuzawa 1978; S. Pozorski and T. Pozorski 1987). The sunken circular court is elliptical in outline, with sloping walls retained by a circular wall cut by two opposing winged staircases. The interior diameter of the stone-walled court is 18.15 × 16 m (Fung Pineda 1969: 32); the pit was at least 149 cm deep (S. Pozorski and T. Pozorski 1987: 23). Although Fung Pineda and Grieder report the floor was not plastered, S. Pozorski and T. Pozorski (1987: 28) discovered a 5 cm thick layer of plastered flooring along the interior perimeter. Grieder (1975: 101) suggests that the sunken circular court was not roofed or surrounded by high stone walls.

In spite of its spectacular isolation, Las Aldas apparently was linked to other Initial Period settlements in the Casma Valley. Matsuzawa (1978: 669–670) has briefly discussed the evidence for economic interactions between communities at Las Aldas and the large Formative sites located in the fertile Casma Valley. More specifically, S. Pozorski (1987: 23) suggests Las Aldas and Sechín Alto existed in "coastal–inland symbiosis," occupying the nodes "of an intersite hierarchy of at least three levels." Certainly the inhabitants of Las Aldas had access to agricultural foods, crops which could not be grown at the site, but the precise nature of the interaction between Las Aldas and sites like Sechín Alto remains hypothetical.

Sechín Alto, Casma Valley

Sechín Alto is one of the most impressive Formative constructions in the Andes, yet its very size seems to have hampered excavations. Dominating the junction of the Sechín and Casma Valleys, Sechín Alto has been described by a number of archaeologists (Fung Pineda and Williams León 1979; Kosok 1965; Tello 1956; Thompson 1961, 1964; S. Pozorski and T. Pozorski 1987, 1992), but excavations at the site are

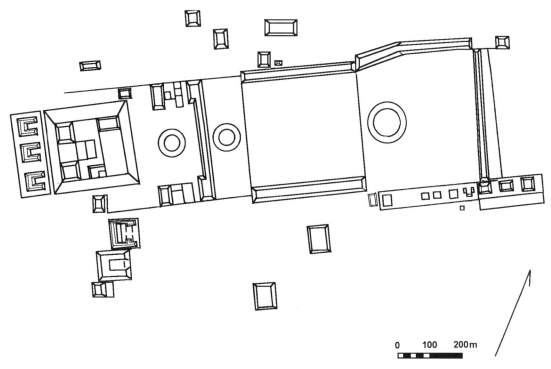

Figure 2.16 Schematic site plan of Sechín Alto (Redrawn from S. Pozorski and T. Pozorski 1987)

limited to six small test pits excavated by Donald Collier and Donald Thompson (Collier 1960). Shelia and Thomas Pozorski (1992) have described Sechín Alto as one part of a larger complex of sites including Sechín Bajo, Taukachi-Konkán, and the well-known Cerro Sechín. Sechín Alto was the monumental center of this group (Figure 2.16).

The principal mound has a base of 300 × 250 m, and it rises 44 m above the surrounding floodplain. Partially constructed from conical adobes, it is estimated that the mound contains some 2,000,000 m³ of fill, masonry, and mudbricks making it one of the largest and earliest prehistoric constructions in the New World. The principal mound is the terminus of a series of plazas which runs 1,400 m to the east. Three sunken circular courts are aligned on the central axis of the mound and plazas; the largest of the sunken circular court is 80 m in diameter (Fung Pineda and Williams León 1979: 114). Although the principal mound is the largest structure at Sechín Alto, flanking mounds range from 40 × 40 m to 120 × 120 m in their basal dimensions. The eastern end of Sechín Alto terminates in a large (500 × 500 m) but low H-shaped mound.

Sechín Alto is considered to be an Initial Period settlement, which – as noted above – is believed to be contemporary and culturally symbiotic with Las Aldas (S. Pozorski and T. Pozorski 1987, 1992). But again, the absence of extensive archaeological investigations at the site limits knowledge of the cultural and ideological frameworks which produced this enormous Andean monument.

Cerro Sechín, Casma Valley

The famous site of Cerro Sechín is located on the southern bank of the Rio Sechín, approximately 15 km inland from the Pacific Ocean. The site is a distinctive temple complex built into the base of a cliff of crumbly granodiorite, but Cerro Sechín's notoriety stems from its 300 etched bas-reliefs depicting axe-wielding warriors, disarticulated body parts, decapitated and mutilated victims, figures ranging from the fearsome to the grotesque. Since Tello's 1937 discovery, this imposing display of public art has sparked intense debate, such as Cerro Sechín's relationship with Chavín de Huántar and the question of the temporal priority of coastal vs. highland complex societies (Larco Hoyle 1938; Tello 1956; Burger 1981). The magnificent bas-reliefs at Cerro Sechín have also spawned some of the silliest writings to be found in Andean archaeology (e.g., Grollig 1978; Paredes Ruiz 1975; Wickler and Seibt 1982), a body of literature not further discussed.

The most recent archaeological published summary of Cerro Sechín is by Samaniego, Vergara, and Bischof based on data as of 1983 (Samaniego et al. 1985). Most excavations have been near the central building (Figure 2.17), a rectangular construction with rounded corners covering an area of 52.7 × 52.7 m and built from stone and conical adobes. Based on Tello's reconstruction, the exterior walls were faced by the famous bas-reliefs and stand up to 4.15 m in height. This represents the last public construction at Cerro Sechín, and it overlies at least two earlier building phases obscured and partly destroyed by later structures.

The chronology of Cerro Sechín is complex. While the temple has been designated as 'Chavín' or from the Initial Period based on stylistic grounds, the most complete set of absolute dates comes from a stratigraphic cut placed outside and adjacent to the western wall of the stone-faced structure. The resulting series of radiocarbon samples provides dates that predate the wall's construction, which Samaniego et al. (1985: 182) interpret as dating the temple of Cerro Sechín and its associated art as before 1300 BC (Table 2.4). Bonavia (1985: 21–22) has argued that the lower constructions are actually intrusive deposits built within the walls defined by the stone stelae, but it seems more plausible that the lower structures were built sometime before 3740 ± 40 bp.

This Central Temple was built on a triple-stepped platform measuring 34 × 34 m on its uppermost plane. A stairway on the northern façade leads to a vestibule 10.6 × 6.15 m in area; two small (5.55 × 2.7 m) lateral rooms flank the vestibule, separated by low benches (Jimenez Borja and Samaniego 1973; Samaniego 1973: 44; Samaniego et al. 1985: 173).

From the vestibule, the central chamber or *la cámara sagrada* (Samaniego 1973) is entered by stepping up onto a 60 cm bench and through an entrance 1.6 m wide. The front exterior walls of the chamber are massive constructions of adobe and mud mortar 1.25 m thick, and even after the damages of subsequent constructions and energetic looters, the walls still stand in places 2.62 m tall (Samaniego 1973: 42; Samaniego et al. 1985: 173). The chamber interior is small, measuring 5.65 × 5.65 m; unfortunately, pothunters have destroyed all but a tiny section of the floor and any features it once contained. A final feature of the central chamber is a small

Table 2.4. *Absolute dates from Cerro Sechín*

sample	material	uncalibrated	corrected	construction
HdTLK 326	burnt clay	na	1290 ± 240 BC	post
H7205–6977	charcoal	3240 ± 20 BP		post
H7206–6958	mixed	3740 ± 40 BP		Temple
H7207–6959	charcoal	3820 ± 50 BP		pre-Temple
H7208–6938	charcoal	7560 ± 70 BP		pre-Temple
H7208–7068	charcoal	7250 ± 65 BP		pre-Temple

Source: From Samaniego et al. 1985

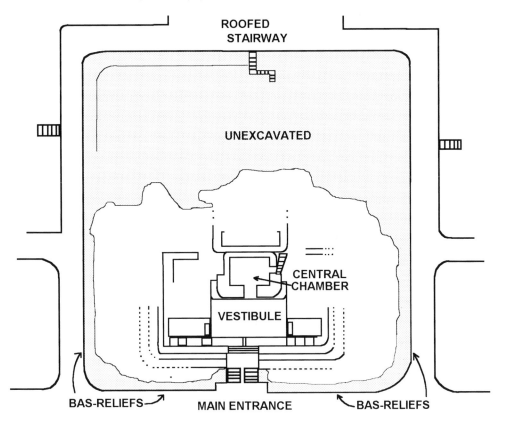

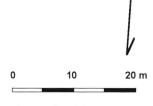

Figure 2.17 Plan of Central Temple, Cerro Sechín (Redrawn from Samaniego et al. 1985)

staircase which leads from a narrow passage (55 cm) through the west wall (Samaniego 1973: 43). This staircase goes up five steps to a group of poorly preserved small buildings located above the chamber (Samaniego 1973: 43; Samaniego et al. 1985: 173).

This central building is decorated with large murals, their reconstruction and possible "elaboration" being a point of some controversy (Bonavia 1985: 13–19; cf. Samaniego et al. 1985: 173–176). The entrance into the central chamber was flanked by two feline figures on the north façade. The upper portion of the mural had been damaged when Tello discovered it in 1937, with the upper portions of the feline figure poorly preserved (Tello 1956: 252). While Tello illustrated the feline on the east side of the chamber entrance, he either did not discover or did not describe the other matching mural, a point of debate (Bonavia 1985: 16; cf. Samaniego et al. 1985: 174). Published photographs suggest that a second mural was uncovered during the 1971–72 excavations at Cerro Sechín (Samaniego et al. 1985: 176), and that a pair of feline figures decorated the façade of the central chamber.

Another example of art associated with the early construction at Cerro Sechín is a human figure carved into one of the large pillars that front the vestibule. The excavators of write: "A human wearing a loincloth of the type frequently depicted on the stone carvings is shown in the act of tumbling down headfirst, a victim of combat or some sacrificial rite. The eye is closed, the mouth is tense in suffering, and a triple stream emerges from the broken or truncated head" (Samaniego et al. 1985: 176). Although this figure is not identical to the later carved decapitations on the stelae of Cerro Sechín, there are definite continuities in the depictions leading Samaniego et al. (1985: 176) to infer "that the artists at work during the first phase of the adobe building and the sculptors of the stone facade both participated in the same stylistic tradition."

Cerro Sechín is not prosaic; its art and architecture place the site outside the course of humdrum affairs. Yet, little is known about the communities associated with this site or the meaning and functions of Cerro Sechín within a broader social context. The ceremonial nature of Cerro Sechín seems unquestionable; the nature of its ceremony is unknown.

Chavín de Huántar, Mosna Valley

The site of Chavín de Huántar is one of the touchstones of Peruvian prehistory, a point captured by Julio Tello's (1960a) reference to it as *la cultura matríz*. Its prominence stems from the coincidence of a number of historical facts (Burger 1992). Chavín de Huántar entered the general literature about the Andes through the accounts of travelers who visited the site during the seventeenth to nineteenth centuries (e.g., Middendorf 1973 [1886]; Raimondi 1874; Vásquez de Espinoza 1968 [ca. 1620]; Weiner 1880), and by the late nineteenth century, the magnificent stone sculptures of Chavín were well known and prized (Lumbreras 1989: 119–121). Tello's (1943) recognition of Chavín de Huántar as an early, preincaic, and uniquely Andean horizon – a sharp departure from the diffusionist theses of his time – justly remains a major point in the development of Andean archaeology, even if, as Burger

(1988) argues, the designation "Chavín" has been extended too far. And finally, Chavín culture became an important element in the development of a national intellectual tradition of Peru, a movement which sought to discover the roots of an independent identity in the prehispanic achievements of Andean peoples (Lumbreras 1989: 111). But if, as Gordon Willey (1951) noted over forty years ago, Chavín has meant many things to many people, there is unanimity that the site itself was a major center, the architectural manifestation of a religious tradition which extended well beyond the narrow valley of the Rio Mosna.

The principal ceremonial sector of the site was built over some six centuries, marked by three ceramic styles as formulated by Burger (1984; cf. Lumbreras 1977, 1989). It is difficult to sort through the welter of proposed relative sequences for Chavín de Huántar. Part of the difficulty stems from the different contexts of the ceramics; the ceramics recovered by Lumbreras and Amat from the central ceremonial structures (i.e., the Ofrendas Gallery [Lumbreras 1977: 14–19]) probably are offerings made at different times and from different places and then mixed, whereas Burger's (1984, 1992) excavations in residential deposits recovered different ceramic styles in stratigraphic context.

Radiocarbon dates do not neatly resolve the chronological problems (Lumbreras 1989: 107–110). Burger (1984: 277–281) has published a series of radiocarbon dates which provide absolute dates for the Urabarriu and Chakiani phases, but poor chronological control for the Janabarriu phase. Lumbreras (1989: 111–114) has written a critical summary of the different radiocarbon dates and their associations at Chavín de Huántar, arguing persuasively that the absolute dates cannot be evaluated in isolation, separated from other sources of information (e.g., stratigraphy or ceramic associations). It is virtually impossible to sort through the chronological problems of Chavín de Huántar based on published information, so I will simply follow Burger's (1984: 277) suggested chronology – Urabarriu 850–460 BC, Chakiani 460–390 BC, and Janabarriu 390–200 BC – recognizing that the chronology is provisional and debated (cf. Lumbreras 1989: 186).

The principal structure at Chavín underwent major modifications, referred to as the Old Temple and New Temple (Lumbreras 1974, 1977, 1989). Unfortunately, Burger's ceramic chronology does not tightly date the different building phases, although a circumstantial argument suggests that the Old Temple construction dates to the Urabarriu phase. While some limited modifications of the temple occurred during the Chakinani phase (Rowe 1967; Burger 1984: 232), the major reconstruction associated with the New Temple probably dates to the Janabarriu phase, which is also characterized by a significant expansion in the size of the resident population at Chavín de Huántar (Burger 1984: 324–326). The balance of this discussion will focus on the Old Temple at Chavín de Huántar.

The Old Temple (Figure 2.18) consists of three stone platforms arranged into a squared "U" shape surrounding an open plaza with a sunken circular court. With a maximum length of 123 m and a maximum width of 73 m, the three-sided platform stands 12 m above ground and extends at least 2 m below the current ground surface (Lumbreras 1977: 2–3), suggesting a total construction volume of roughly

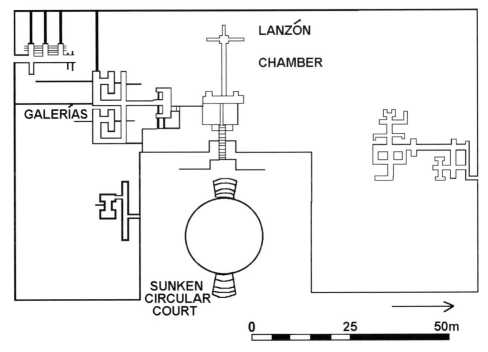

Figure 2.18 Plan of Old Temple, Chavín de Huántar (Redrawn from Moseley 1992)

103,306 m³. The Old Temple at Chavín de Huántar was an impressive construction, but certainly not as large as many Initial Period constructions of the coast. The
Old Temple was cleverly constructed; the platforms were created by building a
series of retaining walls interfilled with stone and mud. Some spaces between retaining walls were left empty and then were spanned with large stone blocks thus
forming hidden passages, the famous "galerías" (Lumbreras 1977: 3).

Within one gallery is the Lanzón, a stone obelisk, 4.5 m tall, located on the central
axes of the Old Temple (Rowe 1962b: 9). Since the Lanzón was incorporated directly
into the Temple's construction, it presumably was the principal cult object at Chavín
de Huántar: "Carved in low relief, the stela depicts a being with a human body in
simple attire and fingers and toes terminating in claws . . . Variously called the
'Smiling' or 'Snarling God', the deity faces the eastward entry of the narrow
chamber, forcefully confronting an arriving viewer" (Moseley 1992: 155–156).

The eastern entry Moseley refers to connects the central plaza to the Lanzón
galería. The central plaza is approximately 40 × 40 m (Lumbreras 1977: 3), and contains a sunken circular court. The sunken court is 21 m in diameter and approximately 2.5 m deep. The court's interior originally was covered in superb reliefs
depicting jaguars and human-feline figures with staffs (see Rowe 1962b).

It is not known if additional Urabarriu structures exist at Chavín de Huántar.
Burger (1984: 231) notes, "It is tempting to speculate that the Urabarriu occupation of the Temple area was primarily related to religious activity and to the construction and maintenance of the religious buildings," and goes on to suggest "that

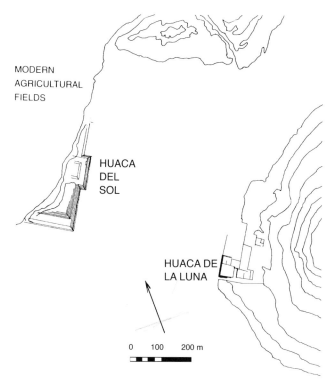

MODERN
AGRICULTURAL
FIELDS

HUACA
DEL
SOL

HUACA DE
LA LUNA

0   100   200 m

Figure 2.19 Site plan of Moche
(Redrawn from T. Topic 1977)

pilgrims from other areas might have camped on Temple grounds, fasting and awaiting ceremonies," as at Pachacamac. Yet to date, no additional excavations have documented such structures at Chavín de Huántar.

The interpretation of Chavín de Huántar as a religious center has become nearly indisputable. Burger (1988: 113–117) has outlined a model of Chavín de Huántar as the center of a prehispanic regional cult, roughly analogous to Pachacamac, in which the religious network centered on Chavín easily co-existed with other contemporary religious traditions (e.g. the later phases at Huaricoto). Yet, perhaps Chavín was the first Andean religious center which created such a widely distributed network of belief, such a broad sacred geography. In earlier religious centers, there is evidence for regional traditions in ceremonial architecture, but only with Chavín de Huántar are there hints that a religious system had pan-Andean converts and consequences.

Moche, Moche Valley
The famous site of Moche is located approximately 6 km inland on the southern side of the Moche Valley. Dominated by two massive adobe brick pyramids, Huaca del Sol and Huaca de la Luna (Figure 2.19), Moche has attracted visitors and scholars since the mid-nineteenth century (e.g. Squier 1973 [1877]; Kroeber 1925, 1930), but archaeological investigations have been remarkably rare. Although Moche ceramics and iconography have been studied extensively (Benson 1972; Donnan 1978; Larco Hoyle 1938), archaeological investigations of Moche itself

and particularly the architecture of Moche awaited Theresa Topic's research (T. Topic 1977, 1982). Recent excavations by Santiago Uceda and others (Uceda et al. 1994) have produced significant insights into the chronology, construction, and iconography of Huaca de la Luna, raising new issues about the development of the site and the spread and nature of Moche culture (Bawden 1994; Shimada 1994; Uceda and Mujica 1994).

Moche covers a minimum of 60 hectares. The western extent of the site is unknown because in 1602 Spanish treasure hunters diverted the Rio Moche to erode the Huaca del Sol and expose its hidden treasure, destroying three-quarters of Huaca del Sol and other low-lying deposits to the west. Based on Topic's map (1977: 12), the remaining site area covers roughly 550 × 1,050 m (Figure 2.19) although Moseley (1992: 167) states the site covers slightly more than 1 km^2.

The site was occupied from AD 1 to AD 600 (i.e., phases Moche I to Moche IV, T. Topic 1977: 336–341), although the settlement underwent major expansion only after Moche III. Much of Huaca del Sol was built during during Moche III – ca. AD 200–400 – (Donnan and Mackey 1978: 6, 65; cf. Moseley 1992: 168), but recent data (Uceda et al. 1994: 293) suggest that construction at Huaca de la Luna began at Moche II (before AD 200) and continued into the end of Moche IV (AD 450–550), possibly into Moche V (AD 550–650/700). Moche became a major seat of power, "for the [Moche] valley itself and for the newly acquired territory outside the valley" (T. Topic 1977: 341). During Moche IV the site reached its "maximum population, prestige, power, and wealth" (T. Topic 1977: 340). The settlement must have been extraordinary, as Moseley (1992: 166–167) reconstructs it:

> Magnificent buildings once sprawled around Huaca del Sol and Huaca de la Luna and included grand courts with niched walls, low platforms that served as mausoleums, multitudes of adobe residences for the aristocracy, workshops producing elite ceramics and corporate arts, and extensive cemeteries of the kuraka [local lords] nobility. Yet little of the once splendid metropolis survives, for during Moche Phase IV, shortly before AD 600, severe El Niño flooding struck the capital. The city was repaired only to be abandoned when enormous sand dunes swept inland, burying everything except the towering huacas.

Moseley's scenario may overstate the El Niño's impact. As Uceda et al. observe (1994: 291–292, 298), the flanks of Cerro Blanco contain numerous looted graves with Moche V ceramics, indicating that the site was not abandoned after the El Niño and suggesting the importance of other factors in explaining the socio-political trajectories of Moche culture.

The two great huacas are impressive structures. Huaca del Sol is the largest adobe construction built in the Andes, and its construction spanned multiple building phases (Hastings and Moseley 1975). The remnant base of Huaca del Sol measures 340 × 160 m and it is 40 m at its tallest point (Figure 2.20); the mound contained over 143 million adobe bricks (Hastings and Moseley 1975: 197). The four sections of the huaca rose in step-like planes. Unfortunately, the extensive destruction of

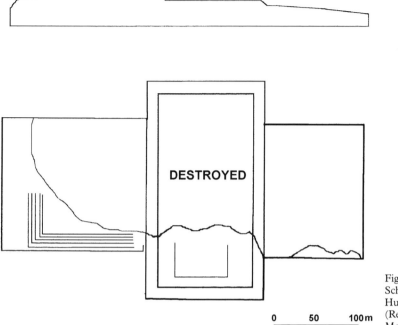

Figure 2.20
Schematic plan of
Huaca del Sol
(Redrawn from
Moseley 1992)

0   50   100 m

Huaca del Sol, while exposing the construction of the pyramid, virtually prevents detailed insights into its use (for summary see T. Topic 1977: 35–70).

Less destroyed, Huaca de la Luna sits opposite Sol, 500 m to the east at the foot of Cerro Blanco. The complex covers an area of approximately 290 × 210 m (Uceda et al. 1994: 253) consisting of three platforms which were once enclosed by a large wall. Unlike Sol, there is not a pyramid on top of the platforms of Huaca de la Luna (Kroeber 1925: 194). The largest platform mound (Mound I) measures 95 × 95 m (Uceda et al. 1994: 253), the medium-size mound (Mound III) measures 8 × 12 m, and the smallest (Mound II) 5 × 15 m (Figure 2.21; Hastings and Moseley 1975: 197).

Mound I was built in several phases supplemented by nearly continuous remodeling and additions (Uceda et al. 1994: 257–268). The mound was constructed to a height of 20 m, 3 to 4 meters of adobes were added to the top, and moundtop structures were built and decorated with murals; subsequently the rooms were filled (Hastings and Moseley 1975). Moseley (1992: 178) observes that the smallest mound was never remodeled, suggesting to him that it "must have had considerable sanctity." Like Sol, Huaca de la Luna has been looted extensively, and the functions of the moundtop structures are poorly documented.

The moundtop structures were not common domestic residences as suggested by the magnificent polychrome murals which line the remaining walls (Kroeber 1930; Bonavia 1985: 72–97; Mackey and Hastings 1982; Uceda et al. 1994). These murals combine strong geometric patterning with anthropomorphic figures, whose stylistic and ideological antecedents Mackey and Hastings (1982: 307–308) see as linked to the well-known Andean motif of the Staff God, an interpretation vigorously attacked by Bonavia

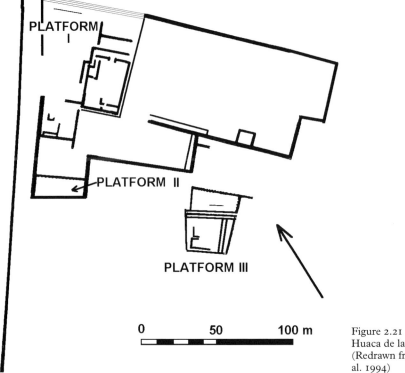

Figure 2.21 Plan of
Huaca de la Luna
(Redrawn from Uceda et
al. 1994)

(1985: 93–95). The recent excavations of extraordinary high-relief polychrome murals identified another "personaje mayor," a fanged anthropomorphic figure surrounded by serpent-like designs (Uceda et al. 1994). Significantly, the murals were painted on the interior walls (Mackey and Hastings 1982: 303), paralleling the placement of the famous "revolt of the objects" mural recorded by Kroeber (1930: 71–73, Plate 27), subject of yet another iconographic controversy (cf. Lyon 1981; Quilter 1990). Thus the hypothesized ceremonies of Huaca de la Luna (Uceda et al. 1994: 271, 296) apparently were directed to people on the mound rather than visible to the entire community.

Moseley (1992: 178) has suggested that Huaca del Sol and Huaca de la Luna reflect a symbolic dichotomy: "If Huaca del Sol was a huaca sepultura where the heads of state reigned and were interred, then Huaca de la Luna seems to have been the imperial huaca *adoratorio* where the national pantheon was attended to." This hypothesis awaits extensive documentation.

Sometime during Moche V, the site declined as a regional center (Mackey and Hastings 1982; Moseley 1992; T. Topic 1977). The reasons for this change are unclear. Topic (1977: 385–387) suggests the interplay of three factors: (1) the expansion of Huari, (2) the occurrence of an El Niño followed by desertification which affected the agricultural base, and (3) heightened class differences expressed in the great emphasis on personal display and the esoterica of rank marking a "class of social parasites" (T. Topic 1977: 387). Whatever its causes, there seems to have been a diminution of construction and occupation at Moche while other sites grew in size

Figure 2.22 Site plan of Pampa Grande (Redrawn from Shimada 1976)

and signficance, most notably the site of Pampa Grande located in the Lambayeque Valley 165 km to the north.

Pampa Grande, Lambayeque
Pampa Grande is an enormous Moche V settlement in the Lambayeque Valley (Figure 2.22), encompassing some 6 sq km of densely constructed space surrounding

a large pyramid referred to as Huaca Grande (also known as Huaca Fortaleza, Huaca La Capilla or Huaca Iglesia [Shimada 1990: 334]). Pampa Grande may have expanded as the Moche capital at Cerro Blanco waned, a possibility which has led to an intense discussion about the shifting boundaries of the Moche polity (see Anders 1981; Haas 1985; Moseley 1992; Shimada 1976, 1978, 1987, 1990; T. Topic 1982). This reorganization was accompanied by "a wide range of material, organizational, and ideological changes" (Shimada 1987: 136), expressed in ceramic styles, iconographic displays, and architectural forms. These attendant changes lead to Moseley's observation (1992: 213) that although Pampa Grande "preserved some of the earlier Moche traditions, such as building gigantic pyramids . . . if it were not for the corporate arts, few relationships with the old capital at Cerro Blanco would be evident."

The monumental architecture of Pampa Grande is extraordinary. Huaca Grande, shaped like a thick "T" (Figure 2.23), is 270 m long, 185 m wide, and 54 m at its highest point, a construction volume totaling 1.26 million m^3 (Haas 1985: 393). The huaca is enclosed by a complex of walled patios and courts, giving the pyramid a fortified appearance and one of its several names.

The access patterns at Huaca Grande are very different and more restrictive than the open pattern at the Moche pyramids. For example, Huaca Grande is approached via a 290 m long corridor, and partial crosswalls jut into the corridor at three points, presumably to restrict the flow of traffic. A series of ramps traverses the face of Huaca Grande, ultimately leading to the top of the huaca, where a wall and a pair of platform mounds "effectively create a large walled enclosure on the huaca top" (Haas 1985: 402).

On top of Huaca Grande there is the relatively intact Room Complex (Haas 1985: 404), a set of medium-sized rooms and patios, some with baffled entrances (Figure 2.24). Access to the Room Complex was via a short ramp with a subfloor chamber that held the partial remains of a child and the skeleton of a juvenile llama, and a necklace of turquoise, *Spondylus* shell, and azurite (Haas 1985: 404). In general the artifactual assemblage underscores the special nature of the Room Complex. There is no evidence of food preparation, but there are serving and storage vessels and limited food remains. Ceramic drums, quartz crystals, *Spondylus* shell, a stone macehead, and curious ceramic replicas of a macehead and of *Spondylus* shells all suggest the special nature of the Room Complex. Haas (1985: 407) concludes that the Room Complex was a residence of the ruling elite of Pampa Grande.

The architectural remoteness of the Huaca Grande is distinct from the plan of Moche. What makes this so interesting is the possibility that these differences in monumental architecture reflect not stylistic changes, but greater social stresses between commoners and elites on the North Coast (cf. T. Topic 1977: 387). This pattern and the hypothesis it raises also may be expressed in the Moche V settlement of Galindo.

Galindo, Moche Valley

Twenty kilometers inland on the Rio Moche, Galindo is a Moche V settlement which covered approximately 6 sq km (Bawden 1982a: 289–290). Galindo's built

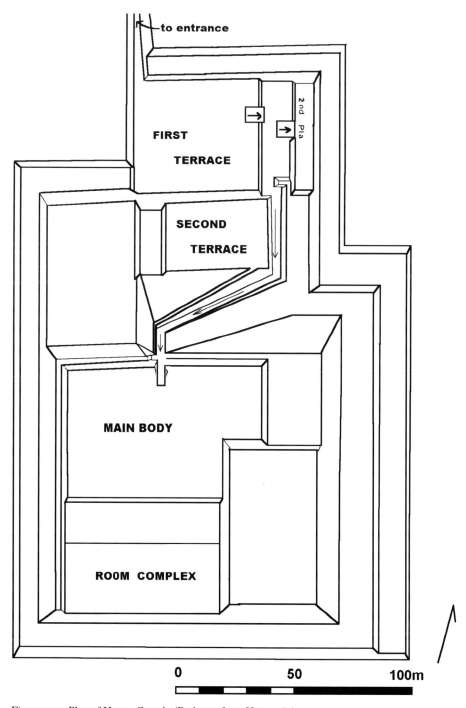

Figure 2.23 Plan of Huaca Grande (Redrawn from Haas 1985)

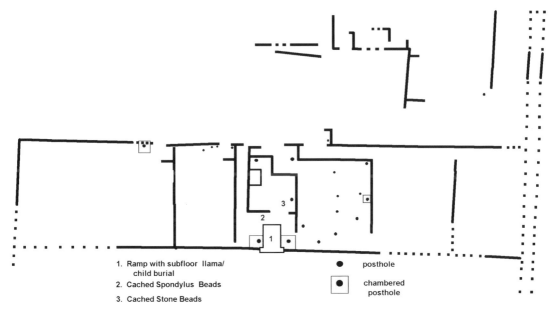

1. Ramp with subfloor llama/
   child burial
2. Cached Spondylus Beads
3. Cached Stone Beads

● posthole

▣ chambered
   posthole

Figure 2.24 Plan of Room Complex, Huaca Grande (Redrawn from Haas 1985)

environment (Figure 2.25) consists of zones of residential architecture, platform mounds, small mound and ramp constructions called tablados, large walled enclosures of presumed administrative focus dubbed cercaduras, and large walls that separate different sectors of the site (Bawden 1977). Galindo is the largest Moche V settlement in the Moche Valley, and it has been interpreted as the frontier remnant of the Moche state. Briefly mentioned by Kosok (1965), principal work at the site awaited Garth Bawden's 1971–73 excavations. Bawden's research at Galindo had two primary emphases: (1) the nature of social differentiation within the settlement of Galindo, and (2) the degree of continuity or rupture of Middle Horizon urban traditions. Both inquiries intersect in the interpretation of architecture.

Social differentiation at Galindo, Bawden (1982b) argues, is evidenced by significant differences in residential architecture and by large walls designed as mechanisms of social control. Residential architecture, built from cobblestone foundations with cane wall superstructures, covered half the site of Galindo. The smallest and poorest residences at Galindo (Bawden's Areas B and C) were located on the slopes of the site and behind large stone walls, while the most elite residences (Bawden's Areas A and D) were situated on relatively level ground. Such variations between barrios suggested to Bawden (1982b: 178) "that the residential occupation of Galindo was divided into rigidly demarcated geographical segments that constituted the dwelling areas of different social classes, each with its own formalized access to wealth, status, and economic control."

The largest, most formal and best constructed residential architecture at Galindo is directly articulated with an administrative complex. Bawden argues that Area D was home to the ruling elite of Galindo (Bawden 1982b: 177).

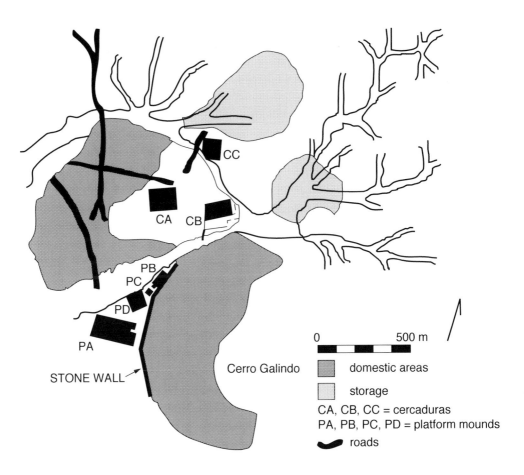

Figure 2.25 Site plan of Galindo (Redrawn from Bawden 1977)

Four platform mounds, reminiscent of the Moche huacas but much smaller, are located on the lower plain of Galindo (Bawden 1982b: 293–297). Platform A is 8 m tall and covers an area 50 × 50 m; the huaca sits on the western end of a set of walled patios enclosing a total area of approximately 250 × 130 m (Figure 2.26). Platform B measures 70 × 50 m and one end has been built into the hillside. A third huaca, Platform C, is a mere 10 × 3 m in area and only 3 m tall, while the fourth mound, Platform D, is 40 × 30 m at its base but only 1.5 m tall. The Galindo platforms may reflect earlier architectural antecedents, but their small size and rudimentary form suggest "significant changes in this architectural form" (Bawden 1982b: 295).

Three rectangular walled compounds at Galindo (Figure 2.25) are referred to as "cercaduras" (Bawden 1982b: 297). Cercadura A sits in the center of Galindo, a walled compound of 170 × 135 m, enclosing patios, terraces, and platform mounds (Figure 2.26). Cercadura A has been looted extensively although evidence for food preparation and a miscellany of fine pottery, copper, and decorated textiles were recovered.

CERCADURA B

CERCADURA C

CERCADURA A

well

PLATFORM A

O   50   100m

Figure 2.26 Plans of Platform A and Cercaduras A, B, and C, Galindo (Redrawn from Bawden 1977)

Cercadura B was all but destroyed by the time of Bawden's (1982a: 299) field-work, but older aerial photographs indicated a large walled compound, 150 × 150 m, with a single entrance with an open patio connected to other platforms and ter-races by ramps and steps (Figure 2.26). Cercadura C is well preserved; the smallest cercadura, it covers 60 × 45 m (Figure 2.26). Because Cercadura C is laid out on a slope, the internal divisions consist of terraced spaces linked by ramps and steps.

Galindo is important in the debate about the architectural and social changes associated with the Middle Horizon on the North Coast (T. Topic 1991). Various scholars (e.g., Schaedel 1951; Lanning 1967; Lumbreras 1974) have suggested that the Middle Horizon marked a major break in North Coast cultural traditions, including the Huari Empire's introduction of the urban tradition. For example, Gordon McEwan, who has worked extensively on the Huari state and its architectural expressions, has argued (1990) that strong formal similarities between Wari walled enclosures (e.g., Pikillacta) and the royal compounds of Chan Chan indicate that these constructions derive from a similar architectural tradition, one distinct from that expressed at Galindo. McEwan (1990: 113) writes: "Chan Chan resembles Wari architecture more closely than its alternative purported antecedent at Galindo." Nothing could be further from Bawden's view of Galindo, since he draws an unbroken line of architectural descent between the cercaduras of Galindo and the ciudadelas of Chan Chan. "Galindo," Bawden (1983: 231) writes, "marks the first appearance of these architectural expressions of a centralized, secular government." The secular nature of governance is inferred from the physical separation of platform mounds and cercaduras, and from the presumed role of the cercaduras in controlling "access to corporate storage facilities. This arrangement duplicates that of the Chan Chan ciudadelas although in a less integrated manner" (Bawden 1977: 125–126).

A second issue involves the use of architecture as a means of social control at Galindo. The construction of large walls at Galindo has been dubbed "a wall obsession" (Conklin 1990: 53), but two less psychoanalytic explanations have been proposed. The first, as noted above, is Bawden's "internal stress" model. Arguing (Bawden 1982b: 179) that the barriers between barrios are evidence (1) that "a large inferior class was kept in a state of formalized deprivation in terms of access to wealth, economic participation, and status," and (2) that the maintenance of such social divisions involved "great energy output by the ruling authority . . . to construct, maintain, and manage the elaborate regulatory system physically manifested by the barrio walls," Bawden (1982b: 180) concludes that Moche V Galindo was "an unsuccessful experiment in cultural integration."

A second interpretation, advanced by John Topic and Theresa Topic (1987), is that the Galindo walls were defensive, designed to thwart outside threats (T. Topic 1991). Calling the Galindo wall "one of the clearest examples of purposive fortification construction that we have encountered on the north coast," the Topics (1987: 49–50) describe the parapet on the uphill side of the wall, the distribution of slingstones, and the existence of dry moats on the downhill side of the wall. This leads them to conclude that the defensive wall served to protect Galindo society from outside attack, rather than to separate distinct social strata.

But if the walls were not constructed as a means of social control, the cercaduras may have been designed to restrict access. The analysis of architecture as a means of

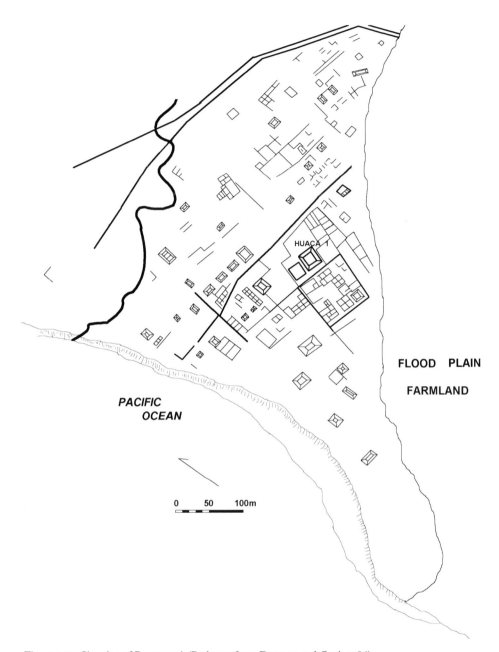

Figure 2.27 Site plan of Pacatnamú (Redrawn from Donnan and Cock 1986)

controlling access is discussed in Chapter 5, but it is a recurrent element in North Coast architecture in sites like Pacatnamú and later Chimu sites.

Pacatnamú, Jequetepeque Valley
Situated on a triangular bluff wedged between the Pacific Ocean and the mouth of the Jequetepeque River (Figure 2.27), Pacatnamú was first studied by Kroeber

(1930: 88–89), who made brief notes and a sketch map of the site he called Ciudad de la Barranca. Subsequent, sporadic excavations by Heinrich Ubbeholde-Doerning uncovered numerous tombs, and his 1962–63 investigations resulted in a general site map and plans produced by Giesela and Wolfgang Hecker (1977, 1985). These maps were made without extensive excavation of architecture, and therefore one goal of the Pacatnamú Project, directed by Christopher Donnan and Guillermo Cock, was to amplify the architectural detail available for Pacatnamú through excavation and mapping. The resulting monograph (Donnan and Cock 1986) and recent discussions with Donnan (personal communication) are the sources of the following information.

The occupation at Pacatnamú began with the Moche, approximately at AD 300, but at ca. AD 1050–1100 was interrupted by an occupational hiatus thought to be associated with an El Niño/Southern Oscillation event. At ca. AD 1100–1150 Pacatnamú was reoccupied, marking the Lambayeque presence (Christopher Donnan, personal communication; cf. Donnan 1986a: 22). The Lambayeque occupation lasted until AD 1370, at which time the settlement diminished, perhaps due to the conquest of the Jequetepeque Valley by the Kingdom of Chimor.

The core of Pacatnamú covers 1 sq km and its built environment is dominated by two architectural features: walls and huacas (Figure 2.27). Large walls form roughly parallel, irregularly spaced arcs across the bluff where Pacatnamú sits, all dating to the post-AD 1110 Lambayeque occupation (Donnan 1986b: 54). The Southern Wall is relatively small, but the Inner and Outer Walls were massive barriers, originally 5–7 meters tall, with dry moats 2 m deep. Large gateways cut through the walls at various points, and some of the entrances are aligned with each other and the doorways of huaca compounds. The large walls and dry moats lead Donnan (1986b: 59) to infer "that defense was a primary motivation for their construction."

These walls protected one of the largest concentrations of ceremonial architecture on the North Coast. The site contains fifty-three huacas – truncated pyramids with moundtop structures (Donnan 1986a: 19) – all but one of which are oriented north and toward a mountain, Cerros de Catalina (Conklin 1990: 65–68). The number of huacas led Keatinge et al. (1975: 129) to suggest that Pacatnamú was a pilgrimage center possibly dedicated to the worship of the moon, an important deity in the Jequetepeque Valley, whereas Conklin (1990) suggests that mountain-worship was central at the site. At one point, Pacatnamú was thought to be the principal Chimu administrative center in the Jequetepeque Valley (Kosok 1965: 123), but Richard Keatinge (Keatinge 1982; Keatinge et al. 1975) and Geoffrey Conrad (Conrad 1990; Keatinge and Conrad 1983) have argued persuasively that the site of Farfán was the Chimu center. Instead, Pacatnamú was seen as an Andean pilgrimage center, analogous to Pachacamac, exemplifying "a coast-wide religious tradition characterized by pilgrimage to centers of oracle worship" (Keatinge 1982: 221). Donnan (1986a: 23) casts doubt on this hypothesis, pointing out that the Pacatnamú ceramics are local and utilitarian, not interregional and fine as one would expect from offerings from different parts of the Andes. Yet the large numbers of huacas which dot Pacatnamú certainly suggest it was a major ceremonial center.

The largest huaca and most impressive compound is Huaca 1 (Figure 2.27), located in the central portion of the site (Donnan 1986c). Huaca 1 and its associated features were the objects of extensive investigations, and specific individual reports (e.g., Bruce 1986; Donnan 1986c, 1986d; Verano 1986; Verano and Cordy-Collins 1986) contain detailed information not covered in the following brief summary.

The Huaca 1 Complex (Figure 2.28) is defined as the large (70 × 70m) huaca, standing 10 m tall, surrounding courtyards, a two-level mound named the East Pyramid, and a large enclosure filled with complex architecture known as the Major Quadrangle. The primary entrance is a ramped causeway that crosses the dry moat and passes through a large doorway in the Inner Wall. This opens onto the North Courtyard, which contains two low ramped platforms (the West and East Altars) that align with ramps which lead up the face of the East Pyramid. A narrow doorway on the northeast corner of Huaca 1 opens onto a corridor which leads to the various east and northeast courtyards, areas where refuse deposits suggest food and drink were prepared (Donnan 1986c: 65, 79). A narrow entrance on the northwest side of Huaca 1 leads to the West Courtyard, featuring an elaborately niched room and smaller rooms with baffled entries.

A central ramp leads to the top of Huaca 1, which is an open plaza, roughly 18 × 18 m in area. Two alternative access routes connect the North Courtyard and the Main Quadrangle, located on opposite sides of Huaca 1. The western, "right-hand" route is architecturally more impressive, passing through a massive pilastered portal, while the eastern, left-hand route is nondescript and littered with debris. Donnan (1986c: 79) suggests that the architectural elegance associated with the right-hand route represents a culturally significant dichotomy, possibly an important tenet of architecture at Pacatnamú, a matter further discussed in Chapter 5.

The Major Quadrangle measures 175 × 170m and its large walls were originally 5 m tall. The entrance is on the northern wall of the Major Quadrangle, opening onto a baffled entrance. Near the entrance the West Corridor leads to the southwestern quarter of the Quadrangle, and eventually into Room Complex A, notable for its *audiencia* (Bruce 1986) and a magnificent textile fragment showing a ceremony in progress (Donnan 1986d). Although the audiencia had been looted, Bruce (1986) uncovered three disturbed burial chambers and an amazing collection of miniature ceramics and 93 miniature textiles, including tiny ponchos, loincloths, and a crown.

Elsewhere in the Major Quadrangle, circuitous corridors and niched rooms characterize Room Complexes B, C, D, and E. The niches in Room Complex E, for example, exhibited well-preserved, thin layers of plaster, indicating they were not used for storing heavy materials; the niches show no evidence of burning, spillage, or abrasion. Donnan (1986d: 77–78) suggests that the niches held ceremonial items like wooden idols, which is interesting given their hidden placements in the Major Quadrangle.

The funerary mound HIMI is located in the southeastern portion of the Major Quadrangle. It was built with case-and-fill construction approximately 30 m in diameter and 2.5 m tall (Verano and Cordy-Collins 1986). Four intact burials were found, of two female adults and two infants, and disturbed bones suggested the presence of

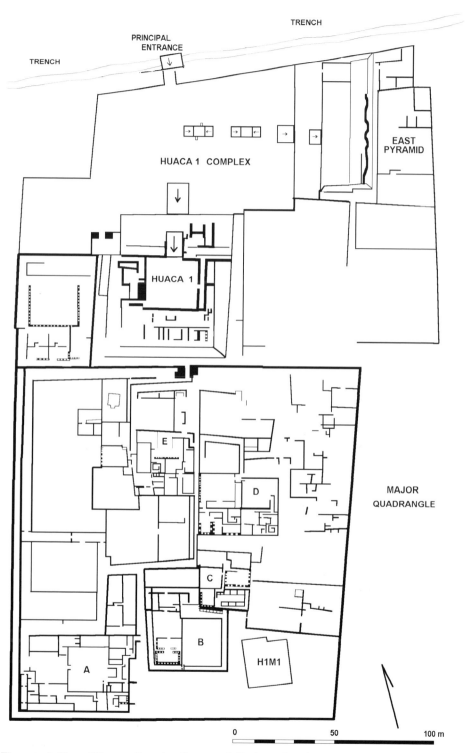

TRENCH

PRINCIPAL
ENTRANCE

TRENCH

HUACA 1 COMPLEX

EAST
PYRAMID

HUACA 1

E

D

MAJOR
QUADRANGLE

C

B

H1M1

A

0   50   100 m

Figure 2.28 Plan of Huaca 1 Complex, Pacatnamú (Redrawn from Donnan and Cock 1986)

ten other individuals, males and females of various ages. The location of HIMI is similar to the burial platforms in the Chan Chan ciudadelas, but HIMI represents the interment of a markedly different social group.

Conklin (1990: 65–69) has suggested that the architecture of Pacatnamú – and of Huaca 1 in particular – exhibits patterns which are "deeply related to those of the Moche Valley tradition," a connection which probably should be reconsidered given that Pacatnamú is now viewed as associated with the Lambayeque culture rather than the later Chimu. Further, Conklin (1990: 69) opines, the pattern of convoluted corridor and well-plastered niches seen in Huaca 1 "may be explicable by a functional activity model, but the labyrinth is difficult to imagine as other than a visual and psychological form. Even the niches seem arranged more for display than for storage. The dualism of the maze and the niche seems to permeate the meaning of the architecture of Pacatnamú's Huaca 1." Such basic questions about access, visibility, and their material expressions become major themes in understanding Chimu architecture, particularly at the capital of Chan Chan.

Chan Chan, Moche Valley

Located 7.5 km northwest of the mouth of the Rio Moche, the site of Chan Chan covers some 20 sq km; it is a densely built, complex urban environment. Chan Chan lacks a single unifying plan or a readily discernible pattern (Conklin 1990: 64), but the architectural confusion reflects dynamic changes in the Chimu polity and its urban expression at Chan Chan. The 6 sq km of Chan Chan's urban core contains four principal classes of architecture: (1) non-elite commoner dwellings and workshops that housed an estimated 20,000–40,000 people spread throughout the city; (2) intermediate architecture associated with Chan Chan's non-royal elites; (3) ten large walled compounds, called ciudadelas, thought to be the palaces of the Chimu kings; and (4) four huacas located in the eastern half of the city (Conrad 1974, 1982; Day 1973, 1982; Klymyshyn 1976, 1982, 1987; Kolata 1978, 1982, 1990; Moseley 1975b, 1990; J. Topic 1982, 1990; Topic and Moseley 1983; West 1967, 1970). The following discussion considers the two classes of really monumental constructions – the ciudadelas and the huacas (Figure 2.29).

The chronology of monumental construction at Chan Chan is a matter of debate as the alternative sequences of Table 2.5 suggest. The Chimu sequence begins ca. AD 900 and Chan Chan was conquered by the Inca ca. AD 1470; beyond that lies controversy. Radiocarbon dates collected from Chan Chan have overlapping standard deviations producing an ambiguous absolute sequence. Relative chronologies based on different material classes – ceramics, adobe bricks, and burial platforms – have resulted in varying sequences with significant differences and no obvious means of resolution.

In general terms, most of the sequences suggest three relative groups of ciudadelas: *Early* (Chayhuac, Uhle, Tello, Laberinto), *Middle* (Gran Chimu), and *Late* (Rivero, Tschudi, Bandelier, Velarde) with Squier's position uncertain.

The Chan Chan ciudadelas are enormous public constructions, and Table 2.6 provides basic data on their size and internal complexity. Separated from the rest

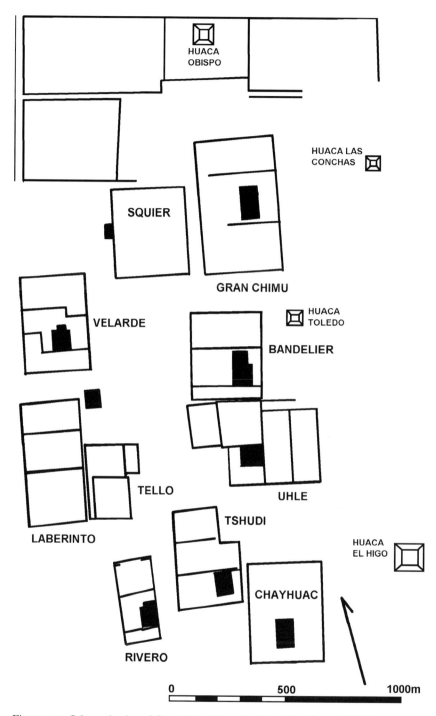

Figure 2.29 Schematic plan of Chan Chan (Compiled from Moseley and Mackey 1974)

Table 2.5. *Alternative sequences for the Chan Chan ciudadelas*

Day (1973)	*Conrad* (1982)	*Topic and Moseley* (1983)
Squier	Tschudi-Rivero	Tschudi-Rivero
Laberinto	Squier?	Bandelier-Velarde
Velarde	Bandelier-Laberinto	Gran Chimu
Gran	Chimu Squier?	Laberinto
Uhle	Velarde	Chayhuac
Chayhuac	Gran Chimu	Uhle-Tello
Bandelier	Uhle	
Tschudi	Chayhuac	
Rivero		

Williams León (1987)	*Kolata* (1990)	*Cavallaro* (1991)
Rivero	Tschudi-Rivero	Bandelier-Velarde
Tschudi	Bandelier-Velarde	Tschudi-Rivero
Bandelier	Squier-Gran Chimu	Laberinto
Velarde	Laberinto-Tello	Gran Chimu
(or Squier?)	Uhle-Chayhuac	Uhle
Gran Chimu-Squier	Tello	
Laberinto	Squier	
Tello	Chayhuac	
Uhle		
Chayhuac		

Table 2.6. *The Chan Chan ciudadelas – basic data*

	area[1] (ha)	rooms[2] (n)	burial[3] platform	storerooms[4] (n)	storage (m^2)	audiencias (n)
Tschudi	10.65	285	+	242	3,020	17
Rivero	7.01	278	+	180	1,730	11
Bandelier	13.53	300	+	175	1,840	8
Velarde	18.11	534	+	396	4,270	11
Squier	13.71	???	*	28	110	0
Gran Chimu	21.09	411	+	259	7,620	8
Laberinto	21.20	907	*	641	7,010	13
Tello	6.73	423	–	260	1,680	3
Uhle	15.56	278	+	175	1,830	22
Chayhuac	15.41	113	+	67	1,800	0

Notes:

[1] To nearest 0.01 ha; does not include annexes.

[2] Does not include burial platforms, walk-in wells, or destroyed areas.

[3] Squier and Laberinto are associated with burial platforms which are outside their walls*;
Tello is not associated with a burial platform.

[4] Data on number and area of storerooms from Klymyshyn 1987.

of Chan Chan by battered adobe walls up to 9 m high, the ciudadelas contain plazas, royal burial platforms, walk-in wells, possible storerooms, and distinctive three-sided constructions called U-shaped rooms or audiencias. The ciudadelas are a distinct architectural set, but they are not identical. There has been a tendency to use Rivero as a model of ciudadela design (e.g., McEwan 1990) because it was the subject of Day's (1973) excellent dissertation. Yet, as Kolata (1990: 122–124) has observed, ciudadelas exhibit significant formal variations, although the variations are not easily interpreted. Using Kolata's (1990) sequence, for example, there is no unidirectional increase in area, number of rooms, number or size of storage, or the numbers of audiencias.

Mere numbers give a sense of the size but not of the complexity and order of the Chan Chan ciudadelas. The following brief descriptions are designed to give a sense of the architectural achievements represented by the ciudadelas, rather than a detailed guide to the compounds (for more details the reader may consult Day 1973, 1982; Conrad 1974, 1982; Guttierez Rodriguez 1990; Klymyshyn 1987; Kolata 1978, 1982, 1990). The descriptions are based on the plans published by Moseley and Mackey (1974) and certain conventions are followed. For example, the ciudadelas are described from north to south by principal sectors as defined by major interior walls. Plazas are large open spaces and courtyards are small ones. Storerooms refer to contiguous blocks of rooms with step-over thresholds, while "cell-like" rooms are unconnected, isolated small rooms. Audiencias refer to a variety of three-sided rooms (Kolata 1990), walk-in wells are areas excavated down to water-table and possibly used as gardens, and burial platforms are the large *tapia* mortuary constructions for the Chimu king and his sacrificed companions. I have not provided detailed definitions of other architectural features (cf. Shimada 1978), hoping that a combination of illustrations and brief exposition will be sufficient. The discussion is organized based on the relative sequence suggested by Kolata (1990), in full recognition of the chronological problems as discussed above.

Ciudadela Chayhuac　Chayhuac is thought to be a very early compound, partially due to the simplicity of its architectural plan (Kolata 1990: 122). Chayhuac (Figure 2.30) is a large, empty rectangular compound containing basically two zones of architecture – a northern architectural group of unclear function and a southern group associated with a burial platform. Like later compounds, Chayhuac is entered via a single northern doorway, but unlike other compounds, the entrance is simple and not baffled, although the immediate presence of blocks of rooms partially restricts the entrance. The largest block of rooms has been extensively destroyed and its internal layout is unclear. In addition, there are five sets of isolated room blocks, two sunken wells, and destroyed or uncompleted scraps of walls.

The south-central portion of Chayhuac contains a now-looted burial platform. The burial platform is fronted by a forecourt, and south and west of the platform is a group of cell-like rooms which Conrad (1982: 97) identifies as a primary-stage addition, but which have also been considered as storerooms (Klymyshyn 1987: 103). Although there are some traces of additional walls in Chayhuac, the compound does

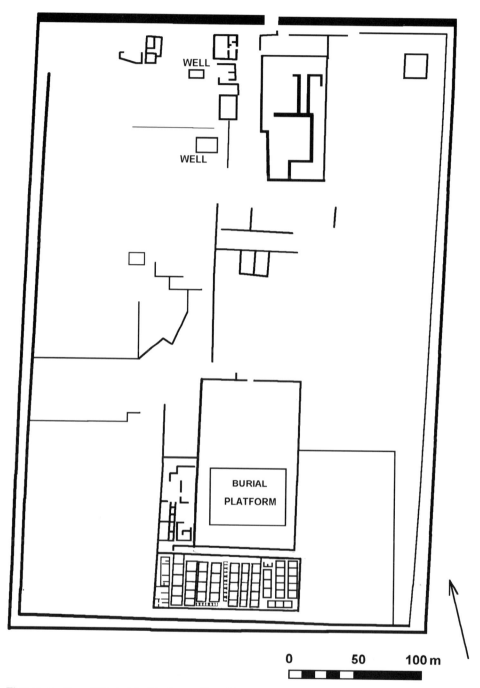

WELL

WELL

BURIAL
PLATFORM

0   50   100 m

Figure 2.30 Plan of Ciudadela Chayhuac, Chan Chan (Redrawn from Moseley and Mackey 1974)

not exhibit major subdivisions and was not designed with a tripartite plan like other, probably later ciudadelas.

Ciudadela Uhle   Uhle contains five large sectors defined by major interior walls (Figure 2.31). The two eastern sectors of Uhle contain a cluster of four audiencias and associated niched rooms and a second group of niched rooms and possible store-rooms; they are otherwise empty. The northwestern sector contains no architecture.

The most architecturally complex portions of Uhle are two of the western sectors. One sector contains a dense cluster of audiencias and storage rooms located south of a plaza. Access was via two offset entrances in secondary interior walls that led into the plaza, and from the plaza via a corridor and up a ramp to a single, small doorway which opened onto an audiencia/storage complex. A second and larger set of store-rooms and niched rooms is associated with the all but destroyed burial platform at Uhle. This complex is completely cut off from the rest of the ciudadela; there are no discernible entrances in the walls surrounding the burial platform and storerooms.

Ciudadela Tello   Ciudadela Tello is the smallest compound (Figure 2.32), and con-tains two sectors: (1) a rectangular, southern sector (Tello South) completely enclosed by a rectangular compound, and (2) a second, northern area (Tello North) that appears to be a later addition. Topic and Moseley (1983) suggest that Tello North was built at least a century after Tello South, but the absolute dating is uncer-tain although the order of construction seems sound.

Tello South is entered through a single, simple door on the north wall. A cluster of cell-like rooms and storerooms is located in the northeast corner of Tello South, the southeastern corner has a large simple patio, and the northeastern corner is empty. The remainder of Tello South contains storerooms, courtyards, cell-like rooms, and a large trough-lined plaza with a tablado – a small raised dais analogous to those described by Bawden (1982b) for Galindo; Topic and Moseley (1983: 160) cite this as evidence of direct continuity between the Moche V site and the early Chan Chan ciudadelas.

Ciudadela Tello forms an inverted "L," and most of its architecture is in the short, northern stem. Tello North is further divided into three sectors. The eastern sector is all but empty of architecture, while the central sector contains a range of rooms and courtyards, niched rooms, storerooms, and two or three audiencias. The western sector of Tello North contains two large plazas with ramps, a variety of rooms like those found in the central sector, and a small set of storerooms. Because it lacks a burial platform, Kolata (1990: 129) suggests Ciudadela "Tello was not func-tionally equivalent to the other ciudadelas of Chan Chan . . . [it] was probably intended as a residence of an expanding class of bureaucrats" (Kolata 1990: 122).

Ciudadela Laberinto   The reason for Laberinto's name is obvious at a glance – the ciudadela is an extraordinarily complex piece of architecture (Figure 2.33). Laberinto's design is pivotal in the architectural tradition at Chan Chan. Kolata (1990: 124) argues that Laberinto represents a threshold of architectural coherency;

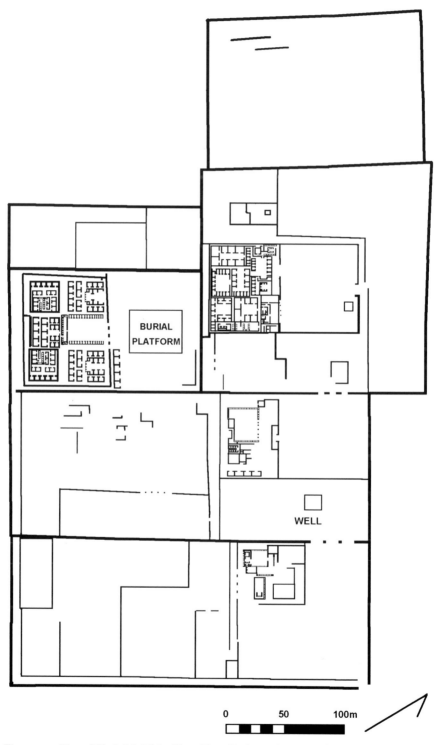

Figure 2.31 Plan of Ciudadela Uhle, Chan Chan (Redrawn from Moseley and Mackey 1974)

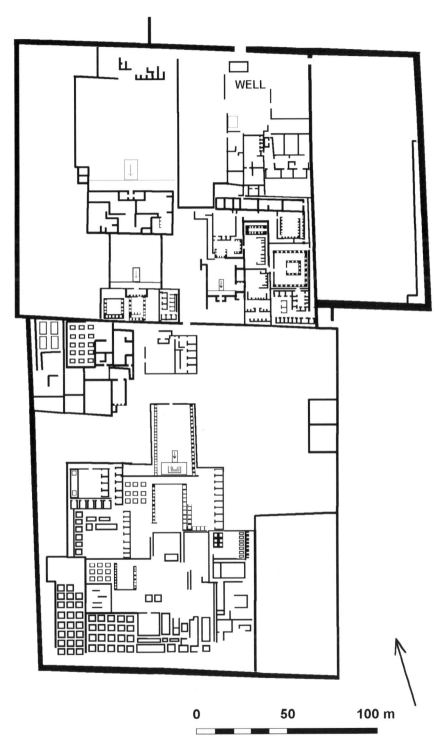

WELL

0   50   100 m

Figure 2.32 Plan of Ciudadela Tello, Chan Chan (Redrawn from Moseley and Mackey 1974)

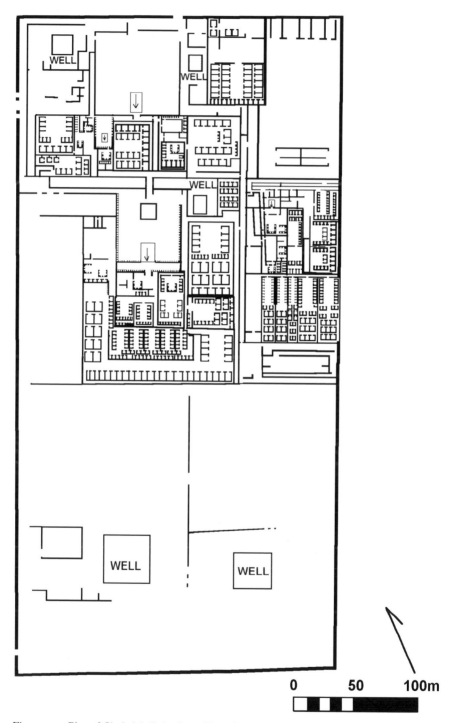

WELL

WELL

WELL

WELL

WELL

WELL

0   50   100m

Figure 2.33 Plan of Ciudadela Laberinto, Chan Chan (Redrawn from Moseley and Mackey 1974)

the ciudadelas built after Laberinto more closely follow the a "classic" ciudadela model, consisting of tripartite layout, the spatial association between audiencias and purported storerooms, burial platform, and empty southern sectors frequently containing walk-in wells. If the subsequent descriptions seem monotonous, it is not because I am an uncreative writer; the repetitions simply reflects the standardized execution of monumental construction at Chan Chan.

Ciudadela Laberinto is entered through a baffled entry on the northern wall leading into a plaza. A door in the northeast plaza wall opens onto a walk-in well and a set of storerooms. A ramp rises from the plaza to a passage into a dense zone of courtyards, storerooms, and audiencias. The central sector contains a plaza lined by three niched walls, banks of storerooms, nine audiencias, courtyards, and a walk-in well. Laberinto lacks a burial platform in its central sector, although a burial platform located northeast of the compound may be associated with the ciudadela.

There is no visible passage between the northern and central or central and southern sectors; the only entrance to the southern sector is through a doorway in the southwestern corner of the compound wall. The southern sector contains two, possibly unfinished, architectural complexes of unknown function and a walk-in well.

Ciudadela Gran Chimu   Gran Chimu is the largest ciudadela (Figure 2.34), due to its enormous northern annex that covers 9.127 ha. The main complex alone is one of the largest ciudadelas at Chan Chan, exhibiting a tripartite division into northern, central, and southern sectors. The baffled entrance in the north wall opens onto the plaza in the northern sector. A passage through the eastern plaza wall leads to a walk-in well and two sets of storerooms. A doorway on the western plaza wall once opened onto a now-blocked corridor that led to a series of courtyards, storerooms, niched rooms, and audiencias. From the plaza, a large ramp leads to a passage through the southern wall and into a complex of storerooms, courts, and an audiencia.

Looting in the central sector has obliterated the burial platform that once dominated the area. A large plaza with the remains of storerooms and a niched room are located in the northern part of the central sector. A walk-in well is located in the northwest corner of the central sector, and a group of storerooms and courtyards sits in the northeast corner. Additional storerooms and a very small walk-in well (12 × 10 m) are found west of the burial platform. The southern sector of Gran Chimu contains little evidence of architecture, although a large walk-in well is located in the southwestern corner of the ciudadela.

Ciudadela Squier   Squier is the most enigmatic ciudadela; it apparently was never finished and subsequent destruction has obscured details of construction, pattern, and access (Figure 2.35). There is no clear entrance into the compound, although a set of corridors, ramps, and a plaza suggests the northern sector was the "front" of Squier. It is not divided into three sectors like other ciudadelas. Squier does not contain a burial platform, although one is located on the outside of its western wall. One three-sided room may represent an audiencia (though it

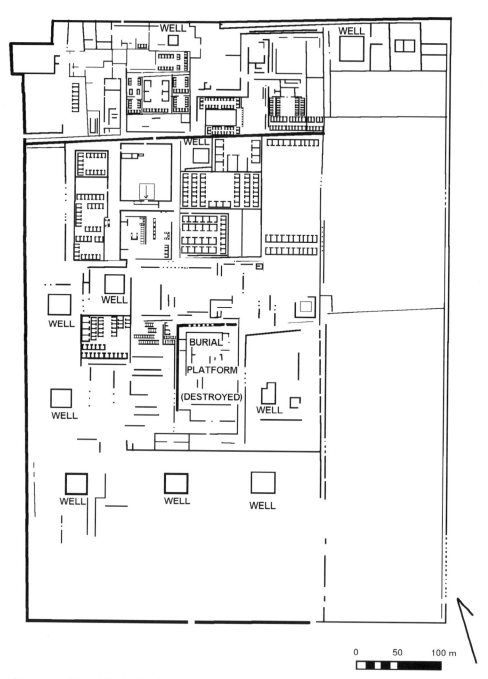

Figure 2.34 Plan of Ciudadela Gran Chimu, Chan Chan (Redrawn from Moseley and Mackey 1974)

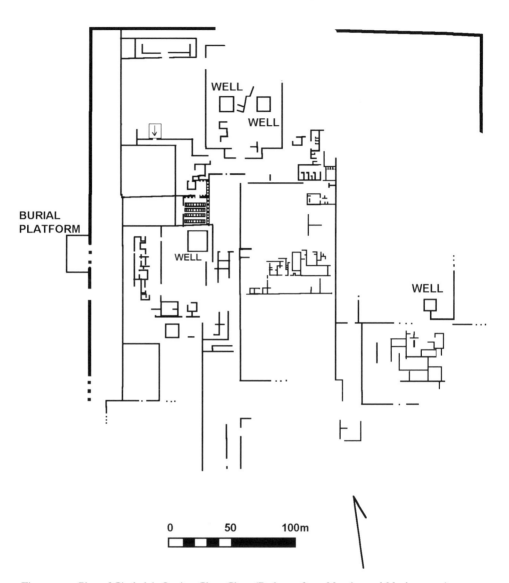

Figure 2.35 Plan of Ciudadela Squier, Chan Chan (Redrawn from Moseley and Mackey 1974)

lacks niches), but it stands alone in a large patio in the south-central portion of the compound. Squier contains two walk-in wells which may postdate the compound. A group of fifty possible storerooms is located in the northern quadrant of Squier, but most of the ciudadela is open and unbuilt, emphasizing the unfinished nature of the compound.

Ciudadela Velarde   Ciudadela Velarde is one of the larger compounds and its plan is rather complex, partly due to the addition of a large annex on the northern end of the compound (Figure 2.36). The northern annex contain large plazas, storerooms, seven audiencias, and a sunken well. It is not clear how the northern annex is linked

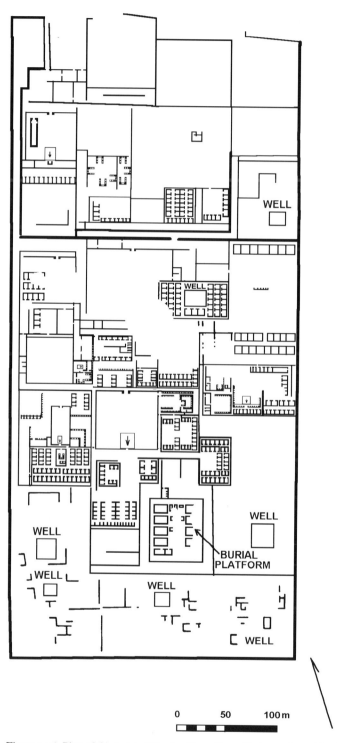

Figure 2.36 Plan of Ciudadela Velarde, Chan Chan (Redrawn from Moseley and Mackey 1974)

to the main body of the compound, although a doorway may have existed in a portion of now-destroyed wall.

The body of the compound is divided into three sectors. The northern sector consists of plazas, banks of storerooms built within walled units, and three audiencias. The central sector of Velarde contains courtyards with niches and storerooms, audiencias, a sunken well in the southeastern corner, and the burial platform, which has been looted heavily. The third and southernmost sector of Velarde contains four walk-in wells and miscellaneous wall sections of unclear plan.

Ciudadela Bandelier   Bandelier is laid out as a simple rectangle, subdivided into three parts by principal interior walls (Figure 2.37). A baffled entrance on the north wall is connected by a corridor to a large plaza. Two opposing doors on the plazas lead to different portions of the compound, and a ramp rises from the plaza to a cluster of niched rooms, audiencias, and storerooms. The northwestern plaza door leads to an area of open courtyards and storerooms, and the northeastern plaza door connects to a set of large rooms, patios, storerooms, and a walk-in well.

The central sector is subdivided into three areas. The eastern subsector contains the burial platform and a walk-in well. The central subsector has a plaza that is connected by a ramp to an area of storerooms and audiencias. The western sector contains few walls but two walk-in wells. The southern sector of Bandelier is empty of architecture, except for a walk-in well.

Ciudadela Rivero   Ciudadela Rivero is one of the best known compounds due to the research conducted by Kent Day (1973, 1982). By most accounts, it is one of the latest ciudadelas and it exemplifies classic ciudadela form (Figure 2.38). Originally, Ciudadela Rivero was laid out as a long rectangle divided into three sections. Three subsequent annexes were added on the north, east, and southern sides of the ciudadela (Kolata 1990: 124), but the original entrance is clearly visible in the plans. The northern entrance opens onto a baffled corridor that leads to a large plaza. Two doorways are located on opposite walls at the north end of the plaza, and a ramp rises to a southern doorway that gives access to a set of storerooms and audiencias. The northeastern plaza door connects to a set of small courts, plazas, and storerooms. The northwestern door leads from the plaza to a corridor that ends in a small plaza and a group of storerooms; by winding through the storerooms, passage is gained to a very long corridor which runs to the southern portions of Ciudadela Rivero. This corridor provides the only access to the southern sector of the compound, which contains a sunken well.

The central and largest sector of Rivero contains a large plaza, three areas of storerooms, and the burial platform. Set off from the rest of the ciudadela by secondary walls, the burial platform has a forecourt lined with niched walls.

Ciudadela Tschudi   Ciudadela Tschudi is one of the best preserved and most formal compounds at Chan Chan. It has been cited as an example of tripartite ciudadela division, although it is not a simple plan (Figure 2.39). The exterior walls form a

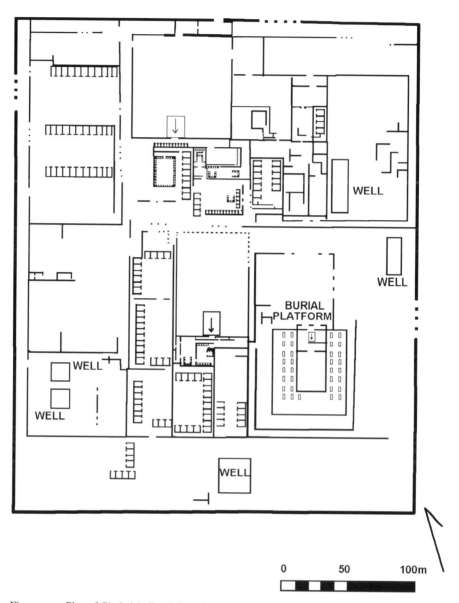

Figure 2.37 Plan of Ciudadela Bandelier, Chan Chan (Redrawn from Moseley and Mackey 1974)

thick-bodied "L"; the majority of the storerooms and audiencias are located in the stem of the "L," and a burial platform sits in the southeastern base of the "L." Tschudi is entered through a baffled doorway on the northern wall of the compound, which opens onto a plaza. Two doorways on opposite walls of the plaza lead to different parts of the ciudadela, while a ramp leads from the plaza to a densely built area of storerooms, audiencias, and smaller plazas. Circuitous corridors then connect to the central sector of Tschudi which is dominated by a large plaza, sets of storerooms, three audiencias, and an enormous (140 × 58 m) walk-in well.

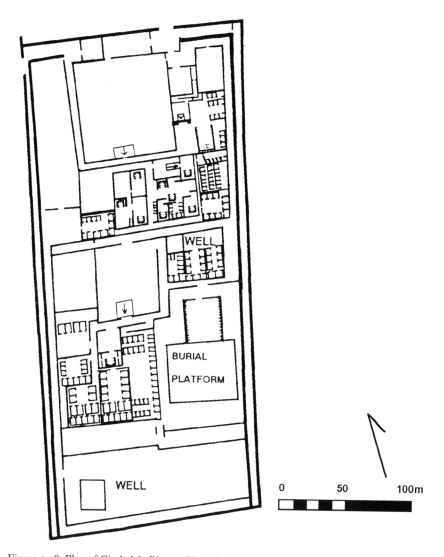

Figure 2.38 Plan of Ciudadela Rivero, Chan Chan (Redrawn from Moseley and Mackey 1974)

To the east, a smaller sector of Tschudi contains storerooms, two audiencias, and a walk-in well. This area is directly connected to Tschudi's entrance by a long corridor, and the burial platform is immediately south of this area. The burial platform is faced by a forecourt, exhibits its cell-like construction, and a secondary-stage addition (Conrad 1982) on its western side. To the west, another division contains a small group of possible storerooms, while the westernmost division holds a miscellany of commoners' residences.

The Chan Chan huacas The Chan Chan ciudadelas have attracted a great deal of study, but the large mounds have been all but ignored. The four Chan Chan huacas are briefly discussed by Day (1982: 62–63) who describes their locations and general states of destruction. Huaca Obispo is located on the far northern margin of Chan Chan

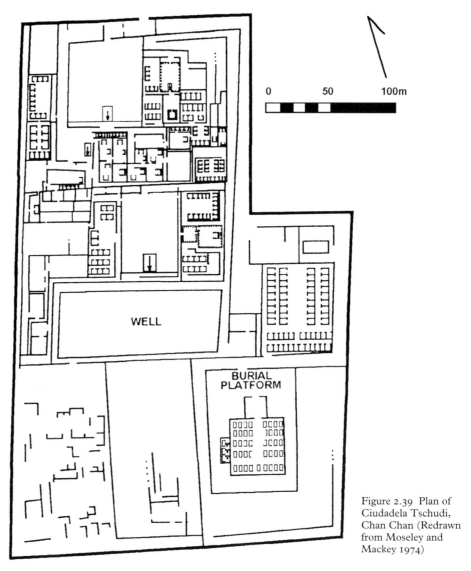

Figure 2.39 Plan of
Ciudadela Tschudi,
Chan Chan (Redrawn
from Moseley and
Mackey 1974)

(Figure 2.29), away from the ciudadelas and urban core of the city. The
remnants of the heavily looted mound suggest the structure was 100 ×
100 m and perhaps 20 m tall. The mound's core was constructed from
cobblestone chamber and fill, "constructed of water-worn cobbles
packed into 1.5- to 2-meter square 'frames' or blocks of carefully laid
cobbles" (Day 1982: 62). This core was sheathed in adobe bricks and
mud plaster, forming terraces approximately 1.5 m wide. At the lip of
each terrace was an adobe wall, at least 1 m tall, that ran around the
edge of the terrace, "giving the impression that each terrace was like a
corridor that went around the huaca" (Day 1982: 62). Day did not find
evidence of stairways or summit-top structures.

The location of Huaca Obispo is interesting (Figure 2.29). Situated in a large open area enclosed by adobe walls, Huaca Obispo apparently was approached from the south via a doorway that opened onto this plaza. Huaca Obispo was separated from the rest of Chan Chan by a major east–west avenue which ran north of Ciudadela Gran Chimu's northern annex. But in spite of its marginal location, Conklin (1990: 61) suggests that Huaca Obispo was a central focus at Chan Chan, oriented toward the mountains and irrigation canals and sharing those orientations with earlier Moche huacas. Beyond that, Huaca Obispo seems to sit at the northern boundary of Chan Chan, possibly associated with walls that marked the edge of the city (Conklin 1990: 61).

Huaca Toledo is located on the east side of Chan Chan near Ciudadela Bandelier (Figure 2.29), and it was built in a large enclosed open area like Huaca Obispo. The patterns of entrances into this area are unclear. Extensively looted, Day (1982: 62) estimated that the huaca was perhaps 75 × 75 m at its base and 15 m high. The map of the huaca (Moseley and Mackey 1974: Sheets 11) suggests a terraced structure. Little remains but "a heap of cobbles," indicating the persistence of rumors of hidden treasures and suggesting the construction was similar to Huaca Obispo.

Two additional huacas are all but destroyed, scarcely indicated by scant remains. Huaca las Conchas is situated southeast of Huaca Obispo and northeast of Huaca Toledo (Figure 2.29). According to Day (1982: 63), looters' discovery of walls decorated with appliquéd mudplaster shells gives the mound its name. Extrapolating from the Chan Chan base map (Moseley and Mackey 1974: Sheet 1), the mound measured about 70 m square and the looted tailings form a pile 6 to 8 m above ground level. The mound was constructed from adobes (Day 1982: 62). Huaca El Higo is located east of Ciudadela Chayhuac (Figure 2.29) and may have been the largest huaca at Chan Chan. Although the mound "presently consists of mounds of melted adobe and traces of walls" (Day 1982: 63), the Chan Chan map (Moseley and Mackey 1974: Sheet 1) suggests the mound may have covered some 120 × 100 m with a height of over 8 m. Like Obispo and Toledo, Huaca El Higo apparently was surrounded by a walled enclosure; however, the extensive destruction in the area makes it impossible to reconstruct.

Recent relative chronologies outlined by Topic and Moseley (1983) and Kolata (1990) correlate the construction of the huacas with relative sequences for the Chan Chan ciudadelas; the two chronologies are in basic agreement. Based on his seriation of adobe bricks from the huacas and ciudadelas (Kolata 1978: 82–94), Kolata (1990) suggests that Huaca El Higo was built early in the development of Chan Chan, i.e. in his phase Early Chimu 1A, ca. AD 900–1100; Topic and Moseley (1983: 159) suggest absolute dates of AD 850–1000. With the expansion of constructions to the north of Chan Chan during Middle Chimu (ca. AD 1200–1300), both Huaca Obispo and Huaca las Conchas appear in the urban landscape, followed by the construction of Huaca Toledo, along with Ciudadela Bandelier, during Late Chimu 1 (ca. AD 1300–1400).

When compared to earlier sites, Chan Chan exhibits a decrease in the size and presumably significance of huacas, a pattern which Topic and Moseley (1983: 163) observe reflects a change in socio-political strategies and objectives. Yet, the social and political roles of the pyramidal huacas of Chan Chan remain unclear, particularly when contrasted with the abundant interpretations of other classes of Chimu architecture (but see Netherly's [1990: 482–484] interpretation of the huacas in the context of Andean dualism). Simply, it is not known how the Chan Chan huacas were integrated into the enormous urban landscape constructed by the desert kingdom of Chimor.

The Chan Chan ciudadelas are a remarkably coherent set of prehispanic monumental constructions. They exhibit a clear architectural pattern represented by the articulations of portal, passage, and plaza in the northern sectors of the ciudadelas. Equally clear is the general spatial association between audiencia and storeroom, although the relationship, as discussed in Chapter 5, is not as simple as some have thought. And, perhaps most of all, there is an unmistakable concern with security, as so many scholars have observed. But was this concern with the control of access widespread among the Chimu or a unique feature of life at Chan Chan? To explore this question, we turn to two sites located in the hinterland of the Chimu state.

Farfán, Jequetepeque

Farfán is located 12.5 km inland from the Pacific Ocean and 3.8 km north of the main channel of the Rio Jequetepeque. Farfán is thought to be the Chimu provincial center in the Jequetepeque Valley (Conrad 1990; Keatinge 1982; Keatinge and Conrad 1983). Farfán runs 3.5 km along the eastern base of Cerro Falco in a narrow 0.25 km strip, totalling about 1 sq km in area. The site consists of six adobe brick walled compounds, various platforms and smaller constructions, cemeteries, and canals; all of the features have been damaged by looters and bulldozers (Keatinge and Conrad 1983: 265). The Panamerican Highway has damaged the west side of Farfán and the eastern portion has been destroyed by modern agriculture.

Much of the discussion of Farfán has centered on whether it – rather than the much larger and imposing site of Pacatnamú – was the seat of power of General Pacatnamú as described by Calancha (1977 [1638]: 1227, 1229). An additional concern is how Farfán, as an example of Chimu provincial constructions, represents the architectural tenets expressed in Chan Chan (e.g., Conrad 1990: 228).

The compounds are strung in a line and numbered from south to north. Compound II (Figure 2.40) was the most complicated structure, it was the only compound with a burial platform, and it was the focus of excavations in 1978. A series of radiocarbon samples from those excavations produced mixed results (Keatinge and Conrad 1983: 274–276); the excavators believe that relative and selected absolute dates suggest an occupation at ca. AD 1200.

Compound II is a rectangular walled compound 374 m long and 130 m wide. A pilastered door on the north side of the compound opens onto a large fore-plaza. From there, access to the main compound is via a pilastered doorway flanked by two sets of three carved figures; four preserved figures depict a feline crouching behind a smaller human (Keatinge and Conrad 1983: 271–272). Beyond this door, additional interior walls have the effect of a baffling passage until a third pilastered entry opens onto the so-called entry court. The open entry court has two low platforms

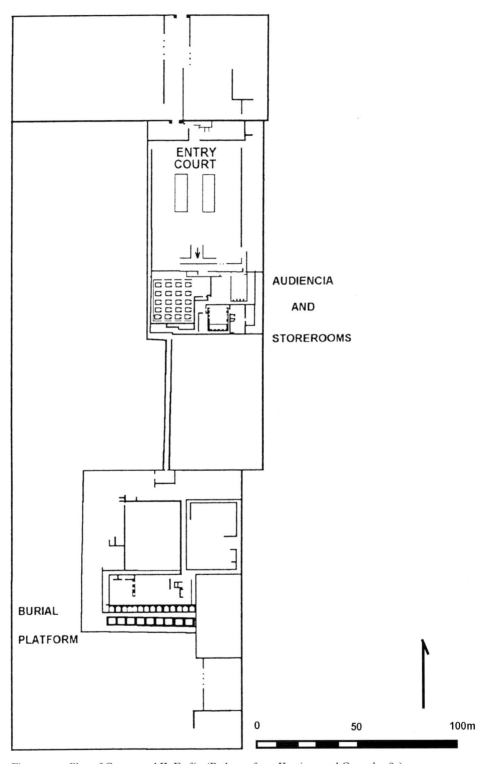

ENTRY
COURT

AUDIENCIA

AND

STOREROOMS

BURIAL

PLATFORM

0   50   100m

Figure 2.40 Plan of Compound II, Farfán (Redrawn from Keatinge and Conrad 1983)

that stand away from the walls and a two-tiered raised platform with niches along the southern wall. A ramp connects the entry court to the raised platform, and from there one enters into a complex of storerooms, an audiencia with bins, and snaking corridors. This portion of Compound II is interpreted as administrative in function.

Access to the burial platform in the southern portion of Compound II is via a long corridor which begins near the northwest corner of the entry court and runs for some 190 meters before terminating in the burial platform complex. The burial platform has been looted, but there are traces of associated bins and storerooms. These features were empty, as were two rooms adjacent to the burial platform in Compound II.

The architectural similarities between Farfán and Chan Chan are important in interpreting the site as an intrusive administrative center representing Chimu expansion into the Jequetepeque Valley. Keatinge and Conrad (1983: 280) write:

> Compound II, the principal structure at Farfán, has many features typical of the most important compounds at Chan Chan. In a general sense, Compound II's overall configuration has the following major similarities to the contemporaneous Uhle compound at Chan Chan: N–S orientation, entry in the north, storerooms in the center and rear, a binned audiencia, a burial platform in the rear. Compound II, however, is smaller and simpler than the Uhle compound and does not represent an attempt to duplicate the structure as closely as possible.

In short, Farfán shares some, but not all, of the architectural traits noted at Chan Chan. It also shares traits with another Chimu provincial center, Manchan, located on the opposite frontier of the Chimu state.

Manchan, Casma Valley
Manchan is located on the southern margin of the Casma Valley, approximately 9.5 km from the Pacific Ocean; it is the largest known Chimu provincial center south of the Virú Valley (Figure 2.41; Mackey and Klymyshyn 1981, 1990, n.d.; Mackey 1987; Moore 1985). Barely mentioned by Tello (1956: 25, 30, 68) and briefly studied by Thompson (1961: 106–108, 232–236), Manchan appears to be a site-intrusive settlement constructed by the Chimu (Mackey and Klymyshyn 1990: 198), not a Middle Horizon settlement as Thompson (1961) suggested. Manchan covers approximately 63 hectares. Mackey and Klymyshyn (1990: 205) tentatively suggest that the construction of Manchan may have begun by AD 1305 and certainly before ca. AD 1450. The site contains various classes of archaeological remains: a large cemetery in the southwestern portion of the site, a cobbled enclosure thought to be a llama corral, five areas of cane-walled structures associated with the commoners of Manchan (Moore 1981, 1985, 1988), five isolated, adobe-walled compounds, a chain of agglutinated compounds that runs across the northern edge of the site, and a tapia walled enclosure on a hillside on the northeastern corner of the site.

The agglutinated compounds of Manchan are a series of simple walled enclosures built from adobe brick. Wall abutments show the compounds were built from east

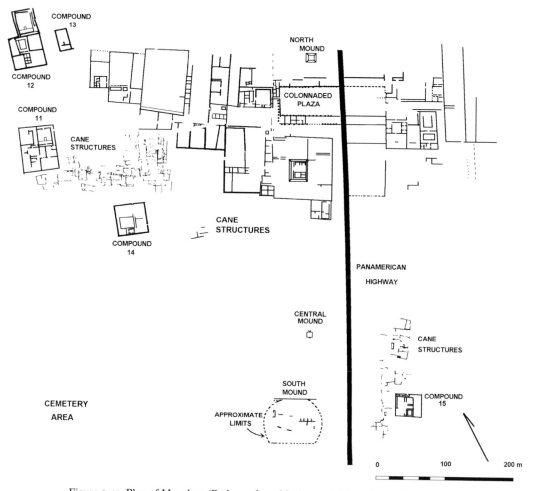

Figure 2.41 Plan of Manchan (Redrawn from Mackey and Klymyshyn n.d.)

to west without interconnecting doorways (Mackey and Klymyshyn 1990: 205). The easternmost compound is the largest and most architecturally complex, and it has a very large plaza, roughly 160 × 85 m in area. The west end of the plaza has a wide bench and an elaborate doorway, and the bases of 65 rounded adobe columns – some painted with ocher and red paint – line the plaza, suggesting the importance of the space (Mackey and Klymyshyn 1990: 205; Moore n.d.). North of the plaza is a mound which has been all but destroyed; south of the plaza is an area of elite residences (Mackey and Klymyshyn 1990: 205).

West of the colonnaded plaza are open patios and patio-and-room clusters (Mackey and Klymsyhyn n.d.: 11–12). Two types of patio-and-room clusters may have served administrative functions (Mackey and Klymyshyn n.d.: 11). Manchan lacks structures formally identical to the audiencias of Chan Chan, but Mackey (1987) argues that the key spaces in Type II patio-and-room clusters were the functional equivalents of audiencias. Mackey (1987: 126) writes: "Manchan differs from the rest of the [Chimu] centers in that *audiencias* at the site do not conform totally to the formal characteristics identified at Chan Chan. However, audiencias at Manchan do share the function of guarding access to storerooms [i.e., as suggested for the Chan Chan audiencias]." Three such audiencia variants are located in Manchan (Mackey 1987: 126).

The isolated compounds more closely follow the grammar and form of built spaces at Chan Chan. The northwestern example (Compound 12) has baffled entries, a roughly tripartite plan, ramps that lead from patios, a couple of storerooms, and an audiencia variant "which is the most similar to the U-shaped structures in Chan Chan" (Mackey and Klymyshyn 1990: 206). To varying extents, the rest of the Manchan isolated compounds share these features, although each differs in scale, access, and internal complexity. The discovery of elite burials in these compounds with Chimu hats and loincloths, and wooden statues and staffs similar to those found in Chan Chan reemphasize the connection between these structures and the heartland of Chimor (Mackey and Klymyshyn 1990: 200).

There are three small, unimpressive mounds at Manchan roughly aligned down the center of the site. Extensively disturbed, the northern mound was approximately 18 × 18 m at its base and 3m tall. The mound has been salvaged for adobe bricks that comprise its core, exposing traces of red-ocher paint. The central mound is approximately 5 × 5 m and less than 2 m tall. To the south and distant from the adobe buildings is the largest mound at Manchan. This mound covers an area of approximately 60 × 60 m and it is about 4 m tall. The mound consists of adobe walls that retain their artificial fill of wall rubble and organic material.

Examining both continuities and variations, Mackey and Klymyshyn (1990; Mackey 1987) have discussed regional patterns of Chimu provincial administration, particularly as expressed in public architecture. One point of variation concerns differences in access patterns from patios to storage areas. Estimating that there were fewer than fifty storerooms at Manchan, Mackey and Klymyshyn (1990: 210) write:

> Although access to storerooms was highly restricted in the capital, Manchan has storerooms with both restricted and unrestricted access. The restricted storerooms were accessible through corridors and/or guarded by audiencia variants. The majority of the storerooms, however, had unrestricted access, that is, they were directly accessible from plazas, and were relatively large.

They conclude that the storage was for short-term storage of bulk utilitarian items, rather than for more permanent warehousing of elite goods suggested by the numerous, highly restricted storerooms of the Chan Chan ciudadelas (Mackey and Klymyshyn 1990: 210). And thus, as a provincial center, Manchan had a different role in the Chimu political economy, a role which is partially reflected in its architecture.

Conclusion

The sample of ancient Andean architecture covers a broad spectrum of social units, from bands to empires, and spans approximately 5,900 years of Peruvian prehistory.

To repeat my introductory disclaimer, this sample of sites was selected because of the quality of the available data, the fact that each site contained public architecture, and my personal familiarity with the sites and the region. But more importantly, the sites in the sample reflect important differences in the social uses of prehistoric architecture. Some sites seem clearly to have been used within ritual contexts while others seem just as obviously secular, but such a rough dichotomy is too crude to be interesting. And so in the following chapters, three topics are considered – the architecture of monuments, the architecture of ritual, and the architecture of social control – in an attempt to understand the social dynamics that produced such intriguing prehistoric constructions.

3

The architecture of monuments

Monuments themselves memorials need.

George Crabbe, 1810

Within twenty years of Pizarro's landfall on the west coast of South America, the word "huaca" was applied to native religious monuments by Spanish speakers throughout the Americas. Derived from the Quechua *waka*, the first written use of the word was in Juan de Betanzos' *Suma y narración de los Incas* completed in 1551, and "huaca" eventually was incorporated into the dialects of Spanish spoken in Central America and the Caribbean (Corominas 1974: 800). Betanzos (1987 [1551]) used *waka* to refer to a sacred place or temple or a priestly residence, but by the late sixteenth and early seventeenth centuries the word's meaning had loosened considerably. With the onslaught of extirpation, the definitional boundaries widened to include any burial place, any shrine, any object or construction that materially marked the indigenous concepts of sacred. As the word spread, its definition stretched. The laxity of categories is paralleled in archaeological approaches to ancient Andean monuments. The word *huaca* has been attached to enormous pyramids (Huaca del Sol at Moche), tell-like accumulations of midden (Huaca Prieta in the Chicama Valley), and burial crypts (Huaca las Avispas at Chan Chan). Only two concepts unify such different structures – they are artificial and they are large – and a moment's reflection suggests such a classification obscures more than it illuminates.

Yet how can one begin to classify and to understand the differing social uses and meanings that prehistoric monuments had for Andean people? First, there is the issue of defining what a monument is. Bruce Trigger (1990: 119) writes of monumental architecture: "Its principal defining feature is that its scale and elaboration exceed the requirements of any practical functions that a building is intended to perform." Although referring to the large monuments of ancient civilizations, Trigger touches on a key element: monuments are non-domestic, non-prosaic structures, separate from the everyday. Monuments are public, although the public may range from a few families to a nation-state of millions. Monuments are structures designed to be recognized, expressed by their scale or elaboration, even though their meanings may not be understood by all members of a society.

Which leads to the problem of the meaning of monuments. In the Andes, the ethnohistoric record is an important and under-utilized source of insight, but it is also insufficient. As others have discussed in detail (e.g., Murra 1975, 1980; Urton 1990; Zuidema 1990a) Andean ethnohistory can provide extraordinary insights into Inca society and culture, and occasional vistas into societies which immediately preceded the Inca. Beyond that, the written record dims. It is possible some basic principles of Inca cosmology have legacies of millennia, such as worship of ancestors (Doyle 1988), sacrifice of crops and animals (Murra 1960), and the deification of mountains and rivers, sun, and sea (MacCormack 1991; Rheinhard 1985; Rostworowski 1983), but these broad concepts also are held by people around the world who have never heard of Cuzco. Within this broad frame, different Andean societies gave unique expression to these cultural values, clearly different from Inca concepts of cosmos and rite. For example, the Sun was the focus of state worship in Inca society, but coastal peoples gave greater reverence to the Moon and Sea. Headhunting was important in Nasca society, but apparently not among the Inca. While the Inca created magnificent works in stone – palaces, terraces, fountains, and sculpture – they did not build great artificial mounds; coastal societies did. The magnificent detail of specific Andean accounts (e.g., the *Huarochiri Manuscript* [Salomon and Urioste 1991] or Guaman Poma de Ayala's *Buen gobierno* [1987]) can be extended into the past only so far until we are forced to recognize earlier Andean societies' utter otherness. There is every reason to believe that, although ideological continuities existed between Inca and other Andean societies, there were significant disjunctures in their systems of belief, their cultural frameworks, and their architectural aesthetics. For such reasons, Andean monuments are the most obvious archaeological remains and among the most difficult to understand.

The following chapter outlines an approach to Andean monuments that is built from three concepts. First, I assume that Andean monuments exhibit socially significant differences, and I am primarily interested in understanding that variation rather than emphasizing continuities of tradition. I contend that even structures which form similar architectural classes (e.g., "pyramids") often exhibit important variations that reflect differing social uses and/or contexts. Second, I argue that it is possible to discover and measure architectural variation such that the inquiry can be replicated and/or disproved by other investigators. I outline a set of analytical techniques below.

And third, I suggest that it is important to analyze monuments within the context of their constructed landscapes. If archaeologists are interested in understanding the social purposes of prehistoric architecture, if we are intrigued by the question "Why was this monument built?" then it is important to focus on the architectural context of a construction. By taking this approach to a small sample of prehispanic monuments – all artificial mounds, all huacas – my goal is to build on the suggestions of others (most notably the work of Richard Blanton [1989] and Tadahiko Higuchi [1983]) and to outline an archaeological perspective on monuments.

Archaeological approaches to monuments

The Enlightenment's fascination with monuments gave birth to archaeology, but it was a fascination shaped by centuries of debate about the relative merits of ancient and modern, tradition and progress (Lowenthal 1985). Views of the past are never static, and since monuments are physical eruptions of the past, their interpretations have been shaped by such changing views. Not only did these changes affect the public's awareness of historical places, but they also molded archaeological and "pre-archaeological" approaches to monuments (Abrams 1989: 47). As the contemplation of ruins was alternately shaped by antiquarianism or colonialism, romanticism or racism (Trigger 1989), the interpretation of monuments shifted. American archaeology's inquiry into the past shifted from unfettered speculation to detailed culture history, and the archaeological approach to monuments paralleled the changing goals of the discipline (*vide* Willey and Sabloff 1974: 30–36, 43–50).

Similarly, as the New Archaeology appropriated Leslie White's (1943, 1949, 1959) theory linking energy and social evolution and applied it to the archaeological record (e.g., Binford 1972), it was paralleled by an approach to prehistoric monuments which Elliott Abrams (1989: 53) has called "the energetic analysis of architecture." The relationship between monumental constructions and levels of social evolution had been stated explicitly by V. Gordon Childe, but it was only with the increasing emphasis on energy (e.g., Adams 1975) that the energetics approach became a common analytical theme in American archaeology (e.g., Arnold and Ford 1980; Peebles and Kus 1977: 432; Renfrew 1983; Sanders and Price 1968; Sanders and Santley 1983). The analysis was predicated on a straightforward proposition: greater levels of social complexity are marked by increased control over resources, including labor, and the scale and complexity of monuments reflect the labor invested in them; thus calculations of prehistoric labor investments represented by monuments serve as an index of social complexity. This logic, expanded to included entire communities, led Price (1982: 728) to refer to prehistoric settlement systems as being "a virtual material isomorph of infrastructure and political economy." When applied to public constructions, the relationship between material remains and social effort was an analytical fulcrum which served "to better understand the dynamics of processual cultural change" (Abrams 1989: 53) by explicitly linking the scale and complexity of architecture to levels of social development. Abrams provides a succinct sketch of the energetics approach:

> architectural energetics seeks to reconstruct the scale of social differentiation and inequality as reflected in the energy expended in various architectural features. For example, architecture, by virtue of its capacity to absorb relatively large amounts of energy during production, can hypothetically reflect a significant range of organizational behaviors requisite for such construction, an important index of cultural complexity.
> (Abrams 1989: 53)

And yet one wonders, "Why invest social effort in architecture?" The energetics approach generally avoids this issue, treating architecture as a dependent variable that passively reflects labor investment marshalled by social forces. After listing the wide variety of prehistoric public architecture – such as temples, defensive walls, storerooms, or burial chambers – Abrams (1989: 58) briefly states: "The increased expenditure in public architecture is caused by a number of variables relating to technological/utilitarian functions . . . and integrative/symbolic functions . . . 'financed' in essence by the growing surplus energy produced by that system."

But what triggers this investment or channels it into architecture? Abrams (1989: 62) suggests that monumental architecture enhances social integration and thus, "Large, state-authored public architecture may provide the central and conspicuous symbol of group identity in the context of the increasing linguistic, ethnic, social, and economic heterogeneity that characterizes states." Further, the author suggests that monumental constructions are undertaken when the need for group cohesion is greatest, during times of stress, "as an attempt to offset symbolically the loss of social cohesion and thus political power by those in authority" (Abrams 1989: 62). In short, public architecture represents energy investments in visible and meaningful social constructions; investments increase when cohesion is threatened during periods of economic, political, or environmental stress.

There must be a relationship between social complexity and the scale of monumental architecture, but the nature of the explanation and the logic of the above hypothesis remain murky. A few points of clarification are in order. First, different forms of public architecture evoke different meanings and distinct social responses. For example, in Washington, DC, the towering obelisk of the Washington Monument, its base ringed by flags snapping in the wind, evokes a public response in a way the nearby squat, massive offices of the Internal Revenue Service never will. The IRS building represents a monumental construction, but the IRS building was never designed as a pure symbol of national identity, although more Americans deal with the IRS than any other government agency. Not all public buildings create social cohesion.

A number of scholars have examined the notion of monuments as foci of social cohesion, but I have found work by Richard Blanton (1989) particularly useful. In his analyses of changes in public architecture in the valley of Oaxaca, Blanton outlines a model in which specific attributes of monumental architecture "pertain to the communicative function of the building, or how it transmits a message" (Blanton 1989: 413). Immediately behind this idea is the notion that artifacts convey information (Conkey 1978; Wobst 1974, 1977). By extension, such intentionally obvious artifacts as public architecture should communicate information obviously, but how is this achieved?

Second, it is important to clarify and limit the notion of "stress." Abrams suggests that monumental constructions may be associated with periods of stress, but monuments are not built during periods of all-out catastrophe. Some of the best documented prehistoric monuments are the pyramids constructed during the Old Kingdom and First Intermediate Period of Egyptian dynastic history (e.g. Bell 1974; Kemp 1983; Mendelsshon 1974; Trigger 1983; Wenke 1989), and they exhibit a marked growth and decline in overall volume, workmanship, and monumentality (Figure 3.1). The decline in pyramid construction and the end of the first dynastic cycle is associated with the end of the Neolithic wet phase and the onset of drought,

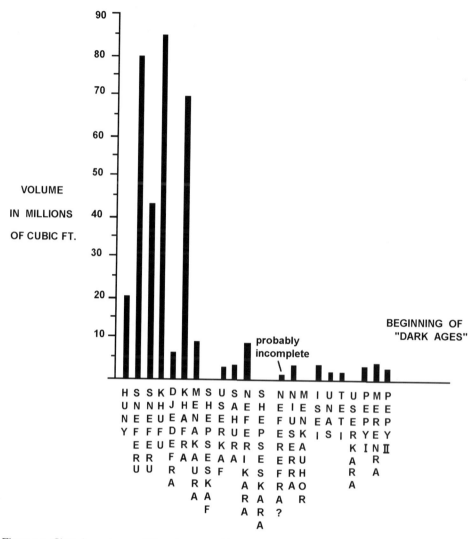

Figure 3.1 Changing volumes of Egyptian pyramid construction, Old Kingdom (Data from Kemp 1983)

famine, and political chaos, a Dark Ages recorded in the inscriptions known as the Lamentations (Bell 1974). But there was more than a simple positive correlation between the volume of the Nile flood and the size of monumental architecture. Those two phenomena were linked by an ideology summarized in the concept of *ma'at*, the notion of cosmic equilibrium, created by the gods at the beginning of time, and maintained by the pharaoh through the completion of proper ritual. *Ma'at* was the conceptual arch that connected natural phenomena and pharaonic authority. The droughts of the First Intermediate Period were tangible evidence of the pharaoh's failure to maintain *ma'at*, and his authority was eroded, quite literally, by the dry winds that blew across the Nile creating a time, as one of the Lamentations record, "when death stalked the land."

Monuments are not constructed during disasters, but less cataclysmic stresses may be resolved in formalized social encounters that occur at and are symbolized by public architecture. Gregory Johnson (1978, 1982) has outlined a model linking increasing difficulties in the transfer of information with the development of decision-making hierarchies; the model predicts that as social groups increase in size, information transfer and processing will be formalized at certain thresholds. This formalization may be expressed in various material means, including public architecture. In their cross-cultural study of "integrative facilities" (i.e., any artificial structure where people come together, from plazas to temples), Adler and Wilshusen (1990) suggest there is a positive relationship not only between group size and the size of integrative facilities, but also between group size and the exclusive use of such facilities for ceremonial purposes. Fewer non-ritual activities occur in larger integrative structures, suggesting an increasing dedication to the formalized modes of communication associated with ceremony.

Adler and Wilshusen consider only non-state societies, but their insights can be extended to the construction of monumental architecture in more complex societies. While the scale of public architecture may reflect a society's ability to produce and direct surplus labor, the creation of monuments takes predictable forms because of their differing communicative potentials. As social networks increase in size, the resolution of ambiguities becomes a premium concern. Monuments serve as unambiguous markers of social relationships, not only because of their scale, but because of their functional unity and visual prominence. The key to monuments, following Lynch (1960), is their *imageability* and *legibility*: their capacity for conveying meaning and the clarity with which meaning can be read.

Blanton clearly outlines the communicative function of monumental constructions: "As a communications media, monumental architecture is actually relatively efficient. The initial costs of construction may be great, but once built a massive building or plaza can be seen by thousands of people over great lengths of time, broadcasting continuously for even thousands of years" (Blanton 1989: 413).

Monumental constructions potentially communicate information for thousands of years, but that potential is not always realized. This chapter opens with a profound verse from an obscure poem that alludes to monuments' loss of meaning (Crabbe 1916 [1810]). Monuments of different materials and configurations do not have equal communicative potentials, as shown by a survey of prototypes for marking nuclear waste dumps (Kaplan and Adams 1986). In response to an Environmental Protection Agency directive that nuclear wastes must be marked with symbols which would last 10,000 years, Kaplan and Adams reviewed the construction and communicative properties of six ancient monuments: the Pyramids of Giza, Stonehenge, the Parthenon, the Great Wall of China, the Nazca Lines, and the Serpent Mound in Ohio. Their insights about the legibility of monuments are fascinating. Monuments built from earth and stone last longer than those of metal because metals are valued, scavenged, and reused. Monuments combining texts and symbols have a greater chance of accurate decoding than those with only symbols. Monuments made from stone blocks at least twice the size of a human tend not to be moved. Further, Kaplan and Adams (1986: 53) also had some very pragmatic insights into legibility:

> The Nazca lines indicate that the primary emphasis of the marking system should be on detectibility at ground level. There is also a subtle relationship between the size and placement of the individual components and the size of the entire monument. Stonehenge, the Acropolis, the [Giza] pyramids, and the Serpent Mound can all be taken in at a single glance. The patterns and forms of the monuments are immediately perceptible. The inability to perceive a monument in its entirety may hamper the investigator's ability to understand it.

In other words, there is a direct relationship between a monument's design and its communicative potential, and thus its ability to serve as a marker of social cohesion. Visible at a distance, comprehended at a glance, the Washington Monument is designed to communicate effectively in a way the headquarters of the IRS was never intended to do. And this leads to an analytical approach to the architecture of monuments.

Visual analysis of monuments

In a very direct manner, the imageability and legibility of monuments are shaped by what can be seen. The issues of visibility and perception are raised again in Chapter 4, but an introduction to this analysis is derived from Tadahiko Higuchi's (1983) study, *The Visual and Spatial Structure of Landscapes*. Although primarily an analyis of Japanese natural landscapes, Higuchi's work is directly relevant to a study of monumental architecture because it emphasizes the viewer's perception and the cultural significance of point of view. Higuchi fuses traditional Japanese responses to landscape with more general observations by students of space (e.g, Kevin Lynch, Edward T. Hall, Christian Norberg-Shulz), producing a clear methodology for transforming ideas about landscape into measurable properties of physical forms. For example, Higuchi (1983: 183), citing Lynch, points out that landmarks ideally have four qualities – they have clear forms, they contrast with their backgrounds, they are prominent, and "they must have sufficiently solid mass to emphasize their presence." Because of the properties of the human eye, such ideal qualities can be expressed as specific, measurable variables (Figure 3.2). Different ranges of vision can be measured as angles above and below a level, horizontal line of sight. Thus, vision is limited to 50–55 degrees above and 70–80 degrees below the horizontal line of vision, but within this range certain visual modes have even more restricted fields. As Figure 3.2 illustrates, color discrimination is restricted to between +30 degrees and –40 degrees, while maximum eye rotation is +25 degrees and –35 degrees. Normal line of sight while standing is approximately 10 degrees below the horizontal. This last fact has an interesting implication for thinking about monuments. With an angle of view of 10–15 degrees below the horizontal (Figure 3.3), it is relatively easy to walk across irregular surfaces because there is sufficient lagtime between seeing an obstacle and stepping on it. But when the point of view is forced upwards it becomes more difficult to see

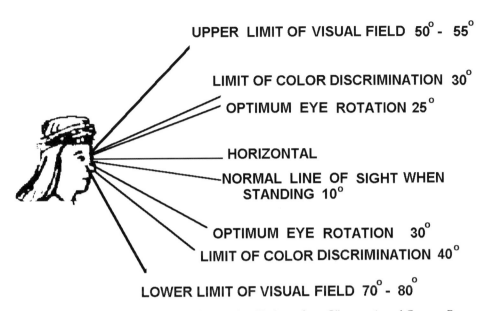

UPPER LIMIT OF VISUAL FIELD 50° - 55°

LIMIT OF COLOR DISCRIMINATION 30°

OPTIMUM EYE ROTATION 25°

HORIZONTAL

NORMAL LINE OF SIGHT WHEN STANDING 10°

OPTIMUM EYE ROTATION 30°

LIMIT OF COLOR DISCRIMINATION 40°

LOWER LIMIT OF VISUAL FIELD 70° - 80°

Figure 3.2 Angles of vision and ranges of perception (Redrawn from Gibson 1960 and Guaman Poma de Ayala 1620)

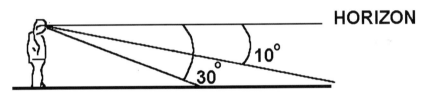

HORIZON

10°

30°

Figure 3.3 Normal lines of sight when standing (Redrawn from Higuchi 1983)

and walk. As one approaches any construction taller than a human, seeing the top of the construction requires tilting the head. Higuchi observes:

> A downward view is free and open whereas an upward view is limited and apt to be closed because *the process of looking up at an object tends to limit the mobility of the human body and to cut off the line of vision at a point above the horizontal.* With the most stable line of vision for the average person being about 10 to 15 degrees below the horizontal, it follows that the very process of looking up involves a certain amount of stress. *Presumably this is why the term "look up to" connotes the idea of paying respect or reverence. "Looking up to" someone or something requires a visual effort.*
> (Higuchi 1983: 46; emphasis added)

But the visual perception of artificial mounds is not only a matter of the height of the building; it is also shaped by the relative position of the viewer. Obviously, objects loom larger as the distance between object and viewer decreases, but the

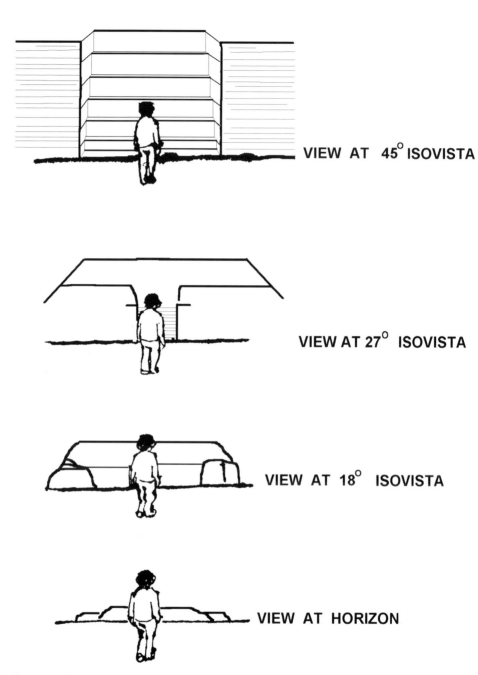

Figure 3.4 Changing fields of view at varying isovistas (Redrawn with modifications from Higuchi 1983)

properties of the human eye create rough thresholds of vision. The angle of view between viewer and tall object varies as the object progressively fills the individual's vision (Figure 3.4). Visual perception changes at 18 degrees when an object first takes on monumental nature, 27 degrees when it fills the viewer's range of vision,

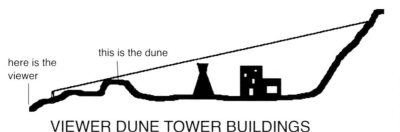

Figure 3.5
Obstructed
viewsheds
(Redrawn from
Higuchi 1983)

and 45 degrees at which details are visible (Higuchi 1983: 47). In addition, visual perception may be blocked by intervening structures, shaping a monument's viewshed (Higuchi 1983: 32–35). As Figure 3.5 illustrates, the visibility of a construction is created by the relative positions of object and viewer and by other constructed forms; the tower and buildings, although significantly different in height, are equally invisible to a beachgoer. Thus, visibility changes with the relative position of object and viewer – not only because of innate thresholds of vision – but because constructed landscapes can be manipulated intentionally to block, enhance, or punctuate visual perception and the communicative potential of monuments.

Before I discuss methods to discover these cultural manipulations, it is important to reiterate some fundamental points. Public works reflect the investment of social resources, but they are never passive reflections of social effort. Within the category of public works, which includes everything from palaces to irrigation canals, monuments form a particular subset designed to convey culturally recognized meaning. Various types of monuments exhibit different communicative potentials reflected in their physical forms. The communicative potential of a monument is partly shaped by the intersection of dimensions like visibility and imageability, which in turn can be specified based on what we know about the properties of human vision. In the following analysis, I attempt to understand the relationship between prehistoric viewer and monumental object.

Mound construction in the Andes: preliminary considerations

A few considerations set the limits of the analysis, and, again, Blanton's (1989) study of prehistoric architecture in Oaxaca is a useful guide. Recognizing that the complexities of meaning in prehispanic Zapotec architecture probably are undecipherable to the archaeologist, an alternative approach

> would be a kind of watered-down semiology in which the concern is not so much with meaning itself as with how meaning is conveyed . . . Thus pertinent questions include: Is there change through time in how architects manipulated perception through variation in such things as scale, verticality, formal arrangements of buildings, "city planning"? If so, does this tell us something about [social] scale, integration, and complexity? Considering our interest in regional integration, if architectural formulas can be found, were these widely adopted in the region or was there a possibility for local variance? (Blanton 1989: 413)

Table 3.1. *Ceremonial sites in the Santa Valley*

Relative period	Absolute dating	Total sites	Huacas/ ceremonial centers	Large huacas	Estimated population
Late Tambo Real	(AD 1350–1532)	58	0	0	10,480
Early Tambo Real	(AD 1150–1350)	34	0	0	11,660
Late Tanguche	(AD 900–1150)	34	0	0	18,435
Early Tanguche	(AD 650–900)	349	8	1	35,930
Guadalupito	(AD 400–650)	84	7	6	22,020
Late Suchimancillo	(AD 200–400)	112	7	0	29,765
Early Suchimancillo	(AD 100–200)	103	5	0	20,110
Vinzos	(350 BC–AD 100)	44	3	0	7,855
Cayhuamarca	(?–350 BC)	49	8	0	5,960
Las Salinas	(>1800 BC)	36	1	0	900

Source: Wilson 1988: Tables 6, 8, 10.

Thus Blanton sets out a research agenda with implications beyond the valley of Oaxaca; for example, the discussion of Chimu architectural patterns (see Chapter 5) considers the relationship between political integration and architectural form in the core and periphery of that North Coast state. But more immediately relevant is Blanton's question about diachronic variation in the architectural manipulation of perception, because archaeological evidence suggests this occurred on the North Coast of Peru.

At certain periods in prehistory large artificial mounds were the focus of public architecture in coastal Peru. At other times, they were not. In valley after valley, there were significant fluctuations in the relative importance of ceremonial centers and large mound construction, suggesting ritual architecture underwent great variations through time.

For example David Wilson's (1988) Santa Valley data (Table 3.1) indicate major shifts in the significance of ceremonial constructions. The data indicate that the varying importance of *huaca* constructions in the Santa Valley was not a simple function of either the total number of sites or the total estimated population. Table 3.1 does not present data on the significant increase in the size of mounds associated with the Guadalupito and Early Tanguche Periods (see Wilson 1988: 207–213, 238–243), which would underscore the importance of large huacas in these times.

Similarly, Proulx's (1973, 1985) survey data from the Nepeña Valley suggest major changes in the nature of public architecture (Table 3.2). Although the temporal divisions and site categories used by Proulx differ from Wilson's chronology for the Santa Valley, an increased proportion of sites were "ceremonial sites" during the Moche occupation of Nepeña, which would approximately correlate with Wilson's Late Suchimancillo and Guadalupito phases (Proulx 1985: 26).

Further south in the Casma Valley, survey data (Thompson 1961) suggest that major mound building occurred during certain periods (e.g., Formative/Initial

Table 3.2. *Ceremonial sites in the Nepeña Valley*

Relative period	Absolute dating	Total sites	Ceremonial sites
Late Horizon	AD 1460–1532	4	0
Late Intermediate Period	AD 900–1460	42	11
Middle Horizon	AD 540–900	131	14
Early Intermediate Period (Moche)	370 BC–AD 540	23	7[1]
Early Horizon	1300–370 BC	40	7
Initial Period	2050–1300 BC	9?	1?

Note: [1] Four of the sites consist of Pañamarca and three associated mounds.
Source: Data from Proulx 1973: 67, 80–83; 1985: Tables 1, 2.

Table 3.3. *Pyramid mounds in the Virú Valley*

Relative period	Total sites	Pyramid mounds
Estero	18	0
La Plata	41	3
Tomaval	114	13
Huancaco	110	16
Gallinazo	117	6
Puerto Moorin	88	10 (11?)
Guanape	21	0
Cerro Prieto	5	0

Source: Data from Willey 1953: 42, 60, 101, 177, 233, 296, 320, 333.

Periods) but not in others (e.g., during the Late Intermediate Period). The extensive excavations in the Casma Valley directed by Shelia and Thomas Pozorski (1987, 1992) have documented the importance of large mound construction in the Initial Period, a pattern not seen at Chimu sites in the valley (Mackey and Klymyshyn 1990). Additional data for the Casma Valley will supplement these findings (Wilson 1992), allowing for more detailed information on changes in the nature and organization of public architecture, but the basic fact is established that certain periods were characterized by large mound construction and others were not.

Such fluctuations in the construction of large pyramids are reflected in Willey's data from the Virú valley (Table 3.3). Again, the temporal divisions and site categories are different from either Wilson's or Proulx', but a clear pattern emerges with the increase in the number of large pyramids during the Huacacao and Tomaval

Periods (ca. AD 300–1000). Further north, Brian Billman's survey of the Moche Valley has documented a similar pattern in which large mounds tend to be constructed during the Initial Period and Early Intermediate Periods, but not during the Chimu or Inca occupations of the valley (Brian Billman, personal communication).

The archaeological data from the North Coast illustrate the fluctuating importance of highly visible monumental mounds, and these variations appear to be partially independent of either total population (i.e., the size of the labor pool) or the centralized nature of political authority. For example, the Chimu devoted little attention and few social resources to the construction of large mounds – in contrast to the Moche state – even though the Chimu state marshalled significant corporate labor groups and directed them to large-scale projects like agricultural developments or the construction of the Chan Chan ciudadelas. The lack of monuments, highly visible massive constructions which dominated the built landscape, does not imply that the Chimu had less political authority or access to labor than did the Moche state. Instead, I argue, it represents a changing role for public architecture, and it is possible to explore the communicative potential of ancient Andean monuments by applying basic methods of visual analysis.

Sample and analyses

The selective sample of seventeen ancient monuments is drawn from eleven sites: La Galgada, Cardal, Garagay, Las Aldas, Pampa de las Llamas-Moxeke, Sechín Alto, Moche, Pampa Grande, Chan Chan, Pacatnamú, and Manchan. The sites all have mounds, though of different sizes and configurations. All things being equal, the monumentality of prehispanic mounds could be simply measured as the height of the mound, yet all things are seldom equal and the monumentality of a construction may be restrained and intensified by various factors. First, there are the limits set by construction methods that may create similarities between structures which are more apparent than real. For example, Chippindale (1992: 263) writes:

> since ancient Egyptian and ancient Mesoamerican building technology lacked any means to secure very high vertical faces, any very tall and heavy structure had to be of a form that would stand by its own mass, that is, sloped to a stable grade. Given the impetus to build massive stone structures, a pyramid is the only building form which is possible.

While similar cultural motives and structural limits produced pyramids in Egypt and Mesoamerica, differences in construction materials and techniques can affect the monumentality of a structure. For example, a mound made from earth fill will have a lower angle of repose than one made from adobe brick, and thus a steeper face and different form. But within such structural limits, there is room for manipulation and a selected set of variables are used to measure that variation in the sample of Andean monuments.

The first variable is the *angle of incidence* of a monument which measures the angle of the slope of a monument from 0 to 90 degrees. Higuchi (1983: 66–70) notes

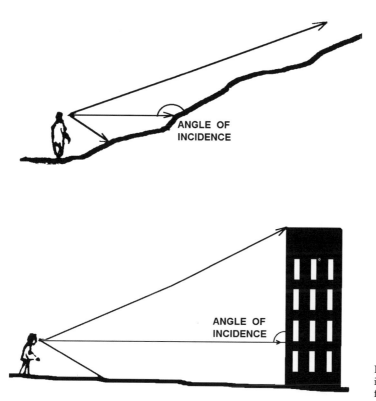

ANGLE OF
INCIDENCE

ANGLE OF
INCIDENCE

Figure 3.6 Angles of
incidence (Modified
from Higuchi 1983)

surfaces that are perpendicular to the viewer provide a well-marked sense of depth while gently sloping surfaces do not, and Figure 3.6 illustrates that difference. Angles of incidence of less than 15 degrees are perceived as gentle slopes, slopes of 15 to 30 degrees as frontal surfaces, and slopes of 30 degrees or more are visually interpreted as vertical planes. Slopes of 15 to 30 degrees deprive the viewer of depth perception, cutting across the individual's range of vision, "which may account in part for the sense of visual oppression that one experiences when climbing mountains" (Higuchi 1983: 70) as one slogs up long, steady slopes. The angle of incidence is simply the angle of the slope between the top of a mound and someone standing at its nearest viewing point. With extremely disturbed mounds like the Chan Chan huacas, the nearest point of view was estimated at one-half the width of the mound. Two values were calculated for Huaca del Sol, one for the gentle slope on the eastern end and another for the steep southern side of the mound.

Another set of variables concerns the ways in which the constructed spaces around a monument may affect its visibility by enhancing or obstructing the view. For example, the height of a monument may be constrained by engineering factors, but the visual impact can be enhanced by creating an intervening concave surface between viewer and monument; this is referred to as the *angle of depression*. Higuchi notes (1983: 50) that when the angle of depression is added to the angle of elevation a mountain appears larger. This last effect occurs in natural landscapes when a deep gorge separates the viewer and a mountain top; "the effect of the concavity is to make

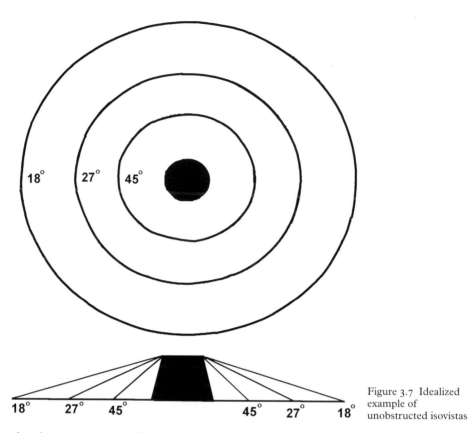

Figure 3.7 Idealized example of unobstructed isovistas

the view more majestic" (Higuchi 1983: 72). In artificial monuments a similar effect is attained by excavating sunken plazas in front of the mound, artificially increasing the visual impact. The angle of depression could be treated as a continous scale, but for my purposes it is enough to treat it as a nominal variable (i.e., a depression between viewer and object is either present or absent).

A final approach attempts to reconstruct the visual impact of a monument as viewed from different points in a ceremonial complex. As one moves across a complex built environment, the visual effect of a construction changes. Depending on the location of the viewer, a monument may fill different visual ranges; as discussed above, a viewer approaching a monument crosses different visual thresholds as the monument progressively occupies 18, 27, and 45 degrees of vision, measured above the horizontal line of vision (Higuchi 1983: 32–35). Of course, a large ceremonial complex will have an enormous number of points from which a monument could be seen. With 3D modeling and video output, it is possible to reconstruct a monument's viewshed from every point in a site, but the output cannot be presented in book format. An alternative approach is to use a simple analysis based on isovistas (i.e., "same views"). Based on the angles of different visual thresholds (18, 27, and 45 degrees), an isovista map (Figure 3.7) simply displays selected angles of view as continuous lines, like contours on topographic maps or the isotherms of a weather map. For each monument the focal point of the principal monument – usually the

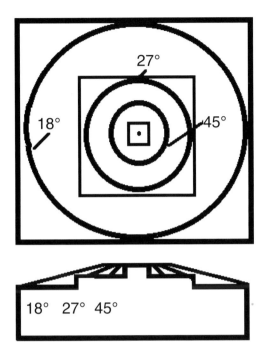

Figure 3.8 Idealized example of obstructed isovistas

highest point – is selected, and using simple trigonometry the alternate isovistas are "back-shot." This produces a series of contour lines which mark the locations at which a person would have a view of a monument that filled the 18, 27, and 45 degree angles of vision. In addition, it is possible to calculate the distance between a monument's focal point and the different isovista contours, and then make inferences about the kind of information which could be communicated over those different distances. For example, two viewers might be standing on the 45 degree isovistas of two different structures one 5 meters tall, the other 50 meters tall. The first viewer is separated by only 7.07 meters from the smaller structure, the second viewer is separated by 70.7 meters; obviously different types of information can be heard or seen over those distances. This matter is discussed further in Chapter 4; for the moment, the primary objective of the isovistas is to force our attention to the architectural context of a monument.

The architectural context shapes the pattern of isovista contours, as does the overall configuration of a monument. For example, a monument with a base larger than its height creates a situation like that in Figure 3.8, where the lower levels of the monument intersect the isovistas, foreshortening contour width.

By looking at the distributions of isovista contours, one can begin to determine if views were obstructed by other buildings, enhanced by intervening depressions, or given a greater sense of depth by surrounding constructions. Prehispanic architects could enhance the visibility of a monument in a number of ways, increasing the communicative potential of a mound. The following analysis explores how such architectural strategies were employed in the sample of Andean monuments.

Table 3.4. *Angles of incidence for selected North Coast monuments*

	Angle of incidence		
	0–15°	15–30°	30° <x
La Galgada			75
Las Aldas	15		
Pampa de las Llamas			
Huaca A			45
Moxeke		23	
Sechín Alto			31
Garagay			41
Cardal			36
Pampa Grande			32
Moche–Huaca del Sol		16 – or – 60	
Chan Chan			
Huaca Obispo			36
Huaca Toledo			36
Huaca de las Conchas		20	
Huaca El Higo	14		
Pacatnamú-Huaca 1		26	
Manchan			
North mound		30?	
Central mound	12		
South mound	12		

Discussion of results

The analysis of the visibility of monuments demonstrates that prehispanic mounds in the sample had different spatial organizations and distinct visual impacts, variations masked by the single class "huaca." These differences can be expressed, at least partially, by the variables of angle of incidence, the organization of adjacent spaces, patterns of isovistas, and the existence of visual obstacles.

The angle of incidence affects the perception of monumentality, and prehistoric Peruvian architects manipulated monuments to create different visual impacts (Table 3.4). Two inferences can be drawn from the data in Table 3.4. First, the visual impact of the monuments at Las Aldas, Huaca El Higo, and the central and southern mounds at Manchan was much less than the towering structures and vertical planes of monuments like La Galgada and the Huaca del Sol. Second, the data in Table 3.4 suggest that the three classes of angle of incidence that Higuchi proposes (i.e., 0–15°, 15–30°, and 30° < x) were not followed by the builders of huacas. The histogram of angles of incidence (Figure 3.9) appears tentatively trimodal, suggesting that the basic division of "gentle slope," "frontal surface," and "vertical plane" was recognized by the monuments' designers although with different values for the modal angles. Alternatively, La Galgada and Huaca del Sol may represent outliers in a data set which represents two architectural classes: gentle sloping monuments

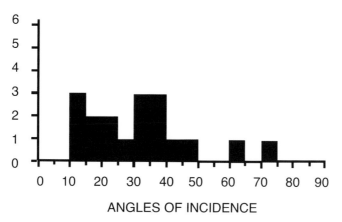

ANGLES OF INCIDENCE

Figure 3.9 Histogram of angles of incidence

and frontal surface monuments. If the latter pattern is true, then perhaps two types of monuments were constructed on the Peruvian coast: monuments with low visibility and monuments with high visibility, with the approximate dividing line being angles of incidence of 20–25 degrees.

Some qualifications are required. This is a very small sample, and additional data might transform a histogram like Figure 3.9. Further, the angle of incidence is a static measure of visibility, whereas the visual impact of a monument depends on the relationship between viewer and object, a fluid relationship. And so the analysis of angles of incidence suggests that differences in visibility exist among monuments, but it does not expose all the differences significant to the designers of ancient Andean monuments.

Therefore isovista maps were used to explore how the physical arrangements of architectural features affected the visibility of different sites (Figures 3.10 to 3.20). In one group of sites – Las Aldas (Figure 3.11), Sechín Alto (Figure 3.13), Garagay (Figure 3.14), Cardal (Figure 3.15), and Pampa Grande (Figure 3.16) – the isovista contours cluster on the principal construction. In other words, the structure does not fill the angle of vision until one has moved onto the monument itself. One does not cross these different visual thresholds until one has gained access to the monument. This does not mean that these monuments are visually unimpressive, but that in this visual sense, these huacas do not appear monumental until the viewer has stepped onto the monument.

Another group of monuments is quite different. The North Mound of La Galgada (Figure 3.10), Huaca del Sol (Figure 3.17), and Huaca 1 at Pacatnamú (Figure 3.19) were constructed such that one or more of the isovistas contours falls at the base of the principal construction. These constructions appear monumental even before the viewer has moved onto the mound. The monuments were constructed such that the visual field is filled from the base of the mound. Finally, a third group of mounds – such as the huacas at Manchan (Figure 3.20) – were simply small and unimpressive.

But beyond this gross categorizations, there are a number of intriguing elements which the isovista maps suggest. First, the design of the monuments shapes the visual impact of the constructions *independent of the mounds' heights*. For example, La

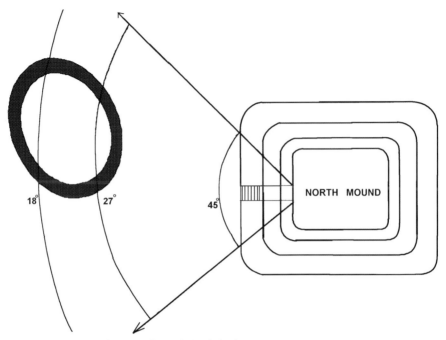

Figure 3.10 Isovistas for North Mound, La Galgada

Galgada's North Mound (12 m) is one-fourth the height of Sechín Alto, but the North Mound has a dramatic, steeply sloped face that enhances its visual impact.

Second, it is possible that these different angles of view were intuitively recognized and intentionally incorporated into the design of some Andean monuments. The best case from the sample is Huaca 1 from Pacatnamú where the isovista contours intersect with specific architectural features (Figure 3.19). The 18 degree contour falls at the base of the ramp which leads from the North Courtyard, the 27 degree line intersects the top of that ramp, and the 45 degree isovista intersects the base of the ramp which leads to the top of Huaca 1. The intersection of angles of view and architectural spaces of transition may reflect the cultural intent of the architects at Pacatnamú.

The isovistas maps also highlight the use of angles of depression and the presence of obstructed views. For example, at Sechín Alto (Figure 3.13) the 18 degree isovista falls in the plaza at the base of the mound, but the stepped nature of the construction obstructs the monument to viewers in the plaza. The sunken circular court immediately east of the mound might have increased the visual prominence of the mound, but the relatively small diameter of the depression suggests that visual enhancement was not its intent. The plan of Las Aldas is quite similar (Figure 3.11); the sunken circular court and sunken plazas probably did not enhance the visual prominence of the mound.

The architectural plans of Sechín Alto and Las Aldas are very similar, and they may represent a basic kind of public architecture utilized in processional rites. The architectural plans of these two sites were not designed to emphasize the height of the

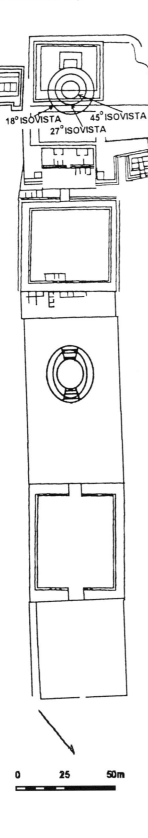

18° ISOVISTA   45° ISOVISTA
27° ISOVISTA

0   25   50m

monument, but instead *the distance between one end of the complex and its mound-top terminus.* This was achieved in different ways. For example, the placement of a series of planes parallel to the line of vision creates a greater sense of depth (Higuchi 1983: 65–66). This is one of the visual effects of the rising plazas in front of Sechín Alto and Las Aldas; the low retaining walls across the plazas serve to mark the planes and thus enhance the perception of depth. Similarly the low lateral mounds at Sechín Alto (Figure 3.13) and the flanking mounds of U-shaped ceremonial centers like Garagay (Figure 3.14) and Cardal (Figure 3.15) make the principal mound seem more distant and larger, creating a concave surface as the focal object. Although occurring within a completely different ideological and architectural context, the concave surfaces of U-shaped ceremonial centers are roughly analogous to a Japanese landscape form which Higuchi (1983: 136–144) refers to as the secluded valley type (from *komoriku* "hidden valley"). The symbolic referents of such a landscape are distinctly Japanese (Higuchi 1983: 144), but its visual properties are similar to U-shaped ceremonial centers: the flanking mounds create parallel planes that lead the eye to the principal mound while the large open plaza in the foreground emphasizes the distinctive volume and shape of the mound.

The natural visual environment of coastal Peru may condition human perception of space. A relatively well-developed body of theory suggests that our physical environments shape the perceptual inferences one habitually makes (for an overview see Brislin 1980: 52–53; Deregowski 1980; Segall et al. 1966). This theory is based on the concept of the "ecological cue," in which learned experience allows for the interpretation of "how a three-dimensional world is mapped onto our two-dimensional retinae" (DeValois and DeValois 1988:

Figure 3.11 Isovistas for Las Aldas

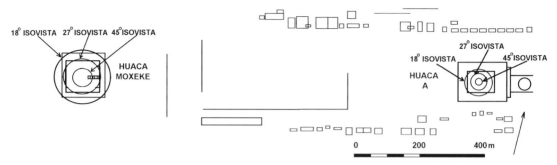

Figure 3.12 Isovistas for Pampa de las Llamas-Moxeke

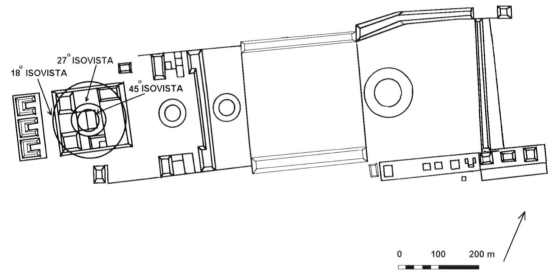

Figure 3.13 Isovistas for Sechin Alto

291–315). In their collaborative research, Segall, Campbell, and Herskovits (1966) conducted psychological tests of specific optical illusions among a large cross-cultural sample of informants living in diverse environments. This led to the "carpentered world hypothesis" (Segall et al. 1966: 83–97), which suggested that individuals living in a world of right angles (i.e., Western societies) would perceive certain visual patterns differently from people who came from habitats where other angles dominate. One hypothesis is that people who experience long uninterrupted horizontal planes tend to make errors of judgment in the horizontal–vertical illusion, thinking the vertical line is longer than the horizontal when they are actually of equal length. For example, the ocean is characterized by uninterrupted vistas, and Pollnac (1977) found a positive correlation between making this error and numbers of year at sea among Costa Rican fishermen. Although the Peruvian coastal desert is seldom flat, broad vistas occur on both land and sea. In such a visual environment, architectural features that divide the landscape into smaller units or create a sense of scale may have been effective ways to emphasize the height and depth of prehispanic monuments.

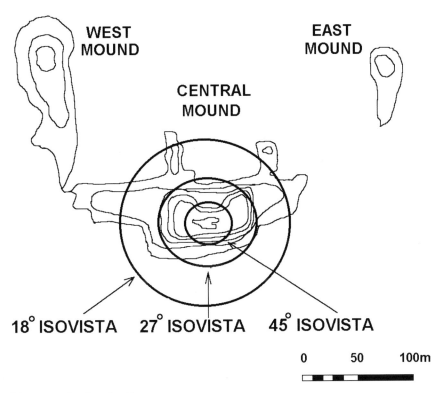

Figure 3.14 Isovistas for Garagay

The huaca at Pampa Grande is a paradoxical monument (Figure 3.16): it is a highly visible structure to which access is tightly controlled. At Huaca Grande access to the enormous structure is via a narrow corridor which runs 290 m and the entire base of the structure is surrounded by a walled compound (Haas 1985). Yet, at 4 m high the compound walls do not obstruct the view of Huaca Grande from most of the site. Based on the available site maps (Figure 2.22), the upper portion of Huaca Grande is visible from at least 80 percent of the site, including from small residential structures on the slopes behind the huaca. The view of Huaca Grande only was obscured to those who wanted to walk up the enormous artificial mound.

It is not clear if this same pattern holds for the great Moche monument, Huaca del Sol (Figure 3.17). So much of the mound has been destroyed that the access patterns are obliterated and severe erosion on the plain between Sol and Luna has erased most traces of walls. The architectural remains preserved in this area suggest the existence of elite residences, not large open plazas. Thus it seems likely that the huge masses of Huaca del Sol and Huaca de la Luna visually dominated the residential sectors of the site of Moche, although it is impossible to be more specific about the nature of its visual impact.

It is unfortunate that the Chan Chan huacas were destroyed before they were studied; the available data suggest these were very impressive constructions (Figure 3.18). If Huaca Obispo's height is estimated correctly, the mound would have been

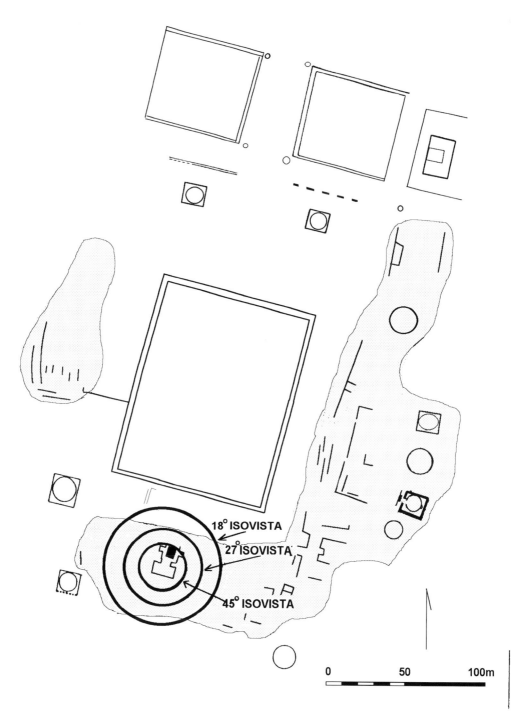

Figure 3.15 Isovistas for Cardal

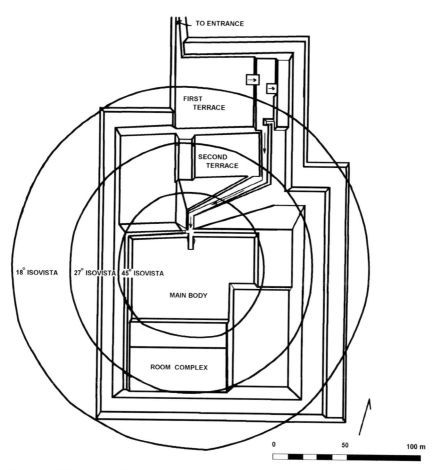

Figure 3.16 Isovistas for Huaca Grande, Pampa Grande

visible from several kilometers away, *but not from inside Chan Chan*. The average person, walking through the densely constructed built environment of Chan Chan, would not have a clear view of Huaca Obispo until reaching the northern margins of the city. Not only would the ciudadela walls obstruct the view, but even the wattle-and-daub walls of lower class residences would block the view of Huaca Obispo from most of Chan Chan. More intentionally, Huaca Obispo was placed inside of a large walled plaza. The height of the walls is not recorded, but if the walls were 6 to 9 meters tall, the view of Huaca Obispo was obstructed for anyone outside of the plaza. Because of the placement of walls around Huaca Obispo, the mound top would be visible only if someone stood at least 42–56 m north of the mound, 157–200 m east of the mound, or 860–1,090 m west of the mound. In other words, when Chan Chan took on its final form, the visual impact of Huaca Obispo was diminished, its view-shed obstructed by the walls of its compound and the constructed labyrinth of Chan Chan.

The blocked view of Huaca Obispo may reflect unplanned growth and urban sprawl at Chan Chan, but screening of huacas may have been an intentional aspect

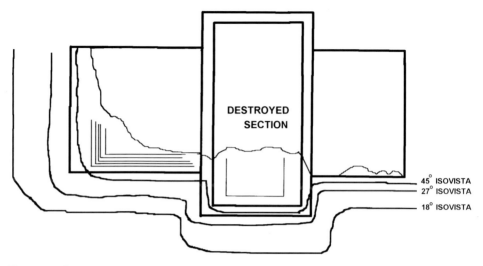

DESTROYED
SECTION

45° ISOVISTA
27° ISOVISTA
18° ISOVISTA

Figure 3.17 Isovistas for Huaca del Sol, Moche

of architecture at other North Coast sites like Pacatnamú. Huaca 1 is 10 m tall and the Inner Wall runs about 100 m north of the mound with an estimated height of 5 m (Donnan 1986b: 50). A person standing 1.5 m tall could not see the top of Huaca 1 until they were at a point 220 m from the huaca, unless they were *inside* the North Courtyard (Figure 3.19). Huaca 1's compound probably was designed to obstruct the view to outsiders, limiting it to those who entered into the impressive North Courtyard. The other huacas at Pacatnamú are similarly placed in walled enclosures, and their visual impact is both defined and obstructed by the surrounding constructions. This pattern is not found among Formative Period monuments, which could be seen from a distance and viewed along a line of approach unobstructed by walled enclosures. Monumental mounds were built at different epochs in Peruvian prehistory, but they did not all have the same communicative potentials.

Conclusions

The communicative potential of mounds as monuments was shaped by Andean architects in a number of ways, and it is possible to outline three broad patterns. Some large mounds were constructed such that they had high angles of incidence, broad isovistas, and surrounding constructions that emphasized the height of the structure; examples of such constructions include La Galgada, Garagay, and Cardal. Other large mounds – most notably Las Aldas and Sechín Alto – have low to moderate angles of incidence, narrow isovistas, and are fronted by plazas and low lateral mounds that emphasize the spatial depth of the architectural complex. In such cases, the mounds mark one end of an architectural axis which bisects the site, the axis further anchored by the locations of sunken circular courtyards and the alignment of doorways. Pampa de las Llamas-Moxeke could be included in such a group,

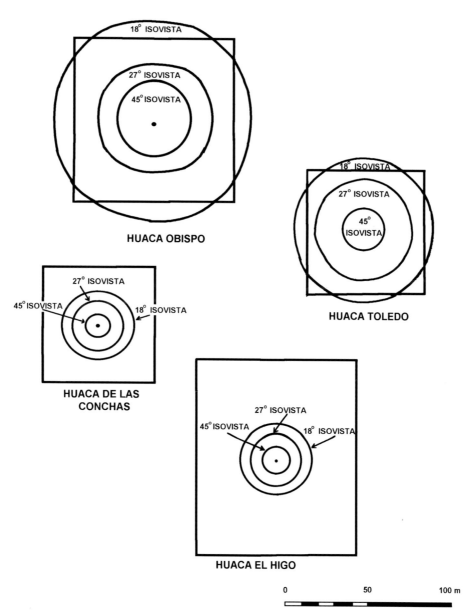

Figure 3.18 Isovistas for the Chan Chan huacas

although Huaca A is a unique construction (as discussed in Chapter 2). A third pattern is the enclosed mound, a pattern which is certainly present at Pacatnamú and Chan Chan. In these sites, the presence of walls around the base of the mound significantly obstructs the view unless one is inside the enclosure, but from the inside the high angle of incidence heightens the monumental scale of the construction. On Huaca 1 at Pacatnamú the 18, 27, and 45 degree isovistas intersect with points of transition marked by ramps; unfortunately, the Chan Chan huacas are too destroyed

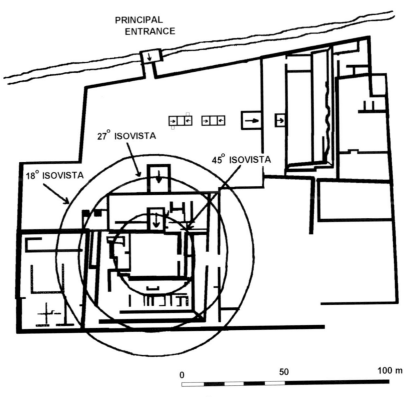

PRINCIPAL
ENTRANCE

27° ISOVISTA

45° ISOVISTA

18° ISOVISTA

0   50   100 m

Figure 3.19 Isovistas for Huaca 1, Pacatnamú

for their architectural forms to be constructed. It seems certain that huacas at Pacatnamú and Chan Chan were designed to be impressive, highly visible constructions – but monuments viewed closely by a small, select group.

Such different architectural patterns suggest diverse social patterns. The enclosed monuments of the Late Intermediate Period suggest a select audience composed of less than the entire community. In contrast, the highly visible monuments of earlier periods suggest a larger social group, one which could have included large and diverse segments of the population, but perhaps brought together in different ways. For example, the principal mounds at sites like La Galgada, Cardal, Garagay, and Moche appeared monumental to audiences standing at the base of the mound, perhaps suggesting a social divide between the participants in moundtop ceremonies and the audience below. In contrast, monuments at Las Aldas, Pampa de las Llamas-Moxeke, and Sechín Alto seem designed to emphasize horizontal distance rather than vertical planes, and it may be that ceremony based on processionals occurred in such spaces, a matter discussed further in Chapter 4. For the moment, it is sufficient to note that the spatial organization of Andean monuments differed, variously shaping their communicative potentials.

The communicative potential of ancient monuments is reflected in their legibility, a dimension which ancient architects manipulated and modern archaeologists intuitively recognize. Thus Wilson (1988: 77) observes of the Santa Valley survey data:

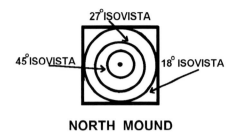

NORTH MOUND

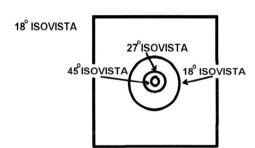

CENTRAL MOUND

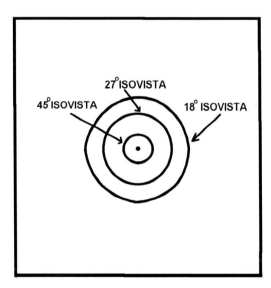

SOUTH MOUND

Figure 3.20 Isovistas for the Manchan huacas

"all sites having a primarily ceremonial-civic function are found in relatively accessible and visible positions throughout the survey area." Bawden (1977, 1983) has noted the shift of monuments to inside enclosures, contrasting the pyramids of Moche with the burial platforms of Chan Chan. Conklin (1990) offers a number of observations about the continuities and changes reflected by monumental architecture on the North Coast. In a recent summary of their research on the development of early complex societies in the Casma Valley and the coeval florescence of monumental architecture elsewhere in Peru, Shelia Pozorski and Thomas Pozorski (1992: 863) note: "The tendency so far has been to stress general similarities; perhaps we should be looking harder at the differences."

But how are we to do this? What differences should we examine and how are they to be measured? I have attempted to provide an example of one approach. By thinking about architecture as a communicative medium (the "watered-down semiology" in Blanton's apt phrase), then one must consider its legibility, its ability to be seen and experienced. The analytical concepts devised by Higuchi for the visual analysis of the natural Japanese landscape are appropriate for analyzing the artificial, monumental landscapes of ancient Peru. This, in turn, leads to new insights about the visibility of monuments and inferences about their potential social functions. Such information can then be used – in concert with other classes of archaeological data – in our efforts to understand ancient Andean societies.

But the ancient communities of coastal Peru built other forms of architecture and their lives were not spent in gap-jawed admiration of tall mounds of mud brick. Monuments were just one class of building, although an important one, raised by prehispanic architects. Ancient buildings also expressed and were the settings for those basic activities of sacrifice and search, consecration and transformation, expressed in an architecture of ritual.

4

The architecture of ritual

For religious man, space is not homogeneous.
                    Mircea Eliade, *The Sacred and the Profane*

The Andean world was populated by gods and ancestors. Throughout the colonial period, Spanish priests learned of the vast array of shrines and altars, the many feast days, and the numerous acts of devotion, small and large, with which Andean peoples honored the deities and the dead. Catholicism responded with the rough hand of righteousness, directed by guidebooks for persecution, like Pablo Joseph de Arriaga's (1968 [1621]) *The Extirpation of Idolatry in Peru* or Cristobal de Albornoz' 1555 *Instructions for the Discovery of All the Guacas of Peru* . . . (Duviols 1967). In spite of that effort, elements of native Andean religion persisted. One reason was the omnipresence of the sacred; as Sabine MacCormack (1991: 146) notes, "everywhere in the Andes, the plains and the mountains, the sky and the waters were both the theatre and the dramatis personae of divine action." The indivisible interweaving of the natural and spiritual worlds is expressed in Father Arriaga's (1968 [1621]: 115) simple, elegant observation that "Some of the huacas are hills and high places which time cannot consume."

And yet the archaeological perspective on the Andean past has taken an uneven view of ritual. On the one hand, there is a body of archaeological literature on Inca temples, shrines, and *ceques* which draws heavily on ethnohistoric literature, identifying specific places and ceremonial functions described in the colonial chronicles (e.g., Niles 1987; Rowe 1979; Urton 1981, 1990; Zuidema 1964, 1990a). But as we move away from the ethnohistoric moment, the archaeological studies of ritual become infrequent. This is not to imply that there are no archaeological discussions of Andean ritual (see, e.g., Donnan 1985; Gero 1990; Isbell 1978b; Isbell and Cook 1987; Rheinhard 1985), but ritual has not held a central *theoretical* role in studies of the prehistoric Andes. Partially this is because many Andeanists, as Burger and Salazar-Burger note (1985: 114), "living within a desacralized cosmos, have found it difficult to accept the profoundly religious nature of Prehispanic societies." Thus, Andeanists have been more comfortable with explanatory models of Inca society and government which emphasize their totalitarian (Karsten 1949), socialist (Baudin 1961), redistributive (Murra 1980; Service 1975: 200–202), or expansionist natures. And even a study like Conrad and Demerest's (1984) *Religion and Empire*, which highlights the significance of ideology, places ritual in a functionalist framework, a cog linking the distribution of wealth (based on split inheritance) to the expansion of empire. But given what we know of Andean societies, this marginal role for ritual almost certainly is misplaced.

The treatment of ritual as marginal to explanation is not unique to Andeanists, but a common reluctance among archaeologists. As Hodder (1982b: 159) observes, "Ritual is often taken [by archaeologists] to include things and acts which are not essential but are peripheral to the mainstream of human behaviour." Insofar as ritual is viewed as non-essential and non-functional, it is considered "odd" and by extension impervious to archaeological understanding. This leads to "the standard joke on archaeological sites that features and artifacts are called ritual when they are not understood" (Hodder 1982b: 164). Even explicit archaeological approaches to ritual, like Merrifield's (1987) *The Archaeology of Ritual and Magic*, treat rite in a fragmented, particularistic manner. Not surprisingly, there is not a coherent archaeological theory about prehistoric ritual as there is for hunter-gatherer subsistence systems, the development of Central Places, or the emergence of social stratification.

Based on data from the ethnographic present and vast references to the ethnohistoric past, the central significance of Andean ritual is certain. Everything we know about the Andes points to the essential nature of rite, and the historical significance of Andean ritual is a simple fact whether or not archaeologists acknowledge it. Ritual is not insignificant, epiphenomenal, or unamenable to archaeological inquiry. Patterned ritual behaviors leave material remains in the same way that patterned economic or political behaviors do (or do not), and prehistoric economic or political motives may be just as elusive as ritual ones. Archaeologists of a hyper-materialist bent who categorically exclude ritual as a field of archaeological inquiry violate one of the fundamental tenets of scientific archaeology, "[t]hat there is no a priori limit on the degree of success attainable in the search for law-based explanations of past human behavior" (Spaulding 1988: 267). Those "law-based explanations" to which Spaulding referred are not rigidly deterministic or exclusively universal laws of human behavior, but may include probabilistic statements that express patterns (e.g, co-occurrence) in specific fields of behavior. Nor does such a point of view "assume that such subjective conditions as human motives, emotions, and dispositions are causally irrelevant. Mental events can be treated as theoretical entities inferred from publicly observable events" (Spaulding 1988: 264). The lack of archaeological study of prehispanic Andean ritual reflects limits which are self-imposed, anthropologically unsound, and scientifically invalid.

But to allege this is one thing, to demonstrate it another. I consider it true that "archaeological theory should match in complexity the complexity of human behavior" (Spaulding 1988: 269), and the following is an attempt to summarize a body of theory about ritual, delineate some of its observable manifestations, and then search for patterns in our sample of Andean public architecture. I begin with an intentionally narrow, focused example: the nature and physical qualities of two classes of Andean shrines, ancestral shrines and oracular shrines. Following Turner (1974), I sketch out a set of predictions that link the physical qualities of the shrines to their social and ideological properties. I then review the ethnohistoric data on other types of ritual architecture, to give some sense of the complexity of the topic. At this point I shift to a more general level which emphasizes the communicative potential of rite. I suggest that we can identify key measures of communicative potential, and then I examine the sample of public architecture in terms of those variables with an eye to finding patterns – and variations in those patterns – within the archaeological data.

Perhaps we live in a desacralized world, but the Andean cosmos was complex and motivating. Andean peoples behaved in certain ways because of their beliefs and shared values, and elements of those values, beliefs, and behaviors shaped Andean architecture.

Andean shrines: patterned behavior and material expressions

It may seem odd to begin a discussion of Andean shrines with an ethnography based in Africa, but Victor Turner's (1967, 1969, 1974, 1982, 1985; Turner and Turner 1978) work contains a body of theory about shrines and their social networks which is immediately relevant to the Andean case. Turner focused on shrines as centers of pilgrimage, foci of interactions which develop under certain social and economic situations:

> the optimal conditions for flourishing pilgrimage systems of this type [i.e., organized massive pilgrimage in which the social order is largely maintained, interrupted by "rare bouts of nomadism"] are societies based mainly on agriculture, but with a fairly advanced degree of division of craft labor, with patrimonial or feudal political regimes, with a well-marked urban–rural division but with, at the most, only a limited development of modern industry.
> (Turner 1974: 171)

Drawing on ethnographic data from west and central Africa, Turner pointed out that pilgrimage cults may emerge around different types of shrines – ancestral and political cults vs. earth and fertility cults. He (1974: 184) observed:

> Each of these opposed types of cults tends to be focused on different types of shrines situated in different localities, resulting in overlapping and interpenetrating fields of ritual relations, each of which may or may not be hierarchically structured. To simplify a complex situation, it may be said that ancestral and political cults and their local embodiments tend to represent crucial power divisions and classificatory distinctions within and among politically discrete groups, while earth and fertility cults represent ritual bonds between those groups.

Turner (1974: 191–197) discussed the peripherality of pilgrimage shrines, noting that in many – but not all – cases pilgrimage shrines tend to be located "not in the centers of towns and cities but on their peripheries or perimeters or even at some distance beyond them" (1974: 193), a pattern exhibited by pilgrimage centers like Tepeyac, Canterbury, Lourdes and Pachacamac. Such shrines create their own networks –

forming what Werbner (1989) calls "cult regions" – often marked by subsidiary shrines which mark the pilgrims' route:

> [the] pilgrimages for which I have evidence exhibit the same picture of a multiplicity of routes converging on a great shrine, each lined with sacred way stations. It is as though such shrines exerted a magnetic effect on a whole communications system, charging up with sacredness many of the geographical features and attributes and fostering the construction of sacred and secular edifices to service the needs of the human stream passing along its arterial routes. Pilgrimage centers, in fact, generate a "field." I am tempted to speculate whether they have played at least as important a role in the growth of cities, markets, and roads as economic and political factors. (Turner 1974: 225–226)

Turner's description of pilgrimage centers neatly characterizes some of the important aspects of prehispanic, colonial, and modern Andean pilgrimage centers. Even today, as David Sallnow (1987) described in *Pilgrims of the Andes*, modern Andean pilgrimage centers form "religious ethnogeographies" in which modern Christian shrine sets reflect "the application of a cosmological model that is derived directly from [an] aboriginal one"; however, "these contemporary, locally focused shrine sets are no mere survivals. Rather, they are part of people's *current* conceptions of space" (Sallnow 1987: 96, emphasis in the original). Pilgrimage centers are documented throughout the Andes, some of which have exclusively modern histories (e.g., Crumrine 1991; Schaedel 1991; Silverman 1991; Vreeland 1991), but many with long, prehispanic heritages (e.g. Urton 1990). Pilgrimage, of course, has a long tradition in Christian Europe (Turner and Turner 1978), and this tradition was flourishing during the Spanish colonial period when it was translated to the Americas, remaining a vital religious tradition (Nolan 1991). Not every pilgrimage center is a prehispanic survival, but the significance of pilgrimage shrines is well documented for the prehistoric Andes.

Ethnohistoric and ethnographic data demonstrate that pilgrimage shrines and related classes of ritual composed an essential part of the Andean reality. At least two types of pilgrimage shrines are documented from Andean ethnohistory, ancestral shrines and oracular shrines, and the written descriptions allow us to generate specific archaeological expectations. This does not imply that ancestral and oracular shrines are the only forms of ritual behavior discernible in the archaeological record; in fact, the analyses in the later sections of this chapter treat quite different types of ritual constructions. But because ancestral shrines and oracular shrines are well documented in the Andean ethnohistoric record, they are good preliminary tests for developing an archaeological approach to ritual architecture.

Machay and *malquis*: ancestors and sacred spaces

The importance of ancestral shrines is documented in Mary Doyle's (1988) superb analysis of seventeenth- and eighteenth-century ancestral cults. Drawing on detailed information from the archives of the archbishopric of Lima, Doyle documents the significance of the ancestors, or *malquis*, in three arenas: creation myths, the social definition of the local kin group or community (*ayllu*) through ceremony and cele-bration, and the ritual restatement of an individual's ties to a community as a deceased ayllu member was transformed into yet another ancestor and buried with the malquis. Not surprisingly, the ritual of burial and reverence occurred in a dis-tinctive space, the *machay*. Doyle (1988: 103–104) writes: "The actual burial place of the sacred ancestors and their descendants, the *machay* was where the ritual and ceremonies in honor of them took place. The *machay* constituted a sacred space due to its sacralization by the *malquis* and by the rituals performed there. In this sense, *machay*s should be considered to some extent as ceremonial centers."

Yet, there are important differences between ancestral shrines and ceremonial centers – such as oracular shrines – in their social functions and architectural pat-terns. Although both malquis and oracles were consulted, consecrated, and revered, there were striking differences. Malquis were honored with sacrifices of chicha, llama blood, and guinea pigs; oracles were honored with gold and fine cloth. Malquis were worshiped by ayllus; oracles cross-cut kin and ethnic boundaries. For its conse-quences of the organization of sacred space, one difference was perhaps most sig-nificant (Doyle 1988: 162–165): malquis were seen and oracles were not.

This difference was expressed in the architecture of machays. Most frequently, machays were natural or modified caves, but the category also included construc-tions variously described as small houses, rooms, chapels, simulacres, or temples (Doyle 1988: 106). Bernabe Cobo (1990 [1653]: 246–249) made a rough typology of burial structures, dividing them into subterranean and above-ground constructions. Observing differences between coastal and highland architectural patterns, Cobo was awed by the number and scale of the coastal tombs, writing: "we are just as amazed by the vast number of them as by their size" (Cobo 1990 [1653]: 247). The coastal tombs, Cobo observed:

> were made with thick huge earthen walls, in the same form and design as the
> main houses of their caciques, on a square plan with many divisions and
> rooms . . . These large guacas or tombs located on the plains are filled with
> earth, and some of them are even covered with large piles of small stones
> [like apachetas?]; as they buried their dead in them, they filled them in.
> (Cobo 1990 [1653]: 247)

In contrast, highland machays were smaller, either masonry above-ground structures or subterranean chambers roofed with slabs of stones (Cobo 1990 [1653]: 248). Interestingly, the doorways of machays were small and frequently compared to the opening of an oven (*horno*); the openings of machays in caves were partially blocked, intentionally reducing the size of the entrance (Doyle 1988: 110).

One parallel between machays and oracular shrines is the presence of plazas where devotees gathered, but these open areas differ remarkably in scale. Called the *cayan*, Doyle (1988: 111) writes: "This was a flat area often formed by terracing, where indi-viduals or groups could gather to carry out activities related to the *malquis* or other individuals buried in the *machay*" (see Grieder 1978).

Doyle refers to Grieder's (1978) excavation of a Recuay Period burial structure at Pashash, Department of Ancash, which was surrounded by an open area roughly 1,110 m² in area, a feature Doyle interprets (1988: 111) as analogous to the cayan, a gathering place for ancestral worship. Thus machays were enclosed architectural or natural spaces with purposefully small entrances, and with associated small, unroofed open areas. These architectural features reflect the need to restrict, but not prevent – access to the malquis and, the gathering together of relatively small social groups. Both malquis and oracles were worshiped, consulted, and consecrated in the Andes, but there were marked differences in the social and ritual relations between ayllu members and their ancestors and between pilgrims and oracular shrines, differences partially reflected in architecture.

Andean oracular shrines: ritual topography and sacred places

Oracular shrines held a special place in the Andean pantheon, and their uniqueness is expressed in three ways. First, oracles created a network of interaction that cross-cut boundaries of kinship, ethnicity, and language. For example, the oracle of Pachacamac drew pilgrims from an enormous region, as far north as Catamez on the northern coast of Ecuador, a distance of 1600 km. It is probable that the lords from Chincha, Mala, and other southern valleys regularly paid tribute to Pachacamac. Pachacamac was widely known in the Andes, and Weiss (1986) has suggested that the deity was known to the Amuesha, Campa, and Machiguenga of the Peruvian Amazon.

A similar pattern has been attributed to the site of Chavín de Huántar by Burger (1988) who contends that the wide distribution of objects exhibiting Chavín iconography reflects the broad network of pilgrimage centered on the Rio Mosna. Based on his 1616 visit, Antonio Vásquez de Espinoza (1968 [ca. 1620]: 491) recalled:

> Near this village of Chavín there is a large building of huge stone blocks very well wrought; it was a guaca [sic], and one of the most famous of the heathen sanctuaries, like Rome or Jerusalem with us; the Indians used to come and make their offerings and sacrifices, for the Devil pronounced many oracles for them here, and so they repaired here from all over the kingdom.

Oracular shrines like Pachacamac and Chavín de Huántar drew from a large territory of the Andes, cross-cutting political boundaries and forming an enormous ritual landscape of pilgrimage centers, creating what Victor Turner (1974: 184) has called "ritual topography."

Second, oracles were not passive entities, but active forces who were consulted via their priests and who were rewarded or punished according to the accuracy of their predictions. The personification of oracles is quite clear in the annual Inca ceremony in which the huacas of distant oracles were brought to Cuzco and placed on elaborate display in the central plaza (MacCormack 1991: 103–104). The idols were consulted, their priests' answers considered, and sacrifices offered. The following year the huacas' prophecies were evaluated; accurate predictions were rewarded by offerings of llamas, cloth, and precious metal, while "those who had put forth equivocations and lies were not given a single offering in the coming year, thus losing their reputation" (Cieza de Leon 1985 [1553]: 89).

Such vivid interaction between rulers and oracles was exemplified during the last days of the Inca Empire. To ransom himself, Atahualpa ordered that the treasure of Pachacamac be brought to Cajamarca, a sacrilege justified because the oracle had lied. Pedro Pizarro relates (1921 [1571]: 209–210) that as a party of Spaniards, led by Hernando Pizarro, were off to loot Pachacamac, Atahualpa called for the priests of Pachacamac who accompanied the Inca and commanded them to give the shrine's treasure to the Spaniards:

> for that Pachacama of yours is no God, and even though he be so, give it, nevertheless, and all the more since he is not [a God]. The Marquis, on learning from the interpreter what it was that Atabilipa [*sic*] had said, asked him why he had said that that Pachacama of theirs was not a God, since they held him to be so. Atabilipa replied: Because he is a liar. The Marquis asked him in what resepect he had been a liar. Atabalipa replied: You should know, Lord, that when my father was sick in Quito, he sent to ask him [Pachacama] what should be done for his health. He [Pachacama] commanded that he be taken out into the sun, and when he was taken out, he died; Guascar, my brother, sent to ask him [Pachacama] who was to win the victory, he or I, and [Pachacama] said that he would, and I won it. When you came, I sent to ask him who was destined to conquer, you or I, and he sent to tell me that I was. You conquered. Therefore he is a liar, and is no God, for he lies. The Marquis said to him that he [Atabalipa] knew much. Atabalipa replied that [even] shopkeepers know much.

Atahualpa's sense of betrayal is palpable. The oracle was wrong, not merely incorrect. Pachacamac had lied and sacking his treasure was justified.

The personification of oracles is also reflected by expressing relationships between shrines in kinship terms, relationships which were more than metaphoric. In 1555 Cristobál de Albornoz (Duviols 1967: 34) listed the huacas associated with Pachacamac, expressing its relationship to branch shrines as the oracle's kin. Thus *sulcavilca*, the primary huaca of the Lunaguana Indians of the *parcialidad* of Mala was a hill at the edge of the sea, who was Pachacamac's brother, and *urpai guachgac* was an island revered by the fishermen of Chincha and was also Pachacamac's wife.

Third, oracular shrines were significant politically having direct influence over public discourse. MacCormack (1991: 59) writes:

> Oracular shrines both great and small abounded in the Andes; their principal role was to legitimate political power by establishing and articulating consensus. In the course of doing this, the oracular shrines also predicted the future. Because such predictions were capable of generating either support or dissent at times of political uncertainty, they were taken most seriously and were carefully remembered.

MacCormack (1991: 157) develops her argument further, translating the opinion of the "perspicacious lawyer" Santillán:

The religion that existed among these people was most carefully observed and comprised many ceremonies and sacrifices, because people were devoted to such things. Lords and Incas in particular held frequent converse with huacas and houses of religion and communicated to everyone else that they approximated more closely to the gods they adored than did other people, and that they knew the future. The principal means whereby they held all other people in subjection was this profession of observing their religion and worship.

Oracular shrines had great significance for the course of human actions in the Andes. Representing more than some marginal pursuit, oracular shrines occupied central roles in Andean societies. To ignore the importance of Andean ritual is to engage in a stunning oversight. But just as the worship of ancestors created certain patterns of Andean ritual architecture, the presence of oracular shrines was expressed in specific built environments. Again, the shrine of Pachacamac is an instructive case.

Three Spanish eyewitnesses documented the search for the treasure of Pachacamac – Hernando Pizarro (1970 [1533], Pedro de la Gasca, and Miguel de Estete (1985 [1533]). Each author describes the search for Pachacamac's treasure and the struggle against Satan embodied in the oracle, and providing a last glimpse into the workings of a prehispanic oracular shrine (Patterson 1983). Of the three, Estete provides the most detailed account of the architecture, but Pizarro's *relación* has the greatest narrative sweep.

After descending the western slope of the Andes to the Pacific, Pizarro and his men followed the well-marked coastal road south to Pachacamac, which Hernando Pizarro – a true conquistador – refers to as "the mosque." Arriving at Pachacamac, Pizarro was told that there was no treasure, but he concluded the loot had been whisked away since flecks of gold dust glittered on the floor of the shrine. Pizarro carefully collected the gold dust and demanded "gifts" from the *kurakas* of Chincha, Mala, Cañete, and other neighboring valleys, amassing booty worth 85,000 castellanos and 3,000 marcos of silver.

Pizarro conducted some rough interviews into the workings of the shrine. Convinced that the priests of Pachacamac did not actually speak with the devil, but simply lied so as to deceive the kurakas and other Indians, Pizarro had one of the chief priests tortured, "and he was so stubborn in his evil creed, that I could never gather anything from him, but that they really held their devil to be a god" (Pizarro 1970 [1533]: 124). But eventually, Pizarro turned his attention from the treasure to the town:

> This town of the mosque is very large, and contains grand edifices and
> courts. Outside, there is another great space surrounded by a wall, with a
> door opening on the mosque. In this space there are the houses of the
> women, who, they say, are the women of the devil. Here, also, are the
> storerooms, where the stores of gold are kept. There is no one in the place
> where these women are kept. Their sacrifices are the same as those to the

Sun [i.e., of llamas and chicha], which I have already described. Before entering the first court of the mosque, a man must fast for twenty days; before ascending to the court above, he must fast for a year. In the upper court the bishop used to be. When messengers of the chiefs, who had fasted for a year, went up to pray to God that he would give them a good harvest, they found the bishop seated, with his head covered. There are other Indians whom they call pages of the Sun. When these messengers of the chief delivered their messages to the bishop, the pages of the devil went into a chamber where they said that he speaks to them; and that devil said that he was enraged with the chiefs, with the sacrifices they had to offer, and with the presents they wished to bring.
(Pizarro 1970 [1533]: 123)

Pizarro was convinced that Pachacamac was worshiped not "from feelings of devotion, but from fear." According to Pizarro the kurakas, seeing the strength of the Spaniards, now wanted to serve the Spaniards. Pizarro led the kurakas into the presence of the shrine: "The cave in which the devil was placed was very dark, so that one could not enter it without a light, and within it was very dirty" (Pizarro 1970 [1533]: 124). Exposing this *santa sanctum* to the kurakas, Pizarro proudly states, "for want of a preacher, I made my sermon, explaining to them the errors in which they lived."

Miguel de Estete (1985 [1533]: 136–139) provides another independent account of the Spanish conquest of Pachacamac, paying special attention to the architecture and functioning of the pilgrimage center. Estete describes the idol as being in "a finely painted house, in a very dark room, foul-smelling and tightly enclosed [*hedionda muy cerrada*] in which they had a filthy wooden idol and that they said was their god." Estete reports that only the pages and servants of Pachacamac could enter the shrine, and that others could only touch the outside walls of the shrine. Estete continues, "They come to this devil in pilgrimage from three hundred leagues with gold and silver and cloth, and when they arrive they go to the gatekeeper and make their request, and he enters and speaks with the idols and he says what it authorizes." Estete describes the streets and gates of the town as covered with wooden idols and states that the lords from throughout the land paid annual tribute to the shrine, maintaining houses and overseers to manage the payment of tribute. After briefly mentioning that the people believed Pachacamac would drown them if he was not well served, Estete (1985 [1533]: 138) writes:

The town of Pachacama is a great thing; next to the mosque is a house of the sun, placed on a hill . . . with five walls; there are houses with terraces as in Spain. The town appears to be old because of the fallen buildings that there are, most of the nearby ones are fallen. The principal lord of the town is named Taurichumbi.

The Spanish accounts of Pachacamac contain rare detail about this important pilgrimage center (MacCormack 1991). First, Estete refers to the existence of the oracle's shrine and the Temple of the Sun constructed by the Inca with the grudging acquiescence of the priests of Pachacamac. Second, there is a consistent theme of the hidden nature of the oracle, a theme expressed both in believers' behavior and in architectural plan. The shrine itself was hidden away, invisible to all but a select priesthood who themselves did not face the shrine. The central image was in a darkened room – described as a cavern by Hernando Pizarro – an unlit space, decorated with images of land and sea animals. There were two court-yards to the shrine, delineated by adobe brick walls, placed on two horizontal planes, and linked by a staircase. The stairway wound around the mound through various doors before finally entering the forecourt of the shrine. The head priest – dubbed "the bishop" by Pizarro – was in the upper court, accessible only to pil-grims who had fasted a year. The lower court apparently was a less sacred space, entered by pilgrims who had fasted merely twenty days. The closest pilgrims could get to the shrine was to touch the well-painted outer wall of the shrine. The hidden sacredness of Pachacamac was violated by Pizarro when he burst through the doorway of the shrine, an act which the Indians believed would destroy them all.

Third, the shrine was surrounded by auxiliary structures and features. There were houses for pilgrims staffed by religious officials (*mayordomos*) charged with the col-lection of tribute; some houses had terraces like buildings in Spain. The town of Pachacamac was not an empty ceremonial center, but a large community ruled over by a lord and his *principales*, political leaders distinct from the priesthood of the shrine. Yet, the religious nature of the town was reflected in the numerous wooden idols which ringed the shrine, lined the streets, and framed the entrances to the town.

Pachacamac is a fascinating case, but how do we move from it to more general inquiry about Andean pilgrimage centers? Not every pilgrimage center was like Pachacamac; the oracle's significance was extensive and unique, thus producing the tribute that attracted the Spaniards. But there are some striking continuities between the shrine of Pachacamac and other shrine centers.

For example Silverman (1991) describes the modern pilgrimage center of Yauca, Ica, and draws parallels between the modern material remains and the archaeologi-cal record of Cahuachi, a Nazca center which Silverman (1986, 1988) interprets as a prehistoric ceremonial center. For most of the year an abandoned neo-colonial church in the empty, windswept desert of coastal Peru, Yauca is visited by thousands of people in early October celebrating a regional cult dedicated to the Virgen del Rosario. The pilgrims erect impermanent structures of poles and matting and cook over temporary hearths; their debris is blown away by the sand or swept away each year in the ritual sweeping of the plaza (1991: 220). This leads Silverman (1991: 222–225) to point out that (a) open plazas, (b) temporary structures (e.g., postholes without floors), and (c) evidence of sweeping and the absence of accumulated domestic debris are material patterns shared by Yauca and Cahuachi. She writes (1991: 225): "These shared patterns of material remains and space have led me to identify Cahuachi's open areas as plazas for the congregation of nonresidential pil-grims and to attribute a pilgrimage function to the site." Equally, some of these fea-tures could be found at Pachacamac.

Drawing on Pachacamac and Pashash as models, the varying material correlates of pilgrimage centers vs. ancestral cults can be recognized. One significant difference is the size of open areas where participants congregate. The sector of Pachacamac where the oracle worshipers probably gathered (Tello's Plaza de los Peregrinos) consisted of a large courtyard with columns and a smaller forecourt to the north, two spaces which roughly match Estete's descriptions. The Plaza de los Peregrinos measures approximately 42,336 m^2, and the smaller forecourt 5,880 m^2, a total of 48,216 m^2 – much larger than any cayan. It is not just that one ritual space was large and the other small. The difference in size reflects different social units; these buildings differ in *scale*, a variable defined and discussed below.

Ancestral shrines and oracular shrines also vary in *visibility*, reflecting differences in the ritual associated with each type of site. The shrine at Pachacamac was designed to be both prominent and remote; the exterior was visible, but not the inner sanctum. The cayan was designed so there was access to the dead ancestor; the interaction between the living and dead was intimate. Structures associated with ancestral cults and oracular shrines also differed in *permanence*; Pachacamac was built to last forever, a monument to omnipresence, while the burial structure at Pashash probably was not. The two sites differ in their *uniqueness*; Pachacamac was one of a handful of interregional shrines in the Andes, but cayan-like structures could be found throughout the Andes. Finally, the ceremonial structures are roughly similar in their spatial association with human settlements, a variable I call *centrality*. Pachacamac sat in the middle of a large settlement, while at Pashash a few domestic structures are on the hilltop with the cayan-like feature, and the bulk of the prehistoric population may have been on the valley floor (Grieder 1978: 15).

A comparison of ancestral shrines and oracular shrines suggests that there are specific variables that distinguish ritual architecture, illuminating the social contexts and ceremonial patterns associated with those constructed spaces. Archaeologists have classified Andean architecture for at least a century, but those classifications have been based on stylistic traditions and broad functional categories. I contend that we can deepen our understanding of ancient Andean societies by examining ceremonial architecture in terms of social context and ceremonial patterns, which in turn illuminate key developments in the nature of power in Andean societies. The ethnohistoric record contains important information on that process, but equally provides a limited range of analogy, as even a brief review will show.

Ritual architecture and the ethnohistoric record: limits to analogy

It is beyond the scope of this section to summarize current knowledge of native Andean religions (for critical essays see Millones 1979; Urbano 1982). A number of overviews exist that summarize basic information on the subject (e.g., Duviols 1977; Murra 1960; MacCormack 1991; Rostworowski 1988; Rowe 1946; Urton 1978; Zuidema 1990a). In addition, there is a growing corpus of native documents, dealing with rite, which have been published and translated (e.g., Salomon and Urioste 1991) as well as anthologies of legends and myths (Pease 1982; Toro 1990, 1991a, 1991b). Some key documents have been the subjects of repeated intensive study, the most famous being Felipe Guaman Poma de Ayala's (1930, 1987) *Nueva crónica y buen gobierno* and Francisco de Avila's accounts of Huarochiri (e.g., Arguedas and Duviols 1966; Salomon and Urioste 1991; Spalding 1984; Taylor and Acosta 1987), but even smaller documents – like Rodrigo Hernandez Principe's (1923) 1622 *visita* to Recuay, Allauca, and Ocros – have been studied repeatedly (e.g., Mariscotti de Görlitz 1973; Romero 1923; Zuidema 1973). Additional studies have considered native beliefs as they underwent fundamental changes during the Colonial Period (e.g. Gisbert 1980; Millones 1990; Ossio 1973). Finally, there are many ethnographic studies which consider ritual and cosmology (e.g., Bastien 1978; B. Isbell 1978), some specifically emphasizing the interaction between rite and political process (e.g., Gelles 1990). The literature on Andean ritual is enormous and growing, reflecting the different points of views of investigators refracted by the complexities of more than five centuries of turbulent, post-contact change.

Such a body of information defies generalization, but a few points are relatively clear. First, there never was a single pan-Andean religion. Even such notable deities as Wiracocha, touted as the widely recognized Supreme Creator of the Andes (e.g., Demerest 1981; Pease 1973), was not a primary god throughout the Andes. Although certain natural objects like mountains (Rheinhard 1985), the Sun and the Moon (Rostworowski 1983) were commonly revered, the meanings attributed to such physical features differed enormously from one region to another. Second, there was not a "highland" religion versus a "coastal" religion. María Rostworowski (1983) properly has emphasized the need to recognize the differences between coastal and highland societies and beliefs, but then seems to suggest the existence of a generic coastal culture, citing ethnohistoric data from such different regions as Chincha, Canta, and Lima. Clearly these areas had certain elements in common, but they exhibited significant differences as well.

One possible reason why archaeologists have minimized the differences between coastal regions is that population collapse and aggressive colonization wiped out obviously native populations. In coastal Peru, ethnic differences are not preserved by language and traditional dress as they are in the highlands, but linguistic data suggest the pre-contact diversity of the northern Andes, a diversity not seen today or reflected in historic sources influenced by the Inca. Torero (1986, 1989) has discounted the existence of a "lengua pescadora" as a separate language (cf. Rabinowitz 1982; Rostworowski 1977), and instead argued persuasively that the language Quingam was spoken in the area between Paramonga and Pacasmayo while Mochica was spoken between the Chicama and Pacasmayo Valleys (Torero 1989, 1990). South of Paramonga, Torero suggests that coastal and highland zones spoke Quechua as early as AD 500. Inland the linguistic reconstructions suggest that Culle was spoken in the Otuzco-Huamachuco basins, Den from the headwaters of the Rio Chicama north to the area around Cutervo, Cat spoken in the vicinity of Cajamarca and north of the Den region – two zones separated by an eastward expansion of Den speakers – and, finally, Chacha on the eastern side of the Marañon.

Such distributional data do not directly bear on matters of cosmology, but they suggest one basic point: it is very unlikely that such different language groups would share a uniform religious ideology. These languages were mutually unintelligible, with non-cognate words for the sun, the moon, the stars, the sea. Even though certain deities were widely revered and particular oracles were broadly attended, there probably was no single coastal system of belief, let alone a unified pan-Andean one.

Ideally information about cosmology would be preserved in indigenous texts, but only scraps of native languages survived both the Spanish conquest and the imposition of Quechua as a lingua franca by the Inca. For the North Coast in general the linguistic data are not as rich as from highland zones, although a handful of word lists remain (e.g., Altieri 1939; Martinez de Companion 1978; Rabinowitz 1982; Schaedel 1988). Given the impact of Christianity, the word lists provide only a few glimpses into indigenous belief systems. For example, de la Carrera (1939 [1644]) was moved to write his *Arte de la lenga yunga* (i.e., Quingam) when, as a newly appointed priest to the pueblo of San Martin de Reque in 1633, he discovered that his parishioners did not understand the difference between Saint Martin and Almighty God. His grammar is an instrument for conversion and not a record of indigenous belief, but a few phrases preserve the intimations of idolatry:

> *Macyæc, macyæro*: the huaca's idol
> *Licapæcoz mæcha macyæc*: you frequently worship the idols
> *?Ecapæcoz xllom pæn pæna pæn fæpiÇaær, ñañissapeÇcæn, pucu, fiñ, pocpoc, licapæcoz mæcha, macyæc, pong, echallo?*: Do you believe in dreams and birds, worshipping the stones, idols and other things?

In the records of repeated attacks on idolatry (e.g., Arriaga 1968 [1621]; Augustinians 1865 [1560]; Hernandez Principe 1923 [1622]), it is very clear that Andean peoples worshiped a wide range of natural and human-made objects, all of them covered by the term "huaca." In his 1555 "Instructions for the destruction of all the huacas in Peru," Cristobal de Albornoz provided a typology of huacas (in Duviols 1967). He distinguished between Incaic and local observances and between those rites which were common throughout the Andes versus those restricted to specific ethnic groups, but ultimately he classified objects of worship based on their physical properties and religious meanings. Thus, Albornoz (Duviols 1967: 17–19) describes regional deities which were incorporated into the Incan pantheon, huacas associated with agricultural and pastoral rites, and burial grounds for ancient principales. Included in the category were offerings made to lightning bolts, the roadside shrines of piled stones called *apachetas*, and an entire subcategory called *guacanqui*, which included small figurines made from leaves and feathers, certain stones, vipers, and a mythical hairless rat faced with a bird's beak (Duviols 1967: 22–23). Mountain peaks, caves, stones that looked like humans, rivers, and springs – a vast array of objects were huacas.

Although the term "huaca" is often attached to prehispanic buildings, the majority of huacas in Albornoz' account were non-architectural. A handful of huacas in Albornoz' list also had houses, though sometimes away from the actual huaca; for example, a huaca was associated with a mountain peak but the huaca had a house in a nearby town. Another class of architectural huacas were the *illiapas*, which referred both to the places where embalmed ancestors were maintained and to the locations where lightning struck. Albornoz (in Duviols 1967: 19) writes:

> There are other types of huacas called *illapas* which are the embalmed corpses of former lords which they worship and revere. This is not a general worship, but specific to the *parcialidad* or *ayllu* which descended from these dead. They preserve them with great care between walls and [they include] their clothes and goblets [*vasos*] of gold and silver and wood and other metals or stone. Also called illapas are other guacas that are the places where lightning bolts have struck and in the same way they revere these places and the house that is devoted to the lightning bolt is walled up [*cierran*] with all that is inside it and they do not touch or use it.
> (translation mine)

Another category of huaca, the *usnu*, often was associated with specific built spaces, either plazas or buildings. Writing from Huamachuco, the Augustinians (1865 [1560]: 16) warned of rites that occurred in the open plazas; kurakas would gather in the plaza to drink and eat, and surreptitiously sprinkle chicha on the earth, a camouflaged "benediction that they make to their Creator, or better said, the devil." The Augustinians warn that many parish priests "think [the kurakas] do this to clean [the plaza] and thus they are tricked" (translation mine). Similarly, Albornoz (Duviols 1967: 24) specifically mentions sites like Vilcas, Pucara, Huanuco Viejo, and Tiahuanaco where such public ceremonies occurred. He praises their towers made from very beautiful stonework, but then retreats to disapproval of the drinking and sacrifices which native *señores* made to the usnu and, thus, the Sun. Beautiful architecture or not, Albornoz (Duviols 1967: 24) instructs: "It is essential to command the destruction of these buildings that, since they are public, offend by what they signify" (translation mine).

Thus, in most cases, architectural features were not huacas, but religious ceremonies directed to specific huacas were conducted in specific built spaces. An exemplary discussion of the ritual use of Andean architecture is found in the 1560 Augustinian account of a sacrificial rite in honor of Ataguju, the principal deity of Huamachuco. It is rich with ethnographic detail:

> To adore and honor this false Trinity they have great patios [*corrales*] and these have a very tall wall and inside the patio they place posts to make their fiestas and in the middle they set a post and wrap it with straw and anoint it [*ponyan un palo y revolbánle con paja y atábanle* [sic] *untávala*] and the man who is going to sacrifice climbs up the post dressed in white garments and they kill a guinea pig and offer the blood to Ataguju and he eats the meat; and others kill alpacas [*ovejas*] and pour the blood on the post and they eat the meat and none of the meat saved or taken away after all that work. There are many niches in the walls for storing the relics which the alpaca or llama has and the land is filled with these *corrales* and we have destroyed many, and

in the tambos and roads there are many niches and, to this day, many who
see them in Peru do not know what they are. All of these are destroyed in
Guamachuco and the posts have been pulled out; at the foot of these posts
the chief priest would mix *chicha* [maize beer] and *zaco – zaco* is a little maize
flour mixed in hot water – and with that make a communal meal [*una comida
general*] for all of the huacas and this they said Ataguju eats.
(Augustinians 1865 [1560]: 14–15, translation mine)

The *corrales* were open patios, the spatial setting of large public fiestas. The use of
wall niches to contain the offerings associated with animal sacrifices is a fascinating
detail – as is the Augustinian's warnings about their significance. But the fundamental importance of such spaces was their use in public ceremony and rite. As
Rostworowski (1984: 58–59) writes: "Dance in the Andean universe had deep roots
in the past. The physical expressions were not only ritual manifestations, the ceremonies of powerful elites or propitiatory representations, but were communal
expressions in which all the inhabitants of a pueblo participated without distinctions
of sex or age. This created a sense of integration and cohesion between ayllu groups"
(translation mine). Not surprisingly, the Augustinian was much less tolerant:

> And in these corrals they make great fiestas of their sacrifices that last five
> days and they make great dances and songs [*taquis y cantos*], dressed in their
> best clothes, and there is great drunkenness, and all this time they never stop
> drinking, some falling down as others are getting up, and this is how they
> celebrate their disgraceful fiestas.
> (Augustinians 1865 [1560]: 15, translation mine)

Drawing on the works of Albornoz, Arriaga, Hernandez Principe, and the
Augustinians, one could outline a brief list of ceremonial architecture, but a list
doomed to be incomplete. First, all the records come from a time when native ceremonies were suppressed and only surreptitiously celebrated in public. Second, we
cannot assume that the Spanish descriptions *ever* captured the full range of meanings associated with a specific ritual or described ritual acts accurately. We lack con-
fidence at etic and emic levels.

But more importantly, the ethnohistoric record is a thin veneer of literacy placed
over the last decades of a tradition of ceremonial architecture which stretched over
four millennia. Even if the ethnohistoric record were a perfect rendering of Andean
beliefs (which it is not), it could never capture the full range of prehispanic Andean
religion or the historical depth of ritual practice. At some point, our ethnohistoric
analogies become brittle.

Thus the need for a body of theory relating to Andean ceremonial architecture
which is not limited to specific ethnohistoric analogies, but is sufficiently robust to
include the ethnohistoric cases. One theoretical approach can be summarized in
four points: (1) ritual ceremony is communication; (2) communication is shaped
by a wide range of variables, but is fundamentally limited by thresholds of human
perception; (3) different rites involve distinct sets of perception as they appeal to

different-sized audiences and transfer information of various levels of detail and complexity; and (4) ceremonial architecture materially reflects those different social contexts and ritual patterns. This very programmatic sketch is developed below, but the approach was sparked by an observation made by Cieza de Leon (1985 [1555]: 90), who wrote of the spatial settings for Inca ceremonies: "And in the middle of the plaza they have arranged . . . a great stage."

An archaeological approach to ritual architecture

Throughout the Andes, as throughout the world, humans define, reify, and contact the forces of the cosmos in rite. Ritual, as Tambiah (1985: 128) writes: "is a culturally constructed system of symbolic communication. It is constituted of patterned and ordered sequences of words and acts, often expressed in multiple media, whose content and arrangement are characterized by varying degrees of formality (conventionality), stereotypy (rigidity), condensation (fusion), and redundancy (repetition)."

A detailed review of anthropological approaches to ritual is outside the scope of this study but is readily found in works by Bell (1992), Douglas (1973), Firth (1975), Grimes (1987b), Leach (1968), Moore and Meyerhoff (1977), Morris (1987), Smith (1987), Tambiah (1985), Turner (1969), Zuesse (1987) and the anthropological classics anthologized by Lessa and Vogt (1972). The definition of ritual used here emphasizes its behavioral and performative aspects, an approach which is commonly found in the anthropological literature. Catherine Bell (1992) outlines a vigorous critique of the separation between practice and meaning, an argument difficult to ignore (cf. Oosten 1993). But I sidestep Bell's point for expedience's sake. The archaeological perspective is necessarily etic, and I am willing to emphasize the material record of ritual practice rather than ignore the 90 percent of human existence which was prehistoric and non-literate. But real problems remain.

The archaeological approach to ritual architecture is founded on three questions: (1) How do we distinguish ritual from non-ritual architecture? (2) How can we identify and characterize different types of ritual architecture? (3) How can we define variation such that it informs us about the nature and organization of social life? The common crux of their answers is the communicative nature of ritual.

Independent of the kaleidoscope of ritual actions or the layers of associated meanings, rituals are designed to communicate, a point made by Leach (1972), who emphasizes that ritual is the communication of highly redundant, stylized, and condensed information. These formal aspects of ritual allow for an archaeological approach because some rites become sufficiently formalized to be associated with established material forms, including architecture.

Ritual architecture is an example of what Miles Richardson (1980: 217) refers to as the "objectification of social experience." Richardson (1980: 217) uses a dramaturgical model of society to highlight "the constructed artificiality of human life," constructions of meaning given behavioral form on a variety of human stages. And while the specific meanings of a "stage" are brought to it by the actors, "Yet . . . the material setting, having been constructed by man, already contains a preliminary definition of the situation. The meaning of interaction has already been located in it, at least in a provisional sense" (Richardson 1980: 218).

Hilda Kuper (1972: 420–421) makes a similar point writing about a site "as a particular piece of social space, a place socially and ideologically demarcated and separated from other places. As such it becomes a symbol within the total and complex system of communication in the total social universe." Like Richardson, Kuper (1972: 421) discusses the ways a special place "conveys and evokes a range of responses. The importance of these sites is not only their manifest and distinctive appearance, but their qualifying and latent meaning."

Ritual may be objectified via the definition of distinctive, constructed spaces associated with rites. As Johan Huizinga (1970: 23) pointed out in *Homo Ludens*, one aspect of "play" includes ritual, which occurs in defined and delineated space. He noted: "one of the most important characteristics of play was its spatial separation from ordinary life. A closed space is marked out for it, either materially or ideally, hedged off from the everyday surroundings. Inside this space the play proceeds, inside it the rules obtain" (Huizinga 1970: 38). Thus, it is understandable why the classic analysis of rite is based on an architectural metaphor. Arnold van Gennep's (1960 [1909]) tripartite division of rites of passage – *preliminal* rites of separation, *liminal* rites of transition, and *postliminal* rites of reincorporation – are ritual categories characterized by their relationship to the *limen*, Latin for threshold. Because of its transitional nature between normal and special spaces, the threshold is an important element in ritual architecture of many cultures, "a locus of architectural symbolism" with the "characteristics of both a path and a space" (Grimes 1987a). In such ways, anthropological theory and ethnographic practices converge in their architectural definitions of ritual spaces.

Similarly, objectification may involve the special features and spatial arrangements within a ritual construction. Ritual spaces are formally defined because they communicate basic information about the relations between members of society and between society and the cosmos. Based on his analysis of small-group interaction, McFeat (1974: 85) observes:

> Rituals and games, two of our prime examples of model-building in small-group cultures, rely upon controlled environments and the material culture that is appropriate to them. Furnishings in formal situations are designed to facilitate communication based upon assumptions about human relationships. Thus, churches, courtrooms, theaters, parade squares, classrooms, seminars and the like all have "basic" patterns that reflect the relations among interacting members who are senders, receivers or observers.

Because ritual architecture and sacred places have this communicative potential, they tend to be formalized; their plans, features, and contents may be recognizably different from other classes of structures. The relations among interacting members may be variously structured: as an egalitarian community of participants, as a congregation with discrete but non-hereditary roles, by distinct roles marked by social distance such as between ritual specialist and adherents, or by a rigid barrier between initiates and others. The relations of members may take various forms, and some of those relationships are codified and preserved in ritual architecture.

But the process of recognition first faces some stiff problems. First, as always, is the issue of meaning. As Leach (1972: 337) categorically states: "no interpretation of ritual sequences in man is possible unless the interpreter has a really detailed knowledge which provides the context for the rite under discussion." I doubt any archaeological inquiry can overcome that ethnographic hurdle. Symbols resonate because of their multivocality, literally speaking in different ways to various segments of a society. Symbols do not mean a single thing, and they may be as intentionally layered as the multilingual meanings of the adjectives in *Finnegans Wake*. For these reasons, I do not attempt to understand the meanings of ancient Andean architecture, because the multiplicity of meanings associated with even simple symbols suggests that we cannot arrive at verifiable accounts of meanings in the absence of informants or written texts.

A second difficulty is the transformation of patterned ritual behavior into the material record. The archaeological approach emphasizes group ritual over individual ritual simply because group ritual creates a behavioral redundancy which may be materially expressed and archaeologically recognized. The individual is seldom visible in the archaeological record, and environmental conditions rarely preserve the material evidence of unrepeated individual actions. Finally, the only rites we can discern are those reflected by distinctive sets of material remains. For example, in traditional Ainu society (Ohnuki-Tierney 1974) the household hearth was ritually cleaned after a family member's death to purify the house and to honor Grandmother Hearth, a deity who resided in the domestic hearths of Ainu houses; only after this cleansing was the house reoccupied and the hearth reused. Regardless of its importance to Ainu society, the hearth-cleaning ritual would not be discernible in the archaeological record. Material remains imperfectly reflect social actions.

Third, sacred and profane may be spatially indivisible (Rabuzzi 1987). On the one hand, sacred spaces may be incorporated into everyday life, as suggested by household altars in such disparate societies as the Ainu (Ohnuki-Tierney 1974) or ancient Romans (Dumézil 1970), or domestic and cosmic may be inseparable, as when dwellings are conceived as *imago mundi*, projections of the cosmos (Eliade 1959: 52–58). Further, the sacrality of spaces may fluctuate, as an otherwise "ordinary" place becomes charged with special meaning during a rite, whether it is a village plaza, a devotee's house, or an evangelist's circus tent. As Leach (1978: 390) points out, a rigid Durkheimian distinction between sacred and profane may be relevant for some distinct classes of architecture, but for many constructions "a fundamental distinction can [not] be made between 'sacred' and 'profane' buildings. Almost all buildings are sometimes one and sometimes the other." And so the problem for the archaeologist is the recognition of ritual architecture, given the fluid nature of sacredness. Fortunately, not all aspects of ritual space are so chameleon-like, and this allows for some rough generalizations about the architectural expressions of rituals which are repeated, public, and corporate.

Ritual spaces are distinguished from other constructed environments in that they are public, special, and unique. For example, public spaces are designed to be entered, approached, or viewed by large groups of people (i.e., more than would fit into an average-sized room of a dwelling). We can identify the special nature of such spaces by contrasting them with residential structures (identified by domestic features and food debris) and from other architectural features which are non-residential and non-ritual (e.g., drying areas, threshing floors, or animal corrals). Finally, there is the issue of uniqueness. This is the inverse of the so-called "principle of abundance," which assumes that the most numerous architectural class is residential, or to place it within its Mesoamerican context, "since there are so many of these small mounds, they must be houses" (Ashmore and Wilk 1988: 10). Obviously, just because a certain architectural form occurs rarely does not mean it is a ritual structure, but we do expect ritual structures to be less numerous than dwellings, since they presumably served more than one household. And so the dimension of uniqueness leads to questions such as: To what extent does the area or space form a unique architectural class when compared to other structures within the site? Is the building or space distinctive in terms of its size, layout, construction, decoration, or location within the site? Does the building or space contain artifacts or features not found elsewhere in the site?

These sets of variables distinguish ritual spaces from other classes of architecture within a site, but only spaces which are used for rites which are public, repeated, and, in Tambiah's (1985) sense, performative. All the archaeological sites analyzed below contain such spaces, but the goal of the analysis is to gain new insights into the societies which built these special places.

As outlined in Chapter 1, this approach is based on the hypothesis that public structures represent political processes, which are "public, goal-oriented and that [involve] a differential of power" (Swartz et al. 1968: 7). Changes in the size, function, and organization of monumental constructions reflect – at least dimly – changes in the nature of social power. One reflection of this involves changes in the communicative potentials of public architecture. Simply, it is impossible to communicate information of the same detail in identical media in public architecture of different sizes and configurations. Thus, when we contrast a monumental construction like the huge Initial Period mound at Sechín Alto with the huge walled royal compounds of Chan Chan, we are seeing more than just two architectural traditions; we are seeing the physical expresssions of different conceptions of power.

The following variables are tentative and preliminary, designed to capture some of the elements that distinguish different types of ritual architecture. Again, the variables attempt to identify the social behaviors associated with different ritual structures rather than to distinguish sacred places by architectural form or artistic styles. These variables include permanence, scale, centrality, uniqueness, and visibility.

Permanence simply refers to an anticipated duration of a ritual construction – was it constructed to last a month or a lifetime? Was it constructed of perishable materials or from the most durable materials available in a particular place? Were the materials carefully utilized or haphazardly arranged?

Table 4.1. *Selected characteristics of Pakao ritual architecture*

	Seclusion lodge	Plaza	Mosque
Permanence	low	high	high
Centrality	peripheral	central	central
Ubiquity	village	village	village
Scale	small	large	moderate
Visibility	moderate	high	high

Scale refers to overall size of the structure, but also the relative size of the ritual structure. For example, if we used average house size as a standard unit of measure, assuming that it reflected in some way a residential group size, how much larger than a residence is the ritual structure? Note that, given the differing complexities of ritual structures, it is important to measure scale for different units within the structure (e.g., open plazas and inner sancta) as well as for the structure as a whole.

Centrality refers to the location of a ritual structure in reference to the nearest settlement; it may be situated in the center or periphery of a settlement or it may be located away from all residences in an isolated locale.

Ubiquity refers to the relative distribution of the ritual structure as measured against some scale of settlement complexity. Is the ritual structure found in every residence, within each barrio, in every village, only in certain villages or is there only one in a large region?

Visibility is an attempt to measure the relative publicness of a ritual space. A proxemic model derived from Edward T. Hall is developed below, but in general visibility refers to the effects of distance and artificial barriers on human perception. Some public spaces are designed for intimate, fine-scaled interactions, others for more public displays of more stylized communications. Visibility expresses this continuum.

By way of example, these variables are used to characterize three classes of ritual architecture found among the Pakao (also known as the Mandinko) of Senegal (Table 4.1). It may seem odd to use an ethnographic case from western Africa in a book on Andean architecture, but the ethnographers Schaffer and Cooper (1987) provide valuable architectural details and excellent maps that illustrate three ritual structures: the seclusion lodge, the plaza, and the mosque. The *seclusion lodge* houses circumcision initiates, keeping them separate from the rest of the community. The lodge is built from millet stalks and demolished when the rite of passage is completed. The seclusion lodge is constructed around a sacred tree whose branches hold protective spirits; this place may be located on the edge or in the center of the settlement. The seclusion lodge is relatively small, it is not connected to other spaces, and within it visibility is extremely fine scale. In contrast, the *village plaza* is a permanent architectural feature, centrally located in each village, and large enough to contain large groups of people during funeral ceremonies or elders' conferences. Visibility is high in the plaza.

Finally, the *mosque* is the most prominent structure in the Pakao village. Mosques are substantial, permanent structures of whitewashed brick with tall pole and thatch conical roofs. Covering some 400 square feet (Schaffer and Cooper 1987: 39), the mosque is a smaller space than the plaza. The mosque is enclosed by a palisaded fence, and between this palisade and the mosque walls is formed a larger sacred space. This creates two "nested" spatial divisions, making the mosque internally more complex than either the seclusion lodge or the plaza. Yet, even these divisions do not represent a significant barrier to communication and visibility is high.

The Pakao example illustrates the variables and another point: these built spaces reflect the rituals conducted in them. The rite of passage associated with circumcision is designed to be transitional and liminal, with a small group of initiates in seclusion, and this is reflected by the impermanence, peripheral location, and small scale of the structure. The plaza is a place where recurrent, highly visible, community-wide rituals occur and this is reflected by the plaza's permanence, central location, large scale, and high visibility. The mosque serves only a portion of the village population (i.e., men), but it is a permanent place for the worship of a timeless God.

Similarly, variations in ritual architecture may reflect differences in the social networks and ideological principles in prehispanic Andean societies, and those differences are explored below.

Analysis of permanence

The analysis of permanence attempts to understand the cultural vision behind a particular public construction and to find evidence of intention in the archaeological record. This is an important architectural dimension, sensitive to emic conceptions of belief. For example, temples are imposing structures in many Western architectural traditions because they are the dwellings of eternal gods (Fox 1988: v), but not every class of ritual architecture is meant to be the dwelling of the everlasting. Substantial structures may be built to honor ancestors, but yet lack the timeless nature of a god's residence. More ephemeral constructions may define special places associated with rites of passage or they may be continuously reconstructed as devotees signal their piety through the act of building. In short, the intended permanence of a ritual structure is an important vista into fundamental ideology.

It is difficult to estimate the absolute number of years a building was intended to last; instead, a rough ranking can be used based on qualitative differences in architectural treatments and evidence for renovations. *Ephemeral* constructions are constructed from highly perishable materials which are never refurbished. Ephemeral constructions are built, used, and decay. *Episodic* constructions are more substantial, with some evidence of refurbishing, but no evidence that they were constructed to last long periods of time. *Generational* and *multi-generational* constructions are two classes of more permanent constructions, made from non-perishable materials. Generational structures are rebuilt and modified, but their functions may change. Multi-generational structures are meant to be used in basically the same manner through time, although they may be refurbished.

Table 4.2. *Relative permanence of Andean ritual architecture*

	Ephemeral	Episodic	Generational	Multi-generational
CA-09–27	+			
Gavilanes		?		
Huaynuná			?	+
Huaricoto			+	
Galgada			+	+
Aspero				?
Cardal				+
Garagay				+
Paraíso				+
Pampa de las Llamas				+
Salinas de Chao				+
Las Aldas				+
Sechín Alto				+
Cerro Sechín				+
Chavín de Huántar				+

Turning to the sample of sites (Table 4.2), the small structure at CA-09–27 in the Zaña Valley appears to have been a single-component, ephemeral construction (Dillehay et al. 1989). The "public structure" at Los Gavilanes (Bonavia 1982) appears to be an episodic structure, but somewhat by default: the evidence of terracing suggests more than an ephemeral structure, but there is no evidence of repeated use. The hillside terraces at Huaynuná almost certainly represent a multi-generational structure, though the small moundtop structure with the ventilator shaft may represent a generational construction (T. Pozorski and S. Pozorski 1990).

The ritual structures at Huaricoto are substantial constructions, but the structures were buried intentionally and removed from use; this leads Burger and Salazar-Burger (1985: 116) to suggest that the structures were used for only short, discontinuous periods. While ritual activity at Huaricoto as a site was repeated over long periods of time, the individual constructions apparently were built to last a generation before being filled in.

A similar situation occurred at La Galgada (Grieder et al. 1988), but with a significant difference: generational structures were replaced by a large, multi-generational structure, the plaza and related features on top of the North Mound. The ritual chambers at La Galgada are an excellent example of generational structures. The chambers are relatively small, they are not extensively remodeled while in use, they are converted into burial chambers, and then new ritual chambers are constructed.

Perhaps the structures at Aspero (Feldman 1980, 1985, 1987) were also generational, since the mounds were the result of intentional abandonment, filling, and new construction, yet there was not the same rapid reconstruction as at La Galgada, suggesting that Huaca de los Ídolos and the other Aspero mounds may have been designed as relatively permanent, multi-generational ceremonial structures.

The remaining sites in the sample contain multi-generational ceremonial structures. Sites like Cardal, Garagay, El Paraíso, Salinas de Chao, Pampa de las Llamas-Moxeke, Las Aldas, Sechín Alto, Cerro Sechín, and Chavín de Huántar are all multi-generational constructions based on their size, architectural coherence, and long-term unity of intent.

The transformation from generational to multi-generational ceremonial structures must reflect a significant change in the organization of prehispanic Andean societies. It is tempting to assume that this threshold of permanence represents the transition from relatively egalitarian, kin-based social organizations to hierarchical, ranked societies, but some caution is required. The structures designed to last for multi-generations also represent a wide array of ceremonial constructions, presumably the products of different social institutions. Such a simple dichotomy masks social differences too interesting to be hidden, as the discussion of centrality suggests.

Analysis of centrality

There is an important relationship between the placement of ceremonial structures and the location of resident population, and this is seen in such different examples as barrio churches, national cathedrals, and isolated shrines. The meanings of such placements are diverse. For example, as Wheatley (1971: 478) suggested, the temples of the great cities of Mesopotamia served to project "images of cosmic order on to the plane of human experience, where they could provide a framework for social action." The central location of the ziggurat was thus the conduit between sacred and secular, an *axis mundi* on which revolved the world of human affairs.

But not all ritual structures occupy such a central position. Drawing on ethnographic studies from central and west Africa, Turner (1974: 185) discusses the distinction "between *ancestral* cults and cults of *the earth*, and between *political* rituals organized by political leaders of conquering invaders and *fertility* rituals retained in the control of indigenous priests. Each of these opposed types of cults tends to be focused on different types of shrines situated in different localities" (emphasis in the original). Citing Fortes' study of the Tallensi, Turner (1974: 184) notes that "earth shrines are set up *outside* settlements while lineage ancestral shrines are located *within* them."

Not all the ceremonial structures in the sample were shrines and there is no reason to think that the Andean pattern will parallel the Tale case, but there are good reasons to consider the placement of ceremonial structures within prehistoric settlements. Three qualitative categories suggest the different relative locations of ceremonial structure and settlement. When a ceremonial structure is surrounded by residential zones, that structure is *central*, and when the structure is on the margin of a residential zone, it is *peripheral*. If more than one ceremonial structure exists and they are located on the margins of the residential zone (as in the case of Pampa de las Llamas-Moxeke), then their locations are classified as *terminal* (as in terminus).

Table 4.3. *Centrality of Andean ritual architecture*

	Central	Peripheral	Terminal	Unknown
CA-09–27				+
Gavilanes	+			
Huaynuná	+			
Huaricoto		?		
Galgada	+			
Aspero	+			
Cardal	+			
Garagay				+
Paraíso	+			
Pampa de las Llamas			+	
Salinas de Chao	+			
Las Aldas		?		
Sechín Alto			?	
Cerro Sechín		?		
Chavín de Huántar		+		

These relationships are illustrated in Table 4.3. No information exists about the location of residential zones for CA-09–27 or Garagay. Pampa de las Llamas is the only site classified as terminal given the placement of Moxeke and Huaca A. Ceremonial structures are located within residential areas at the sites of Gavilanes, Huaynuná, La Galgada, Aspero, Cardal, El Paraíso, and Salinas de Chao.

Other ceremonial structures are located peripherally – Chavín de Huántar and possibly Huaricoto, Las Aldas and Cerro Sechín. At Huaricoto, no residential architecture was found and the small site (1 ha) appears to have been exclusively a ceremonial center, but it is possible the deeply buried deposits contain dwellings. At Cerro Sechín, no residential areas are reported from the vicinity of the temple, but no archaeological excavations have tested for domestic deposits. Las Aldas is also intriguing; the site is littered with domestic debris, but much of this appears to predate the period of major temple construction (S. Pozorski and T. Pozorski 1987: 27).

Table 4.3 suggests a strong tendency toward centrally located ritual architecture, which may suggest that ritual based on ancestral cults or the worship of culture heroes was critical in early Andean religion. A weak case can be made that sites like Chavín de Huántar represent an earth cult based on its peripheral location, an argument that Lathrap (1971) advanced on iconographic grounds. Whether Cerro Sechín and Las Aldas also fall into this category is more doubtful, yet these sites seem to represent a ritual tradition distinct from that practiced at sites like Huaricoto or La Galgada. Yet, enough variation exists among centrally located sites to suggest that other variables are relevant.

Analysis of ubiquity

The concept of ubiquity refers to whether a certain ceremonial center is replicated and the settlement level at which analogous structures are found. Ideally we would

Table 4.4. *Relative ubiquity of Andean ritual architecture*

	Level of ubiquity			
	Community	Subregional	Regional	Interregional
CA-09–27	+			
Gavilanes	+			
Huaynuná			?	
Huaricoto	?	?		
Galgada	?			
Aspero			?	
Cardal		+		
Garagay		+		
Paraíso			+	
Pampa de las Llamas			+	
Salinas de Chao			+	
Las Aldas			+	
Sechín Alto				+
Cerro Sechín				+
Chavín de Huántar				+

be able to compare a specific prehispanic ceremonial center with contemporary settlement and architectural data for a wide area, but, in fact, the evidence is rarely that good. And thus, the conclusions represented in Table 4.4 are tentative inferences; the evidence leading to them is summarized below.

First, the ceremonial architecture at CA-09–27 and Los Gavilanes probably are unique only at the community level. The small structures at CA-09–27 and Los Gavilanes were the only such structures found at those sites, but one can assume that similar structures would be found elsewhere (although there are no current data to support this). The ritual chambers at La Galgada also may represent constructions unique only at the community level. Although additional sites were not excavated, the presence of eleven other preceramic centers (Bueno Mendoza and Grieder 1988: 8–15) in the vicinity of La Galgada – one (Tirichuco Norte) exhibiting the same niche construction as the ritual chambers – suggests similar ceremonial constructions may be located at other sites.

Huaricoto is difficult to classify because so little known of its settlement context. Based on the scale of the chambers and ceremonial hearths, it seems reasonable to think that it served relatively small social units, but the ceremonial structures are not associated immediately with a specific residential zone. This may indicate that Huaricoto served more than one community in the Callejón de Huaylas, but this must be confirmed by more evidence.

The classification "subregional" is used to indicate that a particular ceremonial architecture is found in more than a single site in a region, but not in every site; a subregional center serves several communities. Thus Cardal and Garagay are subregional centers. It is striking that early U-shaped ceremonial centers were constructed so close to similar centers (Burger 1987; Burger and Salazar-Burger 1991), and in the Lurín, Rimac, Chillon, Chancay, and Huara Valleys there are multiple centers, some within 10 kilometers of each other. The general absence of settlement data for the Formative Period makes it difficult to understand the distribution of these large ceremonial centers *vis-à-vis* the resident populations of these valleys. It seems, though, that (a) within specific valleys at least some of the large centers were occupied contemporaneously, and (b) the valley-wide population was not restricted to the large ceremonial center. On those grounds, Cardal and Garagay can be classified as "subregional."

Stating that a site is unique at the regional level implies that there are no similar sites within a specific area such as a river valley; such an assessment demands faith in an uneven data set. There are no other sites like Huaynuná currently known from the Casma Valley, although future research may change that situation. Aspero would appear to be unique at the regional level, although the purported similarities in construction techniques (Fung Pineda 1988: 76–80) and figurine styles (Feldman 1980) between Aspero and Bandurria, Huacho Valley, may suggest the regional distribution of sites like Aspero. We are on more certain ground classifying sites like El Paraíso, Salinas de Chao, Pampa de las Llamas, and Las Aldas as unique at the regional level. Each site is a large architectural complex without parallels within its region. Although Pampa de las Llamas and Las Aldas may have been contemporary centers in the vicinity of the Casma Valley, their differing architectural plans stongly suggest that the two sites were not the same type of centers or settlements.

Finally, the sites of Sechín Alto, Cerro Sechín and Chavín de Huántar would appear to be unique not only for their own immediate regions but for a larger area as well. The interregional nature of Sechín Alto is generally recognized in the literature (S. Pozorski and T. Pozorski 1987). There is no obvious functional parallel between Cerro Sechín and Formative Period sites from the Nepeña Valley (Daggett 1984; Proulx 1985), although there may be stylistic similarities. It is equally safe to conclude, based on current knowledge, that Chavín de Huántar is unique at the interregional level, although other pilgrimage centers may have existed elsewhere in the Andes.

But in addition to the ubiquity of ceremonial centers, we want to know something about the size of social entities associated with specific classes of ritual architecture, and that leads to a consideration of scale.

Analysis of scale
Ideally one could approach this problem by defining a certain Andean notion of personal space, and then attempt to determine the number of people a certain public space may have held. Burger (1987) implicitly used this approach in his discussion of the large U-shaped ceremonial structure of Cardal. The three wings of the structure enclose a large central plaza covering 3 hectares, an area so large that Carlos Williams León (1985: 234) suggested the plazas were "over-sized relative to human scale and appear most appropriate for fields or orchards." Burger (1985) states that excavations at Cardal showed no empirical evidence for the agro-religious complex

hypothesis (e.g., no irrigation canals), but also discusses the relationship between population and the area of sacred space. Citing Smole's (1976) study of the Yanomamö, Burger (1987: 368) points out that one village contained an average of 21.6 m^2 of open, public space per individual, suggesting that the central plaza of Cardal was not "over-sized." Burger finds the Yanomamö figure more useful than Conklin's suggestion of a minuscule 0.46 m^2 of plaza space per person (a personal communication cited by Burger), a value that would suggest that over 65,000 people could squeeze into the central plaza at Cardal, more people than are estimated for any prehistoric Andean city with the possible exception of Cuzco and its environs (Hyslop 1990: 64–65).

Another source of data on personal spacing comes from the Inca town of Ollantaytambo, located in the Urubamba Valley. Inca ceremonies were celebrated outdoors, the interiors of shrines and temples being reserved for priests and objects of worship (Rowe 1946: 298). While most Inca town plans were modified or destroyed by colonial or modern constructions, the Inca town of Ollantaytambo preserves two public areas where community ceremonies may have taken place (Gasparini and Margolies 1980: 69), a plaza in the middle of the residential zone and the Plaza of Maniaraki. Although Luis Miguel Glave and Maria Isabel Remy (1983: 2) rather categorically state: "La plaza pública no era otra que la actual pampa de Manyaraqui," some form of public ceremonies (e.g., rituals associated with a specific ayllu) could have been in conducted in the smaller plaza. Plans published by Gasparini and Margolies (1980) indicate the residential plaza enclosed 3,204 m^2 and the Plaza de Maniaraki covered 3,564 m^2. Based on their analysis of colonial documents, Miguel Glave and Isabel Remy (1983: 16) record that Ollantaytambo contained 919 residents at 1575. These earliest census data postdate the introduction of European diseases (Cook 1981), suggesting that Ollantaytambo's pre-contact population would have been more than 1,000 people. Using this as an approximate population, this suggests that the ratio of ceremonial space at Ollantaytambo was somewhere between 3.2 m^2 and 3.6 m^2 per person.

This discussion verges on a numbers game, and the prudent reader may squirm at its direction. Simply, comparing public space in a Yanomamö *shabono* and a highland Andean village ignores a crucial fact: these places are not used in the same manner, and they almost certainly were not used in the same manner as was the central plaza at Cardal. Thus the matter of scale indirectly leads to questions of social uses of different types of ceremonial architecture.

The human scale of sunken circular courts

A first step in the analysis of scale is to divide architectural complexes into meaningful classes of constructed space which then can be compared. One architectural class is the sunken circular courtyard, a feature associated with a number of Initial Period and Early Horizon sites. Because they are semi-subterranean, there is an easy analogy between the Andean sunken circular courts and the puebloan kivas (e.g., Ravines and Isbell 1975: 259). Thus, Burger and Salazar-Burger (1991: 292) write of the sunken circular courts which are found away from the central plaza at Cardal:

Table 4.5. *Size and placement of sunken circular courts*

	Diameter (m)	Area (sq m)	Peripheral	Axial
Salinas de Chao	8	50	+	
	10	79	+	
Cardal	9.3	68	+	
	12.8	129	+	
	13.0	133	+	
	13.8	150	+	
Huaricoto	16	201	+	
Las Aldas (west court)	9	64	+	
(main court)	17.3	235		+
Galgada	18	255		+
Pampa de las Llamas	20	314		+
Chavín de Huántar	21	343		+

"This arrangement is reminiscent of sites in the SW United States, where dispersed small kivas for localized sodalities complemented the large 'great kivas' used for community ceremonies." Estimating the number of people who used the small sunken circular courts, Burger (1987: 370) writes: "Only 9.3 m in diameter, the circle probably would have held fewer than 175 people," while Moseley (1992: 140) suggests that the Cardal structures "could accommodate a small standing audience of 150 or so." Both estimates appear to use Conklin's estimate of 1 person per 0.46 m^2 of plaza space cited above, and are problematic for reasons discussed above.

But setting aside the occupancy issue for a moment, how do sunken circular courts vary? Two variables are size and placement – some circular courts are larger than others, and some are placed directly on the principal axis of a ceremonial complex while others are on the peripheries. If, as Burger has suggested, the courts on the plaza peripheries reflect smaller social units, then the central, "axial" courts should be larger than the "peripheral" courts.

The data in Table 4.5 address this issue. Sunken circular courts are considered to be "axial" if they fall on a line that bisects the principal ceremonial structure; all other placements are considered peripheral. Size was measured from published maps. The size of the court at Pampa de las Llamas is very approximate because it has been destroyed. The sunken court at Las Aldas is an ellipse 18.15 × 16 m in area; these two values were averaged and it was treated as a circle like the other structures. The sunken circular structure reported for Garagay (Ravines and Isbell 1975) is not included because information on its dimensions, to my knowledge, were not presented in the published sources.

The data are roughly ranked by courtyard size and a rather clear pattern emerges: sunken circular courts located on the main axis of a ceremonial center tend to be larger than those located on the peripheries. This is a very small sample, susceptible to the influences of random differences, but some tentative interpretations may be

Table 4.6. *Scale – estimated audiences for sunken circular courts*

		Estimated area per person		
	Area (m^2)	0.46m^{2a}	3.6m^{2b}	21.6m^{2c}
Salinas de Chao	50	109	14	2
	79	172	22	4
Cardal	68	148	19	3
	129	280	36	6
	133	289	37	6
	150	326	42	7
Huaricoto	201	437	56	9
Las Aldas (west court)	64	139	18	3
(main court)	235	511	65	11
Galgada	255	554	71	12
Pampa de las Llamas	314	683	87	15
Chavín de Huántar	343	746	95	16

Source: [a] from Conklin cited by Burger; [b] estimated from Ollantaytambo data; [c] Yanomamö data from Smole (1976)

outlined. First, it seems likely that different types of social units were using axial vs. peripheral courts, supporting Burger and Salazar-Burger's inference (1991: 292). Second, sunken circular courts are not always the focal ceremonial structure; other classes of architecture – like mounds or ritual chambers – appear more important at other Initial Period/Early Horizon sites like Cardal, Huaricoto, and Salinas de Chao.

Returning to the issue of occupancy, the three values for human density in public plazas produce very different estimates of the number of people who might have used sunken circular courts (Table 4.6). Simply, the estimate of 1 person per 0.46 m^2 results in unacceptably large numbers of people crammed into small circular sunken courtyards (Burger 1987: 370; Moseley 1992: 140). The estimate based on Ollantaytambo data (1 person per 3.6 m^2) may be incorrect, but it certainly seems more reasonable than the alternatives. At best, any estimate of the occupancy of sunken circular courts is a crude approximation. Using a measure of 1 person per 0.46 m^2 results in estimates which painfully stretch credulity. For example, the four circular courts at Cardal for which we have published measurements (of a total of ten) would have contained 1,043 people, three times the population estimated for the entire site (Burger and Salazar-Burger 1991: 278); alternatively, it seems unlikely that the sunken circular courts of Cardal were built for three to seven people. Without accurate estimates, we can only obtain a relative sense of the human scale of these structures, and another approach involves a comparison based on dwelling units.

The idea is to compare the size of the sunken circular court to the size of an average dwelling from the same site, and that allows us to measure architectural spaces in "dwelling units" (Table 4.7). If a sunken circular court was the same size as an average dwelling, then the court measures 1.0 dwelling units, if it is twice the

Table 4.7. *Scale – sunken circular courts in dwelling units*

	Area (sq m)	Dwelling (sq m)	Dwelling units	Placement
Salinas de Chao	50	80 max.	0.6	peripheral
	79		1	peripheral
Cardal	68	33	2	peripheral
	129	"	4	peripheral
	133	"	4	peripheral
	150	"	4.5	peripheral
Huaricoto	201	na	—	peripheral
Las Aldas (west court)	64	na	—	peripheral
(main court)	235	"	—	axial
Galgada	255	14	18	axial
Pampa de las Llamas	314	25 (min)	12.6	axial
	314	1,500 (max)	0.2	axial
Chavín de Huántar	343	na	—	axial

size of a house, then it measures 2.0 dwelling units, and so on. Ideally this would control for cultural differences in notions of personal space, and avoid suspicious estimations, but unfortunately there are some immediate problems. First, domestic structures were not encountered at some sites (e.g., Gavilanes, Huaricoto) or, more commonly, these structures were not excavated or reported fully. For example, in his excavations at Chavín de Huántar, Burger encountered portions of Janabarriu dwellings but only small sections of the houses were exposed (1984: 313–314), and data from more complete excavations in residences by Amat and Fung Pineda have not been published. Second, when data on the size of dwellings are available, they rarely represent a very large sample or a confident average value. Thus the figure for Cardal (33 m²) is based on excavations of a single well-preserved structure (Burger and Salazar-Burger 1985: 279) and the average dwelling size for Galgada (14 m²) was based on four structures (Grieder and Bueno Mendoza 1988: 19). At Pampa de las Llamas, the "range" of values for non-elite domestic structures represents excavations in a small dwelling (25 m²) and a large dwelling (1,500 m²), structures which include open patio areas (Billman 1989: 8; S. Pozorski and T. Pozorski 1986: 394–395). The lack of detailed information for residential architecture at Salinas de Chao requires a somewhat suspect solution: based on maps (Alva Alva 1986: 159) of terrace platforms in Unit D, which Alva Alva (1986: 65) describes as habitational in nature, it seems that no single dwelling was larger than roughly 8 × 10 m.

Las Aldas poses a unique problem. Domestic structures measuring 3 × 2 m were uncovered during the 1969 Japanese excavations, but these structures predate the temple construction (Matsuzawa 1978: 663,671). Grieder (1975: 103) refers to a handful of structures as possibly domestic, but they seem to postdate the principal construction at the site, "the work of impoverished survivors occupying a famous ruin." As S. Pozorski and T. Pozorski (1986: 29) point out, these modest structures were tucked into the lee of the monumental architecture, clearly postdating the ceremonial use of the plaza and mound group. In fact, S. Pozorski and T. Pozorski (1986: 27) write: "we were unable to locate [domestic] refuse which was unequivocally associated with the main mound construction and use. This, plus other data, have led us to conclude that this phase was quite brief, yet visible." Good data on dwelling size are not available from Las Aldas.

The sunken circular courts at Cardal and Salinas de Chao are 2 to 4 times the size of an average dwelling at each site; the sunken circular courts at La Galgada, and possibly at Pampa de las Llamas, are much larger. In absolute terms, the sunken circular court at La Galgada is roughly twice the size of the largest court at Cardal; measured in dwelling units, the La Galgada structure is four times the size of the Cardal sunken circular courts.

There seem to be interesting differences among sunken circular courts, differences in placement and relative and absolute sizes which belie their formal similarities. The data are few and problematic, but suggest some tentative hypotheses for future investigation. First, the evidence supports Burger and Salazar-Burger's (1991: 292) distinction between large axial courts and small peripheral ones, reinforcing their hypothesis that these spaces respectively served the entire community versus smaller social groupings. Second – and this is entirely speculative – it is possible that large axial sunken circular courts become important later on in the Formative, representing a translation of an architectural form from a kin-based to a community-wide social context.

The human scale of plazas

A concern with the human scale of prehispanic plazas threads through the archaeological literature about the large U-shaped ceremonial complexes of the central coast of Peru (e.g., Burger 1987; Williams León 1985). To reiterate, the issue is: What is the relationship between the estimated number of residents at a site and the size of the plaza? Plazas are important constructed spaces because they are often arenas for public gatherings, ceremonies, protests, carnivals, and so on. Understanding the human scale of plazas, in turn, may illuminate the nature of the interactions which occurred in those spaces.

At La Galgada the best-defined plaza-like construction is the space associated with Floor 13 on the North Mound which measures 12.8 × 9 m (Grieder and Bueno Mendoza 1988: 43–44, Figure 14). The data for Las Aldas come from the four central plazas, which from north to south measure 62 × 60 m, 76 × 65.5 m, 107 × 64 m, 65.5 × 58 m (Grieder 1975: Figure 1). The sizes of the central plazas at Cardal and Garagay are from Williams León (1980), and the plaza dimensions for Chavín de Huántar are taken from Lumbreras (1977: Figure 4). The data from Pampa de las Llamas-Moxeke are based on the largest, best-defined plaza at that site which measures roughly 450 × 425 m (S. Pozorski and T. Pozorski 1986: Figure 2). At Salinas de Chao, the large (approximately 43 × 21 m) rectangular plaza in Unit B (Alva Alva 1986: Figure 21) was used; it is the largest architecturally defined open space in the site.

Table 4.8. *Scale – size, estimated occupancy, and dwelling units for plazas*

	Plaza (sq m)	Dwelling (sq m)	@ 1 person/ 3.6 sq m	Dwelling units
Galgada	115	14	32	8
Cardal	30,000	33	8,333	909
Garagay	90,000	na	25,000	—
Salinas de Chao	1,316	80	366	16
Las Aldas	3,720	na	1,033	—
	4,978	"	1,383	—
	6,848	"	1,930	—
	3,799	"	1,056	—
Pampa de las Llamas	191,250	25 (min)	53,125	7,650
		1,500 (max)	"	128
Chavín	1,600	na	444	—

It is difficult to define plazas at Aspero and Huaynuná. Both sites have open spaces, but neither have large culturally modified, open spaces. The hillside terraced structure at Huaynuná, as Thomas and Shelia Pozorski (1990: 24) write, "overlooks a spacious area that would have been suitable for public gatherings and ceremonies," yet what defines that space? This area, roughly 2–3 hectares directly north of the hillside structure, could have held large groups of people, but it also contained dwellings. The space in front of Huaca de los Ídolos and the other mound constructions at Aspero present similar problems, and thus both sites are excluded from Table 4.8. No open plazas are reported for Huaricoto, Gavilanes, or the Zaña Valley sites.

A single adjective captures the data in Table 4.8 – chaotic. Simply there is no pattern which emerges, no hint of even a tenuous relationship between variables. The reason, I would suggest, for such analytical chaos is that plazas represent a distinctive class of ceremonial architecture, one in which the spatial arrangement of people is completely different from either dwellings or sunken circular courts. This difference, I believe, stems from the ways in which people may be distributed across a plaza's space.

To illustrate this point, a modern example of the Andean use of public space occurs annually at the reconstructed celebration of Inti Raymi. Held on the plain of Sacsahuaman, this modern recreation of the Inca Winter Solstice celebration attracts vast crowds of native Andean peoples and foreign tourists (Figure 4.1). Accurate attendance records are non-existent, and claims are made that as many as 100,000 people occupy the Inca fortress which covers the hilltop overlooking Cuzco. The celebrants are not equally spread across this space, however; rather, a relatively small number of participants performs the re-enactment on the large central plaza, while the majority of the crowd cling to small flat perches created by the zig-zag walls of Sacsahuaman. Based on estimates from photographs of the ceremony, the space surrounding participants may average 50–100 square meters per

Figure 4.1 Participants and observers at Inti Raymi celebration, Sacsahuaman, Cuzco, June 1984

person, while observers are crammed together literally shoulder to shoulder. This spatial structure is organized by a simple fact: there are viewers and actors, and they use this public space in different ways.

Such issues may be behind the chaotic patterns observed in Table 4.8. The open spaces listed are all "plazas," but they are quite different as settings for ceremonial activities. Simply, the small plazas of La Galgada, Salinas de Chao, and Chavín de Huántar may represent uses of public space distinct from those in the larger plazas of Las Aldas, Cardal, Garagay or Pampa de las Llamas. In turn, this suggests that even when there seem to be formal parallels between structures – like the suggested similarity in the plans of Garagay, Cardal, and Chavín de Huántar (Williams León 1985: 237) – these constructions were *socially* organized in different ways.

But the use of public space is difficult to discern from architectural plans, although some basic measures help to understand the communicative potentials of different spaces. For example, Burger's and Williams León's approach to Cardal was to think of it as a space to be filled with people; but what about the use of this construction as a setting, a stage for ritual? In short, how would a site like Cardal or other U-shaped ceremonial centers serve as a place where communication took place? Such questions lead to the issue of visibility.

Analysis of visibility
Because of its theatrical uses, ritual architecture partially is shaped by limits of human perception; visibility reflects those limits. Such limits are considered

Table 4.9. *Distance and perception*

	Distance in meters				
Informal distance classes	0 Intimate ——— Social ——————— Public —————————————→ personal	1 2 3	4 5 6	7 8 9 10	
Oral/ aural	Soft voice whisper	Casual or consultative voice	Loud voice when talking to group	Full public-speaking voice, frozen style	
Detail vision	Details of skin, teeth, face visible	Fine lines of face fade; wink visible	Eye color not discernible; smile vs. scowl visible	Difficult to see eyes, subtle expressions	
Scanning vision	Whole face visible	Upper body; can't count fingers	Upper body & gestures	Whole body has space around it in visual field	
Peripheral vision	Head & shoulder	Whole body movement	Whole body visible	Other people become important in vision	

Source: Data from Hall 1966

explicitly by professionals who design signs for use in architectural settings, such as highway signs (Follis and Hammer 1979: 18–23) or interior directories and maps (Ramsey and Sleeper 1988), but archaeologists rarely consider visibility in the built environment in a precise way. A starting point for this analysis is Edward Hall's (1966, 1972) visionary writings on proxemics. Hall describes a series of thresholds for interpersonal interaction, combining the restraints imposed by the physiology of human sensation (Gibson 1960). Distinguishing between intimate distance, personal distance, and social distance, Hall (1966) defines their distances based on the thresholds of communication structured by the abilities of human vision, speech, and hearing. As Table 4.9 suggests, these thresholds, although not rigid, limit modes of interpersonal communication. Hall defines "public distance – close phase" as 12 to 25 feet +/– 5 feet, and "public distance – far phase" as 30 ft to maximum carrying distance of voice (Hall 1972: 147):

> At this distance body stance and gesture are featured; facial expression becomes exaggerated as does the loudness of the voice. The tempo of the voice drops; words are enunciated more clearly. The whole man may be perceived as quite small and he is viewed in a setting. Foeval vision takes in more and more of the man until he is entirely within the small cone of sharpest vision. At this point, contact with him as a human being begins to diminish.
> (Hall 1972: 148)

As the separation between speaker and viewer grows, communication becomes more stylized and less subtle. Thus, a shout may be heard over a distance of hundreds of feet, but multiple-syllable words or complex phrases will be indistinct or inaudible. Instruments other than the human voice – like drums or whistles – may carry further, but obviously convey less information than the spoken word. As distance increases, modes of communication shift; insofar as ritual involves communication and perception, then different classes of ritual will be affected by these different thresholds. And for these reasons, different types of rituals will be conducted in different sized spaces.

Such limits are clearly recognized in the design of open-air theaters, an architectural form with a literature which dates back to Vitruvius (Cheney 1918; Knudsen and Harris 1978). Enclosed theaters solve acoustic problems in ways which are not possible in outdoor theaters (e.g., by hanging ceiling panels). In outdoor theaters, there are two basic design conditions: (1) the sight lines must be clear, and (2) the acoustics must be good (Cheney 1918: 139, 148). Open-air acoustics are usually a matter of the natural setting, and can only be improved by building a back wall or placing an acoustic shell. Knudsen and Harris (1978: 66–67) write that in open-air theaters without sound amplification systems actors can be heard over an area about 85 feet wide and 75 feet deep by an audience of approximately 600 people. This further assumes that the open theater is sheltered from wind. As Cheney (1918: 148–149) observed, "the unfortunate placing of the theatre in an exposed spot leaves the question of hearing dependent upon changing winds and atmospheric conditions," an issue we will return to when discussing exposed ceremonial centers on the Peruvian coast.

Again my observations at the 1984 Inti Raymi ceremony suggested these thresholds of communication. From the walls of Sacsahuaman approximately 75–100 m from the central stage it was impossible to hear clearly the shouted prayers of the leading participants, although it was a superb view of the spectacle and pagentry of costumed dancers and elaborate processions. Speech from the stage was inaudible and most of the crowd was talking, creating a thick layer of white noise. But when six men wrestled a white llama to the stage and the animal's heart was cut out in sacrifice, the crowd went silent. That example of ceremonial communication was perceived clearly.

The following discussion transforms such observations into more explicit, measurable thresholds of perception. Certain types of ceremonies involve specific modes of communication, modes which have different spatial properties. Insofar as ceremonial spaces involve communication, those spaces will be shaped, literally, by the types of ceremonies that occur there.

That issue is explored in three ways. First, I apply Hall's model of perceptual thresholds to the architectural sample, which shows that there are some clear differences between sites. Second, I examine the existence of different communicative zones within one class of ritual architecture, the U-shaped ceremonial center. Finally, I compare two different sites, Las Aldas and Cardal, in an attempt to understand the different types of ceremonies which went on at those sites.

Visibility: an overview
Visibility is explored by applying Hall's (1966) communicative thresholds to architectural spaces and then determining what kinds of ritual communication could be

Table 4.10. *Visibility of Andean ritual architecture*

	Personal	Consultative	Public near	Public far	Public distant
CA-09–27	+				
Gavilanes		?			
Huaynuná				+	
Huaricoto			+		
Galgada			+	+	
Aspero			+		
Cardal			+	+	+
Garagay			?	+	+
Paraíso			?		
Pampa de las Llamas			+	+	+
Salinas de Chao				+	
Las Aldas			+	+	+
Cerro Sechín			+		
Chavín de Huántar			+		

perceived and from where. The analysis assumes that the focal point of a ceremonial space was either the center of small chambers or the highest point of a mound construction.

The sites in the sample vary in visibility (Table 4.10). Although the sample is very small, the data may indicate that communication becomes more public through time. The earlier sites tend to exhibit spaces in which communication would fall into the personal and consultative modes; they are small spaces where perception would be fine-scaled with high resolution perception. For example, in the public structure at the Zaña Valley site of CA-09–27, two people would be able to hear each other breathing. At various sites marked by "public-near" spaces (e.g., Huaricoto, Cerro Sechín, Chavín de Huántar), one could understand innovative spoken messages and perceive facial and body gestures, whereas those modes of communication would not be understood in spaces classified as "public distant."

Later sites tend to have more public spaces, probably reflecting modes of public communication which were more stylized and formalized. It seems as if the spatial and social distances between participants and observers were greater at later Formative Period sites than at earlier ones. Second, there is some suggestion that these modes of communication were combined in an additive pattern. Communication at the public-far level only occurs when there is evidence for public-near communication; communication at the public-distant level only occurs when there is evidence for more intimate levels of interaction as well. In later ceremonial centers, there are multiple arenas for communication and very public spaces were combined with areas in which closer communication also took place.

In short, the sample as a whole indicates that visibility was treated in Andean ritual architecture in a systematic manner, reflecting both diachronic changes and cumu-

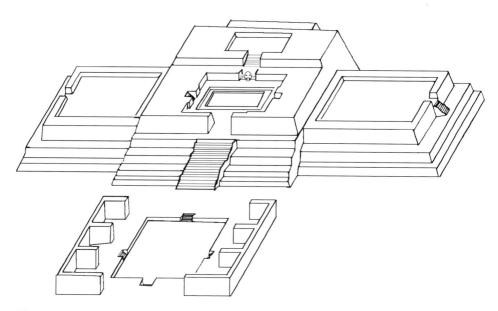

Figure 4.2 Hypothetical reconstruction of Garagay (Redrawn from Ravines and Isbell 1975)

lative additions. Beyond this, the analysis of visibility suggests some interesting differences, with implications for one class of ritual architecture, U-shaped ceremonial centers.

Analysis of visibility: U-shaped ceremonial centers
The following analyzes U-shaped ceremonial structures as potential stages for communicating rituals. These ceremonial centers are a fascinating set of constructions. They are obviously public architecture; the largest such structure, at San Jacinto in the Chancay Valley, required moving more than 2 million cubic meters of material (Fung Pineda 1988: 91). Further, there are a number of these sites, sometimes quite close to one another; Cardal, Mina Perdida, and Manchay Bajo, for example, are three large, contemporary Formative centers within a 5 km radius in the lower Lurín Valley (Burger 1987). These three-sided constructions enclose large areas, not intimate spaces. As Williams León (1980: 98) records, the central plaza areas range from 1 to 30 hectares, averaging 9.2 hectares. The very size of these ceremonial centers placed limits on the kinds of rites that occurred in these spaces.

Although not extensively excavated, Garagay is a good test case because of the detailed, topographic map of the site (Ravines and Isbell 1975). The central mound of the site rises 23 m above the plaza and it is 385 m long and 155 m wide. It is fronted by an atrium; the reconstruction (Ravines and Isbell 1975: 264) shows the relationship between the central mound and the atrium, though the wing platforms are not illustrated (Figure 4.2). The western wing is 260 m long, 115 m at its widest point, and 9 m tall, while the eastern wing is 140 m long, 40 m wide and 6 m tall (Ravines and Isbell 1975: 255).

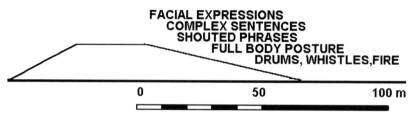

Figure 4.3 Limits of perception for different media at Garagay

Garagay is a classic example of a U-shaped ceremonial center. The scale of the construction limited its use in ceremonies. If we assume that the top of the central mound was the focal point of the ceremonial center, only the largest gestures and only the loudest human sounds could be perceived from most of the plaza (Figure 4.3). Using Hall's suggested threshold between personal and public distances of roughly 25 feet (8 m), then detailed observance of a moundtop ceremony would be restricted to individuals also on top of the mound. Even stylized gestures with the face and hands would be unrecognizable from most of the plaza, and the most visible gestures would be limited to activities like walking up a stairway or lighting a fire. Similarly a spoken human voice could not be heard from the plaza and a shouted voice would be unintelligible to most of the plaza. These considerations eliminate some of the possible ways that Garagay was used as a ritual space. First, it is improbable that Gargay was massed with thousands listening to priestly sermons delivered from the top of the central mound – at least not if the speech was to be understood.

Second, if the moundtop structure was the focus of ceremonial activities, then there were at least two communicative arenas and, possibly, two sets of ritual. If the rite involved subtle gestures or complex speech, then that aspect of the ritual probably took place on the top of the mound. If the rite involved highly visible gestures (such as a procession), such symbolic acts could be perceived by a large number of people within the plaza.

Similarly, we can that predict that other U-shaped ceremonial centers will exhibit two arenas of ritual communication, and recent data from Cardal (Burger and Salazar-Burger 1991) support this hypothesis. First, there is evidence that Cardal was designed for highly visible ceremonies. For example, access to the top of the main mound was via a steep, well-plastered staircase which rises at a gradient angle of over 40 degrees (Figure 4.4); Burger and Salazar-Burger (1991: 283) note that the staircase "is visually very impressive, and its steepness serves to emphasize the great height of the artificial pyramid." Another highly visible feature is a mural representing "a mouth band of interlocking teeth and massive upper fangs" (Burger and Salazar-Burger 1991: 283). The upper fangs were over a meter long, painted yellow, and overlapped the lower lip, which was painted red, a very visible contrast. The mural was designed to enhance visibility. Burger and Salazar-Burger (1991: 285) observe, "The mural is enormous and easily seen from the open plazas. It was intentionally positioned some 80 cm above the landing floor so that the terracing would

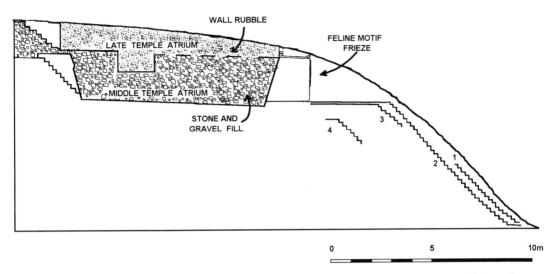

Figure 4.4 Schematic profile of Central Mound, Cardal (Redrawn from Burger and Salazar-Burger 1991)

not obstruct the view from below." Cardal was designed explicitly to be highly public, visible to people located 100 meters away or further.

But Cardal also was designed for less public ceremonies, smaller scale rituals which occurred on the mound itself. For example, a moundtop structure associated with the Middle Temple phase of Cardal (ca. 2950 ± 80 bp) contains a dual altar; similar to the step-block design found on Initial Period pottery, the altar consists of two three-level constructions which share a common wall and were apparently linked by a common window (Burger and Salazar-Burger 1991: 281). Etched into the walls of this room were graffiti which appear to relate to religious ideology. Neither the altar nor the graffiti were visible to people outside of the room; this space is invisible from the plaza. A modeled polychrome mural fragment is another indication of less public ritual associated with the final Late Temple phase at Cardal. Showing a red-painted lower face with flared nostrils and downturned mouth with contrasting white canines, the fragment is relatively small; Burger and Burger-Salazar (1991: 289) note that the modeled fragment was "designed to be seen at close quarters."

Thus the ceremonial focus at Cardal was not restricted to the moundtop structure as viewed from the plaza. Burger and Salazar-Burger (1991: 291) have written:

> the work at Cardal has produced evidence that ritual activity on the summit
> was not limited to the open landings and large inner sanctuaries or atria, but
> also included small enclosed chambers with dual altars isolated from the
> view of the public. These two unprecedented discoveries heighten our
> awareness that the tradition of early religious architecture and ritual on the
> Central Coast remains only dimly understood at present.

Yet there is some reason to think that the pattern observed at Cardal would also be true at other U-shaped ceremonial centers, not necessarily because those prehistoric societies shared a religious ideology expressed in similar symbols (which they may have), but because the limits of human senses and the communicative function of ritual interact to form certain thresholds of perception.

Processional and observational ceremonies: Las Aldas and Cardal
Andean ceremonies did not occur tethered to a single point, and the architectural plans of some sites almost certainly reflect the passage of people across an artificial landscape. At sites like Pampa de las Llamas-Moxeke and Las Aldas there is an obvious linear order. At Pampa de las Llamas-Moxeke the mounds, residences, and plazas are aligned to N 41° E with little variance (S. Pozorski and T. Pozorski 1986: 383). A line drawn through the plaza doorways to the principal stairways at Las Aldas neatly bisects the sunken circular court. Las Aldas is particularly interesting because the aligned features, doorways, and staircases, are specifically associated with foot traffic, and this central line probably represents a route meant to be followed. In turn, that is interesting because visibility changes dramatically along that route, and those changes are patterned consequences of construction.

As discussed above (pp. 98–101), different angles of view afford different levels of perception, visual thresholds which have been recognized by designers (Dreyfus 1959) and architects. Higuchi (1983: 47), discussing the work of the nineteenth-century architect Martens, notes that "Martens took the objective position that the total aesthetic effect of a given object is related to the special characteristics of the human eye's range of vision and to the human being's visual powers." When buildings are being viewed, these characteristics tended to create thresholds of perception (see above, Figure 3.4):

> As the viewer draws closer to a building from a relatively distant point, the building gradually emerges from its background and begins to create a "purely pictorial" impression. It first begins to take on monumental characteristics when its angle of elevation reaches 18 degrees. When this angle increases to 27 degrees, the building fills the range of vision, and the eye sees the larger details. Eventually, when the viewer reaches the point where the angle is 45 degrees, he is at the best place for observing the comparatively small details.
> (Martens 1890: 14, cited in Higuchi 1983: 47)

Obviously, vision differs between individuals and is influenced by cultural dimensions. Yet, these different angles of view are relevant to understanding the shifting dimensions of a complex visual field like the site of Las Aldas.

Figure 4.5 depicts the vision fields of an individual 1.5 m tall moving across the site of Las Aldas. Moving along the central axis, the individual perceives a continuously changing visual field but one with clear transitions: doorways, stairways, and changes of plane. Figure 4.5 reconstructs the angles of elevation and depression from those transition points at angles 18, 27, and 45 degrees above and below the person's horizontal plane of view.

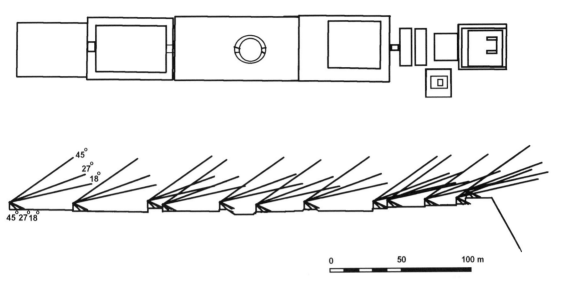

Figure 4.5 Schematic plan and cross-section of Las Aldas, showing vision fields at 18, 27 and 45 degrees

This "cross-sectional" vista of Las Aldas is quite different from the image provided in a plan view, and it suggests different qualities of the built environment. First, the sunken circular court, which seems so focal in the plan view, is hidden from the viewer until he stands on the brink of the pit. Second, as the viewer moves across the site of Las Aldas, the moundtop never fills the range of vision; following Martens, *the mound of Las Aldas never reaches monumental proportions as the viewer moves along this central axis.* Viewed from the north or south, the mound at Las Aldas is highly visible, but not from the central axis which is clearly the intended line of approach.

This suggests that the plazas – rather than the mound – were the culturally significant built spaces at Las Aldas. It may be that the changes in the planes of plaza are also significant. There may be some common significance to the changes in elevations and the stepped motifs present in Initial Period ceramics (Burger and Salazar-Burger 1991: 281). It is intriguing to note that the rhythm of the visual changes increases in tempo as one moves along the central axis to the top of the mound, but again this may be simply a product of topography. But, to reiterate, two points seem quite certain: to people moving along the central axis, the sunken circular court was invisible until the last moment, and the mound itself never filled their visual field. When viewed from the plazas, the Las Aldas mound seems visually insignificant and photographs are not striking; the stunning view is from the top of the mound back to the plazas, which seem to stretch infinitely toward the Cordillera Negra.

The site of Cardal could not be more different, as Figure 4.6 shows. The central platform, rising 17 m above the open plaza area, effectively fills the visual field of anyone standing on the edge of the raised plaza area. The absolute vertical difference between this plaza and the moundtop (ca. 16 m) is actually less than the difference between the top of the mound and Plaza 4 at Las Aldas (approximately 17 m). But at Cardal the monumentality of the mound is emphasized because the elevation

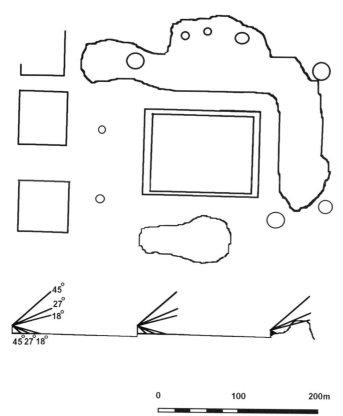

Figure 4.6 Schematic plan and cross-section of Cardal, showing vision fields at 18, 27 and 45 degrees

difference is not broken by a series of planes. At Cardal the mound is important; at Las Aldas the plazas are.

Not every site in the sample fits neatly into the categories represented by Las Aldas and Cardal, but neither is this pair unique. For example, the multiple horizontal planes at Las Aldas are similar to the architectural patterns at Huaynuná, Salinas de Chao, and Sechín Alto. In contrast, the visual domination of the mound at Cardal is obviously analogous to Garagay, but also similar to both Moxeke and Huaca A at Pampa de las Llamas and the last construction phases at La Galgada.

It is frustrating not to know what such differences mean, but one aspect of their meanings may be the difference between the processional vs. the observational elements of these ceremonial centers. The architectural plans of Las Aldas, Salinas de Chao (specifically Unit B during its first phase), and possibly Pampa de las Llamas-Moxeke suggest a transit across the axis of ceremonial spaces including plazas, thresholds, and terraces. At Las Aldas, it may be significant that the doorways and staircases along this axis narrow as the ultimate terrace is reached, from approximately 7 m wide to about 2 m (see Feldman 1980 for a similar discussion of Aspero). The narrowing of doorways and decreasing size of terraces suggest that fewer people could be included in such a procession once it moved out of Plaza 4. From Plaza 4, it is only possible to see the top of the mound from near the center of the plaza, which is more than 100 m from the edge of moundtop. At that distance it is difficult to hear a complex sentence clearly even if it is shouted. Understanding a shouted voice at Las Aldas is made even more difficult by the roar of crashing waves and strong coastal winds that blow up at midday and last until nightfall. The winds of Las Aldas are sufficiently strong and predictable that the 1969 Japanese expedition could not identify stratigraphic details in their excavations because of the whirlwinds created in the sunken circular court (Matsuzawa 1978: 658). This suggests that ceremonies including shouted intonations probably did not occur during the afternoons at Las Aldas, at least not if the ceremonies were meant to be heard.

By decreasing the relative angle of view, the multiple planes of Las Aldas actually interrupt the visual impact of the mound. A similar architectural plan is found at the famous Buddhist temple of Borobudur in Java. The large shrine, broken into a series of planes, can only be experienced through what one scholar referred to as a *marche à l'illumination* in which the secrets of the shrine were revealed gradually during the approach and the ascent (Ashton 1992: 84–85). Borobudur cannot be understood through distant observation. As Eliade (1985: 137) notes: "The temple cannot be 'assimilated' from the outside." Obviously, Las Aldas represents a cultural and ceremonial tradition which is completely independent of Theravada Buddhism, but it is interesting to see such similar architectural treatments. The builders of Las Aldas could have chosen a variety of spatial configurations leading to a moundtop temple or shrine. The fact that they directed movement along the central axis and divided the ascent into a set of horizontal planes seems an explicitly cultural and symbolically significant decision.

The architectural plan of Cardal is quite different, and it suggests that the ceremonies which took place there were differently organized. As noted above, the design of the central platform emphasizes visibility, as indicated by the placement and color of the friezes and the steep frontal surface accented by the sloped main staircase. Although the central platform apparently was the focal point of Cardal, additional ceremonies may have taken place on the lateral mounds; words shouted from the lateral mounds could be heard in most of the raised plaza. It may be that the U-shaped mounds actually improve the acoustics since they mimic an acoustic shell. Based on such observations and inferences, we can suggest that ceremonies at Cardal tended to be divided between those directed to observers in the plazas and those experienced by moundtop participants.

To summarize, there is a basic division between earlier ceremonial structures which were personal/consultative constructions, and later structures which had areas that were more public. Second, within these larger, more public ceremonial centers there were different zones, smaller areas where intimate "high resolution" communication occurred, and larger arenas where less subtle forms of communication took place. Finally, there are notable differences in the organization of highly public communication. One such distinction is indicated by the differences between Las Aldas, which seems processional in purpose, and Cardal, which appears observational in design.

We do not know the specific meanings of Formative Period Andean rituals, but it is possible to understand something about those rites by examining the communicative limits of the built spaces where ceremonies occurred. In a sense, we are trying to establish functional parameters for ceremonial architecture, similar to the way we make inferences between vessel forms and functions. We can reasonably infer that plates were not used for liquids, huge vessels were not used for everyday meals, small pots were not used for bulk storage, and so on because we can set functional limits based on discrete formal classes. Looking at prehistoric public architecture, we may be only able to eliminate alternative modes of ritual communication, but that represents an advance in knowledge. In a roughly analogous manner, we can distinguish between different classes of Andean ceremonial architecture based on their possible ritual uses as shaped by their communicative potentials.

Summary

It may be too obvious to restate, but ritual played a fundamental role in Andean societies. The archaeological record suggests that ritual architecture was the first product of co-ordinated social effort in the Andes, and thus its archaeological examination is of fundamental significance. When we compare the ethnohistoric accounts of ritual against the material traces of Archaic and Formative rites, it seems clear that late prehistoric religions differed in basic ways from the earliest Andean religions. Thus, an archaeological approach to ritual architecture is required, one which could subsume the ethnohistoric patterns but equally illuminate sets of belief and practice unknown to colonial chroniclers or their informants.

One approach is based on a communicative model of ritual and translated into archaeological practice via a set of basic variables. This model first separated the dimensions of ritual practice from ritual meaning, and then considered how and what kind of information could be communicated over different distances given the limits of human perception. I documented how the communicative process of ritual is limited by basic restraints on human vision, hearing, and comprehension, and I argued that insofar as ritual architecture forms the physical setting for that communication, certain elements of the ritual architecture will reflect the nature of the communication. Further, the varying nature of ritual communication illuminates basic questions about the organization of early societies whose corporate efforts were invested in ritual architecture. The subsequent analyses indicated a number of points about the changing nature of Andean ritual architecture and the societies which constructed and worshiped in those buildings.

First, the analysis of permanence suggests that a basic change occurred during the Late Archaic/Early Formative in the conception of ritual architecture: at this time ritual constructions become multi-generational. This is reflected in the continuity of plan and function exhibited by sites like Cardal and Salinas de Chao – among others – and the transition is probably best documented at La Galgada. Although our sample is small, it is sufficient to suggest that such changes mark a real transition in the continuity of political organization in early Andean societies. Prior to this, ritual architecture was paced by the birth and death of a generation; after this transition, ritual architecture began to reflect a continuing social unit and a set of shared belief which cross-cuts generations.

Second, the analysis of centrality indicates that most ritual architecture was directly associated with a resident population. In those cases where ritual architecture is separated from residential architecture (e.g., Huaricoto, Garagay, Las Aldas, Cerro Sechín), it is possible that unexcavated dwellings exist near the architecture. The association between ritual architecture and a settled population may indicate that Archaic and Formative ceremonial centers were tightly associated with kin-based belief systems like the worship of ancestors or culture heroes. This may partially explain the different traditions of ritual architecture known from coastal Peru, and the density of ritual structures in areas like the Lurín Valley. The different architectural traditions may reflect parallel developments in different regions, rather than a more widespread set of beliefs which were expressed in monumental constructions, and the multiplicity of ceremonial centers in the valleys of the Central Coast may suggest a kin-based community of adherents, each associated with a different huaca.

The analysis of ubiquity contrasts with these findings. While the Archaic ritual structures were unique only at the community level, it is surprising to think that a site of the size of La Galgada may have had nearby counterparts at sites like Tirichucho Norte. Similarly, it is intriguing that sites like Garagay and Cardal were unique at the subregional level while sites like Pampa de las Llamas, Salinas de Chao, Sechín Alto, and Las Aldas were unique at the regional level. This is an important difference, one which has been overlooked in the debate over whether Formative monumental constructions were the products of state-level societies (e.g., Burger and Salazar-Burger 1991; S. Pozorski and T. Pozorski 1992). It would seem that the social networks associated with these two classes of sites differed fundamentally, suggesting the need to view ceremonial architecture within its regional context rather than simply consider the size of isolated structures.

The analysis of scale illuminated a number of points. First, there appears to be a pattern among sunken circular courts in which axially located courts are larger than peripherally located ones. Second, there is some reason to revise the estimated number of people who could participate in a ritual held in a sunken circular court; my guess is that no courtyard held more than 100 people and probably held fewer than 50 people. Third, the analysis of the scale of plazas similarly suggested that the estimates of plaza occupants needed to be revised, but more importantly hinted at functional differences among plazas. Some of these smaller plazas were designed to hold a group of people evenly spaced across the area, but others were probably the scene of rituals in which there were participants and observers unevenly distributed across the constructed spaces.

The limits of human perception set communicative thresholds, and the implications of these limits were discussed in the analysis of visibility. The data suggest that there was a progressive addition of increasingly public communication to the ritual repertoire; public-near communication was incorporated into, rather than replaced by, more distant forms of communication. Given the difficulties of communicating over large open spaces, there were probably two different social sets of ritual in large

U-shaped ceremonial centers with two different audiencies, public-near/participants and public-distant/observers. And finally, a consideration of visibility suggests that public rites may have been of two types, which I call observational and processional. The arrangement of the built environment at La Galgada, Cardal, Garagay emphasizes the visual impact of the central mound, creating a steep face which fills the angle of vision. In contrast, the step-like arrangements of Las Aldas and Salinas de Chao diminish the relative difference between the viewer and the focal point of the structure. At Las Aldas in particular, the strong axial alignment of stairways, portals, and circular courts suggests a ritual environment characterized by processions. Thus, roughly contemporary, monumental ceremonial structures appear to have had quite different ritual functions.

Andean ritual architecture exhibits some marked continuities – the importance of ancestor and culture hero worship, the distinction between processional and observational rites – which bear further examination. One key transitional phase occurred during the Late Archaic/Early Formative (ca. 1800–1400 BC) when small ritual constructions were placed on top of mounds. It may be that the architecture reflects the transformation of the initial, preliminal phases of rite into a more visible, public spectacle, while the liminal stages remained basically the same. In short, codified social differences develop at this time which were expressed and reiterated to the entire social group, a social pattern which continued in various manifestations for the next 3,300 years.

Andean ritual architecture also exhibits some marked differences from religious constructions elsewhere. Unlike the Old World temple, Andean ritual architecture does not fall within the tradition of "the house of god." There is no Andean evidence which suggests, as Eliade (1959: 58) contended, that "religious architecture simply took over and developed the cosmological symbolism already present in the structure of primitive habitations." Rather than an elaboration of domestic structures, Andean religious architecture represents a separate branch of architectural development with its origins deep in prehistory. Nor were Andean monumental constructions uniform examples of the *omphalos*, as Wheatley (1971: 429) has argued, symbolic centers "with their pyramids, temples and shrines were raised towards the heavens, the better to facilitate communication with the divine." Andean ritual architecture was more complex than that, and the religious experiences of four millennia resist glib generalities, as the analyses have shown.

But at another level of abstraction, Wheatley (1971: 477–478) offers a profound insight into the relationship between rite and the development of complex societies which seems directly applicable to the Andes:

> But, validating the augmented autonomy resulting from each institutional adaptation [in the development of urbanism], providing the expanded ethical framework capable of encompassing the transformation from ascriptive, kin-oriented groups to stratified, territorially based societies, and from reciprocative to superordinately redistributive economic integration, was a religious symbolization which itself was becoming more highly differentiating

and developing, in Weber's terms, more highly rationalized formulations. The material expression of the symbolization of "the general order of existence" was the ceremonial center, which afforded a ritual paradigm of the ordering of social interactions at the same time as it disseminated the values and inculcated the attitudes necessary to sustain it. In other words it projected images of cosmic order on to the plane of human experience, where they could provide a framework for social action.

It is this communicative potential of ritual architecture which is so important in early Andean societies, and it remains important for the balance of Peruvian prehistory. But over time, as the internal divisions of Andean societies became greater and more codified, the role of monumental constructions also changed, developments which are explored in the analysis of the architecture of social control.

5

The architecture of social control: theory, myth, and method

To establish a government is an essay in world creation.

Eric Voeglin, *Order and History*

The Panopticon may be one of the true oddities of architectural history, but it was more than a mere curio. The model prison was designed by Jeremy Bentham (1748–1832), the British Utilitarian philosopher who unsuccessfully promoted his plan for twenty years, spending a small fortune in the process (Evans 1982: 195–197). Bentham was primarily concerned with the nature of government and the justice of punishment, and, for that reason, a pioneer of prison reform, though a somewhat quirky one. The hidden labyrinths of eighteenth-century prisons led to unobserved abuses, and Bentham's solution was the Panopticon (Figure 5.1) – a circular, glass-roofed structure, with cells along the outer ring all facing onto a central rotunda where a single guard could keep every prisoner under constant surveillance (Johnston 1973: 19–21). Bentham lavished a creator's prose on the project: "The building circular – A cage, glazed . . . The prisoners in their cells, occupying the circumference, the inspectors concealed . . . from the observation of the prisoners: hence the sentiment of a sort of omnipresence . . . One station in the inspection part affording the most perfect view of every cell" (cited in Evans 1982: 195). Bentham's Panopticon was an architectural plan designed explicitly as a means of social control "to induce in the inmate a state of conscious and permanent visibility that assures the automatic functioning of power" (Foucault 1977: 201).

Omniscience was the key to Bentham's project. His sketch for the frontispiece of a book on the project (Evans 1982: 200) shows the trinity Justice, Mercy, Vigilence, under which there is a plan of the Panopticon and the lines of the 139th Psalm: "Thou art above my path, and above my bed, and spieth out all my way." Bentham's ideal was never realized completely, despite near-fanatical efforts on his part; only a handful of examples loosely based on the model were ever built (Johnston 1973).

Seeing humans as a *tabula rasa*, shaped by experience as they sought to gain pleasure and avoid pain, Bentham had a singular vision, as Evans (1982: 196) observes: "How could human behaviour, and through behaviour human existence as a whole, be controlled and made certain by design?" But what makes the Panopticon such a fascinating example – and its only reason for being in a book on Andean architecture – is the explicitness with which Bentham linked ideology, social control, and the built environment. Bentham's Panopticon was the physical expression of a complex ideological statement about the nature of humans, the need for punishment, and the role

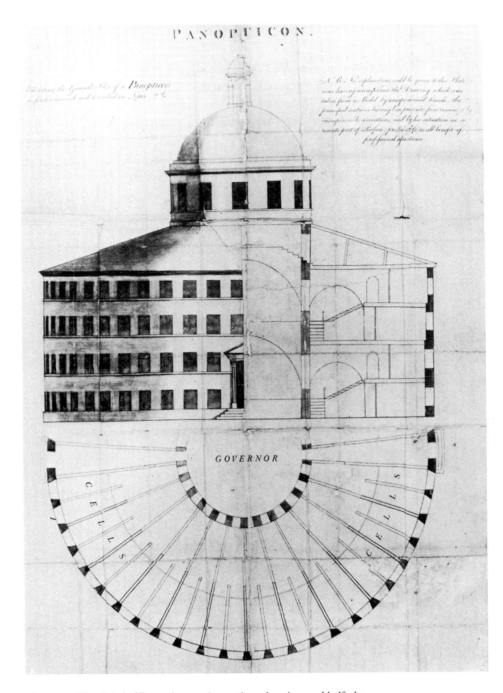

Figure 5.1 The Critchef Panopticon, 1787, section, elevation, and half-plan

of inspection. The Panopticon's specific architectural plan was not the obvious physical outcome of society's desire to control its members. Ideology was the linchpin.

Ideology: concepts and controversies

The ideological expressions of architecture are not easily discerned, particularly when we are looking at another culture's architectural tradition. This problem is not unique to anthropological approaches, as Diana Agrest (1991: 31) has recently noted:

> The specific relationship of architecture to ideology has been generally excluded from consideration in traditional architecture criticism . . . When the cultural dimension has been introduced, it has more often been as a simple explanation of architecture as "reflecting" a particular culture – the notion of style as the expression of the spirit of an age – than as a problem to be confronted from a consistent theoretical standpoint.

Perhaps ideology eludes consistency, as 150 years of debate might suggest (for recent reviews, see Eagleton 1991; Larrain 1979). Although first used by Destutt de Tracy in 1801 as a concept bright with Enlightenment positivism, the dark side of ideology was clearly presaged in the handbooks of governance written by Aristotle, Machiavelli, and Katilya. Eagleton (1991: 29–31) has listed a half-dozen definitions of ideology that progressively limit and sharpen the focus of the concept. Most broadly, ideology can refer to "the general material process of production of ideas, beliefs, and values of social life," while a less general definition views ideology as "the ideas and beliefs (whether true or false) which symbolize the conditions and life-experiences of a specific, socially significant group or class." A third definition more closely focuses on those ideas and beliefs that relate to "the promotion and legitimation of the interests of such [socially significant] social groups in the face of opposing interests." A fourth definition simply limits the third, by restricting ideology to the practice of a dominant social power. A fifth definition considers ideology as "the ideas and belief which help to legitimate the interests of a ruling group or class specifically by distortion and dissimulation." A sixth and final meaning "retains an emphasis on false or deceptive beliefs" but attributes them to "the material structure of society as a whole" and not just to a single, dominant class.

Eagleton's dispassionate taxonomy of definitions fails to capture the bitter debates over ideology, and just as well. Archaeologists have not escaped the maelstrom of debate as arguments have swirled around considerations of the causal priority of material dimensions (e.g., Athens 1977; Seagraves 1982 vs. Parker Pearson 1984; Kristiansen 1984), or the exercise of vulgar materialism (Friedman 1974). But the most consistent current in this literature is the role of ideology in legitimation; for example, a recent symposium on chiefdoms reached consensus on ideology "as the justification for developing political domination" (Earle 1991: 1). A brief, intentionally partisan review of this subject is presented by Conrad and Demerest (1984: 210–221), who offer useful distinctions between various Marxist approaches to ideology and cultural evolution. I think the authors correctly criticize the view that ideology only exists to legitimate class inequalities derived from the material forces of production; such a view dilutes ideology into a mere epiphenomenon.

But Conrad and Demerest dull their critique by confusing legitimation with centralization; they (1984: 219–220) argue that since the Aztec state was decentralized, ideology did not serve a legitimizing function – a curious piece of reasoning that ignores some classic ethnographic studies of political process. For example, Edmund Leach's *Political Systems of Highland Burma* (1954) is an explicit analysis of how shared ideology produces neither fission nor stability, but flux (Vincent 1990: 271). Conrad and Demerest's confusion stems from the idea that elites or centralized authorities have uncontested control over the means of shaping ideology, but that is seldom the case. Rather, as Gailey and Patterson (1987: 7) write: "The state . . . is not a homogeneous entity but a cluster of potentially conflicting priorities."

If ideology is defined as the social production of meaning, then it seems obvious that any number of institutions, groups, classes, clans, and – most importantly – individuals have the potential to create meaning. Clearly some social sectors will have marked advantages in the production of ideology, but the role of even disadvantaged individuals cannot be dismissed, as the examples of Jesus Christ, Karl Marx, and Wovoka sugggest. As populations increase, as factions crystallize, or as multi-ethnic communities develop, multiple sets of meanings can emerge and diverse meanings may be applied to the same symbol, creating the potential for discourse and dissent.

This diversity of meaning is discussed by Rasnake (1988) in his study of political dynamics, ritual, and symbolism in the canton of Yura, located in the arid Bolivian highlands southwest of Potosi. Rasnake provides (1988: 265–266) an insightful analysis of Max Weber's (1978) approach to power and legitimacy, paraphrasing Weber's position on "'domination' (as his *Herrschaft* is usually translated) – power resulting from a socially recognized position of leadership." Rasnake points out that although Weber recognized "all systems of authority have complex and mixed bases of legitimacy," Weber's emphasis on Western structures of power and authority led him to attend more to systems of centralized control, and "less with those cases in which decision-making is either more fragmented or more consensual than it is in the feudal, absolutist, or bureaucratic models he was developing." This leads to the treatment of socio-political structures as static schema, whereas Rasnake (1988: 269) argues:

> social institutions and the cultural precepts associated with them are precarious constructions, created in history by particular social entities. Principles of organization, values, and worldview exist only as they are socially reproduced in interaction and, we might add, in a particular context of power and property relations. Nor is this cultural construction a one-time thing; it must be enunciated again and again, to the current members of society and to future generations.

Shmuel Eisenstadt (1988: 239) – whose *Political Systems of Empires* (1963) remains a seminal analysis of political structures – takes a position similar to that enunciated by Rasnake, but explicitly in regard to ancient states and civilizations:

> The fragility of social structures and their organizational boundaries in very complex societies such as in ancient states and civilizations requires special

mechanisms of control and integration, regulative mechanisms that try to overcome the inherent instability in the construction of such boundaries. Among the most critical mechanisms are those concerned with processing information, settling disputes, and establishing public symbols and their ritualization (various ideological institutions and occasions).

Social control is established by a combination of organizational structures (e.g., bureaucracies, legal symbols) and systematic restructuring – through processing of socialization, communication, and public and semi-public rituals.

Returning to Eagleton's definitions, I have decided to employ the first and most general definition of "ideology" with the important caveat that more specific characteristics are matters for empirical determination. Following Eagleton (1991: 28–29), I use ideology to refer to "the material process of production of ideas, beliefs, and values in social life," but a sphere of cultural life which "involves the relations between these signs and processes of political power." I am not denying that ideology is used to legitimate the inequalities of power; I spend most of this chapter arguing precisely that point. But, it seems to me, the relationships between ideology and power are empirical matters, not a priori ones. Thus, for example, any number of nineteenth-century utopian groups exhibited specific ideologies, ideologies designed to decrease inequality in the distribution of wealth and power (Erasmus 1977).

Ideology is a major tool in the creation of legitimacy, in the justification of power relationships. In small-scale societies, the process of legitimation is dynamic and unstable for a variety of reasons, not the least being the relatively equal access which competing social sectors may have to instruments of ideology. And yet, stable patterns also emerge as specific ideological tenets become so pervasive that they shape the cultural reality of a particular historic moment. And this forms the cornerstone of any historical analysis, as Marx (cited in Larrain 1979: 42) observed: "Men make their own history, but they do not make it just as they please; they do not make it under circumstances chosen by themselves, but under circumstances directly encountered, given and transmitted from the past."

Ideology and the built environment
At least at some times and in some places, ideological circumstances are expressed in spatial relationships of the constructed environment. An explicit archaeological formulation of this *problematique* is Mark Leone's (1984) work on historic landscapes. He writes:

> Ideology's function is to disguise the arbitrariness of the social order, including the uneven distribution of resources, and it reproduces rather than transforms society.
>
> Ideology takes social relations and makes them appear to be resident in nature or history, which makes them apparently inevitable. So that the way space is divided and described, including the way architecture, alignments,

and street plans are made to abide by astronomical rules, or the way gardens, paths, rows of trees, and vistas make a part of the earth's surface appear to be trained and under the management of individuals or classes with certain ability or learning, is ideology.
(Leone 1984: 26)

Similarly, and in the same volume, Tilley (1984) briefly sketches a series of notions linking power and the cultural presentation of time and space as the physical expressions of legitimizing ideology. Tilley suggests that the projection of authority "into the past and onto a mystical place . . . in a manner in which the principles underlying social relationships" appears timeless, inevitable, and unquestionable. This, coupled with the physical separation of legitimizing rites from daily activities, "creates a legitimate form of inequality in an imaginary world dislocated from ordinary experience." Architecture and other objects,

> are affected by their place in the space of others. Presence, position and absence or "negative presence" are of crucial importance. Places stand out and are vested with meanings and significance. They are far more than merely locational nodes in a spatial lattice. Places exist through time and in space, and sacred places, such as the megaliths, command awe and respect and this is an obvious reason for their monumentality.
> (Tilley 1984: 122)

Thus, there are general reasons to think that the ideology of legitimacy may have an architectural expression, but I want to focus on a specific set of archaeological cases. In the following analysis, I examine how major social differences were expressed in Andean society with a particular focus on the public architecture of the Chimu state, a Late Intermediate Period polity of the North Coast. The starting point for this analysis is a brief statement made by John Rowe (1948: 47) linking social stratification with North Coast ideology: "Evidently differences between social classes were great and immutable on the north coast, for the creation legend told at Pacasmayo relates that two stars gave rise to the kings and nobles and two others to the common peoples." In the following I examine this legend and other creation myths to understand more about the ideology and architectural expression of social differences in Andean societies.

Andean ideologies of separation

Cosmogonies "give a rhetorical, stylistic and imaginative portrayal of the meaning of the creation of the world" (Long 1987: 94), and this is certainly true of the creation myths recorded for northern Peru (for an overview see MacCormack 1991; Rostworowski 1983). Although there is a debate about whether specific tales of creation reflect historical facts (Donnan 1990; Moseley 1990), structural principles (Zuidema 1990b), contested narratives (Urton 1990: 5–10), or scraps of history cloaked in legend (Rowe 1948), for my purpose the historical accuracy of a creation myth is less important than the social principles it expresses. When that myth expresses a world view that appears to be prehispanic and non-Incaic, then it may contain statements about the ideology of social differences in late prehispanic North Coast societies.

As Leone (1984: 26) has observed: "Ideology takes social relations and makes them appear to be resident in nature or history, which makes them apparently inevitable." One clear example of this is the creation myth recorded by Antonio Calancha in Pacasmayo (1977 [1638]: 1244). My translation follows:

> It was said in the treatise of Pachacamac that these Indians of the flatlands and seacoasts were certain (and many believe it today) that their initial masses and founding fathers were not Adam and Eve, but four stars, that two gave birth to the Kings, Lords, and nobles, and the other two to the commoners, the poor, and the indentured, which – as the Faith we profess makes precise – are [actually the result of] the chances of this earth and not because it is thought that the rich and powerful are descendants of other beginnings than are the humble and poor, but they see the poor not as naturally equal but as the least valued of Fortune.

Calancha, always striving for a classical analogy, chose his words carefully, recalling the Roman deity, Fortune, who presided over the vagaries of life.

This oft-cited passage about the creation myth of Pacasmayo is wedged into a much larger discussion of celestial bodies and other phenomena worshiped by coastal peoples. A premier deity was the Moon, Si, worshiped at the huaca Sian, located near Guadelupe in Pacasmayo – "more powerful than the Sun because he does not appear at night" (Calancha 1977 [1638]: 1239) – who controlled the elements, protected crops, and caused sea storms, lightning, and thunder. The Sea, Ni, was given the richest offerings so he "would not drown them and would give them fish" (1977 [1638]: 1241) and Calancha refers to certain rocks called *alæcpong* (translated by Rowe [1948: 51] as "cacique stone"), worshiped by specific social units, *parcialidades* (Calancha 1977 [1638]: 1243). Further passages describe the honor given to Patá, the stars of Orion's Belt; the center star was a thief, held by the flanking stars to be eaten by vultures sent by the Moon, a punishment analogous to depictions in Moche art (Donnan 1978: 94–95). Additional paragraphs discuss the annual cycle as measured by the waxing and waning of Fur, the Pleiades (Calancha 1977 [1638]: 1244).

Calancha recorded a second myth which describes the separate creations of different social classes from three eggs (Hellbom 1963: 77). What makes this creation myth particularly important is that Calancha prefaces the tale with a "pre-sociological" discussion about the representativeness of his information; he states explicitly that the myth was registered by more than a thousand witnesses polled in six *informaciones* in the coastal valleys of Huarmey, Huara, Supe, Barranca, Aucayama, Huacho, Vegueta, Carabaillo to Pachacama, and "the peoples along the coast . . . to Arica."

The legend tells the story of the birth of Vichama and the struggles for divine supremacy between the Sun and Pachacamac (Calancha 1977 [1638]: 930–935). Vichama's mother was one of the two first people created by Pachacamac, who failed to create any food for the people. After her spouse died, Vichama's mother was condemned to wander the coast eating the roots of thorny herbs, until she pleaded with the Sun for either help or an end to her misery. The Sun impregnated her with a beam of light, thinking that a son would help her gather food. The child was born in four days and the mother thanked the Sun. Pachacamac – angered at the honor being given to his father, the Sun – stole the newborn from his mother and slaughtered the boy, his own half-brother.

Pachacamac decided to rectify his initial oversight and created food. He took the dead boy's teeth, which became maize, and planted the ribs and bones, which became manioc. Pieces of flesh were planted and became pepinos and pacays. In the fertility of the valleys the plants flourished, "but this abundance did not please the mother, because in every fruit there was a remembrance of her son."

The mother's sadness and tears continued and were heard by the Sun, who gave her another son, a beautiful boy named Vichama. She kept Vichama wrapped in cloth to muffle his cries and protect him from Pachacamac. Growing to maturity, Vichama wanted to follow the path of his father, the Sun, and so, with his mother's assent, Vichama began to wander the world.

But soon after Vichama left, Pachacamac killed Vichama's mother. Pachacamac cut her body into pieces and fed it to the vultures and condors, and "her hairs and bones he held hidden in the waves of the sea." He also "created men and women that possess the world and he named those that govern Curacas and Caziques."

Vichama returned to his home in Vegueta, found his mother had been killed, and flew into a white-hot rage of revenge. He found his mother's bones, rearranged them, and gave life to her. She pleaded with Vichama not to annihilate the God Pachacamac, since Pachacamac was still his half-brother. For all his rage, Vichama listened to his mother and confined Pachacamac to the sea near the place where the shrine of Pachacamac is located. Vichama turned his rage on the curacas of Vegueta who had permitted his mother's murder and with the Sun's help the curacas were turned to stone.

But once his anger cooled, Vichama decided the caciques' punishment was too severe. Calancha writes:

> The Sun and Vichama were unable to undo the punishment, but they wanted to repay the injustice, and they determined to give the honor of gods to the Curacas and Caciques, to the nobles and the valiant, and taking them to the coasts and seashores, they placed some there to be worshiped as huacas, and others they put in the sea, these are the rocky points, the breakers, and the reefs, who are given the titles of gods and who each year are offered silver leaf, chicha and aromatic woods.

The narrative continues:

> Vichama seeing the world without men and the Sun and the huacas with none to worship them, prayed to his father the Sun to make new men, and the Sun sent three eggs, one gold, one silver, and one copper. From the

golden egg came the Curacas, the Caciques, and the nobles they call segunda personas and principales; from the silver one came their women; and from the copper egg the common people, that today are called Mitayos, and their women and families.

(Calancha 1977 [1638]: 934–935)

In short, the celestial origins of social stratification are presented as basic cosmogonic texts, as inviolable as the movement of the moon and stars. These widespread, widely held creation myths which Antonio Calancha recorded are potent examples of the ideology of social differences.

Southward and into the sierra, the Augustinians (1865 [1560]) recorded a creation myth from Huamachuco that tells the tale of Catequil. Described as "first among many evils and the most feared and honored idol that there was in all of Peru, adored and revered from Quito to Cusco," Catequil was one of two sons. Their mother Cautaguan was one of the original *guachemines*, the ancient ones who lived in Huamachuco. Cautaguan's brothers kept her tightly closed in her house and out of public view. But one day when her brothers were gone, an interloper appeared. He was Guamansuri, sent to Earth from the sky by Ataguju. Guamansuri went to Cautaguan and "with entreaties and trickeries he had her and impregnated her. And as her brother *guachemines* saw her pregnant and knew what happened [*supieron el negocio*, lit., "knew the business"] and that Guamansuri had been the deflowerer and aggressor, they . . . burned him and ground him into dust; and the Indians say that the dust goes up into the sky and there he stays with Ataguju" (Augustinians 1865 [1560]: 22).

A few days later Cautaguan gave birth to two eggs, but died during childbirth. Her brothers threw the eggs on a garbage heap, but the eggs broke open and out came two screaming boys. A woman took them and raised them, and their names were Piguerao and Catequil.

Catequil went to where his mother had died and brought her back to life. She gave Catequil two slings which had belonged to Guamansuri. Catequil used these slings to avenge his father, slaying all of the guachemines; some of the slingstones fell to the ground where they remained. With his father's enemies dead, Catequil went up to the sky and said to Ataguju:

"Now the land is free and the *guachemines* are dead and thrown out from the land, and now I beg that you create Indians to live and work the land." And because of the strong deeds he had done, Ataguja sent Catequil to the hill they call Guacat [from *guaca* + *catequil*?] above Sancta Cruz that is where now exists the town of la Parrilla [today's Santa] between Trujillo and Lima (in which hill I have been because there they make many offerings of chicha and cloth and other things which the Indians offer in memory of their Creator) and they [*sic*] went to this hill and they dug with golden and silver foot-plows and hoes, and from there they took out the Indians who multiplied and from them were multiplied everyone; and that is how it was done and from there was their beginning.

(Augustinans 1865 [1560]: 23; translation mine)

The Augustinians concluded that Catequil was greatly feared. Catequil threw lightning bolts and thunder with his sling, and the Indians worshiped him because Catequil could kill them as he had the guamachemines.

The Augustinians also related that three shrines in Huamachuco were associated with this culture hero. Located on the three peaks of a mountain called Porcon, 4 leagues from Huamacucho, the shrines were called Apocatequil, Mamacatequil, and Piguero, associated with the hero, his mother, and brother. Below these shrines "was a great pueblo for the service" of the shrine of Apocatequil with "great houses of worship and many haciendas and five priests, two mayordomos, and many other people and servants; it was where, more than anywhere else in that land, the devil spoke" (Augustinians 1865 [1560]: 25).

The myth of Catequil is markedly different from the Pacasmayo cosmogony recorded by Calancha, but they share certain structural elements. In both cases there is a pair of progenitors, and a mother's death figures in both the legend of the *alæcpong* and the myth of Catequil. Lightning and thunder are associated with deities, although in Pacasmayo these celestial explosions were associated with the moon rather than a personified culture hero as in Huamachuco. Arguably the differences outweigh the parallels, but the fundamental similarity of the accounts is common to all cosmogonic myths: they are "a distinctive expression of a narrative that states a paradigmatic truth" (Long 1987: 94).

This is also true of the dynastic myth of the North Coast, the legend of Ñamlap. Recorded by Miguel Cabello Valboa in 1586, the legend has been glossed by Means (1931: 51–53), Rowe (1948) and Donnan (1990: 243–245), all of whom were primarily interested in the accuracy of the dynastic succession recorded in the tale (for an alternative interpretation see Netherly 1990). Rather than repeat the tale again, I simply will sketch the text drawing on Cabello Valboa's account, although I will emphasize those details which shed light on social stratification and the ideology of separation.

The tale begins in a mythic past "in very ancient, uncountable times" when Ñamlap, the "father of the Company, man of great valor and quality," led a flotilla of balsas to northern Peru. Accompanied by his principal wife, Ceterni, his concubines, forty courtiers, and a great company, Ñamlap landed at the mouth of the Lambayeque. With this retinue of noble courtiers – who watched over Ñamlap's food, drink, face paints, and royal costume – Ñamlap's person and household were "adorned and authorized." Ñamlap and his retinue took land in the lower valley, and half a league from the ocean established palaces at the place called Chot, where he enshrined the idol Yampallec, a green stone carved in Ñamlap's own image. Ñamlap died after a long life of peaceful rule and numerous progeny, but so his vassals would not know that death had jurisdiction over him ("porque no entendiessen sus vassallos que tenia la muerte jurisdicion sobre el"), Ñamlap was secretly buried in the palace where he had lived. It was announced throughout the land that Ñamlap, because of his great virtue, had taken wing and disappeared, escaping death.

Ñamlap's descendants multiplied and spread through the land, and his throne was inherited by his eldest son, Cium, who, in turn, begat twelve sons, each fathers of large families. Having lived and ruled many years, Cium was put in an underground crypt where he died, so that all took him for an immortal and a god.

After nine rulers, Fempellec succeeded to the throne, only to commit a grave error. Fempellec (for obscure reasons) attempted to move the green stone idol, Yampallec, from the Huaca Chot where Ñamlap had placed it. After trying to do this without success, Fempellec was visited by the Devil disguised as a beautiful woman. Due to Satan's trickery and Fempellec's lust, Fempellec slept with the woman and as soon as the union was consummated it began to rain – a thing rarely seen on the coast. The rain lasted thirty days and was followed by a year of sterility and hunger. The priests of the huacas and the principales, knowing of the grave sin that Fempellec had committed, decided to make him pay a penalty equal to that suffered by his people, and they took him and bound him and cast him into the depth of the sea (Cabello Balboa 1951 [1586]: 327–329).

The Ñamlap legend contains a number of fascinating elements that illuminate indigenous concepts of leadership. First, there is the mythic origin of the ruling dynasty whose control over Lambayeque is set in the timeless past and whose hegemony is uncontested. Second, the roles of royal servitors are very much focused on the person of the leader, not divided among different types of administrative responsibilities, but their object is to adorn and authorize the ruler's person and house. Third, there is the theme of separation; Ñamlap and his successor are buried away from the people, a physical separation that marks their divinity by hiding their mortality. And finally, there is this interesting relationship between proper ritual and natural well-being. The catalyst of cataclysm is Fempellec's consorting with the Devil, but his fundamental error is failing to show proper respect to the huacas. Consequently disaster falls on the land in the form of an El Niño, and the priests and lords hold Fempellec personally responsible. The disaster Fempellec brought to his people justified his execution by drowning in the depths of Ni. The violation of proper ritual brought disaster.

Proper ritual is a key theme in another scrap of North Coast dynastic legend, the *Anonymous History of Trujillo*, translated by Rowe (1948) and Kosok (1965). A mythic history of the founding of the royal lineage of Chimor, the fragmented beginnings of the myth start with the arrival of Taycanmayo on balsa log rafts from southern Ecuador. Eventually Taycanmayo founded the dynasty which ruled Chimor, but initially he shut himself up in a house for a year where he practiced his ceremonies and learned the local languages. He used certain yellow powders in these ceremonies that, the Anonymous Historian asserts, were well known in southern Ecuador, as was the style of his cotton loincloth. He married with local families, and took the name Chimo Capac, a title meaning Great Lord of Chimor, which nonetheless incorporates a Quechua word.

These four myths consist of two creation myths and two dynastic legends. They do not represent the corpus of Andean myth that presumably existed in north central Peru; they simply are four available examples. They lack the complex, "biblical" structure of the text from Huarochiri (Salomon and Urioste 1991), nor are they surrounded by multiple layers of mythohistory like the myth of Pacariqtambo (Urton

1990). Instead, these accounts are fragmentary, isolated, and filtered through translation and transcription. But they are what we have.

At least three themes are notable in these legends. First, there are the unique origins of different social groups. In the Pacasmayo legend there is the explicit statement that the great divide between elite and commoner originated at the beginning of time. But no less timeless are the arrivals of founders of the dynasties of Lambayeque and Chimor; these events are also placed in the mythic past. A commoner in North Coast society was separated from the elites not solely by secularized class distinctions, but by the legends of kingship and the myths of creation.

Second, there are strong suggestions of the relationship between proper ritual and natural phenomena. The gods ruled over different natural phenomena – lightning bolts, thunder, and storms – but they could be placated with offerings and sacrifices. Proper ritual was a leader's responsibility, although lords and priests shared these tasks. When the proper worship was violated and natural disaster resulted, any steps could be taken to redress the wrong, including the sacrifice of a wicked king.

But finally, there are interesting references to physical separation and the status it implies. Cautaguan's brothers shut her up in a house to preserve her virginity, Taycanmayo remained indoors for a year while performing rites and solidifying his power, and Ñamlap and Cium were shut up in their crypts, hidden from sight, so that their divine status could not be scrutinized by mere mortals. In different ways and for different reasons, the figures in the cosmogonic myths of northern Peru are kept separated, placed behind walls built with human hands. It would seem that physical separation implies special status, an inference arrived at, on quite different grounds, by a number of archaeologists who have worked on the coast of Peru.

Archaeological approaches to spatial patterns

Archaeologists working in coastal Peru have discussed the cultural significance of spatial patterns in both monumental and residential architecture, specifically by considering access patterns as a medium of social control. For example, in writing about Aspero, Feldman (1985: 85) describes access to the moundtop structure of Huaca de los Ídolos as a "pattern of restricted access" which "can be interpreted as further evidence of differential access to, and control of, ceremonial/religious activity by a small group of people" (see also Feldman 1987).

In their excavations at the Initial Period/Early Horizon site of Pampa de las Llamas-Moxete, Pozorski and Pozorski (S. Pozorski and T. Pozorski 1986; T. Pozorski and S. Pozorski 1988) identified clear evidence that access was limited to the room group on top of Huaca A. In addition to raised thresholds, gates, and bar-closures, the overall architectural plan appears designed to restrict and monitor access to a series of possible storerooms (S. Pozorski and T. Pozorski 1986: 387–390).

Fung Pineda notes a similar pattern at the large U-shaped ceremonial structures of the Central Coast. She writes:

> Access to the upper levels is through a single entrance from this court, via a stairway built along the main site axis. Use of the stairway was restricted: at Garagay, for example, there is no trace of wear on its fine coating of clay . . .

> In all, the marked symmetry of such complexes reveals a considered handling
> of space, aimed at controlling access to the sacred enclosures, through single
> entrances leading to areas which are increasingly elevated, restricted, and
> reserved.
>
> (Fung Pineda 1988: 91)

Occasionally, the *absence* of internally divided space is thought to reflect the lack
of major social divisions between insiders and outsiders. For example, Fung Pineda
(1988: 72–73) describes the relatively open-plan El Paraíso, Chillon Valley: "Absence
of distinctions in the allocation of space and in the architectural form of the principal buildings . . . seems to reflect a social order free from conditions likely to enhance
hierarchical differences, or the power struggle these would engender."

In the Lambayeque Valley, the use of space to restrict access is documented in both
residential and public architecture during the Moche V occupation at Pampa Grande
(ca. AD 600–700). Shimada (1978) argues that patterns of corridors physically articulated workers and workshops. Anders (1981) describes the storage facilities at Pampa
Grande, characterizing access to these rooms as restricted. The main body of Huaca
Grande, located in the central sector of the site, is topped by a room complex interpreted as an elite residence (Haas 1985). Access to the upper surfaces of the massive
platform mound was via a ramp/corridor that passed three small interior walls defined
as "checkpoints" (Haas 1985: 397). Once the top of the main huaca was reached,
access within the room complex was "complicated and almost always indirect" (Haas
1985: 404), with most doorways consisting of baffled entrances. At a more general
level, Shimada (1981: 411) outlines the significance of access patterns in defining religious architecture and as "an effective device for symbolic communication."

One of the most explicit analyses of architecture and access is Bawden's (1982b)
study of the site of Galindo in the Moche Valley. Bawden has identified distinct
sectors in the site, including non-elite barrios that are separated from the rest of the
settlement by walls (for an alternative hypothesis see J. Topic and T. Topic 1987; T.
Topic 1991). Bawden (1982b: 179) writes:

> The extensive residential barrio occupied by the lowest social stratum of the
> population is not only physically removed from other residential and
> corporate portions of the settlement, but confined to these peripheral
> locations by massive artificial partitions. The high wall that bounds [this
> barrio] has few formal openings. The access ways are narrow, enabling
> regulation of movement from the hillside residential area to the centers of
> economic activity and corporate administration on the plain below. All
> evidence points to this wall as forming a device for social control whereby a
> large segment of the population was barred from free access to the sources of
> community wealth and status.

This issue becomes paramount in studies of the Chimu capital of Chan Chan
(Klymyshyn 1982, 1987; Moseley 1975b; Moseley and Day 1982; Moseley and
Cordy-Collins 1990), where considerations of access are a major analytical theme. At

its heydey the Chimu state (AD 900–1470) controlled a 1,000 km section of the Pacific coast (Mackey 1987; Rowe 1948), a territory governed from Chan Chan, a large pre-hispanic city with an urban core covering some 6 square kilometers and inhabited by an estimated 20,000–40,000 people (Topic and Moseley 1983: 157). The built environment of Chan Chan was dominated by ten large enclosures thought to be associated with the kings of Chimor. The royal compounds, or ciudadelas, are separated from the rest of Chan Chan by battered adobe walls up to 9 meters high, and contain plazas, royal burial platforms, rooms thought to be storerooms, and distinctive three-sided constructions called U-shaped rooms or audiencias. The complexity of the plans suggest that controlling access was an important aspect of architectural design in the Chan Chan ciudadelas. For example, Day's (1982) discussion of the ciudadelas of Chan Chan indicates that restricted entrances, maze-like corridors, and associated U-shaped rooms were designed to prohibit and regulate access to storerooms. Day (1982: 65) writes: "The overwhelming concern with security expressed in the controlled access, high walls and tortuous corridors of *ciudadelas* indicates a profound social and economic gulf between royalty and the rest of the populace."

Kolata (1990: 140–142) argues the architectural patterns of the ciudadelas reflect an increasing separation – "a heightened 'social distance' between the king and his subjects." Contending the central sector of the ciudadelas were the residential areas directly associated with the Chimu kings, Kolata posits that these areas become increasingly isolated from other activity areas within the ciudadelas. This separation between royal residence and other administrative activities, "was a direct spatial expression and symbol of increased social differentiation between the king and his subjects. In fact, the physical boundary that was being drawn between the central sector and the rest of the palace enclosure resulted from the evolution of a very special institution: divine kingship" (Kolata 1990: 140). Kolata further suggests that this institution is not reflected in the earliest ciudadelas at Chan Chan, but instead crystallized at ca. AD 1350–1370. "It was at this time that access to the central sector was severely restricted. It finally had become inviolate to the public, it was the locus of the sacred" (Kolata 1990: 141).

Each of these approaches underscores the manner in which hypothesized changes in socio-political divisions were reflected in architectural patterns, particularly access patterns. William Conklin (1990) takes a slightly different tack, suggesting that the gulf between ruler and ruled was not just reflected in the ciudadela walls, but that the architectural patterns symbolically reinforced and created these social divisions. He writes:

> In Chan Chan, the height and thickness of the surrounding compound walls vastly exceed any security threat. Though the walls have some precedent in Moche architectural traditions (i.e., they have a memory base and the walls have security as a functional excuse), the explanation of their scale lies in their intention as expressions of power and in their roles as creators of an image.
> (Conklin 1990: 63)

In the parenthesis, Conklin alludes to a trio of concepts he proposes for understanding architectural meaning: memory, function, and image. *Memory* refers to continuities in "architectural forms that continue to hold power even though their meaning shifted through time" (Conklin 1990: 44). *Function* retains its colloquial and archaeological sense of the way in which a building and its component spaces are used. The final concept, *image*,

> refers not to a technical record such as a photograph or a drawing, but to that which remains in the mind of the viewer after he has turned away from the actual scene. Image refers to that interpreted and censored record remaining after vision itself has been completed. Image is both more and less than a photographic record and involves a memory of associated emotions and impressions as well as a memory of form.
> (Conklin 1990: 45)

But what are we to make of this? How are we to take this cluster of ideas about access patterns, social divisions, and the role of ideology and convert it into a set of archaeological analyses that are verifiable and explicit?

Three points seem reasonably clear. First, on general theoretical grounds we can argue that ideology, broadly defined, may buttress political power by providing a rationale for legitimacy. Second, the coastal cosmogonic myths suggest that social divisions were viewed as eternal verities and that these social divisions may be expressed in the physical separation of ruler and ruled. Third, a significant number of archaeologists consider the relationship between access and social differences to be significant, usually arguing that architectural patterns reflect social changes, although specific architectural patterns may serve, as Conklin suggests, to reify and reinforce those social divisions.

But there remain some important issues of measurement and verification. For example, in each case cited above where the author discusses access patterns, the author views access as binary – it is either "restricted" or "open." Yet even a brief glance at the plans of sites like Huaca de los Ídolos, Aspero, Huaca Grande at Pampa Grande or Huaca A at Pampa de los Llamas-Moxeke, clearly indicates that there are significant differences in their access patterns, all of which have been categorized as restricted. Further, if, as Kolata hypothesizes, there were diachronic changes in the relative accessibility of certain spaces within the Chan Chan ciudadelas, how can we measure such changes? And finally, if, as Conklin suggests, the Chan Chan ciudadelas reflect the architectural "memory" of earlier prehispanic constructions, how can we discover, in other than an impressionistic manner, what those memories were of?

These three issues shape most of this chapter, where I turn to an analysis of public architecture of Chan Chan, other Chimu settlements, and their precursors. But before that analysis can proceed, I discuss the methodology and methods I use to explore the architecture of social control.

Methodology and methods

The following analyses assume that patterns in built spaces are culturally significant, and specifically that variations in access patterns reflect differences in the nature of the social order. Rigid restrictions in movement suggest societies in which certain social sectors can exert coercion, literally forcing others to stay away, while open spaces with few internal barriers may suggest a corresponding lack of strict social divisions. Any archaeologist – and probably any person – glancing at the small public structure at Las Gavilanes and then at the large walled compounds of Chan Chan could conclude that the societies which built these structures were separated by a chasm of social and political difference. Such an inference is almost certainly correct.

Yet it is always easier to define the extremes of a continuum than its gradations, which is the situation facing archaeologists working on Early Intermediate Period (AD 1–600), Middle Horizon (AD 600–900), and Late Intermediate Period (AD 900–1470) sites of the North Coast. The analytical problems are complex, involving the continuities between Moche, Lambayeque, and Chimu socio-political organization, diachronic changes within the evolving Chimu state, synchronic variations between core and periphery of Chimu territory, and the ways such processes are reflected in monumental architecture. As discussed above, archaeologists working at North Coast urban settlements have proposed a number of fairly subtle relationships between architectural patterns and socio-political organizations. Most of these posited relationships are based on "unformalized" observations and "reasonable" inferences, both completely legitimate activities. "Unformalized" observations involve direct inspection of architectural plans and intuitive recognition of notable patterns. There is nothing wrong with such approaches, but they have limits. First, architectural plans can be extremely complex (e.g., the 907 rooms of Ciudadela Laberinto), and even gross patterns may be overlooked. Second, the observed patterns tend to be intuitively obvious such as the orientations of buildings, principal architectural subdivisions, or major functional units, while more subtle relationships may be missed. Third, there is a tendency to search for architectural patterns previously deemed notable in the archaeological literature, which means that new patterns or variations on recognized patterns may be overlooked. Fourth, and following from the above, there is a tendency to treat variations as derivative from central patterns, forcing cases into normative molds. Such limits to unformalized observation shape lines of investigation that emphasize broad norms and leave fine-scaled variations unrecognized.

A final issue involves verification. "Seeing" patterns in an architectural plan entails replicating a procedure as a means of confirmation: Observer A notices a particular pattern in a plan, makes a statement about the relationship, and then Observer B inspects the plan, judging whether the suggested pattern exists. Inevitably Observer B's judgment is influenced by extraneous factors (such as Observer B's familiarity with the site or Observer A's reputation) which have nothing to do with architectural patterns in a prehistoric building.

The problem is the recognition of variation in a verifiable manner; it is a problem which archaeologists have debated for forty years (Ford 1954; Spaulding 1953, 1954). Much of that debate initially revolved around considerations of style, but the central issues are relevant to recognition of any class of patterning of material remains. Following Spaulding (1953, 1960, 1973, 1988), I consider that archaeological patterns are discovered not imposed, that one may investigate selected variables and temporarily ignore others as a means of advancing knowledge, and that this process must be well defined and transparent so that others can verify or reject knowledge claims. I am unconvinced that, simply because data are selected and viewed from various frames of reference, this makes the data "non-objective" (Hodder 1991: 35). And finally, one must note that the basic search for structure in archaeological data equally may serve quite different theoretical masters. Just to cite three ready examples published in a single volume of *Archaeological Method and Theory* (Schiffer 1992), archaeologists contend that patterns in data are discovered rather than created, even if they then interpret the patterns within Darwinian (Neff 1992), dialectical (Marquandt 1992), or cognitive (Whitley 1992) frameworks.

The following methods simplify complex architectural plans by selecting key, relevant variables such that patterns can be recognized and measured (for a discussion of pattern recognition see Washburn and Crowe 1988: 14–41). The problem, as Christopher Chippindale (1992: 257) has written, "is that a *pattern can always be found in any set whatever of characteristics that artifacts present*" (original emphasis). In the balance of this chapter, I explore evidence for structure in architectural plans which relate to prehistoric access patterns, a focus justified on theoretical grounds and ethnohistoric evidence on Andean ideology of social differences. The analysis is derived from an explicit – though nascent – archaeological theory linking access patterns and social control. The inquiry is implemented with a small set of analytical methods. No single method illuminates every analytic question, just as no single tool is good for every task. Even within a relatively focused field like architectural patterns of access, different methods highlight different relationships, and the methods used form two groups, access graphs and route graphs.

Access Graphs and Indices

One approach to understanding architectural patterns is to reduce a plan of interconnected rooms to an access graph, a standardized drawing in which spaces are represented by points and their connections by linking lines. The general relevance of graph theory to anthropological problems has been reviewed by Hage (1979), but the application of graph theory to architecture is most commonly associated with *The Social Logic of Space* by Hillier and Hanson (1984), although it was preceded by the writings of Steadman (1976, 1983). The access plans (also called gamma maps) have a number of properties (Figure 5.2). First, they ignore the differences in the size of rooms, instead emphasizing their interconnections. Second, the access graphs may be "justified" (Hillier and Hanson 1984: 149–150), i.e. each space has a depth value defined as the number of rooms one must pass through to get from a given, initial reference point. For example, if from the front door of a house, you could only get to the bathroom by passing through (1) the living room, (2) a hallway, (3) a bedroom, before entering (4) the bathroom, the bathroom would have a depth of 4. The depth of any room could be compared to any other room and its relative depth assessed.

A third property of access graphs is they can form different configurations. For example, Hillier and Hanson (1984: 148–149) describe forms in terms of two

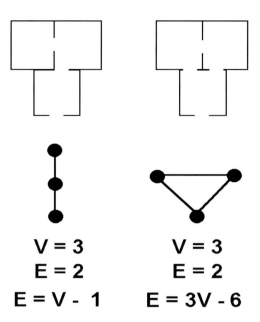

Figure 5.2 Access patterns for two three-room plans. "V" equals "vertices," "E" equals "edges"

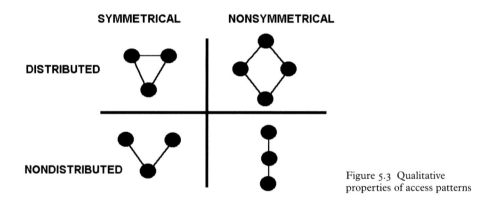

Figure 5.3 Qualitative properties of access patterns

nominal variables, symmetry and distributedness (Figure 5.3). Thus graphs are *symmetric* if *a:b* is the same as *b:a* with regard to the outside point; in other words if access to *b* is not controlled by *a*. Graphs are *distributed* if there is more than one way to get from *a* to *b*, including passing through *c*. Similarly, a graph which is characterized by large numbers of interconnected rooms is said to exhibit *ringiness*, while a symmetric, non-distributed graph is said to be *tree-like* and a non-symmetric, non-distributed graph is *chain-like*.

These diagrams allow for visual comparisons of different access patterns. One successful application is Foster's (1989) analysis of changes in Early Iron Age vs. Middle Iron Age residential structures in Scotland; there is a marked increase in the size, depth, and asymmetry of the later structures. The difference is notable at a glance, leading Foster (1989: 49) to suggest that the change reflects a social order that

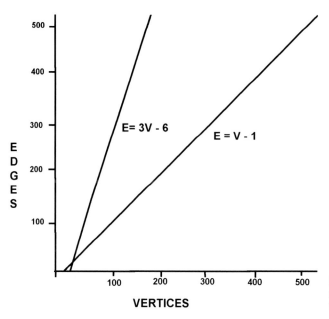

E
D
G
E
S

E= 3V - 6

E = V - 1

VERTICES

Figure 5.4 Maximum and minimum slopes for edges and vertices in a network

"required strict control in order to be both established and maintained." In a similar approach, Brewster-Wray (1983) devised a network graph for the plan of the Moraduchayuc sector of the site of Huari, pointing out the similarity between different subgraphs representing room clusters and suggesting that rooms of different depths had different functions, and in a related study Isbell et al. (1991: 37–38) use simple network graphs to make inferences about room functions. Chiswell (1988, 1989) applied network graphs to search for repetitive components in the plans of Pacatnamú. In each case, inspection of access graphs produced insights unnoticed in basic architectural plans.

But a point is quickly reached when descriptive terms are unwieldly and inspection is insufficient. A set of descriptive measures and concepts borrowed from graph theory (Steadman 1976, 1983) and locational geography (Haggett et al. 1977: 313–324) enhances our abilities to inspect and compare. As noted above, *depth* is a useful measure, and we can compare the depths of individual spaces or the maximum, modal, or mean depths for the graph as a whole. We can count the number of rooms (called "vertices" in network graphs) and the number of connections (referred to as "edges") and describe the degree of interconnectedness of access within the structure. With these two counts we can establish the limits of access plans (Figures 5.2, 5.4). At one extreme, if each room opens onto one and only one other room, then there will be one less connection than the number of rooms or $E = V - 1$, and the result is a chain of rooms. In an ideal network, unconstrained by structural considerations, a completely interconnected network is expressed by the slope of $E = 3V - 6$ (Figure 5.4).

But in the real world it is impossible for all rooms to be connected directly, and thus the "actual maximum" slope will be less than $E = 3V - 6$. The "actual maximum" degree of interconnectedness is based on the number of wall segments representing the interfaces of adjacent rooms (see Steadman 1976 for discussion of the adjacency problem in architecture). This "actual maximum" is influenced by the shape of the room, the size of the rooms, and the difficulties of living in a three-dimensional world. For example, circular rooms do not pack as densely as rectangular rooms do (Chippindale 1992: 261; Flannery 1972) and have different levels of adjacency. Rooms of different sizes and perimeters also will have different potential levels of adjacency; for example, if one room in a five-room structure is twice the size of every other room, it will have a different potential adjacency from a structure with five equal-sized rooms. As the number of rooms increases, so does the divergence from $E = 3 V - 6$. A practical, though tedious, solution to the problem is simply to count the number of shared walls in a given plan, and then contrast that number with the number of connecting passages. As a caution, small differences in the relationship between E and V are probably insignificant, but large variations indicate distinctive organizations of space and access.

In addition to graphic presentations, access patterns can be expressed with various indices, each having a different property and measuring a slight difference in a network. The simplest index, the *beta index*:

$$b = \frac{E}{V}$$

measures the overall complexity of a graph. Tree-like and disconnected graphs tend to have beta indices less than 1.0, while as the number of edges (connections) increases the value approaches a maximum of 3.0 in planar graphs (Smith 1975: 284).

Networks may contain distinct subgraphs, and as the number of subgraphs increases the graph becomes more complicated. To characterize the overall complexity of the total graph, the *cyclomatic number* is given by:

$$N = E - V + G$$

where N is the cyclomatic number, E the number of edges, V the number of vertices and G the number of subgraphs. As the number of connections and complexity of a graph increase, the cyclomatic number increases also (Smith 1975: 282–283).

Another advantage of these measures and indices is that they can be used as a set of variables for comparing different buildings. One must avoid spurious relationships between non-independent variables (e.g., a high positive correlation between the vertices and the cyclomatic number is meaningless), but with minimal prudence these techniques are powerful methods for comparing the similarities and differences between prehistoric buildings, relationships not obvious by scrutinizing architectural plans.

Route maps
Access patterns may be expressed as routes and paths (Tabor 1976b), and a simple method is used below to examine paths in the sample of North Coast sites. It consists

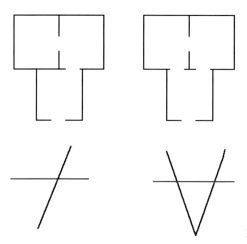

Figure 5.5 Route maps for two three-room plans

of a route map (Figure 5.5), which simply shows the architecturally formalized paths between spaces and not the spaces themselves. The route maps are used to examine Donnan's (1986c: 79) proposed dichotomy between right-hand and left-hand routes, specifically his suggestion that "the right hand route is consistently more elegant and leads to higher status that the route to the left." Although Donnan only proposed this pattern for Pacatnamú, the broad cross-cultural significance of right vs. left (see, for example, Needham 1973; Martin 1987) suggests such a pattern might occur at other sites and that organization of access patterns had a symbolic content in North Coast societies.

Summary of data

For Pampa Grande, Galindo, Pacatnamú, Chan Chan, Manchan, and Farfán, architectural data were recorded from the best available maps and plans (Bawden 1977; Donnan and Cock 1986; Keatinge and Conrad 1983; Mackey and Klymyshyn n.d.; Moseley and Mackey 1974; Shimada 1976). Blocked doorways were assumed to be post-occupation features. Sets of rooms with no clear connections to other rooms were treated as separate subgraphs. Walk-in wells, burial platforms and their associated rooms were excluded, as were areas where walls were poorly preserved. Only the main compounds of the ciudadelas (i.e., no annexes) were analyzed. The resulting access graphs are illustrated in Figures 5.6 to 5.19. Basic descriptive measures and indices derived from the access graphs are presented in Table 5.1.

Analysis of access patterns

The prehistoric constructions in the sample differ greatly in terms of raw values of the variables (Table 5.1); the number of edges ranges from 0 to 854, the number of vertices from 1 to 907, depth from 1 to 26, and number of subgraphs from 1 to 41. That variation makes the tight relationship between edges and vertices all the more surprising. As Figure 5.20 shows, there is a strong linear relationship between the two variables. This relationship is also expressed by beta indices that cluster tightly around 1.0 (Figure 5.21). Note that the strong linearity is not

Table 5.1. *Basic access graph data, selected North Coast sites*

Site	Unit	E	V	Depth	Subgraph	Beta	Cyclomatic
Pampa Grande	Huaca Grande	19	18	11	1	1.06	2
Galindo	Cercadura A	24	27	9	4	0.89	1
Galindo	Cercadura B	7	10	6	1	0.70	−2
Galindo	Cercadura C	23	22	6	1	1.05	2
Pacatnamú	Huaca 1	145	147	21	4	0.97	2
Chan Chan	Chayhuac	90	113	5	19	0.80	4
Chan Chan	Uhle	312	278	21	14	1.12	48
Chan Chan	Tello South	79	211	7	26	0.37	−106
Chan Chan	Tello S & N	260	423	9	41	0.61	−122
Chan Chan	Laberinto	854	907	15	13	0.94	−40
Chan Chan	Gran Chimu	416	411	13	9	1.01	14
Chan Chan	Velarde	506	534	26	3	0.95	−25
Chan Chan	Bandelier	298	300	24	4	0.99	2
Chan Chan	Rivero	282	278	17	7	1.01	11
Chan Chan	Tschudi	296	285	18	1	1.04	12
Farfán	Compound II	24	24	12	3	1.00	3
Manchan	Compound 11	19	17	8	1	1.12	3
Manchan	Compound 12	21	22	14	2	0.96	1
Manchan	Compound 13	0	1	1	1	0.00	1
Manchan	Compound 14	6	7	5	1	0.86	0
Manchan	Compound 15	11	10	7	1	1.10	2

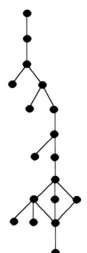

Figure 5.6 Access pattern for Huaca Grande, Pampa Grande

created by outliers. The basic pattern throughout the architectural sample is that each space is connected to one other space by a passageway. It is extremely rare to see examples of double entrances into specific spaces, although they occur in Chimu plazas.

In general, all the monumental constructions are extremely tree-like regardless of

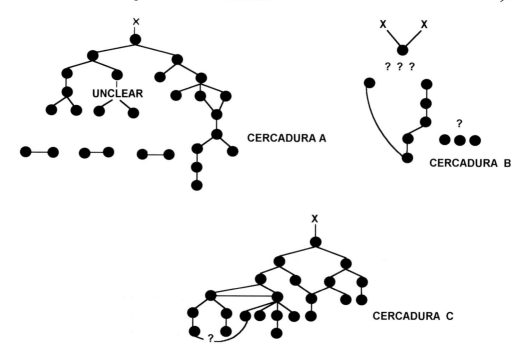

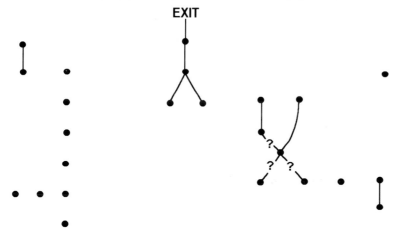

Figure 5.7 Access patterns for Cercaduras A, B, and C, Galindo

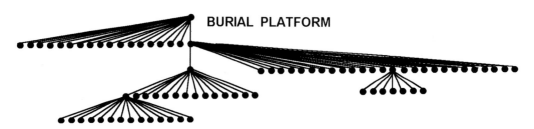

Figure 5.8 Access pattern for Ciudadela Chayhuac, Chan Chan

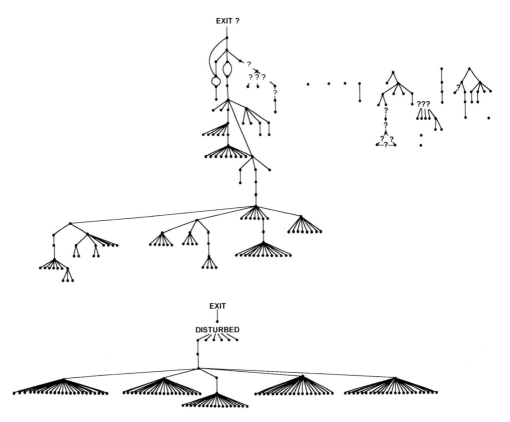

Figure 5.9 Access pattern for Ciudadela Uhle, Chan Chan

overall size, and this is illustrated by plotting beta indices against values for depth (Figure 5.22); in this case depth is a rough measure of the size of the constructions independent of the number of vertices or edges. The tight patterning of beta indices shows no relationship to depth, suggesting that the organization of access reflects cultural intent rather than numeric chance. The patterns evident in these data illuminate key questions about the development of North Coast monumental architecture.

North Coast monumental architecture: disruptions or continuities?
A recurrent issue in North Coast archaeology is whether the monumental constructions of Chan Chan represent an abruptly new architectural tradition or instead an elaboration of previous North Coast traditions. It is possible to partially address that question by examining access patterns for the Moche V sites of Pampa Grande and Galindo, and the Chan Chan ciudadelas.

The plot in Figure 5.20 suggests the Chan Chan ciudadelas represent a dramatic change in the development of monumental architecture on the North Coast, but a shift of scale not pattern. The Chan Chan ciudadelas reflect a massive increase in the number of spaces inside a single building; the smallest ciudadela (Chayhuac, V = 113) has four and a half times as many interior spaces as the largest cercadura at Galindo (Cercadura A, V = 27) and five times as many as Huaca Grande (V = 18).

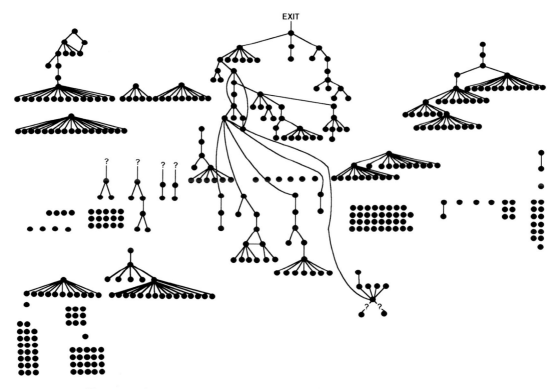

Figure 5.10 Access pattern for Ciudadela Tello, Chan Chan

It may be, as Bawden (1977: 408) suggests, that "the architectural and governmental innovations which emerged at Galindo led directly to the socio-political and ideological structure of Chan Chan" but only in a rather generic way. *The Chan Chan ciudadelas were not merely cercadura architecture writ large; the ciudadelas represent fundamental changes in the scale of public architecture.*

The ciudadelas also reflect a significant change in the organization of architectural space as measured by depth (see Figure 5.22). With the exception of Chayhuac and Tello, which are relatively shallow, the Chan Chan ciudadelas are significantly deeper than any of the Galindo cercaduras. For the other ciudadelas, access depth ranges between 13 (Gran Chimu) and 26 (Velarde), while the Galindo cercaduras range from 6 to 9 in depth. Note that this difference is not simply a matter of structure size, since if the Galindo cercaduras were organized as a chain of rooms with a single entrance, depth could have ranged from 9 to 26, i.e. V − 1. There are important differences between Galindo and Chan Chan in the organization of internal space. It was not a smooth development, but rather a dramatic threshold of change. The analysis of access patterns suggests that the Chimu state approached the architecture of social control differently from Moche. If, as Bawden (1977) suggests and Haas (1985) implies, Moche V architecture reflects the development of secular elites, an innovative pattern on the North Coast, those elites nevertheless differed in fundamental ways from the ruling elite of Chan Chan.

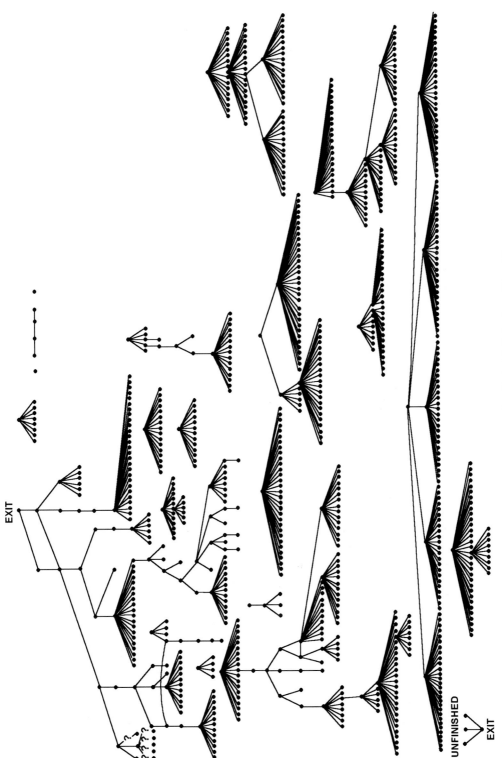

Figure 5.11 Access pattern for Ciudadela Laberinto, Chan Chan

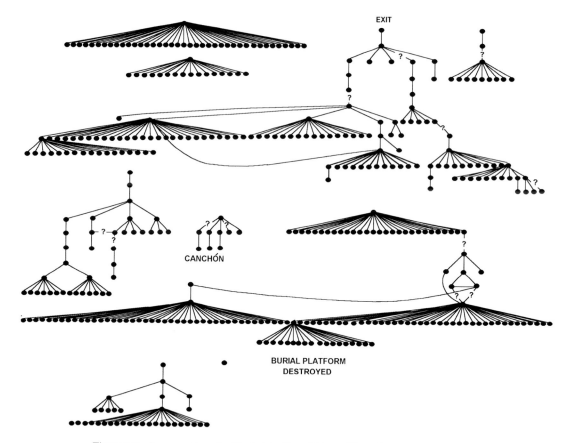

Figure 5.12 Access pattern for Ciudadela Gran Chimu, Chan Chan

The development of Chan Chan: ciudadelas and access patterns

The occupation at Chan Chan spanned some 500 years, centuries marked by important socio-political changes as the Chimu state consolidated its core, expanded its territory, and carried out a wide range of agricultural and other projects in response to episodic environmental catastrophes. Not surprisingly, the ciudadelas of Chan Chan – so often treated as a coherent architectural set – exhibit differences in scale, plan, and select architectural features. Such hypothesized differences include a change in the amount of storage in ciudadelas (Klymyshyn 1987), formal differences in burial platforms (Conrad 1982), variations in the forms and placement of audiencias, and, among other developments, changes in the organization of access patterns within the ciudadelas (Kolata 1990).

Kolata (1990: 128–130) hypothesized that through time administrative activities, as represented by audiencias, were concentrated in the northern sector of the ciudadelas, segregating the more public activities from the central sector, which became "the specific locus of residence for the king" (Kolata 1990: 140). Based on his relative chronology, Kolata (1990: 129) argues that "Beginning with Late Chimu (ca. AD 1300), there was a trend toward an inverse gradient of (administrative) use intensity

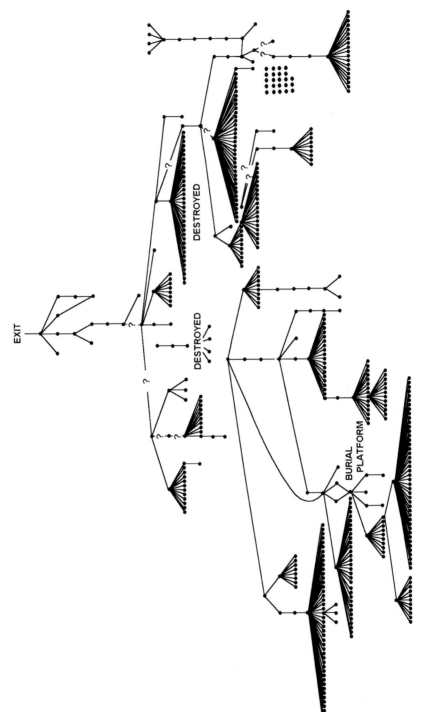

Figure 5.13 Access pattern for Ciudadela Velarde, Chan Chan

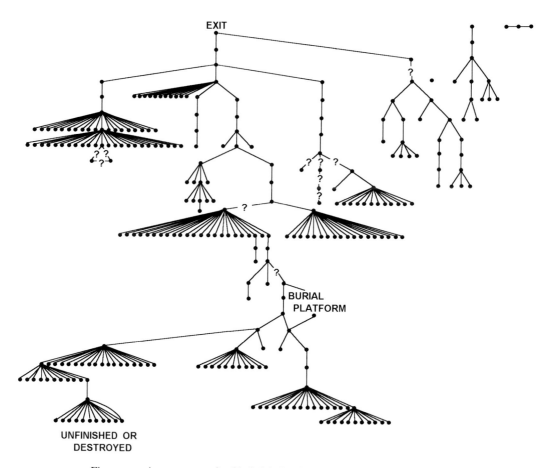

Figure 5.14 Access pattern for Ciudadela Bandelier, Chan Chan

in ciudadela design." Progressively, access was restricted to the central sectors of later ciudadelas like Velarde, Bandelier, Tschudi, and Rivero, implying that "as access was reduced, this [central] sector was becoming an exceptionally private space" (Kolata 1990: 130). This perceived pattern leads Kolata (1990: 140) to conclude:

> This increasingly physical isolation of the central sector – the king's residence – from public activities was a direct spatial expression and symbol of increased social differentiation between the king and his subjects. In fact, the physical boundary that was being drawn between the central sector and the rest of the palace enclosure resulted from the evolution of a very specific institution: divine kingship.

Thus, Kolata clearly posits a link between changes in access patterns and the architecture of social control. This hypothesis will be tested, but first I want discuss patterns of access at Chan Chan in more general terms.

As noted in Chapter 2, any discussion of the development of Chan Chan immediately stumbles on the problem of relative chronology. To sidestep this issue, I

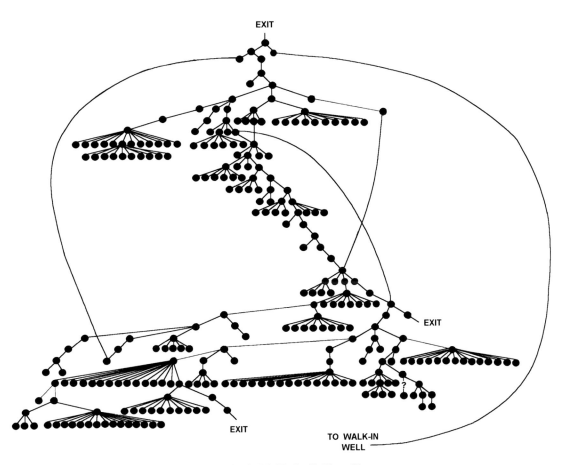

Figure 5.15 Access pattern for Ciudadela Tschudi, Chan Chan

consider patterned changes in the Chan Chan ciudadelas based on the three relative sequences proposed by Topic and Moseley (1983), Kolata (1990), and Cavallaro (1991). The basic data on the Chan Chan ciudadelas are presented in Tables 5.2, 5.3, 5.4, each ordered according to a different relative chronology, the rankings from oldest (rank = 1) to most recent.

There are no easily discerned patterns in the various iterations. The Chan Chan ciudadelas do not neatly increase through time in the number of vertices, edges, depth, number of subgraphs, or overall complexity as measured by the cyclomatic number, with one exception: there is a possible relationship between increasing depth and time based on Cavallaro's sequence. The Chan Chan patterns resist simple diachronic inferences.

This may partially express the surprising uniformity of access patterns at Chan Chan. Access is tree-like and restrictive in the Chan Chan ciudadelas, and that is true of the earliest and latest ciudadelas. This apparent continuity of form leads back to Kolata's insights into the emergence of divine kingship. Kolata (1990: 141) writes that at ca. AD 1350–1370, and coterminous with major Chimu territorial expansion,

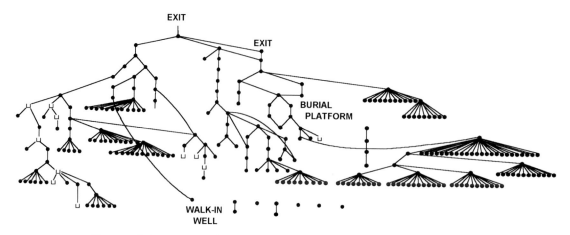

Figure 5.16 Access pattern for Ciudadela Rivero, Chan Chan

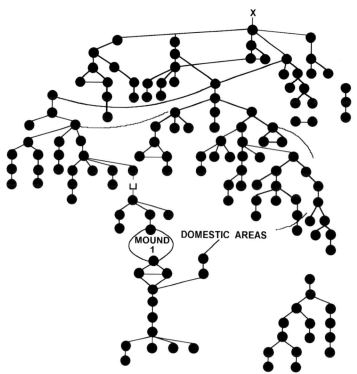

Figure 5.17 Access pattern for Huaca 1, Pacatnamú

"access to the central sector was severely restricted. It had finally become inviolate to the public, it was the locus of the sacred."

Examination of the Chan Chan plans suggests the germ of Kolata's inference. There does seem to be a change in the concentration of storerooms and audiencias with a higher proportion of those structures concentrated in the northern sectors of the ciudadelas (Table 5.5), but this change in architectural layout does not mean that access to the central sector was increasingly restricted. Kolata has conflated two

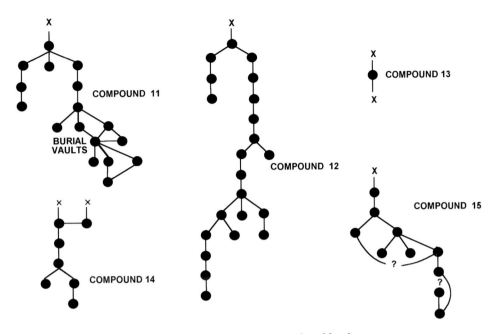

Figure 5.18 Access patterns for Compounds 11, 12, 13, 14, and 15, Manchan

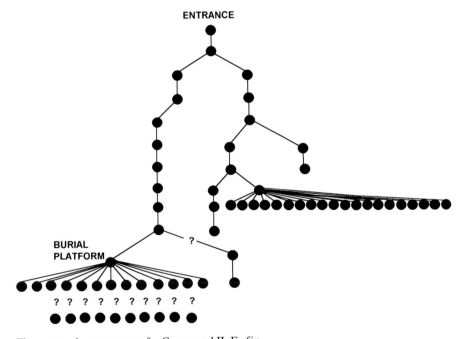

Figure 5.19 Access patterns for Compound II, Farfán

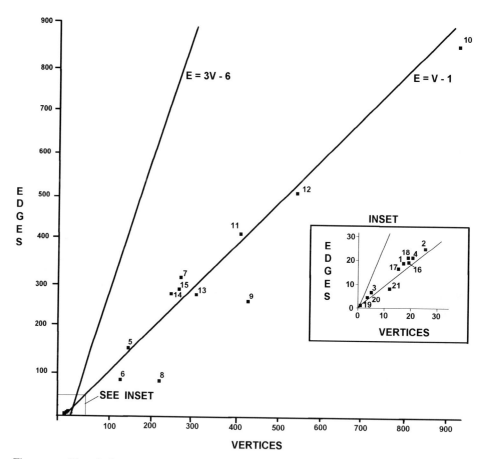

Figure 5.20 Plot of edges x vertices for selected constructions: 1 Huaca Grande, Pampa Grande;
2 Cercadura A, Galindo; 3 Cercadura B, Galindo; 4 Cercadura C, Galindo; 5 Huaca 1, Pacatnamú;
6 Ciudadela Chayhuac; 7 Ciudadela Uhle; 8 Ciudadela Tello – South; 9 Ciudadela Tello – South and
North; 10 Ciudadela Laberinto; 11 Ciudadela Gran Chimu; 12 Ciudadela Velarde; 13 Ciudadela
Bandelier; 14 Ciudadela Rivero; 15 Ciudadela Tschudi; 16 Compound II, Farfán; 17 Compound 11,
Manchan; 18 Compound 12, Manchan; 19 Compound 13, Manchan; 20 Compound 14, Manchan;
21 Compound 15, Manchan

different variables, "location of storerooms" and "access to central sector"; they are
related but not the same.

If access to the central sector is measured by the depth of the shortest route
from outside the compound to the central sector, Kolata's hypothesis is not supported (Table 5.6). Tello, Squier, and Chayhuac are excluded because they either
lack internal divisions (Squier, Chayhuac) or a burial platform (Tello). As Table
5.6 suggests, *the central sectors of later ciudadelas may actually be less deep than in
earlier ciudadelas.* Interestingly, ready access to the burial platforms in Rivero and
Tschudi is due to a set of corridors on the east side of the compound that lead
to the central sector, almost like a service entrance. These corridors were
not later additions, suggesting that access to the burial platforms was an
important aspect of ciudadela design. It is notable that these corridors represent

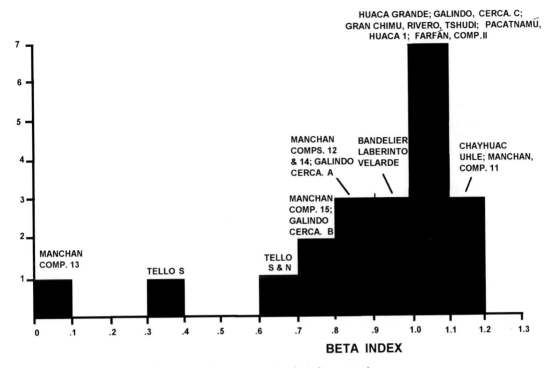

Figure 5.21 Histogram of beta indices for selected constructions

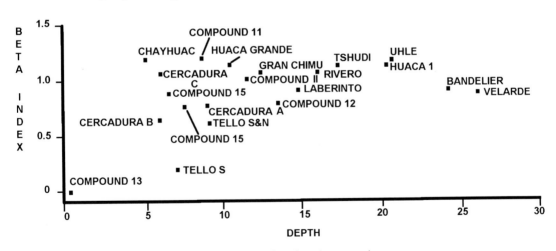

Figure 5.22 Plot of beta index x depth for selected constructions

"lefthanded routes" as noticed by Donnan (1986c) at Pacatnamú, a matter considered below.

It appears that Kolata (1990) observed a spatial segregation of storage-administrative functions vs. funerary functions in the Chan Chan ciudadelas; that observation is valid and seems to co-occur with the greater standardization of later ciudadelas. Klymyshyn (1987) has discussed the reorganization of storage at Chan

Table 5.2. *Chan Chan ciudadelas ordered in relative chronology by Topic and Moseley (1983)*

Ciudadela	Rank	E	V	Depth	Subgraphs	Beta	Cyclomatic no.
Rivero	6	282	278	17	7	1.01	11
Tschudi	6	296	285	18	1	1.04	12
Velarde	5	506	534	26	3	0.95	−25
Bandelier	5	287	300	24	4	0.96	−9
Gran Chimu	4	416	411	13	9	1.01	14
Laberinto	3	854	907	15	13	0.94	−40
Chayhuac	2	130	113	5	19	1.15	36
Tello S & N	1	260	423	9	41	0.61	−122
Uhle	1	312	278	21	14	1.12	48

Table 5.3. *Chan Chan ciudadelas ordered in relative chronology by Kolata (1990)*

Ciudadela	Rank	E	V	Depth	Subgraphs	Beta	Cyclomatic no.
Rivero	5	282	278	17	7	1.01	11
Tschudi	5	296	285	18	1	1.04	12
Velarde	4	506	534	26	3	0.95	−25
Bandelier	4	287	300	24	4	0.96	−9
Gran Chimu	3	416	411	13	9	1.01	14
Squier	3	no data					
Laberinto	2	854	907	15	13	0.94	−40
Tello S & N	2	260	423	9	41	0.61	−122
Chayhuac	1	130	113	5	19	1.15	36
Uhle	1	312	278	21	14	1.12	48

Table 5.4. *Chan Chan ciudadelas ordered in relative chronology by Cavallaro (1991)*

Ciudadela	Rank	E	V	Depth	Subgraphs	Beta	Cyclomatic no.
Velarde	8	506	534	26	3	0.95	−25
Bandelier	8	287	300	24	4	0.96	−9
Rivero	7	282	278	17	7	1.01	11
Tschudi	7	296	285	18	1	1.04	12
Laberinto	6	854	907	15	13	0.94	−40
Gran Chimu	5	416	411	13	9	1.01	14
Uhle	4	312	278	21	14	1.12	48
Tello S & N	3	260	423	9	41	0.61	−122
Squier	2	no data					
Chayhuac	1	130	113	5	19	1.15	36

Table 5.5. *Distribution of audiencias in ciudadelas*

	Ciudadela sectors		
	North	Central	North Annex
Rivero	10	1	0
Tschudi	12	5	2
Bandelier	6	2	0
Velarde	2	4	6
Gran Chimu	0	8	1
Laberinto	5	8	1
Uhle	(NE) 8	(NW) 7	(S) 7

Source: Data from Kolata 1990: Table 1.

Table 5.6. *Chan Chan ciudadelas, depth of central sectors*

	Depth to central sector
Rivero	16
Tschudi	15
Bandelier	18?
Velarde	8?
Gran Chimu	17?
Laberinto	18?
Uhle	16?

Note: ? reflects unclear connections to northern sector.

Chan in persuasive detail, arguing that different patterns of association between storerooms and burial platforms reflect changes in administrative structures correlated with phases of Chimu territorial expansion.

But access did not become more restricted in the Chan Chan ciudadelas, and the data do not support the hypothesis that divine kinship developed with the construction of Ciudadela Laberinto. Neither do the data allow us to state when divine kingship developed, partially because the notion is imprecisely defined (for a review of the concept see Grottanelli 1987; Hocart 1927). As discussed above, the North Coast ethnohistoric accounts suggest a relatively stark separation between deities and rulers. Although a ruler's responsibility for cosmic well-being is suggested by Fempellec's fate, nothing indicates that dead rulers were worshiped as anything other than extremely important ancestors and culture heroes.

But when the ciudadelas are contrasted with the cercaduras of Galindo or the walled-in approaches to Huaca Grande, it is almost certain that the separation

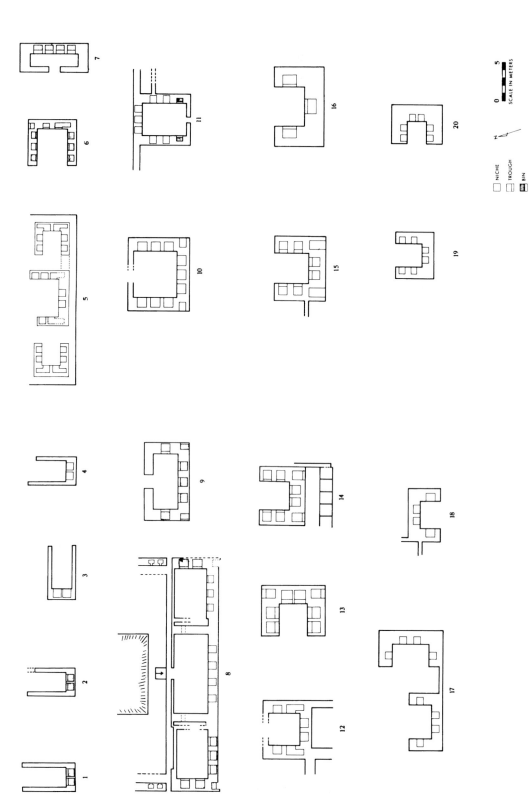

Figure 5.23 Formal typology of U-shaped rooms (From Kolata 1982; courtesy A. Kolata)

Figure 5.24 Depiction of an audiencia-like structure on Moche pottery (From Larco Hoyle 1939)

between ruler and ruled was well established when the initial course of adobes were laid for the first ciudadela. That enormous social divide, based in cosmogony and manifested in mud brick, existed from the earliest phases of Chan Chan.

The coherence of its architectural expression is partially observed in the organization of access within the ciudadelas of Chan Chan, a pattern which fluctuates in scale but not in its essential order or intent. Architecture was a medium of social control from Chan Chan's beginnings, spatially defining a divide between king and subject which, as the legends claimed, was spawned by the heavens.

Access in Chan Chan: the problem of the U-shaped rooms

A basic model of Chimu political organization views power as centralized, hierarchical, and redistributive, a model I refer to as the bureaucratic model (Moore 1985). Key elements of this model are: (1) there was a bipartite division of status, wealth, and power in Chimu society; (2) political power was centralized in the person of the Chimu king and exercised by noble administrators whose authority was derived from their position in the bureaucracy; and (3) the Chimu state directly controlled the direction and flow of goods and labor, governing exchange via a non-monetarized, command economy. The bureaucratic model has been used to explain evidence for corvée labor (Moseley 1975b), the development of irrigation systems (Kus 1972; Nials et al. 1979; T. Pozorski 1987), and the organization of craft production at Chan Chan (J. Topic 1977, 1982, 1990). The bureaucratic model is the ruling paradigm for most archaeological research at Chan Chan (cf. Netherly 1976, 1984, 1990).

Within this model, the U-shaped room (Figure 5.23) plays a central role because it is interpreted as the architectural manifestation of administration. U-shaped rooms are adobe brick structures consisting of three walls, open at one end, and essentially rectangular or square in plan (Andrews 1974: 247). The U-shaped rooms also have a variety of niches, troughs, or bins associated with them; these differences and distinctions in overall layout have led Kolata (1982) to define some twenty different types of U-shaped structures, an expansion on the seven types initially defined by Andrews (1974). At least certain U-shaped rooms appear similar to features illustrated in Moche iconography (Figure 5.24), showing a high-status individual sitting on a raised bench-like throne (Donnan 1976: 67,69), and this apparent analogy has led to calling some types of U-shaped rooms audiencias and to suggesting that such structures were occupied by bureaucratic overseers.

The administrative interpretation of U-shaped rooms is not solely based on form and analogy; it is also based on a perceived association between U-shaped rooms and storerooms, specifically that U-shaped rooms control access to the storerooms. Day presents the argument very clearly: "Storerooms in *ciudadelas* housed many more goods than did storerooms elsewhere in the site. These storage facilities could only be reached by a system of corridors that passed the *audiencias*. It is the strategic position of these U shaped structures rather than anything inherent in their form that indicates *audiencias* were administrative control points in *ciudadelas*" (Day 1982: 64).

The suggested strategic role of U-shaped rooms in controlling access to storerooms has been echoed by others. For example, Parsons and Hastings (1988: 193) wrote: "In particular, the role of distinctive U-shaped buildings in controlling access to storerooms throughout Chan Chan seems undeniable and highly significant."

The hypothetical administrative function of U-shaped rooms has been extrapolated beyond the walls of the Chan Chan ciudadelas. For example, Keatinge and Conrad (1983: 264) discuss the association of audiencias with other Chimu sites in the Chimu heartland of the Moche Valley and the northern valley of Jequetepeque:

> The occurrence of *audiencias* within the main structures of these administrative centers [outside of Chan Chan] is assumed to be symbolic of the regional extension and economic unity of state control and authority centered at the capital [of Chan Chan]. In summary, the association of *audiencias* with contiguous rooms thought to have been storerooms, as well as their location in state rural administrative centers, has led to the development of a model of Chimu socio-economic organization in which *audiencias* are seen as *the architectural expression of state control over the production, storage, and redistribution of goods.*
> [emphasis mine]

In short, the characterization of U-shaped rooms as having a general administrative function and/or meaning throughout Chimu territory is largely based on their specific role in controlling access to the purported storerooms in the ciudadelas of Chan Chan. Yet, this hypothesized relationship has not been tested, probably because of the lack of methods for the analysis of access patterns. Access graphs provide an effective means of testing the relationship between audiencias and storage in the Chan Chan ciudadelas.

Ciudadela Rivero has been cited as an exemplar of the relationship between U-shaped rooms and storage (Day 1982), and it will illustrate how the hypothesis was tested. Figure 5.25 depicts the basic plan of Ciudadela Rivero showing the U-shaped structures and the storerooms; the caption accompanying this figure in Day's 1982 article states, "Note the strategic position of U-shaped *audiencias* in relationship to storerooms in the north and central sectors." Based on an earlier passage in the same article (Day 1982: 64), "strategic" would seem to imply that it is impossible to gain

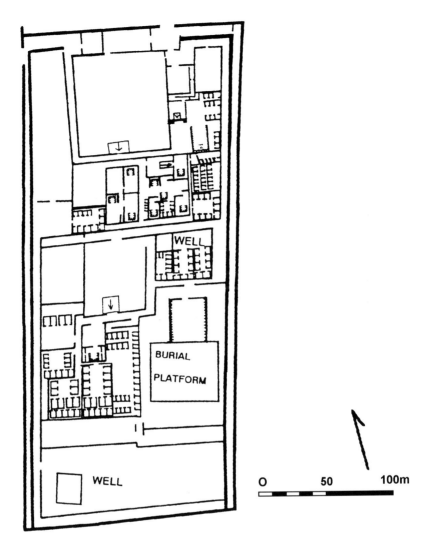

Figure 5.25 Plan of Ciudadela Rivero, Chan Chan

access to the storerooms without passing by or at least being seen from U-shaped rooms.

The access pattern graph for Ciudadela Rivero (Figure 5.16), however, shows that the association between U-shaped rooms and storage is not clear-cut. I use association in its statistical sense: a patterned, non-random relationship between entities. The U-shaped rooms are not located in the most strategic or pivotal nodes of the graph; if one really wanted to control access within the ciudadelas, it would be more effective to locate the U-shaped rooms elsewhere. Also, while some U-shaped rooms are located such that they control access to storerooms, not all U-shaped rooms are associated with storerooms. The inverse is also true: while some storerooms are associated with U-shaped rooms, the vast majority are not (Table 5.7).

Table 5.7. *Association of U-shaped rooms and storerooms, main compounds, Chan Chan ciudadelas*

	No. of U-shaped rooms without storerooms	No. of U-shaped rooms with storerooms	No. of storerooms with U-shaped rooms	No. of storerooms without U-shaped rooms
Tello	2	I	4I	2I9
Velarde	8	3	63	233
Laberinto	0	3	132	509
Chayhuac	0	0	0	67
Tschudi	13	4	29	22I
Bandelier	2	6	37	138
Uhle	II	II	107	68
Rivero	8	3	19	I6I
Gran Chimu	0	8	82	177
Total	44	49	460	1,793

Note: Chi square = 0.23, not significant, alpha = 0.1 level, degrees of freedom = 1.

A similar lack of association between U-shaped rooms and storerooms is manifested by some of the other ciudadelas in Chan Chan. Table 5.7 presents frequencies for U-shaped rooms and storerooms in the nine completed ciudadelas, and a few conclusions are clear. First, there are some ciudadelas in which the majority of U-shaped rooms are, in fact, associated with possible storerooms: Laberinto, Gran Chimu, and Bandelier. Second, at least in the case of Ciudadela Uhle, some storerooms are very much associated with U-shaped rooms. But for Chan Chan as a whole and for certain ciudadelas like Tschudi, Tello, Velarde, and Rivero, the relationship does not exist. For Chan Chan as a whole, a one-sample test of the null hypothesis that the association between U-shaped rooms and storage is the result of chance, the resulting chi-square is .23, which is not significant at the .05 level with 1 degree of freedom. In other words, *there is no significant relationship in the co-occurrence of U-shaped rooms and storage.* Neither is there a statistically significant relationship between storage and U-shaped rooms, since storerooms *not* associated with U-shaped rooms outnumber storerooms associated *with* U-shaped rooms almost 4 to 1. Simply, audiencias do not control access to storerooms in the Chan Chan ciudadelas.

These results suggest the need to reconsider previous archaeological approaches to the meaning of U-shaped rooms in Chimu society. On the one hand, the architectural categories may be poor ones; the twenty different types of buildings linked by Kolata (1982) on formal grounds may cross-cut different functional classes, and, alternatively, there may be more than one kind of storeroom at Chan Chan. It is equally possible that the relationships between U-shaped rooms and the purported storerooms changed through time at Chan Chan, a hypothesis immediately snagged on the difficulty of seriating the ciudadelas. It is worth while noting that the ciudadelas with the least association between U-shaped rooms and storage include supposedly early (Tello) *and* late (Velarde, Rivero, Tschudi) ciudadelas (Kolata 1982; Topic and Moseley 1983).

The data also suggest the need to rethink the administrative interpretation of the meaning of U-shaped rooms. For example, Keatinge and Conrad (1983: 261) refer to the "*audiencias* hypothesized to have functioned as administrative 'offices'," but it would seem that we have been captured by our analogies. The interpretation of the U-shaped rooms as offices in Chan Chan was based on their hypothetical association with storage and their suggested function in controlling access. On this basis, the U-shaped rooms were interpreted as "symbolic of the regional extension and economic unity of state control and authority" (Keatinge and Conrad 1983: 264). Obviously, if the U-shaped rooms did *not* control access to storage in Chan Chan's ciudadelas, then their symbolic association with the administrative state cannot be extended to other territories of the Chimu state. In short, analysis of the architectural plans in the ciudadelas suggest that the hypothesized "function" of U-shaped rooms in Chan Chan and their suggested "meaning" elsewhere on the North Coast simply are not supported by the data.

The emphasis on the administrative functions of audiencias – and the ready acceptance of the untested hypothesis – stems from two factors. First, the selective examination of ciudadela plans suggested the relationship was sound. Ciudadela Rivero and Ciudadela Tschudi were the best known compounds because of Day's (1973) research in Rivero and the Instituto Nacional de Cultura's restoration of Tschudi for tourism beginning in 1964 (Ocas C. 1986); by chance, these are also the two ciudadelas where audiencias are most tightly clustered in the northern sector. The apparent patterns in these ciudadelas were extrapolated to ciudadela architecture as a whole, contributing to the ready acceptance of the administrative interpretation of audiencias.

But beyond this, audiencias were interpreted as "checkpoints" or "offices" because that interpretation neatly fitted the bureaucratic model of the Chimu state, a model derived from general concepts of state organization which emphasized redistributive economic organizations (e.g., Polanyi et al. 1957; Service 1975; Steward 1973) and from studies of Inca political organization (e.g., Morris 1967; Murra 1980) which emphasized similar dimensions. These ideas formed the intellectual background for the Chan Chan research (e.g., Moseley 1975b) and coupled with Rowe's (1948) suggestion that the Inca may have borrowed administrative structures from the Chimu they led to the bureaucratic model of the Chimu state and its emphasis on the redistributive public economy. In this context, the audiencias looked like "offices."

An alternative model was considered originally by Andrews (1974: 257), who discussed the possible role of religious activities in the functions of U-shaped rooms. Yet, Andrews was swayed by the apparent administrative role of U-shaped rooms: "However, the associations with storerooms, other U-shaped structures, ciudadela entrances, and other important features argue for a primarily administrative role for these structures; in such a predominantly secular context, religion would have been relegated to a secondary role" (Andrews 1974: 257).

Similarly, Keatinge (1977: 232) suggested that audiencias developed from a religious-ceremonial context although they "through time became increasingly associated with the socio-administrative activities of the compounds, activities that are represented in their most developed form by the audiencia-storage complexes at Chan Chan," but remarking on the "religious aura" of the audiencias as reflected in the dedicatory burials found in the floors of the audiencia (Keatinge 1977: 232). It is unclear if audiencias were incorporated into displays of legitimation – similar to the dais depicted in Moche presentation scenes – but neither were they desacralized, administrative offices.

Architecture and empire: core and periphery in the Chimu state

The expansion of the Chimu state over a 1,000 km territory from Tumbez to Huarmey was accompanied by the construction of monumental public buildings. Political expansion did not occur in a political or architectural vacuum, and imperial integration was a dynamic process. Thus, consolidation of the Chicama– Moche– Virú core preceded further expansion, the northern conquests occurred before successes to the south, and effective rule was an ongoing problem (Rowe 1948; Mackey 1987; T. Topic 1991). The political problems of empire are never solved, they are simply held at bay. Similarly, the architectural expressions of conquest are rarely uniform. Even empires with a single-minded desire to place their architectural stamp on newly conquered territories – such as the Inca (Niles 1987) or Imperial Rome (Rykert 1976) – must conform to local circumstance, and this was equally true of the Chimu.

As documented in Table 5.1 and discussed above, a strong similarity exists in the access patterns of the Chan Chan ciudadelas, Compound II at Farfán, and the isolated compounds at Manchan. These structures follow a coherent pattern of access, characterized by relatively deep structures with beta indices which cluster around 1.0. But the agglutinated compounds at Manchan do not exhibit this pattern. The agglutinated compounds are shallow, chain-like, and their maximum depth equals 5. The most common architectural feature is large open plazas. None of the plazas has a baffled entryway, few of the doors are oriented north, and none of the plazas exhibit the trilinear routes found in other Chimu constructions (see below).

The architectural analysis supports Mackey's (1987) general model that Manchan reflects a political strategy of control by incorporating local elites. Mackey (1987: 129) argues this point based on the stylistic differences in the architecture of Manchan and Chan Chan, but the same inference can be made on other grounds. If the access patterns at Chan Chan are the architectural expression of enormous status divisions and relatively rigid social control, then the opposite situation was at work at Manchan. The large plazas of Manchan were not hidden behind 9 m high walls, but were easily entered from the lower class barrios at the site (Moore 1981, 1985). Storerooms could be entered directly from the plazas (Mackey 1987: 127), unlike the storerooms at Chan Chan. And finally, the co-existence of isolated compounds that emulate Chan Chan's architecture and agglutinated compounds unlike anything at the Chimu capital suggests a mixture of architectural forms and perhaps the political arrangements they mirror. The amalgam of local and Chimu architectural patterns reflected in access graphs is also seen in an alternative method of analyzing architecture, the analysis of route paths.

Route maps: paths, functions, and ceremony in Chimu architecture

Corridors and passages give the Chan Chan ciudadelas their labyrinthine structure, but similar complexities have been observed in North Coast architecture outside the Moche Valley. Christopher Donnan (1986c) has given special attention to the organization of routes in his study of Huaca 1 at Pacatnamú. As noted above, Donnan observed that two routes connected the North Courtyard to the Main Quadrangle of Huaca 1: a right-hand route which passed through architecturally elaborated passages and corridors, and a left-hand route which was narrow, nondescript, and led to areas where food preparation may have taken place. "Spaces reached by the right-hand route imply ceremonial or administrative functions, while those accessed by the left-hand route normally have refuse and thus imply a domestic function or an area where ceremonial food and drink were prepared and/or stored" (Donnan 1986c: 79). Proposing that the right–left dichotomy was culturally significant, Donnan hypothesizes that the pattern was an important tenet of architectural design at Pacatnamú, in a footnote acknowledging Cristobal Campana's suggestion that differential routing was frequently used in the monumental architecture of Chan Chan. Donnan suggests access routes were bilaterally organized and that the right-hand side represented higher status, ceremonial, and/or administrative activities marked by architectural elaborations while left-hand side routes led to more mundane work areas.

One can explore this intriguing suggestion using route maps. Route maps simply describe possible paths through an architectural plan without depicting the actual buildings; in this sense, route maps are derived from the axial maps devised by Hillier and Hanson (1984; for alternative route notation systems, see Appleyard et al. 1964; Lynch 1968). With their selective emphasis on pathways, route maps are an effective means of searching for patterns of access as expressed in built space. The route map for Pacatnamú's Huaca 1 (Figure 5.26) demonstrates the efficacy of the method. By highlighting paths, the basis of Donnan's hypothesis is obvious – there are clear right-hand and left-hand routes in Huaca 1. But the route map indicates a third path, the central path which proceeds to the top of the huaca. While the right and left routes are defined by doorways and corridors, the central route is no less defined by a line between the principal entrance and the ramps leading up the north side of Huaca 1. Instead of a pattern of bilateral routes, Figure 5.26 suggests a triad of paths – right, left, and central, with the central route marked by a change in elevation. The architectural pattern can be paraphrased as, "Upon entry into a plaza, there will be three possible routes: a central route which runs from the entrance to a doorway incorporating a change in elevation, and a right-hand route and a left-hand route leading out of the plaza via opposing doorways."

This trilinear pattern was not limited to Pacatnamú, but was also incorporated into Chimu architecture. Route maps indicate that trilinear paths were

Architecture and power in the ancient Andes   212

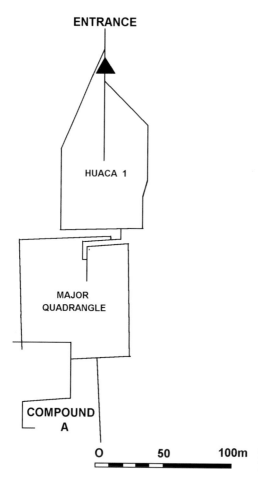

ENTRANCE

HUACA 1

MAJOR
QUADRANGLE

COMPOUND
A

O   50   100m
Figure 5.26 Route map for Huaca 1,
Pacatnamú

incorporated in Ciudadelas Squier, Laberinto, Velarde, Bandelier, Rivero, and Tschudi (Figure 5.27) and at the Chimu provincial centers of Farfán and Manchan (Figure 5.28) In each case, trilinear paths begin at the entrance to an open area or plaza, they are marked by opposing doors and/or corridors on the right and left sides of the plaza, and the central path leads up a ramp to a door which is opposite the main entrance. In some cases, the pattern is repeated; trilinear routes were associated with plazas in the northern and central sectors of the ciudadelas at Laberinto, Bandelier, Tshudi, and Rivero. The trilinear route pattern is not present at Chayhuac, Tello, Uhle, or Gran Chimu, although related patterns are recognizable at the last two ciudadelas. For example, the burial platform at Uhle contains a trilinear pathway which leads to the storerooms behind the platform and the northern plaza of Gran Chimu exhibits a plan with central and right-hand paths but lacking a left-handed route.

Chimu provincial centers also exhibit trilinear routes, and Compound II at Farfán is a particularly clear case. The central route passes between the low platforms and up a ramp into the administrative architecture; the left-hand path unobtrusively

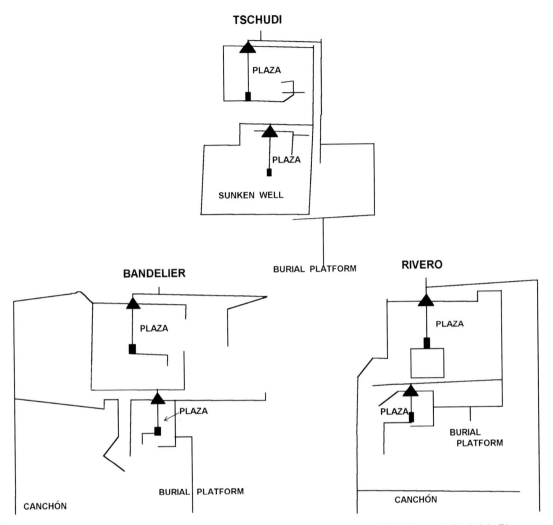

Figure 5.27 Partial route maps for Ciudadela Tschudi, Ciudadela Bandelier, and Ciudadela Rivero, illustrating trilinear paths, plaza and ramp combinations

edges the compound before terminating in the administrative constructions, while the right-hand route runs deep, leading to the burial platform spatially segregated from the rest of the complex. At Manchan, the trilinear pattern is found only in Isolated Compounds 11 and 12; not surprisingly, these compounds were recognized as most closely following Chimu architectural patterns (Mackey and Klymyshyn 1990: 205–206).

There is reason to believe that the trilinear route was designed in the later phases of Chan Chan's development. Again, the relative chronology is problematic, but the ciudadelas with trilinear routes are considered to be later rather than earlier constructions (Cavallaro 1991; Kolata 1990; Topic and Moseley 1983). A later development is suggested by the dates for the provincial structures, believed to represent Chimor's northward expansion at ca. AD 1100–1200 (Donnan 1986a: 22; Keatinge

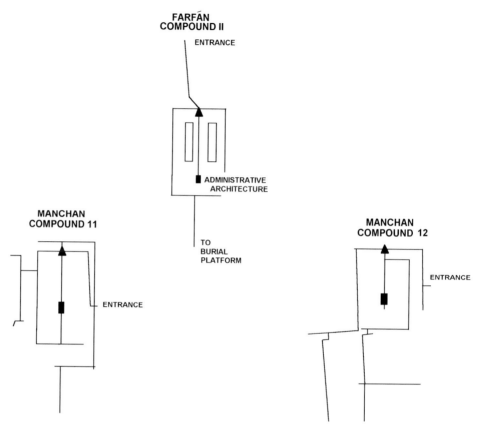

Figure 5.28 Route maps for Compound II, Farfán, and Compounds 11 and 12, Manchan, illustrating trilinear paths and ramp combinations

and Conrad 1983: 274–276) and a later, southern conquest dating to AD 1300–1350 (Mackey and Klymshyn 1990: 205).

But what is the significance of trilinear routes? Donnan (1986c) observed that the right–left dichotomy was paralleled by differences in architectural elaboration and densities of food debris. Unfortunately, it is difficult to test this pattern at the other Chimu sites because of a lack of comparable data. For example, Pillsbury (1993: 120) notes that friezes in the Chan Chan ciudadelas are associated with "areas of transition. Entry courts, corridors, ramps and other features often have friezes," but there is no evidence that right-hand routes consistently were more decorated than left-hand routes. Neither are there consistent data on the distribution of food debris within the compounds, and so an indirect approach is required.

Table 5.8 summarizes the "destinations" of right-hand, central, and left-hand routes, and a great degree of variation is immediately obvious. Yet a weak pattern is suggested by the fact that most of the central and right-hand routes end in sectors containing storerooms and audiencias, and when the route maps are compared to the architectural plans, a potentially significant pattern appears. Right-hand routes lead to storerooms and audiencias, but end among those rooms

Table 5.8. *Alternative routes and destinations, selected North Coast sites*

	Routes		
	Left	Central	Right
Burial Platform	Rivero – N. Plaza Rivero – C. Plaza Velarde	Velarde	Compound 2
Storerooms/ Audiencias	Velarde	Velarde Tschudi – N. Plaza Tschudi – C. Plaza Bandelier Squier Compound II	Tschudi – N. Plaza Tschudi – C. Plaza Rivero – N. Plaza Rivero – C. Plaza Huaca 1 Compound II
Irregular Structures	Huaca 1 Bandelier		
Other	Laberinto – dead end Squier – dead end Tschudi – N. Plaza – wachaque Tschudi – C. Plaza – wachaque Rivero – N. Plaza – central sector	Huaca 1 – mound Tschudi – C. Plaza – wachaque Rivero – C. Plaza – unclear	Laberinto – open area Bandelier – incomplete? Squier – niched room and dead end

without a defining, terminal architectural feature. Central routes generally end in a small narrow anteroom which separates the plaza from the storerooms to the rear. These narrow anterooms are present at Manchan Compounds 11 and 12, Farfán Compound II, and Ciudadelas Squier, Bandelier, Laberinto, Velarde, Rivero, and Tschudi; a similar feature may be present at Gran Chimu. A similar feature appears to be represented in Types I and II intermediate architecture at Chan Chan, as discussed by Klymyshyn (1982: 125–127), non-royal compounds most similar to the ciudadelas.

These rooms are very narrow (2–3 m), often appearing more like corridors; only small groups of people could fit in such spaces. The narrow room is at a right angle to the central axis; people standing in the room could not be seen until they actually stood in the doorway and walked onto the bench. It is a curious feature.

But valuable architectural details are recorded in an amazing wooden model of Chimu architecture; the artifact (Figure 5.29) is held by the Museum für Volkerkunde and is described by Donnan (1975). The wooden model illustrates the ramp, elevated bench, doorway, and narrow structure which is identical to the architectural pattern described above. The only difference, as Donnan (1975: 26) notes, is that the narrow room in the model is an enclosed room while in Chan Chan it is a corridor. The fact that this narrow room was included in the model suggests it was an integral element of the structure. Patterns of inlaid decoration on the model

Figure 5.29 Chimu wooden architectural model (Photograph courtesy C. Donnan)

indicate that it was designed to be viewed "from" the plaza; the exterior walls and the rear of the central wall were undecorated. This suggests the central route – as defined by the ramp, door, and narrow anteroom – comprised a unique route in Chimu architecture, different from left-hand or right-hand routes. The ramp and bench mark a focal point when viewed from the plaza. The narrow anteroom does not always provide access to deeper parts of the structure; for example, in Manchan, Unit 11, the narrow room is basically a dead end. This may indicate that the narrow room served as a prehispanic version of the offstage spaces hidden from spectators' view.

It seems probable that the central ramp and bench were pivotal points of public ceremonies, probably ceremonies which involved presentations to an elite. For example, an elaborate textile discovered in the Major Quadrangle of Huaca 1 at Pacatnamú depicts a high-status individual seated on elevated architecture, raising a goblet, and watching dancers and the sacrifice of llamas (Donnan 1986d). Given the general relationship between raised elevation and high status as depicted in Moche iconography (Donnan 1978: 34), it is reasonable to suggest that the ramp–bench–anteroom was the focal point of presentations to the Chimu elites, nobles in the provinces and in the intermediate architecture, and to the kings of Chimor in the Chan Chan ciudadelas.

At this time, this hypothesis cannot be tested, although we can outline specific test implications. The hypothesis that the central route represented a place of encounter rather than merely another path would be supported by (1) evidence of differential traffic on the right or left vs. central routes (e.g., little evidence of wear on ramps or in the narrow corridors), (2) elaborate artistic treatments of ramps but not other portals, (3) offerings associated with ramps but not right or left portals, and (4) narrow doorways associated with ramps vs. wide doorways associated with alternative routes. This is a testable hypothesis which future research could support or reject.

But for the moment, the analysis of route maps suggested the following points. First, although a right-hand vs. left-hand distinction existed in Chimu architecture, it was complemented by a third, central route; routes in formal Chimu public constructions are trilinear rather than bilateral. Second, trilinear patterns appear to develop in Early Chimu Phase 2 (Kolata 1990), roughly after AD 1100, and trilinear route patterns are found in both the core and periphery of Chimu territory. Third, although variation exists, there is greater regularity in the destinations of right-hand and central routes than in left-hand routes. Right-hand and central routes tend to lead ultimately to areas of storerooms, although only those in the central sectors of ciudadelas. Fourth, the evidence is insufficient to determine if right-hand routes are more decorated than left-hand routes. Fifth, the central route is unique in its association with an elevation change usually marked by a ramp. Finally and most speculatively, the architectural features of ramp, bench, and narrow room may represent the focal point of a ceremony, viewed by spectators in the plaza, in which a ruler or other elite moved from the narrow room and into view on the bench where he was the recipient of presentations from his subjects.

The architecture of social control: power and place

Just as the Panopticon reflected Bentham's Utilitarian philosophy, the architecture of social control is shaped by ideology. Insofar as ideology is the social production of meaning, then meaning and meanings will be expressed in a variety of forms, created and interpreted by different segments and individuals in society. When public buildings are constructed under the direction of elites, such constructions will exhibit values held by elites and meanings understood by the society at large. And such a situation occurred on the North Coast of Peru.

A common element in North Coast cosmogonies is the notion of separation – separate creations for elites and commoners, physical separation of culture heroes from hoi polloi. The creation of nobles from a special star or a golden egg marked the distinct origins of rulers, a chasm between lord and subject established in the beginnings of time. Yet, while nobles could be worshiped as ancestors, they were not quite gods. Lords were responsible for proper ritual and behavior, and their failure could result in natural disaster and legitimate revolt. But neither were they mere mortals; lords were different and lived separate lives, behind large walls. The public architecture of the Chimu state was a direct expression of the ideology of separation, and the formal analysis of Chimu architecture has provided new insights into the relationship between architecture and social control.

First, the analysis compared the access patterns of the Chan Chan ciudadelas with examples of Moche, Lambayeque, and provincial Chimu constructions. Using access graphs, data on the number of edges, the number of vertices, depth, number of subgraphs were collected and allowed for calculations of beta indices and cyclomatic numbers for each construction. A comparison of Chimu to Moche V architecture suggested that there was a fundamental change in monumental constructions on the North Coast; even the simplest Chan Chan ciudadela is a much larger and much more complex structure than any of the Galindo cercaduras. This suggests that a major change occurred in the scale and organization of space with the development of Chan Chan. In that sense, Chimu architecture represents a transition from earlier North Coast traditions. The current evidence suggest that Chan Chan's ciudadelas were innovative architectural expressions of a new configuration of ideology and power, one which may have had roots in the Moche state, but which represents fundamental differences in scale and social distance.

When did this new configuration develop? That is unclear, but it seems to have developed before the construction of the first ciudadela. The analysis considered Kolata's hypothesis that a greater isolation of audiencias and storage from burial platforms after the construction of Laberinto marked the development of divine kingship. The hypothesis, however, combined two different variables (i.e., concentration of storage and isolation of central sector); analysis of the access to the central sector suggested that there was no significant change in its isolation in the later ciudadelas. While storage may have been more concentrated in the northern portions of the ciudadelas, this probably reflects segregation of activities, the increasing formalization of ciudadela plans, and reorganization of storage – all of which may reflect significant changes in the organization of the Chimu state (Klymyshyn 1987) – but not a change in access to the central sector and not necessarily the development of divine kings.

Previous examinations of the ciudadela plans had suggested that U-shaped rooms controlled access to storerooms, and, in turn, that U-shaped rooms were the architectural marker of the administrative state in Chan Chan and beyond. Yet, analysis of the ciudadela access patterns indicated that U-shaped rooms were not significantly associated with the storerooms and that the vast majority of storerooms could be entered without passing by or being seen from an audiencia. This undermines the interpretation of audiencias as "checkpoints" or "offices" and suggests their role in an administrative state needs reconsideration. Does this mean that access within the ciudadelas was unrestricted? Obviously not; it is simply that movement was structured via independent routes, a pattern which is found in Chan Chan and in Chimu provincial centers.

A comparison between the Chan Chan ciudadelas, Farfán, and Manchan suggested differences and similarities in Chimu architecture between core and periphery. On one hand, there are basic similarities in organization and plan between the ciudadelas, Compound II at Farfán, and the isolated compounds at Manchan. In contrast, the large open plazas at Manchan are unlike anything at Chan Chan. In spite of those differences, there are remarkable similarities in the organization of routes within North Coast constructions, similarities recognizable in route maps. Following Christopher Donnan's suggestion that a right–left dichotomy may have been a tenet of North Coast architecture, it was discovered that routes were trilinear rather than bilateral. In addition to right and left routes, a central path led between plaza entrance and a ramp–bench–doorway, creating a third axis. The trilinear pattern was found in six ciudadelas, Farfán, and Manchan, and it may have developed after ca. AD 1100–1200. It seems that right-hand and central routes led towards storerooms and audiencias, but via differently configured, built spaces which suggest distinct social functions. Right-hand routes may lead to storerooms and audiencias, but simply terminate among the rooms. In contrast, the central route usually terminates in a narrow room perpendicular to the route. It may be that this room was designed as a transitional space between the public plaza and the hidden spaces behind the benched wall, although this is speculative. Rather than another corridor, the central route may represent the highly visible focus of public encounter between ruler and subject.

What does this suggest about power and ideology in the Chimu state? First – and most obviously – status differences were clearly marked. Second, Chimu architectural canons were followed to varying degrees in the provinces, but sometimes in concert with distinctly different classes of constructions. Third, and perhaps most important, the architecture of empire was not simply designed to prohibit the free movement of people. Instead, Chimu architecture marked the physical separation of lord and subject, but it also shaped their encounters. That architectural tradition, a material expression of ideology and a constructed representation of social control, marks the development of a unique political achievement on the North Coast of Peru.

6

Summary and implications

... to this day in Peru many who see them
do not know what they are.
The Augustinians on ancient architecture

"Space is never empty," the geographer Edward Relph writes (1976: 10), "but has content and substance that derive both from human intention and imagination and from the character of the space." Relph describes the different kinds of space humans experience and create: the unselfconscious space experienced by an infant moving without reflection, the space shaped by human perception, and space which is cognitive and abstract. Like other elements in the cultural landscape, architecture often contains explicit material statements about human intention and imagination, expressing human desires to literally shape the world. When such material patternings become widespread and shared, we are seeing the physical remains of what Relph calls "existential space":

> Existential or lived in space is the inner structure of space as it appears to us in our concrete experience of the world as members of a cultural group . . . It is intersubjective and hence amenable to all members of that group for they have all been socialized to a common set of experiences, signs, and symbols . . . existential space is not merely a passive space waiting to be experienced, but is constantly being created and remade by human activities. It is the space in which "human intention inscribes itself on the earth" (Dardel 1952: 40) and in doing so creates unselfconsciously patterns and structures of significance through the building of towns, villages, and houses, and the making of landscapes.
> (Relph 1976: 12)

The prehispanic Andean constructions discussed in this book are examples of existential spaces. Their special configurations, symbolic contents, and unique perceptual properties mark them as expressions of human intention. All the structures in the sample – from the small structure in the Zaña Valley to the ciudadelas of Chan Chan – meet those criteria.

The catalyst for this study was the realization that prehistoric architecture had not received the archaeological attention it deserved. Prehistoric architecture had not been considered as existential space. Archaeologists had analyzed ancient constructions as complex artifacts, as labor investments, or as passive backdrops, but we had not – with few exceptions – considered the ways that the built environment shaped and was shaped by social interaction.

Obviously, this is not to sugggest that archaeologists had "ignored" architecture; this book is jammed with references to archaeologists' considerations of prehistoric constructions, particularly in the Andes. Yet, I believe that current archaeological approaches have not exhausted the potential insights which systematic inquiry of architecture may provide. And, as I have argued in the previous chapters, the development of systematic inquiry requires simultaneous advances in theory and methods applied to sets of archaeological data.

This study is an attempt to achieve this by argument and example. I focused on public architecture because it represents social effort and reflects social motives. Domestic architecture represents an overlapping but distinct set of considerations – such as residence patterns, household economy, or status differences – different from those that shape a public construction. Given my interest in the changing political processes and structures that humans created over 4,000 years of Andean prehistory, I examined a sample of prehistoric public architecture. The sample of twenty-two sites was not strictly representative of prehistoric Andean architecture, because our ignorance of the full range of constructions is so profound we really cannot define a statistical universe of structures. But the sample was illustrative, allowing for the application of new analytical methods and the derivation of specific, tentative inferences informed by three sets of anthropological theory. I have attempted to balance theory, method, and data to highlight the intellectual synergy which exists between them.

Synopsis, implications, and hypotheses

Three arenas of inquiry were considered and the results can be summarized briefly. The architecture of monuments explored the ways that Andean construction could serve as communicative media, expressing certain kinds of culturally encoded information. In the absence of informants, cultural meanings usually slip through an archaeologist's grasp, but it is possible to examine *how* monuments mean even if we do not know *what* they mean. Public monuments are designed to communicate, and effective monuments are visible constructions whose messages can be understood. Given the nature of human perception, certain kinds of designs vary in their ability to communicate information to audiences of different sizes. The analysis was based on the assumptions that variations in monuments were socially significant, that those variations could be discovered, and that partial understanding of variation was attainable if the monument was analyzed within its architectural context. This boiled down to a pair of simple questions: What could be perceived and from where?

The analysis suggested that prehistoric mounds, a recurrent form of Andean public architecture, were designed to communicate in different ways at distinct periods. The manipulation of angles of incidence indicated that mounds at some sites (e.g., Moche, La Galgada, Garagay, and Cardal) were shaped to form steep, visually impressive vertical planes, while other sites (e.g., Sechín Alto and Las Aldas) had surfaces that formed gentle slopes. The analysis of isovistas suggested that at structures like Huaca 1 at Pacatnamú, different isovistas intersected with constructed points of transition, suggesting the importance of visual perception and movement. At other sites, the mounds were designed such that the isovistas fall on the structure itself; the visual perception of monumentality is greatest only when one has gained access to the construction. Instead, sites like Sechín Alto and Las Aldas appear designed to emphasize distance and depth rather than vertical planes and height.

Perhaps the most socially significant inference about monuments concerns the intentional obstruction of view at late prehispanic sites like Pacatnamú and Chan Chan, a pattern distinct from Formative sites where the vistas are relatively open, and even at Moche sites (e.g., Huaca del Sol or Huaca Grande) where the principal monument is widely visible. This is very different from Chan Chan, where the dense urban environment blocked the views of huacas and walled enclosures visually separated monuments, effectively obstructing their viewsheds. Similarly, the walls surrounding Huaca 1 at Pacatnamú effectively screened the mound, except to a viewer inside the compound. Such obstructed monuments suggest that the social unit designed to understand the monument's meanings was select, a group smaller than the entire community.

The variation in Andean monuments suggested different modes of communications, and in a similar way the study of the architecture of ritual documented fundamental differences in the constructed expressions of rite. Ethnohistoric sources prove beyond any reasonable objection that ritual was a fundamental dimension of Andean society. And yet, archaeologists have tended to overlook or marginalize the explanatory significance of rite. Again, this is not to suggest that Andean archaeologists have not discussed Andean ritual at all, but rather that Andeanists have not given ritual a central role in understanding the dynamics of prehispanic societies, employing theoretical models that highlight other dimensions (economic, environmental, dialectic, or imperial) of Andean culture. That, I believe, is an oversight.

As an example, the comparison of pilgrimage centers – like Pachacamac – with ancestral shrines – like the machay – indicated the importance of ritual action in the organization of Andean societies and suggested the possibility of an archaeological inquiry into rite. But beyond this, the comparison of pilgrimage centers and ancestral shrines illustrated how a body of anthropological theory, as outlined by Victor Turner and others, could be articulated to a specific ethnographic case and to a well-defined set of material correlates. The point of this example is simple: there is no ethnographic, ethnohistoric, or archaeological justification for the continued lack of inquiry into Andean ritual, even for archaeologists who think of ritual – as one colleague expressed it – as "that touchy-feely stuff."

Though the meaning of rituals may elude archaeological inquiry, I believe that one can make solid inferences about ritual practice. Such inferences are based on a model (a) that ritual is a repetitive, behaviorially dense, and stylized form of communication; (b) that as patterned, repetitive human behavior, ritual may produced specific material remains (at least there is no a priori reason to exclude ritual from archaeological study); (c) that public rituals often occur in constructed spaces which represent the partial objectification of symbolic meanings and serve as the settings for social dramas; (d) that gross classes of ritual communication are associated with distinct thresholds of human perception, thus allowing us (e) to make inferences about the nature of ritual practice based on what kinds of information could be perceived by people in a specific built environment.

From this perspective, it was possible to consider five variables that illuminate different aspects of Andean ritual architecture: permanence, scale, centrality, ubiquity, and visibility. Permanence expresses the intended duration of a structure, providing an important measure of basic ideology. Structures designed to last for a generation are obviously different from structures built as timeless expressions of the divine. This cultural intent reflects different ideological conceptions and it is frequently associated with specific archaeological remains. The most striking example was the site of La Galgada, where ritual chambers used as burial crypts representing generational structures were replaced by a large moundtop plaza and associated features that seem to be multi-generational. The analysis of permanence suggested that the intended duration of ritual structures changed dramatically through time.

Centrality refers to the spatial relationship between ritual structure and secular settlements. The analysis suggests that most of the ritual structures in the sample were located in the center of settlements rather than peripheral to or isolated from residential areas. Rather than "empty ceremonial centers" or shrines without extensive residential occupation like Silverman (1991, 1993) describes for the Nazca site of Cahuachi, the ritual structures in the sample were directly associated with a resident population. It may be that Archaic and Formative ritual structures were associated with kin-based, community-wide sodalities, although the current evidence is insufficient to prove this idea.

In some ways, the analysis of ubiquity produced a more readily interpreted pattern. Ubiquity refers to the level at which a particular kind of ritual structure is encountered by determining if the structure is unique at the community, subregional, regional, or interregional levels. The analysis uncovered examples of each level of ubiquity. Rather than a single category of "monumental constructions," the analysis of ubiquity suggested there were fundamental differences in the extent of social networks associated with structures of different sizes, and that those differences do not form a smooth cline but rather fundamental shifts in the organization of rite and society.

Other hints of such shifts were found in the analysis of scale, a variable that attempts to measure the human dimension of monumental constructions. Because the size of personal space is influenced by cultural patterns, it is difficult to estimate the potential number of occupants of a given space; in turn this makes it difficult to infer the size of the social unit (e.g., nuclear family or moiety) associated with a particular structure. An analysis of the human scale of sunken circular courts (a) suggested that many occupant estimates were probably too high, (b) indicated that there was a tentative relationship between the size of dwellings and the size of sunken circular courts, and (c) demonstrated that sunken circular courts located on the principal axis of a ceremonial complex were larger than courts located in other areas. As discussed in Chapter 4, this last pattern, if substantiated with more evidence, may suggest the translation of a ritual structure from a sub-community to a community-wide context. Yet, when the analysis turned to the human scale of plazas the results were chaotic. Some plazas would contain roughly the number of inhabitants estimated for the site; other spaces seem disproportionately large. This chaos may indicate that the category "plaza" subsumes open spaces that were used in fundamentally different ways, with people unevenly spread across the spaces and with different roles in public rituals. Changes in the human scale of public spaces may suggest a growing social distance between participants and observers in public rituals, another inference about development of ancient Andean societies.

The analysis of visibility highlighted this change from another perspective. If we assume that ritual is a form of communication, then the kind of communication which can take place is partially limited by thresholds of human perception. Using Edward Hall's notions of different communicative distances, one can draw reasonable inferences about the kinds of information perceptible in a specific architectural setting. Thus, the modes of ritual information transmitted at Huaricoto or Chavín de Huántar were fundamentally different from those communicated at Garagay or Sechín Alto. Similarly, the analysis of U-shaped ceremonial centers suggested that (a) complex information communicated from the moundtop was undiscernible to a large crowd standing in the plaza below, although (b) more stylized symbolic behavior could be readily perceived, and (c) more fine-grained forms of ritual communication undoubtedly occurred inside moundtop structures. Further, the analysis of other ceremonial centers suggested the existence of at least two types of public ceremonies, which I call "observational" and "processional." The arrangement of constructed space at some sites (e.g., Cardal and Garagay) seems designed to emphasize the visual impact of the moundtop, the mound rising steeply from the plaza. At other sites (the best example is Las Aldas) the constructed spaces are arranged actually to disrupt visual impact, dissecting the increase of height into a series of intervening planes. The alignment of portals, sunken courtyards, and stairways at Las Aldas marks a well-defined axis obvious from two-dimensional plans, but we get a slightly different perspective by thinking about the movement of people in three-dimensional space. As someone moves across Las Aldas, following the axis from east to west, the rhythm of progress is marked by three doorways, each separated by 60 to 90 meters, then the descent into and ascent from the sunken circular court, followed by a series of doorways and staircases punctuated by brief landings, and finally the climb to the moundtop. This is a very different type of ritual architecture from that at Cardal or Garagay, and a conceptual universe away from later structures that expressed the architecture of social control.

I suggest that the architecture of social control expresses an ideology of separation, the notion that royalty and commoners were divided by birth, myth, and adobe walls. Archaeologists commonly refer to access patterns, arguing that the physical separation of spaces parallels the social separation of people. Yet, the analysis of access has been limited by the notion that access is binary – either open or closed – and by the lack of methods to measure variation. I discussed two sets of methods – access pattern graphs and route maps – and I applied them to sites associated with Moche and Chimu cultures. This analysis suggested a number of points. A fundamental change separates Moche and Chimu public architecture. The access patterns of Chan Chan appear to represent an innovative physical expression of social distance and political power, one which characterizes all of the ciudadelas. The notion that ciudadela architecture expressed increasing social distance between ruler and ruled and the fourteenth-century emergence of divine kingship was not supported by the analysis; instead the latter ciudadelas were more formalized than the earlier compounds, which accounts for the impression. Another finding suggested that audiencias did not control access to storage inside the ciudadelas, and thus were not the secular offices that were the architectural stamp of the Chimu Empire. And yet the Chimu did have well-defined architectural canons that are found in the core and periphery of the empire. From an analysis of route maps, a basic pattern was identified in which there were three paths associated with plazas in compounds. The right and left paths apparently served as routes, passages leading into the depths of the structure, but the central path appears to mark a place of encounter.

Beyond the specific hypotheses and inferences suggested above, the study suggests the need to reconsider some larger issues commonly encountered in Andean archaeology. First, there is the two-edged issue of ethnohistory. On one hand, archaeologists have not spent sufficient time studying primary ethnohistoric documents as opposed to ethnohistoric synopses. As a consequence, Andeanists frequently confuse normative generalizations with ethnographic realities, unwittingly substituting idealized generalities for realized, specific behaviors. For example, the specific details of the Augustinian's account of ritual practice in Huamachuco provides insights lost in generalizations about pan-Andean systems of belief. Too many Andeanists, myself included, have not marshaled the full range of ethnographic information about the dynamism of Andean societies, too often relying on well-known generalizing summaries conveniently available in English.

But on the other hand, archaeologists cannot infinitely stretch ethnohistoric patterns to prehistoric societies. For all the evidence of cultural continuities, there is unassailable evidence that early Andean societies were not diluted versions of Tawantinsuyu. The architectural evidence makes this point unequivocally. The Formative centers of the North Coast do not have counterparts in the Inca Empire, because they represent fundamentally diverse kinds of societies organized by distinct social principles in starkly different environments. We may propose that social structures like dualism or ayllus or bureaucratic states or pilgrimage networks have pre-Incaic roots, but these propositions require proof.

This notion of continuities is variously expressed in the Andean literature; a common variant is the notion of "pre-adaptations." The concept of pre-adaptation was introduced by Moseley (1975a) to suggest the ways in which human aggregations based on the exploitation of marine resources developed social and economic systems that would be elaborated once agriculture was well established. Since then the concept has been extended to cover a wide range of cultural phenomena, including public architecture. I think this is misleading, confusing hindsight with foreordination. Thus, to suggest that Aspero is somehow a prelude to Sechín Alto or other Initial Period sites (Feldman 1987: 14) or that the Huaynuná is a precursor – in anything other than a chronological sense – to Pampa de las Llamas (S. Pozorski and T. Pozorski 1992: 864) masks a fundamental set of basic facts: these are very different kinds of sites built by distinct societies, and none of the parallels were inevitable. Like other emphases on normative approaches (Cordell and Plog 1979), viewing one pattern as the predetermined consequence of another obscures the most revealing vein for archaological analysis: cultural variation.

It was the analysis of cultural variation in public architecture that, in my opinion, produced the two most interesting implications for understanding Andean societies. First, Andean societies underwent a major transformation at ca. 1800–1400 BC, marked by the development of new forms of public architecture. Not only was there an increase in the size of public architecture, but there were basic changes in the modes of public communication associated with the structures. Prior to this time, communication took place over relatively small distances in which complex and new information could be conveyed. Facial gestures could be seen, the spoken word easily heard. The distances – physical, communicative, and symbolic – between speaker and audience were small. After 1800–1400 BC, this changes. Although intimate ritual spaces were maintained, they become auxiliary to larger monumental constructions. The large mounds of the Formative provided visually impressive, symbolically distinctive spaces within which public rituals occurred. The placement of stairways facing plazas suggests that the ascent of mounds was an element in the ceremony. The distance between moundtop and plaza, however, exceeded the perceptual thresholds for understanding complex or new information. At such distances larger gestures, loud noises, or extremely visible signs – murals or fires – could be perceived, but a complex text would be unheard. The architectural patterns suggest an untested hypothesis: *in a sharp departure from previous patterns, the Formative Period was marked by the development of public vs. private religion, by an increasing social distance between participants and observers in public ceremony, and the development of complex social institutions that relied on the legitimacy imparted by highly visible, public ritual.*

The second implication which I think is important relates to the development of the ideology of separation at the beginning of the Late Intermediate Period. There is a close parallel between the architectural access patterns and the mythological tropes relating to the ideology of separation. The architectural data, however, suggest that this ideology of separation was most developed in Chimu society. Access to Moche constructions was more restricted than in the Early Formative centers; the social differences which appear in the Formative certainly became wider and more formalized by the Early Intermediate Period and Middle Horizon. Yet, even in these societies there was simply not the same intentional obstruction of view or the tortuous manipulation of access that is such a characteristic of Chimu public architecture. While Chan Chan is the best example of this pattern, it is also documented for

Chimu sites in the periphery. Although the ciudadelas exemplify the pattern, the same intention characterizes regional administrative centers like Manchan and Farfán. Further, this pattern characterizes the entire sequence at Chan Chan, regardless of which relative chronology is used. This leads to a second hypothesis: *political legitimacy in the Chimu state was based partly on the spatial and ideological separation of social classes; expressed in a variety of architectural settings the basis of legitimacy did not involve highly visible, widely viewed public ceremony but rather the separation of ruler and ruled punctuated by spatially controlled and visually regulated encounters.*

In short, the architectural analysis implies that significant cultural discontinuities mark the developments of complex societies on the North Coast of Peru. Additional data and further analyses may disprove this notion, but I see little evidence for the slow, steady development of social complexity. Rather the architectural evidence suggests disruption and innovation, marked by periods of relatively rapid social change.

Implications for future research

I believe this study has implications for future archaeological research in the Andes and other regions. First, and most obviously, is the need for large-scale excavations which define the spatial properties of the architectural sites. This is an enormous undertaking, leading immediately to problems of massive excavations and complex conservation programs, yet there is no substitute for excavated archaeological data. For all the importance of survey data, surface impressions are no substitute for detailed understanding of architectural patterns. It is no surprise that theoretical frameworks for large-scale survey emphasize broad functional categories and rough labor estimates because such information can be derived from survey data (e.g., Wilson 1988). But more subtle and equally important information is necessary, and accurate architectural plans – like the maps of Chan Chan (Moseley and Mackey 1974) – are fundamental data sets for archaeological analyses because they make it possible to think about people in terms of their built environments.

Second, there is an obvious need to pursue studies of ceremonial structures which, though public, are not monumental. There is a particular gap in our knowledge of Archaic ritual structures (Aldenderfer 1990, 1991, 1993a; Bonnier 1988), a general scarcity of archaeological data. For example the few cases known from the Andes are paralleled by a handful of studies from Mesoamerica (Drennan 1976, 1983), such as Voorhies' excavations at Tlacuachero in coastal Chiapas (Voorhies et al. 1991) or Hole's excavations of Geo Shih in the valley of Oaxaca. The lack of archaeological data about Archaic ritual partly reflects the difficulty of discovering such pre-Formative sites, but it also reflects a theoretical emphasis on subsistence, environment, and settlement which tends to be expressed by relatively small-scale, test-pit excavations rather than broad horizontal exposures. Without such data, the transformations experienced and created by early Formative societies will remain somewhat mysterious, since we will know little about their Archaic predecessors' social achievements.

Beyond illuminating lacunae in our knowledge, this study suggests areas for methodological developments. The crude measures and techniques used in this study were adequate to my task, but they could readily be replaced and supplemented with more sophisticated methods. In particular, the application of computer-assisted design and geographic information systems could result in fuller reconstructions of architectural spaces and potentially more subtle recognitions of constructed patterns. And yet, it is important to design techniques so they address specific archaeological questions and not as an end in themselves. That implies the need to advance simultaneously the three fronts of inquiry – data, method, and theory.

Finally, I hope that this study has made it clear that prehistoric architecture is an understudied domain of archaeological investigation that contains a wealth of insights into the nature of past societies. Architecture is more than a constellation of traits, an index of social effort, or a passive backdrop to human activities. Architecture is molded by human interactions, shaped by the nature of society. I chose to examine how Andean societies used public architecture as monuments, ritual spaces, and as a medium of social control; these do not begin to exhaust the potential lines of inquiry. Yet, certain basic points will be useful for future investigations: the importance of architecture within broader systems of human communication, the necessity of thinking about buildings within the context of specific built environments – and a sense of sincere awe when we consider the diverse ways fellow humans have marked our place upon the earth.

REFERENCES

Abrams, Elliott 1989. Architecture and energy: an evolutionary perspective. In *Archaeological Method and Theory*, vol. 1, edited by M.B. Schiffer, pp. 47–87. University of Arizona Press, Tucson.

Adams, Richard N. 1970. *Crucifixion by Power: Essays on Guatemalan National Social Structure, 1944–1966*. University of Texas Press, Austin.

　1975. *Energy and Structure: A Theory of Social Power*. University of Texas Press, Austin.

　1977. Power in human societies: a synthesis. In *The Anthropology of Power: Ethnographic Studies from Asia, Oceania, and the New World*, edited by R. Fogelson and R. Adams, pp. 387–410. Academic Press, New York.

Adler, Michael and Richard Wilshusen 1990. Large-scale integrative facilities in tribal societies: cross-cultural and southwestern US examples. *World Archaeology* 22 (2): 135–146.

Agorto Calvo, Santiago 1987. *Estudios acerca de la construcción, arquitectura y planeamiento incas*. Cámara Peruana de la Construcción, Lima.

Agrest, Diana 1991. *Architecture from Without: Theoretical Framings for a Critical Practice*. MIT Press, Cambridge, MA.

Aikens, C. and T. Higuchi 1982. *Prehistory of Japan*. Academic Press, New York.

Aldenderfer, Mark 1990. Late Preceramic ceremonial architecture at Asana, southern Peru. *Antiquity* 64: 479–493.

　1991. Continuity and change in ceremonial structures at Late Preceramic Asana, southern Peru. *American Antiquity* 2: 227–258.

　1993a. Ritual, hierarchy, and change in foraging societies. *Journal of Anthropological Archaeology* 12: 1–40.

　(ed.) 1993b. *Domestic Architecture, Ethnicity, and Complementarity in the South-Central Andes*. University of Iowa Press, Iowa City.

Altieri, Radmmes 1939. Introducción. In *Arte de la lengua yunga* by F. de la Carrera, edited by R. Altieri, pp. vii–xxvi. Universidad Nacional de Tucuman, Tucuman, Argentina.

Alva Alva, Walter 1986. *Las Salinas de Chao: asentamiento temprano en el Norte del Perú*. Verlag C.H. Beck, Munich.

Anders, Martha 1981. Investigation of state storage facilities at Pampa Grande, Peru. *Journal of Field Archaeology* 8: 391–404.

　1986. Dual organization and calendars inferred from the planned site of Azangaro – Wari administrative strategies. Unpublished Ph.D. dissertation, Cornell University. University Microfilms International, Ann Arbor.

　1991. Structure and function at the planned site of Azangaro: cautionary notes for the model of Huari as a centralized secular state. In *Huari Administrative Structure: Prehistoric Monumental Architecture and State Government*, edited by W. Isbell and G. McEwan, pp.167–197. Dumbarton Oaks Library and Research Collection, Washington, DC.

Andrews, Anthony 1974. The U-shaped structures at Chan Chan, Peru. *Journal of Field Archaeology* 1: 241–264.

Appleyard, Donald, Kevin Lynch, and John Meyer 1964. *The View from the Road*. MIT Press, Cambridge, MA.

Arguedas, José and Pierre Duviols 1966. *Dioses y hombres de Huarochirí: narración quechua recogida por Francisco de Avila*. Instituto de Estudios Andinos and Instituto Francés de Estudios Andinos, Lima.

Arnold, J. and A. Ford 1980. A statistical examination of settlement patterns at Tikal, Guatemala. *American Antiquity* 45: 713–726.

Arriaga, Father Pablo Joseph de 1968. [1621] *The Extirpation of Idolatry in Peru*, trans. by L. Clark Keating. University of Kentucky Press, Lexington.

Ashmore, Wendy and Richard Wilk 1988. Household and community in the Mesoamerican past. In *Household and Ccommunity in the Mesoamerican Past*, edited by R. Wilk and W. Ashmore, pp. 1–27. University of New Mexico Press, Albuquerque.

Ashton, Dore 1992. *Noguchi, East and West*. Alfred A. Knopf, New York.

Athens, J. Stephen 1977. Theory building and the study of evolutionary process in complex societies. In *For Theory Building in Archaeology*, edited by L. Binford, pp. 353–384. Academic Press, New York.

Augustinians 1865. [1560] Relación de la religión y ritos del Perú, Hecha por los primeros religiosos Agustinos que alli pasaron para la conversión de los naturales. *Colección de documentos ineditos relativos al descubrimiento, conquista y colonización de las posesiones Españolas en América y Oceanía* 3: 5–58.

Balandier, Georges 1970. *Political Anthropology*. Random House, New York.

Bar-Yosef, O. 1986. The walls of Jericho: an alternative explanation. *Current Anthropology* 27: 157–162.

Barthes, R. 1984. *Elements of Semiology*. Jonathan Cape, London.

Bastien, Joseph 1978. *Mountain of the Condor: Metaphor and Ritual in an Andean Ayllu*. West Publishing Co., St. Paul, MN.

Baudin, Louis 1961. *A Socialist Empire: The Incas of Peru*. Van Norstrand, Princeton.

Bawden, Garth 1977. Galindo and the nature of the Middle Horizon in northern coastal Peru. Unpublished Ph.D. dissertation, Department of Anthropology, Harvard University, Cambridge, MA.

    1982a. Galindo: a study in cultural transition during the Middle Horizon. In *Chan Chan: Andean Desert City*, edited by M. Moseley and K. Day, pp. 285–320. University of New Mexico Press, Albuquerque.

    1982b. Community organization reflected by the household: a study of pre-columbian social dynamics. *Journal of Field Archaeology* 9: 165–181.

    1983. Cultural reconstitution in the Late Moche Period: a case study in multidimensional stylistic analysis. In *Civilization in the Ancient Americas: Essays in Honor of Gordon R. Willey*, edited by R. Leventhal and A. Kolata, pp. 211–235. University of New Mexico Press, Albuquerque.

    1990. Domestic space and social structure in pre-Columbian northern Peru. In *Domestic Architecture and the Use of Space: An Interdisciplinary Cross-Cultural Study*, edited by S. Kent, pp. 153–171. Cambridge University Press, Cambridge.

    1994. La paradoja estructural: la cultura Moche come ideología política. In *Moche: propuestas y perspectivas*, edited by S. Uceda and E. Mujica, pp. 389–412. Travaux de l'Institut Français d'Etudes Andines 79: 7–8; Lima.

Bell, Barbara 1974. The dark ages in ancient history. In *The Rise and Fall of Civilizations: Modern Archaeological Approaches to Ancient Cultures*, edited by C. Lamberg-Karlovsky and J. Sabloff, pp. 356–389. Cummings Publishing Co., Menlo Park, CA.

Bell, Catherine 1992. *Ritual Theory, Ritual Practice*. Oxford University Press, New York.

Benson, Elizabeth 1972. *The Mochica: A Culture of Peru*. Praeger, New York.

Berger, R., G. Ferguson, and W. Libby 1965. UCLA radiocarbon dates IV. *Radiocarbon* 7: 347.

Betanzos, Juan de 1987. [1551] *Suma y narración de los Incas*. Ediciones Atlas, Madrid.

Billman, Brian 1989. Land, water, and architecture: political and economic organization of an early Andean state. Unpublished MA thesis, Department of Anthropology, University of California, Santa Barbara.

Binford, Lewis 1972. *An archaeological perspective*. Seminar Press, New York.

Blanton, Richard 1989. Continuity and change in public architecture: Periods I through V of the valley of Oaxaca, Mexico. In *Monte Alban's Hinterland Part II: Settlement Patterns in Tlacolula, Etla, and Ocatlan, Valley of Oaxaca, Mexico*, vol.1., edited by S. Kowaleski, G. Feinman, R. Blanton, L. Finsten, and L. Nichols, pp. 409–447. Museum of Anthropology, University of Michigan, Ann Arbor.

Boas, Franz 1951. *Primitive Art*. Capitol Publishing Company, Irvington-on-Hudson, New York.

Bonavia, Duccio 1982. *Los Gavilanes*. Editorial Ausonia, Lima.

  1985. *Mural Painting in Ancient Peru*, translated by P. Lyon. University of Indiana Press, Bloomington.

Bonnier, Elisabeth 1983. Piruru: nuevas evidencias de ocupación temprana en Tantamayo, Perú. *Gaceta Arqueológica Andina* 8: 8–10.

  1988. Arquitectura precerámica en la cordillera de los Andes: Piruru frente a la diversidad de los datos. *Antropológica* 6: 336–361.

Bonnier, Elisabeth and Catherine Rozenberg 1988. Del santuario al Caserío: acerca de la neolitización en la cordillera de los Andes centrales. *Bulletin de l'Institut Français d'Etudes Andines* 17 (2): 23–40.

Bonnier, Elisabeth, Julio Zegara, and Juan Carlos Tello 1985. Un ejemplo de crono-estratigrafía en un sitio con superposición arquitectónica – Piruru-Unidad II. *Bulletin de l'Institut Français d'Etudes Andines* 14 (3–4): 80–101.

Brewster-Wray, Christine 1983. Spatial patterning and the function of a Huari architectural compound. In *Investigations of the Andean Past*, edited by D. Sandweiss, pp. 122–135. Latin American Studies Program, Cornell University, Ithaca.

Brislin, Richard W. 1980. Cross-cultural research methods: strategies, problems, applications. In *Human Behavior and Environment: Advances in Theory and Research*, vol. IV: *Environment and Culture*, edited by I. Altman, A. Rapoport, and J. Wohlwill, pp. 47–82. Plenum Press, New York.

Bruce, Susan 1986. The audiencia room of the Huaca 1 Complex. In *The Pacatnamú Papers*, edited by C. Donnan and G. Cock, pp. 95–108. Museum of Culture History, University of California, Los Angeles.

Bueno Mendoza, Albert and Terence Grieder 1988. The geography of the Tablachaca Canyon. In *La Galgada, Peru: A Preceramic Culture in Transition*, edited by T. Grieder, pp. 4–18. University of Texas Press, Austin.

Bukert, Walter 1988. The meaning and function of the temple in classical Greece. In *Temple in Society*, edited by M. Fox, pp. 27–47. Eisenbrauns, Winona Lake, (Wisconsin?).

Burger, Richard 1981. The radiocarbon evidence for the temporal priority of Chavín de Huántar. *American Antiquity* 46: 592–602.

  1984. *The Prehistoric Occupation of Chavín de Huántar, Peru*. University of California Publications in Anthropology, no. 14. University of California Press, Berkeley.

  1985a. Concluding remarks: early Peruvian civilization and its relation to the Chavín horizon. In *Early Ceremonial Architecture in the Andes*, edited by C. Donnan, pp. 269–289. Dumbarton Oaks, Washington DC.

  1985b. Prehistoric stylistic change and cultural development of Huaricoto, Peru. *National Geographic Research* 1: 505–534.

  1987. The U-shaped pyramid complex, Cardal, Peru. *National Geographic Research* 3: 363–375.

1988. Unity and heterogeneity within the Chavín horizon. In *Peruvian Prehistory*, edited by R. Keatinge, pp. 99–144. Cambridge University Press, Cambridge.

1989. The pre-Chavín stone sculpture of Casma and Pacopampa. *Journal of Field Archaeology* 16: 478–485.

1992. *Chavín and the Origins of Andean Civilization*. Thames and Hudson, New York.

Burger, Richard and Lucy Salazar-Burger 1980. Ritual and religion at Huaricoto. *Archaeology* 33: 26–32.

1985. The early ceremonial center of Huaricoto. In *Early Ceremonial Architecture in the Andes*, edited by C. Donnan, pp. 111–138. Dumbarton Oaks, Washington, DC.

1986. Early organizational diversity in the Peruvian highlands: Huaricoto and Kotosh. In *Andean Archaeology: Papers in Memory of Clifford Evans*, edited by M. Ramiro Matos, Solveig Turpin, and Herbert Eling Jr., pp. 65–82. Institute of Archaeology, Monograph 27, University of California, Los Angeles.

1991. The second season of investigations at the Initial Period center of Cardal, Peru. *Journal of Field Archaeology* 18: 275–296.

Cabello Balboa, Miguel 1951. [1586] *Miscelanea antártica*. Universidad Nacional Mayor de San Marcos, Lima.

Calancha, Antonio 1974–77. [1638] *Crónica moralizada* (4 vols.). Ignacio Prado Pastor, Lima.

Canziani Amico, José 1989. *Asentamientos humanos y formaciones sociales en la costa norte del antiguo Perú (del Paleolítico a Moche V)*. Ediciones INDEA, Lima.

de la Carrera, Francisco 1939. [1644] *Arte de la lengua yunga*. Universidad Nacional de Tucman, Tucuman, Argentina.

Castagnoli, Ferdinando 1971. *Orthogonal Town Planning in Antiquity*. MIT Press, Cambridge, MA.

Cavallaro, R. 1991. *Large-Site Methodology: Architectural Analysis and Dual Organization in the Andes*. Occasional Papers, no. 5, Department of Anthropology, University of Calgary. Calgary, Alberta, Canada.

Cheney, Sheldon 1918. *The Open-Air Theatre*. Mitchel Kennerley Co., New York.

Childe, V. Gordon 1974. *The Urban Revolution*. Orig. 1936. In *The Rise and Fall of Civilizations: Modern Archaeological Approaches to Ancient Cultures*, edited by C. Lamberg-Karlovsky and J. Sabloff, pp. 6–14. Cummings Publishing Co., Menlo Park, CA.

Chippindale, Christopher 1992. Grammars of archaeological design: a generative and geometrical approach to the form of artifacts. In *Representations in Archaeology*, edited by J. Gardin and C. Peebles, pp. 251–276. Indiana University Press, Bloomington.

Chiswell, Coreen 1988. An analysis of architctural function at Pacatnamú, Peru. Paper presented at the 53rd Annual Meeting of the Society for American Archaeology, Phoenix, Arizona.

1989. Studying "invisible" spatial relations: an analysis of prehistoric architecture on Peru's North Coast. Paper presented at the 60th Annual Meeting of the Southwestern Anthropological Association, Riverside, CA.

Cieza de Leon, Pedro de 1985 [1555]. *Crónica del Perú. Segunda parte*. Pontífica Universidad Católica del Perú, Lima.

Cobo, Bernabe 1990 [1653]. *Inca Religion and Customs*, trans. by Roland Hamilton. University of Texas Press, Austin.

Collier, Donald 1960. Archaeological investigations in the Casma Valley, Peru. *Akten des 34 Internationalen Amerikanstenkongresses* 34: 411–417

Conkey, Margaret 1978. Style and information in cultural evolution: toward a predictive model for the Paleolithic. In *Social Archaeology: Beyond Subsistence and Dating*, edited by Charles Redman, Mary Berman, Edward Curtin, William Langhorne, Jr., Nina Versaggi, and Jeffery Wasner, pp. 61–85. Academic Press, New York.

Conklin, William 1990. Architecture of the Chimu: memory, function, and image. In *The Northern Dynasties: Kingship and Statecraft in Chimor*, edited by M. Moseley and A. Cordy-Collins, pp. 43–74. Dumbarton Oaks Research Library and Collection, Washington, DC.

Conklin, William and Michael Moseley 1988. The patterns of art and power in the Early Intermediate Period. In *Peruvian Prehistory: An Over-view of Pre-Inca and Inca Society*, edited by R. Keatinge, pp. 145–163. Cambridge University Press, Cambridge.

Conrad, Geoffrey 1974. Burial platforms and related structures on the North Coast of Peru: some social and political implications. Unpublished Ph.D. dissertation, Harvard University.

1982. The burial platforms of Chan Chan: some social and political implications. In *Chan Chan: Andean Desert City*, edited by M. Moseley and K. Day, pp. 87–117. University of New Mexico Press, Albuquerque.

1990. Farfán, General Pacatnamú, and the dynastic history of Chimor. In *The Northern Dynasties: Kingship and Statecraft in Chimor*, edited by M. Moseley and A. Cordy-Collins, pp. 227–242. Dumbarton Oaks Research Library and Collection, Washington, DC.

Conrad, Geoffrey and Arthur Demerest 1984. *Religion and Empire: The Dynamics of Aztec and Inca Expansionism*. Cambridge University Press, New York.

Cook, Noble David 1981. *Demographic Collapse, Indian Peru, 1520–1620*. Cambridge University Press, Cambridge.

Cordell, Linda S. 1979. Prehistory: Eastern Anasazi. In *Handbook of North American Indians: Southwest*, edited by Alfonso Ortiz, vol. 9, pp. 131–151. Smithsonian Institution, Washington, DC.

Cordell, Linda S. and Fred Plog 1979. Escaping the confines of normative thought: a reevaluation of puebloan prehistory. *American Antiquity* 44: 405–429.

Corominas, Joan 1974. *Diccionario crítico etimológico de la lengua castellana*, vol. II. Editorial Gredos, Madrid.

Cosgrove, Denis 1984. *Social Formation and Symbolic Landscape*. Barnes and Noble Books, Totowa, New Jersey.

Crabbe, George 1916 [1810]. *The Borough, a Poem, in Twenty-Four Letters*. Hatchard, London.

Crumrine, N. Ross 1991. A pilgrimage fiesta: Easter week ritual at Catacaos, Piura, Peru. In *Pilgrimage in Latin America*, edited by N. Ross Crumrine and Alan Morinis, pp. 269–280. Greenwood Press, New York.

Czwarno, R. Michael 1988. Spatial logic and the investigation of control in Middle horizon Peru. In *Recent Studies in Pre-Columbian Archaeology*, edited by N. Saunders and O. de Montmollin, pp. 415–456. BAR International Series 421. British Archaeological Reports, Oxford.

1989. Spatial patterning and the investigation of political control: the case from the Moche/Chimu area. In *The Nature of Huari: A Reappraisal of the Middle Horizon Period in Peru*, edited by R.M. Czwarno, F. Meddens, and A. Morgan, pp. 115–145. BAR International Series 525. British Archaeological Reports, Oxford.

Daggett, Richard 1984. The early horizon occupation of the Nepeña Valley, north central coast of Peru. Unpublished Ph.D. dissertation, Department of Anthropology, University of Massachusetts, Amherst.

D'Altroy, Terence and Christine Hastorf 1984. The distribution and contents of Inca state storehouses in the Xauxa region of Peru. *American Antiquity* 49: 334–349.

Dardel, E. 1952. *L'homme et la terre: nature et realité géographique*. Presses Universitaires de France, Paris. Cited in Relph 1976.

Day, K. 1973. The architecture of Ciudadela Rivero, Chan Chan, Peru. Unpublished Ph.D. dissertation, Department of Anthropology, Harvard University, Cambridge.

  1982. Ciudadelas: their form and function. In *Chan Chan: Andean Desert City*, edited by M. Moseley and K. Day, pp. 55–66. University of New Mexico Press, Albuquerque.

Demerest, Arthur 1981. *Viracocha: The Nature and Antiquity of the Andean High God*. Peabody Museum of Archaeology and Ethnology, Harvard University, Cambridge, MA.

Deregowski, J. 1980. Perception. In *Handbook of Cross-Cultural Psychology*, vol. III, edited by H. Triandis and W. Lonner. Allyn and Bacon, Boston.

Derrida, Jacques 1976. *On Grammatology*. Johns Hopkins University Press, Baltimore.

DeValois, Russell and Karen DeValois 1988. *Spatial Vision*. Oxford University Press, New York.

Dillehay, Tom, Patricia Netherly, and Jack Rossen 1989. Early preceramic public and residential sites on the forested slope of the western Andes, northern Peru. *American Antiquity* 54: 733–759.

Donnan, Christopher 1975. An ancient Peruvian architectural model. *The Masterkey* 49: 20–29.

  1976. *Moche Art and Iconography*. Latin American Center Publications, University of California, Los Angeles.

  1978. *Moche Art of Peru*. Museum of Cultural History, University of California, Los Angeles.

  (ed.) 1985. *Early Ceremonial Architecture in the Andes*. Dumbarton Oaks, Washington, DC.

  1986a. Introduction. In *The Pacatnamú Papers*, edited by C. Donnan and G. Cock, pp. 19–26. Museum of Culture History, University of California, Los Angeles.

  1986b. The city walls at Pacatnamú. In *The Pacatnamú Papers*, edited by C. Donnan and G. Cock, pp. 47–62. Museum of Culture History, University of California, Los Angeles.

  1986c. The Huaca 1 Complex. In *The Pacatnamú Papers*, edited by C. Donnan and G. Cock, pp. 63–84. Museum of Culture History, University of California, Los Angeles.

  1986d. An elaborate textile fragment from the Major Quadrangle. In *The Pacatnamú Papers*, edited by C. Donnan and G. Cock, pp. 109–116. Museum of Culture History, University of California, Los Angeles.

  1990. An assessment of the validity of the Naymlap dynasty. In *The Northern Dynasties: Kingship and Statecraft in Chimor*, edited by M. Moseley and A. Cordy-Collins, pp. 243–274. Dumbarton Oaks Research Library and Collection, Washington, DC.

Donnan, Christopher and Guillermo Cock (eds.) 1986. *The Pacatnamú Papers*, vol. I. Museum of Culture History, University of California, Los Angeles.

Donnan, Christopher and Carol Mackey 1978. *Ancient Burial Patterns of the Moche Valley, Peru*. University of Texas Press, Austin.

Douglas, Mary 1972. Symbolic orders in the use of domestic space. In *Man, Settlement, and Urbanism*, edited by Peter Ucko, Ruth Tringham, and G.W. Dimbleby, pp. 513–521. Schenkman Publishing Co., Cambridge, MA.

  1973. *Natural Symbols*. Random House, New York.

Doyle, Mary Ellen 1988. Ancestor cult and burial ritual in the seventeenth and eighteenth century, central Peru. Unpublished Ph.D. dissertation, University of California, Los Angeles. University Microfilms International, Ann Arbor.

Drennan, Robert 1976. Religion and social evolution in Formative Mesoamerica. In *The Early Mesoamerican Village*, edited by K. Flannery, pp. 345–368. Academic Press, New York.

  1983. Ritual and ceremonial development at the hunter-gatherer level. In *The Cloud*

People: Divergent Evolution of the Zapotec and Mixtex Civilizations, edited by K. Flannery and J. Marcus, pp. 30–32. Academic Press, New York.

Dreyfus, Henry 1959. The *Measure of Man: Human Factors in Design*. Whitney Publication, New York.

Dumézil, Georges 1970. *Archaic Roman Religions*, trans. by Phillip Krapp. University of Chicago Press, Chicago.

Duviols, Pierre 1967. Un inédit de Cristóbal de Albornoz: la instrucción para descubrir todas las guacas del Pirú y sus camayos u haziendas. *Journal de la Société des Américanistes* 56: 7–39.

  1977. *La destrucción de las religiones andinas: conquista y colonia*. Universidad Nacional Autónoma de Mexico, Mexico D.F.

Eagleton, Terry 1991. *Ideology: An Introduction*. Verso Press, London.

Earle, Timothy 1991. The evolution of chiefdoms. In *Chiefdoms: Power, Economy and Ideology*, edited by T. Earle, pp. 1–15. Cambridge University Press, Cambridge.

Eco, Umberto 1980. Function and sign: the semiotics of architecture. In *Signs, Symbols, and Architecture*, edited by G. Broadbent, R. Bent, and C. Jenks, pp. 11–69. New York: John Willey and Sons.

Eisenstadt, Shmuel 1963. *Political Systems of Empires*. The Free Press, Glencoe, IL.

  1988. Beyond collapse. In *The Collapse of Ancient States and Civilizations*, edited by N. Yoffee and G. Cowgill, pp. 236–243. University of Arizona Press, Tucson.

Eliade, Mircea 1959. *The Sacred and the Profane: The Nature of Religion*, trans. by W. Trask. Harcourt Brace and Company, New York.

  1985. *Symbolism, the Sacred, and the Arts*. New York.

Ember, Melvin 1973. An archaeological indicator of matrilocal versus patrilocal residence. *American Antiquity* 38: 177–182.

Engel, Frederic 1966. Le complexe préceramique d'El Paraíso (Perou). *Journal de Société des Americanistes* 55: 43–96.

  1970. *Las lomas de Iguanil y el complejo de las Haldas*. Universidad Nacional Agraria, Lima.

Erasmus, Charles 1977. *In Search of the Common Good: Utopian Experiments Past and Future*. The Free Press, Glencoe, IL.

Estete, Miguel de 1985. [1533] La relación del viaje que hizo el señor capitán Hernando Pizarro por mandado del señor Gobernador, su hermano, desde el pueblo de Caxamalca a Paracama y de allí a Jauja. In *Verdadera relación de la conquista del Perú* by Francisco de Xerez, pp. 130–148. Historia 16, Madrid.

Evans, Robin 1982. *The Fabrication of Virtue: English Prison Architecture 1750–1840*. Cambridge University Press, Cambridge.

Feijóo de Sosa, Miguel 1984. [1763] *Relación descriptiva de la ciudad y provincia de Trujillo del Perú*. Banco Industrial del Perú, Lima.

Feldman, Robert 1980. Aspero, Peru: architecture, subsistence economy, and other artifacts of a preceramic maritime chiefdom. Unpublished Ph.D. dissertation, Anthropology Department, Harvard University.

  1985. Preceramic corporate architecture: evidence for the development of non-egalitarian social systems. In *Early Ceremonial Architecture in the Andes*, edited by C. Donnan, pp. 71–92, Dumbarton Oaks, Washington, DC.

  1987. Architectural evidence for the development of non-egalitarian social systems in coastal Peru. In *The Origins and Development of the Andean State*, edited by J. Haas, S. Pozorski, and T. Pozorski, pp. 9–14. Cambridge University Press, Cambridge.

Firth, Raymond 1975. *Symbols: Public and Private*. Cornell University Press, Ithaca, New York.

Flannery, Kent 1972. The origins of the village as a settlement type in Mesoamerica and the Near East: a comparative study. In *Man, Settlement, and Urbanism*, edited by P. Ucko, R. Tringham and G. Dimbleby, pp. 23–53. Schenkman Press, Cambridge, MA.

(ed.) 1976. *The Early Mesoamerican Village*. Academic Press, New York.

Flannery, Kent and Joyce Marcus 1976. Evolution of the public building in Formative Oaxaca. In *Cultural Change and Continuity: Essays in Honor of James Bennett Griffin*, edited by C. Cleland, pp. 205–221. Academic Press, New York.

Folan, W., E. Kintz, L. Fletcher, and B. Hyde 1982. An examination of settlement patterns at Coba, Quintana Roo, Mexico and Tikal, Guatemala: a reply to Arnold and Ford. *American Antiquity* 47: 430–436.

Follis, John and Dave Hammer 1979. *Architectural Signing and Graphics*. Whitney Library of Design, New York.

Ford, James 1954. Comment on A.C. Spaulding, "Statistical techniques for the discovery of artifact types." *American Antiquity* 19: 390–391.

Foster, Sally 1989. Analysis of spatial patterns in buildings (access patterns) as an insight into social structure: examples from the Scottish Atlantic Iron Age. *Antiquity* 63: 40–50.

Foucault, M. 1977. *Discipline and Punishment: The Birth of the Prison*, trans. by Alan Sheridan. Pantheon Books, New York.

Fox, Michael V. (ed.) 1988. Preface. In *Temple in Society*, edited by M. Fox, pp. v–vi. Eisenbrauns, Winona Lake (Wisconsin?).

Friedman, Jonathan 1974. Marxism, structuralism, and vulgar materialism. *Man* 9: 444–469.

Frigout, Arlette 1979. Hopi ceremonial organization. In *Handbook of North American Indians: Southwest*, edited by Alfonso Ortiz, vol 9, pp. 564–580. Smithsonian Institution, Washington, DC.

Fritz, J. 1978. Paleopsychology today: ideational systems and human adaptations in prehistory. In *Social Archaeology: Beyond Subsistence and Dating*, edited by Charles Redman, Mary Berman, Edward Curtin, William Langhorne, Jr., Nina Versaggi, and Jeffery Wasner, pp. 37–60. Academic Press, New York.

Fung Pineda, Rosa 1969. Las Aldas: su ubicación dentro del proceso histórico del Perú antiguo. *Dédalo: Revista de Arte e Arqueología* 9–10: 5–208.

1988. The Late Preceramic and Initial Period. In *Peruvian Prehistory*, edited by R. Keatinge, pp. 67–96. Cambridge University Press, Cambridge.

Fung Pineda, Rosa and Carlos Williams León 1979. Exploraciones y excavaciones en el valle de Sechín, Casma. *Revista del Museo Nacional* 43: 111–155.

Gailey, Christine and Thomas Patterson 1987. Power relations and state formations. In *Power Relations and State Formations*, edited by T. Patterson and C. Gailey, pp. 1–26. American Anthropological Association, Washington, DC.

Gasparini, Graziano and Luise Margolies 1980. *Inca Architecture*. Indiana University Press, Bloomington.

Gayton, Anna and Alfred Kroeber 1927. The Uhle pottery collections from Nazca. *University of California Publications in American Archaeology and Ethnology* 24 (1): 1–46.

Geertz, Clifford 1973. *The Interpretation of Cultures: Selected Essays*. Basic Books, New York.

Gelles, Paul 1990. Channels of power, fields of contention: the politics and ideology of irrigation in an Andean peasant community. Unpublished Ph.D. dissertation, Harvard University. University Microfilms International, Ann Arbor.

Gero, Joan 1990. Pottery, power, and . . . parties! *Archaeology* 43 (March/April): 52–54.

Gibson, James 1960. *The Perception of the Visual World*. Riverside Press, New York.

Gill, Brendan 1987. *Many Masks: A Life of Frank Lloyd Wright*. G.P. Putnam's Sons, New York.

Gillin, John 1947. *Moche, a Peruvian Coastal Community*. Smithsonian Institution, Institute of Social Anthropology, Publication no. 3.

Gisbert, Teresa 1980. *Iconografía y mitos indígenas en el arte*. Editorial Gisbert CIA., La Paz, Bolivia.

Glassow, Michael 1972. Changes in the adaptations of the Southwestern Basketmakers: a systems approach. In *Contemporary Archaeology*, edited by M. Leone, pp. 289–302. Southern Illinois University Press, Carbondale.

Glave, Luis Miguel and Maria Isabel Remy 1983. *Estructura agraria y vida rural en una región andina: Ollantaytambo entre los siglos XVI y XIX*. Centro de Estudios Rurales Andinos, "Bartolomé de las Casas," Cuzco.

Goldberger, Paul 1993. Making a street: forget about logos on the skyline. *The New York Times* (January 24, 1993), p. H30.

Goody, Jack (ed.) 1971. *The Developmental Cycle in Domestic Groups*. Cambridge University Press, Cambridge.

Gossen, Gary 1972. Temporal and spatial equivalents in Chamula ritual symbolism. In *Reader in Comparative Religion: An Anthropological Approach*, edited by W. Lessa and E. Vogt, pp. 135–149. Harper and Row, New York.

Gould, Richard 1990. *Recovering the Past*. University of New Mexico Press, Albuquerque.

Griaule, M. and G. Dieterlen 1954. The Dogon. In *African Worlds*, edited by Darryl Forde, pp. 83–110. Oxford University Press, London.

Grieder, Terence 1975. A dated sequence of building and pottery at Las Haldas. *Ñawpa Pacha* 13: 99–113.

    1978. *The Art and Archaeology of Pashash*. University of Texas Press, Austin.

    1982. *Origins of Pre-Columbian Art*. University of Texas Press, Austin.

    1988a. Radiocarbon measurements. In *La Galgada, Peru: A Preceramic Culture in Transition*, edited by T. Grieder, pp. 68–72. University of Texas Press, Austin.

    1988b. Burial patterns and offerings. In *La Galgada, Peru: A Preceramic Culture in Transition*, edited by T. Grieder, pp. 73–102. University of Texas Press, Austin.

    1988c. Art as communication at La Galgada. In *La Galgada, Peru: A Preceramic Culture in Transition*, edited by T. Grieder, pp. 204–216. University of Texas Press, Austin.

Grieder, Terence and Alberto Bueno Mendoza 1988. The history of La Galgada architecture. In *La Galgada, Peru: A Preceramic Culture in Transition*, edited by T. Grieder, pp. 19–67. University of Texas Press, Austin.

Grieder, Terence, Alberto Bueno Mendoza, C. Earle Smith Jr., and Robert Malina 1988. La Galgada in the world of its time. In *La Galgada, Peru: A Preceramic Culture in Transition*, edited by T. Grieder, pp. 192–203. University of Texas Press, Austin.

Grimes, Ronald 1987a. Portal. In *The Encyclopedia of Religions*, edited by M. Eliade, vol. 11, pp. 452–453. Macmillan Publishing Co., New York.

    1987b. Ritual studies. In *The Encyclopedia of Religions*, edited by M. Eliade, vol. 12, pp. 422–425. Macmillan Publishing Co., New York.

Grobman, Alexander, Lawrence Kaplan, Cesar A. Moran Val, Virginia Popper, and Stanley Stephens 1982. Restos botánicos. In *Los Gavilanes*, edited by D. Bonavia, pp. 147–182. Editorial Ausonia, Lima.

Grollig, Francis X. 1978. Cerro Sechín: medical anthropology's inauguration in Peru? In *Advances in Andean Archaeology*, edited by D. Browman, pp. 351–369. Mouton Publishers, The Hague.

Grottanelli, Cristiano 1987. Kingship: an overview. In *Encyclopedia of Religions*, edited by M. Eliade, vol. 8. pp. 313–316. Macmillan Publishing Co., New York.

Guaman Poma de Ayala, Felipe 1987. *Nueva crónica y buen gobierno*, edited by J. Murra, R. Adorno, and J. Urioste. Historia 16, Madrid.

Guttierez Rodriguez, Rudolfo 1990. *Chan Chan: arquitectura e implicaciones sociales del palacio "Tschudi."* Concejo Nacional de Ciencia y Tecnología y el Instituto Indigenista Peruano, Lima.

Haas, Jonathan 1982. *The Evolution of the Prehistoric State.* Columbia University Press, New York.

1985. Excavations on Huaca Grande, Peru: an initial view of the elite of Pampa Grande, Peru. *Journal of Field Archaeology* 12 : 391–409.

Hage, Per 1979. Graph theory as a structural model in cultural anthropology. *Annual Review of Anthropology* 8: 115–136.

Haggett, P., A. Cliff, and A. Frey 1977. *Locational Analysis in Human Geography.* John Wiley and Sons, New York.

Hall, Edwin T. 1959. *The Silent Language.* Doubleday, Garden City, New York.

1966. *The Hidden Dimension.* Doubleday, Garden City, New York.

1972. Silent assumptions in social communication. In *People and Buildings*, edited by Robert Gutman, pp. 135–151. Basic Books, New York.

Haselberger, Herta 1961. Method of studying ethnological art. *Current Anthropology* 2: 341–355

Hastings, Charles and Michael Moseley 1975. The adobes of Huaca del Sol and Huaca de la Luna. *American Antiquity* 40: 196–203.

Haviland, William 1982. Where the rich folks lived: deranging factors in the statistical analysis of Tikal settlement. *American Antiquity* 47: 427–429.

Hecker, Giesela and Wolfgang Hecker 1985. *Pacatnamú y sus construcciones: centro religioso prehispánico en la costa norte peruana.* Verlag Klaus Dieter Vervuert, Frankfurt.

Hecker, Wolfgang and Giesela Hecker 1977. *Archäologische untersuchungen in Pacatnamú, Nord-Peru.* Indiana, Supplement 9. Ibero-Amerikanisches Institut, Gebr. Mann Verlag, Berlin.

Hellbom, Anna-Britta 1963. The creation egg. *Ethnos* 28: 63–105.

Henry, Donald 1989. *From Foraging to Agriculture: The Levant at the End of the Ice Age.* University of Pennsylvania Press, Philadelphia..

Hernández Príncipe, Rodrigo 1923. Mitología Andina por el licenciado Rodrigo Hernández Príncipe. *Inca* 1: 25–68.

Higuchi, Tadakiko 1983. *The Visual and Sspatial Structure of Landscapes.* MIT Press, Cambridge, MA.

Hill, James and Joel Gunn 1977. Introducing the individual in prehistory. In *The Individual in Prehistory*, edited by J. Hill and J. Gunn, pp. 1–12. Academic Press, New York.

Hillier, Bill and Julienne Hanson 1984. *The Social Logic of Space.* Cambridge University Press, Cambridge.

Hocart, A. M. 1927. *Kingship.* Oxford University Press, Oxford.

Hodder, Ian 1982a. Theoretical archaeology: a reactionary view. In *Symbolic and Structural Archaeology*, edited by I Hodder, pp. 1–16. Cambridge University Press, Cambridge.

1982b. *The Present Past: An Introduction to Anthropology for Archaeologists.* Pica Press, New York.

1984. Burials, houses, women and men in the European Neolithic. In *Ideology, Power and Prehistory*, edited by D. Miller and C. Tilley, pp. 51–68. Cambridge University Press, Cambridge.

1986. *Reading the Past: Current Approaches to Interpretation in Archaeology.* Cambridge University Press, Cambridge.

1991. Postprocessual archaeology and the current debate. In *Processual and Postprocessual Archaeologies: Multiple Ways of Knowing the Past*, edited by R. Preucel, pp. 30–41. Center for Archaeological Investigations, Occasional Paper no. 10, Southern Illinois University, Carbondale.

Huaypa Manco, Cirilo 1977–78. El templo de Tizal, valle de Chao. *Arqueología P.U.C,
Boletín del Seminario de Arqueología* 19–20: 127–136.

Hugh-Jones, Christine 1979. *From the Milk River: Spatial and Temporal Processes in Northwest
Amazonia*. Cambridge University Press, Cambridge.

Huizinga, Johann 1970. *Homo Ludens: A Study of the Play Element in Culture*. Harper and
Row, New York.

Hyslop, John 1984. *The Inca Rroad System*. Academic Press, New York.

1985. *Inkawasi, the New Cuzco*. BAR International Series 234. British Archaeological
Reports, Oxford.

1990. *Inka Settlement Planning*. University of Texas Press, Austin.

Isbell, Billie Jean 1978. *To Defend Ourselves: Ecology and Ritual in an Andean Village*.
University of Texas Press, Austin.

Isbell, William 1978a. El imperio Huari: estado o ciudad? *Revista del Museo Nacional* 43:
227–241. Lima.

1978b. Cosmological order expressed in prehistoric ceremonial centers. *Actes du XLIIe
Congrès des Américanistes*, vol. 4, pp. 269–297. Paris.

1987. City and state in Middle Horizon Huari. In *Peruvian Prehistory*, edited by R.
Keatinge, pp. 164–189. Cambridge University Press, Cambridge.

1991. Conclusion: Huari administration and the orthogonal cellular architecture horizon.
In *Huari Administrative Structures: Prehistoric Monumental Architecture and State
Government*, edited by W. Isbell and G. McEwan, pp. 293–315. Dumbarton Oaks
Research Library and Collection, Washington, DC.

Isbell, William, Christine Brewster-Wray, and Lynda E. Spickard 1991. Architecture and
spatial organization at Huari. In *Huari Administrative Structures: Prehistoric Monumental
Architecture and State Government*, edited by W. Isbell and G. McEwan, pp. 19–53.
Dumbarton Oaks Research Library and Collection, Washington, DC.

Isbell, William and Anita Cook 1987. Ideological origins of an Andean conquest state.
Archaeology 40 (4): 27–33.

Isbell, William and Gordon McEwan (eds.) 1991. *Huari Administrative Structure: Prehistoric
Monumental Architecture and State Government*. Dumbarton Oaks Library and Research
Collection, Washington, DC.

Isbell, William and Katharina Schreiber 1978. Was Huari a state? *American Antiquity* 43:
372–389.

Izumi, Seiichi, Pedro J. Cuculiza, and Chiaki Kano 1972. *Excavations at Shillacoto, Huanuco,
Peru*. The University Museum, Bulletin no. 3. The University of Tokyo, Tokyo.

Izumi, Seiichi and Toshihko Sono 1963. *Andes 2, Excavations at Kotosh, Peru, 1960*.
Kadokawa Publishing, Tokyo.

Jett, Stephen and Virginia Spencer 1981. *Navajo Architecture: Forms, History, Distribution*.
University of Arizona Press, Tucson.

Jimenez Borja, Arturo and Lorenzo Samaniego Roman 1973. *Guía de Sechín*. Comisión de
Reconstrucción y Rehabilitación de la Zona Afectada, Lima.

Johnson, Gregory 1978. Information sources and the development of decision-making
organizations. In *Social Archaeology: Beyond Subsistence and Dating*, edited by Charles
Redman, Mary Berman, Edward Curtin, William Langhorne, Jr., Nina Versaggi, and
Jeffery Wasner, pp. 87–112. Academic Press, New York.

1982. Organizational structure and scalar stress. In *Theory and Explanation in Archaeology*,
edited by C. Renfrew, M. Rowlands, and B. Seagraves, pp. 389–421. Academic Press,
New York.

Johnston, N. 1973. *The Human Cage: A Brief History of Prison Architecture*. Walker and
Company, New York.

Kaplan, Maureen F. and Mel Adams 1986. Using the past to protect the future: marking
nuclear waste disposal sites. *Archaeology* 39 (5): 51–54.

Karsten, Rafael 1949. *A Totalitarian State of the Past: The Civilization of the Inca Empire of Ancient Peru*. Helsingfors, Copenhagen.

Keatinge, Richard 1973. Chimu ceramics from the Moche Valley, Peru: a computer application to seriation. Unpublished Ph.D. dissertation, Department of Anthropology, Harvard University.

1977. Religious forms and secular functions: the expansion of state bureaucracies as reflected in prehistoric architecture on the Peruvian North Coast. *Annals of the New York Academy of Sciences* 293: 229–245.

1982. The Chimu Empire in a regional perspective: cultural antecedents and continuities. In *Chan Chan: Andean Desert City*, edited by M. Moseley and K. Day, pp. 197–224. University of New Mexico Press, Albuquerque.

Keatinge, Richard, David Chodoff, Deborah Chodoff, Murray Marvin, and Helaine Silverman 1975. From the sacred to the secular: first report on a prehistoric architectural transition on the North Coast of Peru. Archaeology 28: 128–129.

Keatinge, Richard and Geoffrey Conrad 1983. Imperialist expansion in Peruvian prehistory: Chimu administration of a conquered territory. *Journal of Field Archaeology* 10: 255–283.

Kelly, David and Duccio Bonavia 1963. New evidence for pre-ceramic maize on the coast of Peru. *Ñawpa Pacha* 1: 39–42.

Kemp, Barry 1983. Old Kingdom, Middle Kingdom, and Second Intermediate Period *c*. 2686–1552 BC. In *Ancient Egypt: A Social History*, edited by B. Trigger, B. Kemp, D. O'Connor, and A. Lloyd, pp. 71–182. Cambridge University Press, Cambridge.

Kendall, Ann 1985. *Inca Architecture: Description, Function, and Chronology*. BAR International Series 242. British Archaeological Reports, Oxford.

Kent, Susan 1984. *Analyzing Activity Areas: An Ethnoarchaeological Study of the Use of Space*. University of New Mexico Press, Albuquerque

1990a. Activity areas and architecture: an interdisciplinary view between use of space and domestic built environments. In *Domestic Architecture and the Use of Space: An Interdisciplinary Cross-Cultural Study*, edited by S. Kent, pp. 1–8. Cambridge University Press, Cambridge.

1990b. A cross-cultural study of segmentation, architecture, and the use of space. In *Domestic Architecture and the Use of Space: An Interdisciplinary Cross-Cultural Study*, edited by S. Kent, pp. 127–152. Cambridge University Press, Cambridge.

(ed.) 1990. *Domestic Architecture and the Use of Space: An Interdisciplinary Cross-Cultural Study*. Cambridge University Press, Cambridge.

Kenyon, Kathleen 1952. *Digging Up Jericho*. Frederick Praeger, New York.

1972. Ancient Jericho. In *Old World Archaeology: Foundations of Civilization*, pp. 89–94 (Orig. April 1954). Readings from *Scientific American*. W.H. Freeeman and Co., San Francisco.

Klein, Cecelia 1982. The relation of Mesoamerican art history to archaeology in the United States. In *Pre-Columbian Art History: Selected Readings*, edited by Alana Cordy-Collins, pp. 1–6. Peek Publications, Palo Alto.

Klymyshyn, Alexandra 1976. Intermediate architecture in Chan Chan, Peru. Unpublished Ph.D. dissertation, Department of Anthropology, Harvard University.

1982. The elite compounds in Chan Chan. In *Chan Chan: Andean Desert City*, edited by M. Moseley and K. Day, pp. 119–143. University of New Mexico Press, Albuquerque.

1987. The development of Chimu administration in Chan Chan. In *The Origins and Development of the Andean State*, edited by J. Haas, S. Pozorski, and T. Pozorski, pp. 97–110. Cambridge University Press, Cambridge.

Knudsen, Vern and Cyril Harris 1978. *Acoustical Designing in Architecture*. Acoustical
Society of America, New York.

Kolata, Alan 1978. Chan Chan: the form of the city in time. Unpublished Ph.D.
dissertation, Department of Anthropology, Harvard University.

1982. Chronology and settlement growth at Chan Chan. In *Chan Chan: Andean Desert
City*, edited by M. Moseley and K. Day, pp. 67–85. University of New Mexico Press,
Albuquerque.

1990. The urban concept of Chan Chan. In *The Northern Dynasties: Kingship and
Statecraft in Chimor*, edited by M. Moseley and A. Cordy-Collins, pp. 107–144.
Dumbarton Oaks Research Library and Collection, Washington, DC.

Kosok, Paul 1965. *Life, Land, and Water in Ancient Peru*. Long Island University Press, New
York.

Kramer, Carol 1982. *Village Ethnoarchaeology: Rural Iran in Archaeological Perspective*.
Academic Press, New York.

Kristiansen, Kristian 1984. Ideology and material culture: an archaeological perspective. In
Marxist Perspectives in Archaeology, edited by M. Spriggs, pp. 72–100. Cambridge
University Press, Cambridge.

Kroeber, Alfred 1925. The Uhle pottery collections from Moche. *University of California
Publications in American Archaeology and Ethnology* 21 (5): 191–234.

1930. Archaeological explorations in Peru. Part II: The Northern Coast. *Anthropology
Memoirs*, vol. 2 no. 2. Field Museum of Natural History, Chicago.

1931. Historical reconstruction of culture growths and organic evolution. *American
Anthropologist* 32: 149–156.

1952. Great art styles of ancient South America. In *The Nature of Culture*, pp. 289–300.
University of Chicago Press, Chicago.

Kubler, George 1962. *The Shape of Time: Remarks on the History of Things*. Yale University
Press, New Haven.

1984. *The Art and Architecture of Ancient America* (3 edition; first published 1962).
Penguin Books, New York.

1991. *Esthetic Recognition of Ancient Amerindian Art*. Yale University Press, New
Haven.

Kuper, Hilda 1972. The language of sites in the politics of space. *American Anthropologist* 74
(3): 411–425.

Kus, James 1972. Selected aspects of irrigated agriculture in the Chimu heartland, Peru.
Unpublished Ph.D. dissertation, Department of Geography, University of California,
Los Angeles.

Lanning, Edward 1967. *Peru before the Incas*. Prentice-Hall, Engelwood Cliffs, NJ.

Larco Hoyle, Rafael 1938. *Los Mochicas*. Casa Editorial la Crónica, Lima.

Larrain, Jorge 1979. *The Concept of Ideology*. University of Georgia Press, Athens.

Lathrap, Donald 1971. The tropical forest and the cultural context of Chavín. In *Dumbarton
Oaks Conference on Chavin*, edited by E. Benson, pp. 73–100. Dumbarton Oaks
Research Library, Washington, DC.

Layton, Robert 1981. *The Anthropology of Art*. Columbia University Press, New York.

Lawrence, Denise and Setha Low 1990. The built environment and spatial form. *Annual
Reviews in Anthropology* 19: 453–505.

Leach, Edmund 1954. *Political Systems of Highland Burma: A Study of Kachin Social
Structure*. Bell and Sons, London.

1968. Ritual. In *International Encyclopedia of the Social Sciences*, edited by D. Sills, vol. 13
pp. 520–526. Macmillan Publishing, New York.

1972. Ritualization in man in relation to conceptual and social development. In *Reader in
Comparative Religion: An Anthropological Approach*, edited by W. Lessa and E. Vogt, pp.
333–337. Harper and Row, New York.

1978. Does space syntax really "constitute the social"? In *Social Organization and Settlement: Contributions from Anthropology, Archaeology, and Geography*, edited by D. Green, C. Haselgrove, and M. Spriggs, pp. 385–401. British Archaeological Reports, International Series 47, vol. II.

LeBlanc, Steven 1971. An addition to Naroll's suggested floor area and settlement population relationship. *American Antiquity* 36: 210–211.

Leone, Mark 1984. Interpreting ideology in historical archaeology: using the rules of perspective in the William Paca Garden in Annapolis, Maryland. In *Ideology, Power and Prehistory*, edited by D. Miller and C. Tilley, pp. 25–35. Cambridge University Press, Cambridge.

Lessa, William and Evon Vogt (eds.) 1972. *Reader in Comparative Religion: An Anthropological Approach*. Harper and Row, New York.

Lévi-Strauss, Claude 1966. *The Savage Mind*. Weidenfeld and Nicolson, London.

Long, Charles 1987. Cosmogony. In *Encyclopedia of Religions*, edited by M. Eliade, vol. 4, pp. 94–100. Macmillan Publishing Co., New York.

Lowenthal, David 1985. *The Past Is a Foreign Country*. Cambridge University Press, Cambridge.

Lumbreras, Luis 1969. *De los pueblos, las culturas y las artes del antiguo Perú*. Editorial Moncloa-Campodonico, Lima.

1974. *The Peoples and Cultures of Ancient Peru*, trans. by B. Meggers. Smithsonian Institution, Washington, DC.

1977. Excavaciones en el Templo Antiguo de Chavín (sector R); informe de la sexta campaña. *Ñawpa Pacha* 15: 1–38.

1989. *Chavín de Huántar en el nacimiento de la civilización andina*. Ediciones INDEA, Lima.

de Lumley, Henry 1969. A Paleolithic campsite at Nice. *Scientific American* 220 (5): 42–50.

Lynch, Kevin 1960. *The Image of the City*. MIT Press, Cambridge, MA.

1968. City design and city appearance. In *Principles and Practice of Urban Planning*, edited by William Goodman, pp. 249–276. International City Planners Association, Washington, DC.

Lyon, Patricia 1981. Arqueología mitología: la escena de "los objetos animados" y el tema de "el alzamiento de los objetos." *Scripta Etnológica* 6: 1105–1108.

MacCormack, Sabine 1991. *Religion in the Andes: Vision and Imagination in Early Colonial Peru*. Princeton University Press, Princeton.

MacDonald, William Lloyd 1965. *The Architecture of the Roman Empire*. Yale University Press, New Haven.

McEwan, Gordon 1984. The Middle Horizon in the valley of Cuzco, Peru: the impact of the Huari occupation of Pikillacta in the Lucre basin. Unpublished Ph.D. dissertation, University of Texas, Austin. University Microfilms International, Ann Arbor.

1990. Some formal correspondences between the imperial architecture of the Huari and Chimu cultures of ancient Peru. *Latin American Antiquity* 1: 97–116.

1991. Investigations at the Pikillacta Site: a provincial Huari center in the valley of Cuzco. In *Huari Administrative Structures: Prehistoric Monumental Architecture and State Government*, edited by W. Isbell and G. McEwan, pp. 93–119. Dumbarton Oaks Research Library and Collection, Washington, DC.

McFeat, Tom 1974. *Small-Group Cultures*. Pergamon Press, New York.

Mackey, Carol 1982. The Middle Horizon as viewed from the Moche Valley. In *Chan Chan: Andean Desert City*, edited by M. Moseley and K. Day, pp. 321–331. University of New Mexico Press, Albuquerque.

1987. Chimu administration in the provinces. In *The Origins and Development of the Andean State*, edited by J. Haas, S. Pozorski, and T. Pozorski, pp. 121–129. Cambridge University Press, Cambridge.

Mackey, Carol and Charles Hastings 1982. Moche murals from the Huaca de la Luna. In *Pre-Columbian Art History: Selected Readings*, edited by Alana Cordy-Collins, pp. 293–329. Peek Publications, Palo Alto.

Mackey, Carol and Alexandra Klymyshn 1981. Construction and labor organization in the Chimu Empire. *Ñawpa Pacha* 19: 99–114.

1990. The southern frontier of the Chimu Empire. In *The Northern Dynasties: Kingship and Statecraft in Chimor*, edited by M. Moseley and A. Cordy-Collins, pp. 195–226. Dumbarton Oaks Research Library and Collection, Washington, DC.

n.d. Political integration in prehispanic Peru. Final Report to the National Science Foundation for 1981–1982. Unpublished manuscript, 1983.

MacLean, Margaret 1986. Sacred land, sacred water: Inca landscape planning in the Cuzco area. Unpublished Ph.D. dissertation, University of California, Berkeley.

Mariscotti de Görlitz, Ana María 1973. La posición del señor de los fenómenos meteorológicos en los panteones regionales de los Andes centrales. Historia y Cultura 6: 207–215

Marquandt, William 1992. Dialectical archaeology. In *Archaeological Method and Theory*, vol. IV, edited by M. Schiffer, pp. 101–140. University of Arizona Press, Tucson.

Martin, Richard 1987. Left and right. In *Encyclopedia of Religions*, edited by M. Eliade, vol. 8, pp. 495–497. Macmillan and Co., New York.

Martinez de Companion, Baltasar Jaime 1978. *Trujillo del Perú a fines del siglo XVIII*. Ediciones Cultura Hispánica, Madrid.

Matsuzawa, Tsugio 1978. The Formative site of Las Aldas, Peru: architecture, chronology, and economy. *American Antiquity* 43: 652–673.

Means, Philip 1931. *Ancient Civilizatons of the Andes*. Charles Scribner's Sons, New York.

Mellaart, James 1975. *The Neolithic of the Near East*. Charles Scribner's Sons, New York.

Mendelsshon, K 1974. A scientist looks at the pyramids. In *The Rise and Fall of Civilizations: Modern Archaeological Approaches to Ancient Cultures*, edited by C. Lamberg-Karlovsky and J. Sabloff, pp. 390–402. Cummings Publishing Co., Menlo Park, CA.

Menzel, Dorothy 1959. The Inca occupation of the south coast of Peru. *Southwestern Journal of Anthropology* 2: 125–142.

1977. *The Archaeology of Ancient Peru and the Work of Max Uhle*. Lowie Musem, University of California, Berkeley.

Menzel, Dorothy, John Rowe, and Lawrence Dawson 1964. The *Paracas Pottery of Ica: A Study in the Style and Time*. University of California Publications in American Archaeology and Ethnology, vol. 50. University of California Press, Berkeley.

Merrifield, Ralph 1987. *The Archaeology of Ritual and Magic*. B.T. Batsford, London.

Middendorf, E. 1973 [1886]. *Perú: observaciones y estudios del país y sus habitantes durante una permanencia de 25 anos*, trans. by E. More. Universidad Nacional Mayor de San Marcos, Lima.

Millones Santa Gadea, Luis 1979. *Las religiones nativas del Perú recuento y evaluación de su estudio*. Institute of Latin American Studies, University of Texas, Austin

(ed.) 1990. *El retorno de las huacas: estudios y documentos sobre el Taki Onqoy siglo XVI*. Instituto de Estudios Peruanos, Lima.

Morgan, Lewis Henry 1881. *Houses and House-Life of the American Aborigines*. Government Printing Office, Washington, DC.

Moore, Jerry 1981. Chimu socio-economic organization: preliminary data from Manchan, Casma Valley, Peru. *Ñawpa Pacha* 19: 115–128.

1985. Household economics and political integration: the lower class of the Chimu Empire. Unpublished Ph.D. dissertation, University of California, Santa Barbara. University Microfilms International, Ann Arbor.

1988. Prehispanic raised field agriculture in the Casma Valley: recent data, new hypotheses. *Journal of Field Archaeology* 15: 265–276.

1992. Review of *Large-Site Methodology: Architectural Analysis and Dual Organization in the Andes* by R. Cavallaro. *Latin American Antiquity* 3: 176–178

n.d. Fieldnotes, excavations at Manchan 1981. Notes in author's possession.

Moore, Sally Falk and Barbara Meyerhoff (eds.) 1977. *Secular Ritual*. Van Gorcum, Amsterdam.

Morris, Brian 1987. *Anthropological Studies of Religion*. Cambridge University Press, Cambridge.

Morris, Craig 1967. Storage in Tawantinsuyu. Unpublished Ph.D. dissertation, University of Chicago.

1972. State settlements in Tawantinsuyu: a strategy of compulsory urbanism. In *Contemporary Archaeology: A Guide to Theory and Contributions*, edited by M. Leone, pp. 393–401. Southern Illinois University Press, Carbondale.

Morris, Craig and Donald Thompson 1985. *Huanuco Pampa: An Inca City and Its Hinterland*. Thames and Hudson, New York.

Moseley, Michael 1972. Demography and subsistence: an example of interaction from prehistoric Peru. *Southwestern Journal of Anthropology* 28: 25–49.

1975a. *The Maritime Foundations of Andean Civilization*. Cummings Publishing Co., Menlo Park, CA.

1975b. Chan Chan: Andean alternative of the preindustrial city? *Science* 187: 219–225.

1982. Introduction: human exploitation and organization. In *Chan Chan: Andean Desert City*, edited by M. Moseley and K. Day, pp. 1–24. University of New Mexico Press, Albuquerque.

1990. Structure and history in the dynastic lore of Chimor. In *The Northern Dynasties: Kingship and Statecraft in Chimor*, edited by M. Moseley and A. Cordy-Collins, pp. 1–41. Dumbarton Oaks Research Library and Collection, Washington, DC.

1992. *The Incas and Their Ancestors*. Thames and Hudson, New York.

Moseley, Michael and Alana Cordy-Collins (eds.) 1990. *The Northern Dynasties: Kingship and Statecraft in Chimor*. Dumbarton Oaks Research Library and Collection, Washington, DC.

Moseley, Michael and Kent Day (eds.) 1982. *Chan Chan: Andean Desert City*. University of New Mexico Press, Albuquerque.

Moseley, M. and C. Mackey 1974. *Twenty-Four Architectural Plans of Chan Chan, Peru*. Peabody Museum Press, Cambridge, MA.

Mosley, Michael and Gordon Willey 1973. Aspero, Peru: a reexamination of the site and its implications. *American Antiquity* 38: 452–468.

Murra, John 1960. Rite and crop in the Inca state. In *Culture and History: Essays in Honor of Paul Radin*, edited by S. Diamond, pp. 393–407. Columbia University Press, New York.

1975. *Formaciones económicas y políticas del mundo andino*. Instituto de Estudios Peruanos, Lima.

1980. *Economic Organization of the Inca State*. JAI Press, Greenwich, CT.

Nabokov, Peter and Robert Easton 1989. *Native American Architecture*. Oxford University Press, New York.

Naroll, Raul 1962. Floor area and population settlement. *American Antiquity* 27: 587–588.

Needham, Rodney (ed.) 1973. *Right and Left: Essays on Dual Symbolic Classification*. University of Chicago Press, Chicago.

Neff, Hector 1992. Ceramics and evolution. In *Archaeological Method and Theory*, vol. IV, edited by M. Schiffer, pp. 141–193. University of Arizona Press, Tucson.

Netherly, Patricia 1976. Local level lords on the North Coast of Peru. Unpublished Ph.D. dissertation, Department of Anthropology, Cornell University. University Microfilms International, Ann Arbor.

1984. The management of late Andean irrigation systems on the North Coast of Peru. *American Antiquity* 49: 227–254.

1990. Out of many, one: the organization of rule in the North Coast polities. In *The Northern Dynasties: Kingship and Statecraft in Chimor*, edited by M. Moseley and A. Cordy-Collins, pp. 461–487. Dumbarton Oaks Research Library and Collection, Washington, DC.

Netherly, P. and T. Dillehay 1986. Duality in public architecture in the upper Zaña Valley, northern Peru. In *Perspectives on Andean Prehistory and Protohistory*, edited by D. Sandweiss and D. Kvietok, pp. 85–114. Latin American Studies Program, Cornell University, Ithaca.

Nials, Fred, Eric Deeds, Michael Moseley, Shelia Pozorski, Thomas Pozorski, and Robert Feldman 1979. El Niño: the catastrophic flooding of coastal Peru. *Bulletin of the Field Museum of Natural History* 50 (7): 4–14 (Part I); 50 (8): 4–10 (Part II).

Niles, Susan 1987. *Callachaca: Style and Status in an Inca Community*. University of Iowa Press, Iowa City.

Nolan, Mary Lee 1991. The European roots of Latin American pilgrimage. In *Pilgrimage in Latin America*, edited by N. Ross Crumrine and Alan Morinis, pp. 19–49. Greenwood Press, New York.

Ocas C., José 1986. *Chan-Chan, palacio Tschudi*. Galeria de Arte Jose Ocas, Trujillo, Peru.

Ohnuki-Tierney, Emiko 1972. Spatial concepts of the Ainu of the northwest coast of southern Sakhalin. *American Anthropologist* 74: 426–457.

1974. *The Ainu of the Northwest Coast of Southern Sakhalin*. Holt, Rinehart and Winston, New York.

O'Neale, Lila and Alfred Kroeber 1930. Textile periods in ancient Peru. *University of California Publications in American Archaeology and Ethnology* 28: 23–56.

Oosten, Jarich 1993. Examining the theoretical discourse on ritual. *Current Anthropology* 34: 106–108.

Ortiz, Alfonso 1969. *The Tewa World: Space, Time, Being, and Becoming in a Pueblo Society*. University of Chicago Press, Chicago.

Ossa, Paul 1973. A survey of the lithic preceramic occupation of the Moche Valley, north coastal Peru. Unpublished Ph.D. dissertation, Department of Anthropology, Harvard University.

Ossio, Juan (ed.) 1973. *Ideología mesiánica del mundo andino*. Colección Biblioteca de Antropología, Lima.

Paredes Ruiz, Victor 1975. *Sechín: posible centro de conocimientos anatómicos y de disección en el antiguo Perú*. El Sol, Cuzco.

Parker Pearson, Michael 1984. Social change, ideology and the archaeological record. In *Marxist Perspectives in Archaeology*, edited by M. Spriggs, pp. 59–71. Cambridge University Press, Cambridge.

Parsons, Jeffrey and Charles Hastings 1988. The Late Intermediate Period. In *Peruvian Prehistory*, edited by R. Keatinge, pp. 190–229. Cambridge University Press, Cambridge.

Patterson, Thomas 1983. Pachacamac – an Andean oracle under Inca rule. In *Recent Studies in Andean Prehistory and Protohistory: Papers from the Second Annual Northeast Conference on Andean Archaeology and Ethnohistory*, edited by D. Kvietok and D. Sandweiss, pp. 159–174. Latin American Studies Program, Cornell University.

Patterson, Thomas and M. Edward Moseley 1968. Late preceramic and early ceramic cultures of the Central Coast of Peru. *Ñawpa Pacha* 6: 115–133.

Pearson, Richard 1986. Jomon introduction. In *Windows on the Japanese Past*, edited by R. Pearson, G. Barnes, and K. Hutterer, pp. 219–221. University of Michigan, Ann Arbor.

Pease G.Y., Franklin 1973. *El dios criador andino*. Mosca Azul, Lima.

1982. *El pensamiento mítico*. Mosca Azul, Lima.

Peebles, Christopher and Susan Kus 1977. Some archaeological correlates of ranked society. *American Antiquity* 42: 421–448.

Pillsbury, Joanne 1993. Sculptural friezes of Chimor. Unpublished Ph.D. dissertation, Columbia University.

Pizarro, Hernando 1970. [1533] Letter of Hernando Pizarro to the Royal Audience of Santo Domingo. In *Reports on the Discovery of Peru*, edited and translated by C. Markham, pp. 113–127. Burt Franklin Publishers, New York.

Pizarro, Pedro 1921. [1571] *Relation of the Discovery and Conquest of the Kingdoms of Peru*, trans. by Philip A. Means. The Cortes Society, New York.

Polanyi, Karl, Conrad Arensberg and Harry Pearson (eds.) 1957. *Trade and Market in the Early Empires: Economies in History and Theory*. The Free Press, Glencoe, IL.

Pollnac, R. 1977. Illusion susceptibility and adaptation to the marine environment: Is the carpentered world hypothesis seaworthy? *Journal of Cross-Cultural Psychology* 8: 425–434.

Poole, Deborah A. 1991. Rituals of movement, rites of transformation: pilgrimage and dance in the highlands of Cuzco, Peru. In *Pilgrimage in Latin America*, edited by N. Ross Crumrine and Alan Morinis, pp. 307–338. Greenwood Press, New York.

Porras Barrenchea, Raul 1959. Cartas del Peru, 1524–1543. *Colección de documentos inéditos para la historia del Perú, III*. Sociedad de Bibliofilos Peruanos, Lima.

Pozorski, Shelia 1987. Theocracy vs. militarism: the significance of the Casma Valley in understanding early state formation. In *The Origins and Development of the Andean State*, edited by J. Haas, S. Pozorski, and T. Pozorski, pp. 15–30. Cambridge University Press, Cambridge.

Pozorski, Shelia and Thomas Pozorski 1986. Recent excavations at Pampa de las Llamas-Moxeke, a complex Initial Period site in Peru. *Journal of Field Archaeology* 13: 381–401.

    1987. *Early Settlement and Subsistence in the Casma Valley, Peru*. University of Iowa Press, Iowa City.

    1992. Early civilization in the Casma Valley, Peru. *Antiquity* 66: 845–870.

Pozorski, Thomas 1975. El complejo de Caballo Muerto: los frisos de barro de la Huaca de les Reyes. *Revista del Museo Nacional* 41: 211–251.

    1980. The Early Horizon site of Huaca de los Reyes: Societal implications. *American Antiquity* 45: 100–110

    1987. Changing priorities in the Chimu state: the role of irrigation agriculture. In *The Origins and Development of the Andean State*, edited by J. Haas, S. Pozorski, and T, Pozorski, pp. 111–120. Cambridge University Press, Cambridge.

Pozorski, Thomas and Shelia Pozorski 1988. An early stone carving from Pampa de las Llamas-Moxeke, Casma Valley, Peru. *Journal of Field Archaeology* 15: 114–119.

    1990. Huaynuná, a late cotton preceramic site on the North Coast of Peru. *Journal of Field Archaeology* 17: 17–26.

Pozorski, Thomas, Shelia Pozorski, Carol Mackey, and Alexandra Klymyshyn 1983. Pre-hispanic ridged fields of the Casma Valley. *Geographical Review* 73: 407–416.

Preucel, Robert (ed.) 1991. *Processual and Postprocessual Archaeologies: Multiple Ways of Knowing the Past*. Center for Archaeological Investigations, Occasional Paper no. 10. Southern Illinois University, Carbondale.

Price, Barbara 1982. Cultural materialism: a theoretical review. *American Antiquity* 47: 709–741.

Protzen, Jean-Pierre 1993. *Inca Architecture and Construction at Ollantaytambo*. Oxford University Press, New York.

Proulx, Donald 1973. *Archaeological Investigations in the Nepeña Valley, Peru*. Research Reports no. 13. Department of Anthropology, University of Massachusetts, Amherst.

    1985. *An Analysis of the Early Cultural Sequence in the Nepeña Valley, Peru*. Research Reports no. 25. Department of Anthropology, University of Massachusetts, Amherst.

Quilter, Jeffrey 1985. Architecture and chronology at El Paraíso, Peru. *Journal of Field Archaeology* 12: 279–297.

    1990. The Moche revolt of the objects. *Latin American Antiquity* 1: 42–65.

Rabinowitz, Joel 1982. La lengua pescadora: the lost dialect of Chimu fishermen. In *Investigations of the Andean Past*, edited by Daniel Sandweiss, pp. 243–267. Latin American Studies Program, Cornell University, Ithaca.

Rabuzzi, Kathryn 1987. Home. In *Encyclopedia of Religion*, edited by M. Eliade, vol. 6, pp. 438–442. Macmillan Publishing Co., New York.

Raimondi, Antonio 1874. *El Perú* (vol. 1). Imprenta del Estado, Lima.

Ramsey, Charles and Harold Sleeper 1988. *Architectural Graphic Standards*. Willey and Sons, New York.

Rapoport, Amos 1969. *House Form and Culture*. Prentice-Hall, Englewood Cliffs, NJ.

Rasnake, Roger Neil 1988. *Domination and Cultural Resistance: Authority and Power among an Andean People*. Duke University Press, Durham, NC.

Ravines, Rogger 1979. Garagay como arqueología experimental. In *Arqueología peruana*, edited by Ramiro Matos Mendieta, pp. 75–80. Centro de Proyección Cristiana, Lima.

    (ed.) 1980. *Chanchan: metropolí Chimu*. Instituto de Estudios Peruanos, Lima.

Ravines, Rogger, Helen Engelstad, Victoria Palomino, and Daniel Sandweiss 1982. Materiales arqueológicos de Garagay. *Revista del Museo Nacional* 46: 135–233.

Ravines, Rogger and William Isbell 1975. Garagay: sitio ceremonial temprano en valle de Lima. *Revista del Museo Nacional* 41: 253–275.

Reese, Thomas (ed.) 1985. *Studies in Ancient American and European Art: The Collected Essays of George Kubler*. Yale University Press, New Haven,

Relph, Edward 1976. *Place and Placelessness*. Pion Limited, London.

Renfrew, Colin 1983. The social archaeology of megalithic monuments. *Scientific American* 249 (5): 152–163.

    1984. *Approaches to Social Archaeology*. Harvard University Press, Cambridge, MA.

Rheinhard, Johan 1985. Chavín and Tiahuanaco: a new look at two Andean ceremonial centers. *National Geographic Research* 1 (3): 395–422.

Richardson, Miles 1980. Culture and the urban stage: the nexus of setting, behavior, and image in urban places. In *Human Behavior and Environment: Advances in Theory and Research*, vol. IV: *Environment and Culture*, edited by I. Altman, A. Rapoport, and J. Wohlwill, pp. 209–241. Plenum Press, New York.

Rodman, Margaret 1985. Moving houses: residential mobility and the mobility of residences in Longana, Vanuata. *American Anthropologist* 87: 56–72.

Romero, Carlos A. 1923. Nota final. *Inca* 1: 70–78.

Rostworowski de Diez Canseco, María 1977. *Etnia y sociedad costa peruana prehispánica*. Instituto de Estudios Peruanos, Lima.

    1981. *Recursos naturales renovables y pesca siglos XVI y XVII*. Instituto de Estudios Peruanos, Lima.

    1983. *Estructuras andinas del poder: ideología y política*. Instituto de Estudios Peruanos, Lima.

    1984. El baile en los ritos agrarios andinos (Sierra Nor-Central, siglo XVII). *Historia y Cultura* 17: 51–60.

    1988. *Conflicts over Coca Fields in XVIth Century Peru*. Studies in Latin American Ethnohistory and History, no. 4. University of Michigan, Museum of Anthropology, Ann Arbor, MI.

Rowe, John 1946. Inca civilization at the time of the Spanish conquest. In *Handbook of South American Indians*, edited by J. Steward, vol. 2, pp. 183–330. Bureau of American Ethnology, Bulletin 143. Smithsonian Institution, Washington, DC.

    1948. The Kingdom of Chimor. *Acta Americana* 6: 26–59.

1954a. *Max Uhle, 1856–1944: A Memoir of the Father of Peruvian Archaeology.* University of California Publications in American Archaeology and Ethnology, vol. 46. University of California Press, Berkeley.

1954b. Absolute chronology in the Andean area. *American Antiquity* 10: 265–284.

1962a. Stages and periods in archaeological interpretation. *American Antiquity* 18: 40–54.

1962b. *Chavín Art: An Inquiry into Its Form and Meaning.* The Museum of Primitive Art, New York.

1963a. Review of *The Shape of Time: Remarks on the History of Things* by G. Kubler. *American Anthropologist* 65: 704–705.

1963b. Urban settlements in ancient Peru. *Ñawpa Pacha* 1: 1–27.

1967. Form and meaning in Chavín art. In *Peruvian Archaeology: Selected Readings*, edited by J. Rowe and D. Menzel, pp. 72–103. Peek Publications, Palo Alto, CA.

1979. An account of the shrines of ancient Cuzco. *Ñawpa Pacha* 17: 1–80.

Rybcsynski, Witold 1989. *The Most Beautiful House in the World.* Viking, New York.

1992. Pale fire (Review of *Disfiguring: Art, Architecture and Religion* by M. Taylor). *New York Review of Books* (November 19, 1992) 39 (19): 43–46.

Rykert, Joseph 1976. *The Idea of a Town: The Anthropology of Urban Form in Rome, Italy, and the Ancient World.* Princeton University Press, Princeton.

Sallnow, David 1987. *Pilgrims of the Andes: Regional Cults in Cusco.* Smithsonian Institution, Washington, DC.

1991. Dual cosmology and ethnic division in an Andean pilgrimage cult. In *Pilgrimage in Latin America*, edited by N. Ross Crumrine and Alan Morinis, pp. 281–306. Greenwood Press, New York.

Salomon, Frank and Gary Urioste 1991. *The Huarochirí Manuscript: A Testament of Ancient and Colonial Andean Religion.* University of Texas Press, Austin.

Samaniego Roman, Lorenzo 1973. *Los nuevos trabajos arqueológicos en Sechín, Casma, Perú.* Larsen Ediciones, Trujillo, Peru.

Samaniego Roman, Lorenzo, Enrique Vergara, and Henning Bischof 1985. New evidence on Cerro Sechín, Casma Valley, Peru. In *Early Ceremonial Architecture in the Andes*, edited by C. Donnan, pp. 165–190. Dumbarton Oaks Research Library and Collection, Washington, DC.

Sanders, William and Barbara Price 1968. *Mesoamerica: The Evolution of a Civilization.* Random House, New York.

Sanders, William and Robert Santley 1983. A tale of three cities: energetics and urbanization in prehispanic central Mexico. In *Prehistoric Settlement Patterns*, edited by E. Vogt and R. Leventhal, pp. 242–292. University of New Mexico Press, Albuquerque and the Peabody Museum of Archaeology and Ethnology, Harvard University, Cambridge, MA.

Santillan, Hernando de 1968. Relación del origen, descendencia, política y gobierno de los Incas. In *Crónicas peruanas de interés indígena*, edited by E. Barba. Biblioteca de autores españoles, vol. 209, Madrid.

Saussure, F. de 1966. *Course in General Linguistics.* McGraw-Hill, New York.

Schaedel, Richard 1951. Major ceremonial and population centers in northern Peru. In *The Civilizations of Ancient America: Selected Papers of the 29th International Congress of Americanists*, edited by S. Tax, pp. 239–243. University of Chicago Press, Chicago.

1988. *La etnografía muchik en las fotografías de H. Brüning 1886–1925.* Ediciones COFIDE, Lima.

1991. Locational symbolism: the Fiesta de los Reyes o del Niño in northern Peru. In *Pilgrimage in Latin America*, edited by N. Ross Crumrine and Alan Morinis, pp. 257–279. Greenwood Press, New York.

Schaffer, Matt and Christine Cooper 1987. *Mandinko: The Ethnography of a West African Holy Land.* Holt, Rinehart and Winston, New York.

Schiffer, Michael (ed.) 1992. *Archaeological Method and Theory*, vol. IV. University of Arizona Press, Tucson.

Schreiber, Katharina 1978. Planned architecture of Middle Horizon Peru: implications for social and political organization. Unpublished Ph.D. dissertation, State University of New York, Binghamton. University Microfilms International, Ann Arbor.

1987a. From state to empire: the expansion of Huari outside the Ayacucho Basin. In *The Origins of the Andean State*, edited by J. Haas, S. Pozorski, and T. Pozorski, pp. 91–96. Cambridge University Press, Cambridge.

1987b. Conquest and consolidation: a comparison of Huari and Inca occupations of a highland Peruvian valley. *American Antiquity* 52: 266–284.

1991. Jincamocco: a Huari administrative center in the south central highlands of Peru. In *Huari Administrative Structures: Prehistoric Monumental Architecture and State Government*, edited by W. Isbell and G. McEwan, pp. 199–213. Dumbarton Oaks Research Library and Collection, Washington, DC.

1992. *Wari Imperialism in Middle Horizon Peru*. Anthropological Papers, Museum of Anthropology, University of Michigan, no. 87. University of Michigan, Ann Arbor.

Scully, Vincent 1975. *Pueblo: Mountain, Village, Dance*. Viking Press, New York.

Seagraves, Barbara 1982. Central elements in the construction of a general theory of the evolution of societal complexity. In *Theory and Explanation in Archaeology*, edited by C. Renfrew, M. Rowlands, and B. Seagraves, pp. 287–300. Academic Press, New York.

Segall, M., D. Campbell, and M. Herskovits 1966. *The Influence of Culture on Visual Perception*. Bobbs-Merrill, Indianapolis.

Service, Elman 1962. *Primitive Social Organization*. Random House, New York.

1975. *The Origins of the State and Civilization: The Process of Cultural Evolution*. W.W. Norton, New York.

Shady Solís, Ruth 1982. La cultura Nieveria y la interacción social en el mundo andino en la época Huari. *Arqueológicas* 19: 5–108. Lima.

Shimada, Izumi 1976. Socioeconomic organization at Moche V Pampa Grande, Peru: prelude to a major transformation to come. Unpublished Ph.D. dissertation, Department of Anthropology, University of Arizona.

1978. Economy of a prehistoric urban context: commodity and labor flow at Moche V Pampa Grande, Peru. *American Antiquity* 43: 569–592.

1981. The Batan Grande–La Leche Archaeological Project: the first two seasons. *Journal of Field Archaeology* 8: 405–446

1987. Horizontal and vertical dimensions of prehistoric states in north Peru. In *The Origins and Development of the Andean State*, edited by J. Haas, S. Pozorski, and T. Pozorski, pp. 130–144. Cambridge University Press, Cambridge.

1990. Cultural continuities and discontinuities on the northern North Coast of Peru, Middle–Late Horizons. In The *Northern Dynasties: Kingship and Statecraft in Chimor*, edited by M. Moseley and A. Cordy-Collins, pp. 297–392. Dumbarton Oaks Research Library and Collection, Washington, DC.

1994. Los modelos de organización sociopolítica de la cultura Moche: nuevos datos y perspectiva. In *Moche: propuestas y perspectivas*, edited by S. Uceda and E. Mujica, pp. 359–387. Travaux de l'Institut Français d'Etudes Andines 79: 7–8; Lima.

Silverman, Helaine 1986. Cahuachi: an Andean ceremonial center. Ph.D. Dissertation, Anthropology, University of Texas, Austin. University Microfilms, Ann Arbor.

1988. Cahuachi: non-urban cultural complexity on the South Coast of Peru. *Journal of Field Archaeology* 15: 403–430.

1991. The ethnography and archaeology of two Andean pilgrimage centers. In *Pilgrimage in Latin America*, edited by N. Ross Crumrine and Alan Morinis, pp. 215–238. Greenwood Press, New York.

1993. *Cahuachi in the Ancient Nasca World*. University of Iowa Press, Iowa City.

Small, David 1987. Toward a competent structuralist archaeology: a contribution from historical studies. *Journal of Anthropological Archaeology* 6: 105–121.

1991. Initial study of the structure of women's seclusion in the archaeological past. In *Gender in Archaeology*, edited by D. Waide and N. Willows, pp. 336–342. University of Calgary, Calgary.

Smith, D. 1975. *Patterns in Human Geography: An Introduction to Numerical Methods.* Russak, New York.

Smith, Jonathan 1987. *To Take Place: Toward Theory in Ritual.* University of Chicago Press, Chicago.

Smole, William J. 1976. *The Yanomama: A Cultural Geography.* University of Texas Press, Austin.

Spalding, Karen 1984. *Huarochiri: An Andean Society under Inca and Spanish Rule.* Stanford University Press, Stanford.

Spaulding, Albert 1953. Statistical techniques for the recovery of artifact types. *American Antiquity* 55: 615–633.

1954. Reply to Ford. *American Antiquity* 19: 391–393.

1960. The dimensions of archaeology. In *Essays in the Science of Culture in Honor of Leslie A. White*, edited by G. Dole and R. Carneiro, pp. 437–456. Cromwell Press, New York.

1973. Archaeology in the active voice: the New Archaeology. In *Research and Theory in Current Archaeology*, edited by C. Redman, pp. 337–354. Willey and Sons, New York.

1988. Distinguished lecture: archeology and anthropology. *American Anthropologist* 90: 263–271

Squier, Ephraim George 1973 [1877]. *Peru: Incidents of Travel and Exploration in the Land of the Incas.* AMS Press, New York.

Stanish, Charles 1989. Household archaeology: testing models of zonal complementarity in the south central Andes. *American Anthropologist* 91: 7–24.

1992. *Ancient Andean Political Economy.* University of Texas Press, Austin.

Steadman, Philip 1976. Graph-theoretic representation of architectural arrangement. In *The Architecture of Form*, edited by L. March, pp. 94–115. Cambridge University Press, Cambridge.

1983. *Architectural Morphology: An Introduction to the Geometry of Building Plans.* Pion, London.

Steward, Julian 1973. *Theory of Culture Change: The Methodology of Multilinear Evolution.* University of Illinois Press, Urbana.

Sutro, Livinston and Theodore Downing 1988. A step toward a grammar of space: domestic space use in Zapotec villages. In *Household and Community in the Mesoamerican Past*, edited by R. Wilk and W. Ashmore, pp. 29–50. University of New Mexico Press, Albuquerque.

Swartz, Marc, Victor Turner, and Arthur Tuden 1968. Introduction. In *Political Anthropology*, edited by M. Swartz, V. Turner, and A. Tuden, pp. 1–41. Aldine Publishing Co., Chicago.

Tabor, Philip 1976a. Analysing communication patterns. In *The Architecture of Form*, edited by L. March, pp. 284–351. Cambridge University Press, Cambridge.

1976b. Analysing route patterns. In The *Architecture of Form*, edited by L. March, pp. 352–377. Cambridge University Press, Cambridge.

Tambiah, Stanley J. 1985. *Culture, Thought, and Social Action: An Anthropological Perspective.* Harvard University Press, Cambridge, MA.

Taylor, Gerald and Antonio Acosta 1987. *Ritos y tradiciones de Huarochirí del siglo XVII.* Instituto de Estudios Andinos and Instituto Francés de Estudios Andinos, Lima.

Tello, Julio 1943. Discovery of the Chavín culture in Peru. *American Antiquity* 9: 135–160.

1956. *Arqueología del valle de Casma – culturas: Chavín, Santa o Huaylas Yunga y Sub-Chimú*. Editorial San Marcos, Lima.

1960a. *Chavín cultura matriz de la civilización andina*. University of San Marcos, Lima.

1960b. *Guía de las ruinas de Pachacamac/Guide to the Ruins of Pachacamac*. Tipografía Peruana, Lima.

Thompson, Donald 1961. Architecture and settlement patterns in the Casma Valley, Peru. Unpublished Ph.D. dissertation, Department of Anthropology, Harvard University.

1964. Postclassic innovations in architecture and settlement patterns in the Casma Valley, Peru. *Southwestern Journal of Anthropology* 20: 91–105.

Tilley, Christopher 1984. Ideology and the legitimation of power in the Middle Neolithic of southern Sweden. In *Ideology, Power and Prehistory*, edited by D. Miller and C. Tilley, pp. 111–146. Cambridge University Press, Cambridge.

1991. *Material Culture and Text: The Art of Ambiguity*. Routledge, London.

Topic, John 1977. The lower class at Chan Chan: a qualitative approach. Unpublished Ph.D. dissertation, Department of Anthropology, Harvard University.

1982. Lower-class social and economic organization at Chan Chan. In *Chan Chan: Andean Desert City*, edited by M. Moseley and K. Day, pp. 145–175. University of New Mexico Press, Albuquerque.

1990. Craft production in the Kingdom of Chimor. In *The Northern Dynasties: Kingship and Statecraft in Chimor*, edited by M. Moseley and A. Cordy-Collins, pp. 145–176. Dumbarton Oaks Research Library and Collection, Washington, DC.

1991. Huari and Huamachuco. In *Huari Administrative Structures: Prehistoric Monumental Architecture and State Government*, edited by W. Isbell and G. McEwan, pp. 141–164. Dumbarton Oaks Research Library and Collection, Washington, DC.

Topic, J. and M. Moseley 1983. Chan Chan: a case study of urban change in Peru. *Ñawpa Pacha* 21: 153–182.

Topic, John and Theresa Topic 1987. The archaeological investigation of Andean militarism: some cautionary observations. In *The Origins and Development of the Andean State*, edited by J. Haas, S. Pozorski, and T. Pozorski, pp. 47–55. Cambridge University Press, Cambridge.

Topic, Theresa 1977. Excavations at Moche. Unpublished Ph.D. dissertation, Department of Anthropology, Harvard University.

1982. The Early Intermediate Period and its legacy. In *Chan Chan: Andean Desert City*, edited by M. Moseley and K. Day, pp. 255–284. University of New Mexico Press, Albuquerque.

1991. The Middle Horizon in northern Peru. In *Huari Administrative Structures: Prehistoric Monumental Architecture and State Government*, edited by W. Isbell and G. McEwan, pp. 233–246. Dumbarton Oaks Research Library and Collection, Washington, DC.

Torero, Alfredo 1986. Deslindes lingüisticos en la costa norte peruana. *Revista Andina* 2: 523–548.

1989. Areas toponímas e idiomas en la sierra norte peruana: un trabajo de recuperacion lingüistica. *Revista Andina* 7: 217–257.

1990. Procesos linguísticos é identificación de dioses en los Andes centrales. *Revista Andina* 15: 237–263.

Toro Montalvo, César 1990. *Mitos y leyendas del Perú*, vol. I: *Costa*. A.F.A. Editores Importadores, Lima.

1991a. *Mitos y leyendas del Perú*, vol. II: *Sierra*. A.F.A. Editores Importadores, Lima.

1991b. *Mitos y leyendas del Perú*, vol. III: *Selva*. A.F.A. Editores Importadores, Lima.

Trigger, Bruce 1983. The rise of Egyptian civilization. In *Ancient Egypt: A Social History*, edited by B. Trigger, B. Kemp, D. O'Connor, and A. Lloyd, pp. 1–70. Cambridge University Press, Cambridge.

1989. *A history of Archaeological Thought*. Cambridge University Press, Cambridge.

1990. Monumental architecture: a thermodynamic explanation of symbolic behaviour. *World Archaeology* 22 (2): 119–132.

Tuan, Yi-Fu 1974. *Topophilia: A Study of Environmental Perception, Attitudes and Value*. Prentice-Hall, Englewood Cliff, NJ.

Turner, Victor 1967. *The Forest of Symbols: Aspects of Ndembu Ritual*. Cornell University Press, Ithaca.

1969. *The Ritual Process: Structure and Anti-Structure*. Aldine Publishing, New York.

1974. *Dramas, Fields, and Metaphors: Symbolic Action in Human Society*. Cornell University Press, Ithaca.

1982. *From Ritual to Theatre: The Human Seriousness of Play*. Performing Arts Journal Publications, New York.

1984. Liminality and the performative genres. In *Rite, Drama, Festival, Spectacle, Rehearsals: Toward a Theory of Cultural Performance*, edited by J. MacAloon, pp. 19–41. Institute for the Study of Human Issues, Philadelphia.

1985. The anthropology of performance. In *On the Edge of the Bush*, edited by E. Turner, pp. 177–204. University of Arizona Press, Tucson.

Turner, Victor and Edith Turner 1978. *Image and Pilgrimage in Christian Culture: Anthropological Perspectives*. Columbia University Press, New York.

Uceda, Santiago, Ricardo Morales, José Canziani, and María Montoya 1994. Investigaciones sobre la arquitectura y relieves polícromos en la Huaca de la Luna, valle de Moche. In *Moche: propuestas y perspectivas*, edited by S. Uceda and E. Mujica, pp. 251–303. Travaux de l'Institut Français d'Etudes Andines 79: 7–8; Lima.

Uceda, Santiago and Elías Mujica 1994. Moche: propuestas y perspectivas. In *Moche: propuestas y perspectivas*, edited by S. Uceda and E. Mujica, pp. 11–27. Travaux de l'Institut Français d'Etudes Andines 79: 7–8; Lima.

Uhle, Max 1902. Types of culture in Peru. *American Anthropologist* 4: 753–759.

Urbano, Henrique 1982. Representaciones colectivas y arqueología mental en los Andes. *Allpanchis* 7(20): 33–83.

1991. Mythic Andean discourse and pilgrimage. In *Pilgrimage in Latin America*, edited by N. Ross Crumrine and Alan Morinis, pp. 339–356. Greenwood Press, New York.

Urton, Gary 1978. Orientation in Quechua and Incaic astronomy. *Ethnology* 17: 157–167.

1979. The astronomical system of a community in the Andes. Unpublished Ph.D. dissertation, University of Illinois. University Microfilms International, Ann Arbor.

1981. *At the Crossroads of the Earth and the Sky: An Andean Cosmology*. University of Texas Press, Austin.

1990. *The History of a Myth: Pacariqtambo and the Origins of the Inkas*. University of Texas Press, Austin.

Van Beek, Walter E. 1991. Dogon restudied: a field evaluation of the work of Marcel Griaule. *Current Anthropology* 32: 139–158.

van Gennep, Arnold 1960 [1909]. *The Rites of Passage*. University of Chicago Press, Chicago.

Vásquez de Espinoza, Antonio 1968. *Description of the Indies (c. 1620)*, trans. by C. Clark. Smithsonian Miscellaneous Collections, vol. 102. Smithsonian Institution Press, Washington, DC.

Verano, John 1986. A mass burial of mutilated individuals at Pacatnamú. In *The Pacatnamú Papers*, edited by C. Donnan and G. Cock, pp. 117–138. Museum of Culture History, University of California, Los Angeles.

Verano, John and Alana Cordy-Collins 1986. HIMI: a Late Intermediate Period mortuary structure at Pacatnamú. In *The Pacatnamú Papers*, edited by C. Donnan and G. Cock, pp. 85–94. Museum of Culture History, University of California, Los Angeles.

Villa, Paola 1983. *Terra Amata*. University of California Publications in Anthropology, Berkeley.

Vincent, Joan 1990. *Anthropology and Politics: Visions, Traditions, and Trends*. University of Arizona Press, Tucson.

Voorhies, Barbara, George Michaels, and George Riser 1991. An ancient shrimp fishery in south coastal Mexico. *Research and Exploration* 7: 20–35.

Vreeland, James 1991. Pilgrim's Progress: the emergence of secular authority in a traditional Andean pilgrimage. In *Pilgrimage in Latin America*, edited by N. Ross Crumrine and Alan Morinis, pp. 229–256. Greenwood Press, New York.

Washburn, Dorothy and Donald Crowe 1988. *Symmetries of Culture: Theory and Practice of Plane Pattern Analysis*. University of Washington Press, Seattle.

Watanabe Hitoshi 1986. Community habitation and food gathering in prehistoric Japan: an ethnographic interpretation of the archaeological evidence. In *Windows on the Japanese Past*, edited by R. Pearson, G. Barnes, and K. Hutterer, pp. 229–254. University of Michigan, Ann Arbor.

Weber, Max 1978. *Economy and Society*, edited by G. Roth and C. Wittich. University of California Press, Berkeley

Weiner, Charles 1880. *Pérou et Bolivie*. Libraire Hachette, Paris.

Weiss, Gerald 1986. Elements of Inkarrí east of the Andes. In *Myth and the Imaginary in the New World*, edited by Edmundo Magaña and Peter Mason, pp. 305–320. Centrum voor Studie en Documentatie van Latjins Amerika, Amsterdam.

Wenke, Robert 1989. Egypt: origins of complex societies. *Annual Review of Anthropology* 18: 129–155.

Werbner, Richard P. 1989. *Ritual Passage, Sacred Journey: The Process and Organization of Religious Movement*. Smithsonian Institution Press, Washington, DC.

West, Michael 1967. Chan Chan, Peru: an ancient urban metropolis: results of a settlement pattern study. Unpublished Ph.D. dissertation, Department of Anthropology, University of California, Los Angeles.

   1970. Community settlement patterns at Chan Chan, Peru. *American Antiquity* 35: 74–86.

Wheatley, Paul 1971. *The Pivot of the Four Quarters: A Preliminary Enquiry into the Origins and Character of the Ancient Chinese City*. Aldine Publishing Co., Chicago.

White, Leslie 1943. Energy and the evolution of culture. *American Anthropologist* 45: 335–356.

   1949. *The Science of Culture: The Study of Man and Civilization*. Grove Press, New York.

   1959. *The Evolution of Culture*. McGraw-Hill, New York.

Whitley, David 1992. Prehistory and post-positivist science: a prolegomenon to cognitive archaeology. In *Archaeological Method and Theory*, vol. IV, edited by M. Schiffer, pp. 57–100. University of Arizona Press, Tucson.

Wickler, Wolfgang and Uta Seibt 1982. Toad spawn symbolism suggested for Sechín. *American Antiquity* 47: 441–444.

Wilk, Richard 1990. The built environment and consumer decisions. In *Domestic Architecture and the Use of Space: an Interdisciplinary Cross-Cultural Study*, edited by S. Kent, pp. 34–42. Cambridge University Press, Cambridge.

Wilk, Richard and Wendy Ashmore (eds.) 1988. *Household and Community in the Mesoamerican Past*. University of New Mexico Press, Albuquerque.

Wilk, Richard and William Rathje (eds.) 1982. Archaeology of the household. *American Behavioral Scientist* 25: 611–74.

Willey, Gordon 1951. The Chavín problem: a Review and Critique. *Southwestern Journal of Anthropology* 7: 102–144.

   1953. *Settlement Patterns in the Virú Valley, Peru*. Bureau of American Ethnology, Bulletin 155, Government Printing Office, Washington, DC.

Willey, Gordon and John Corbett 1954. *Early Ancon and Early Supe Cultures, Chavin Horizon Sites of the Central Peruvian Coast*. Columbia University Press, New York.

Willey, Gordon and Jeremy Sabloff 1974. *A History of American Archaeology*. W.H. Freeman, San Francisco.

Williams León, Carlos 1980. Complejos de pirámides con planta en u: patrón arquitectónico de la costa central. *Revista del Museo Nacional* 44: 95–110.

    1985. A scheme for the early monumental architecture of the central coast of Peru. In *Early Ceremonial Architecture in the Andes*, edited by C. Donnan, pp. 227–240. Dumbarton Oaks Research Library and Collections, Washington, DC.

    1987. Inicios de la tradición arquitectónica andina. In *Arquitectura y arqueología: pasado y futuro de la construcción en el Perú*, edited by Victor Rangel Flores, pp. 27–34. Consejo Nacional de Ciencia y Tecnología, Chiclayo.

Wilson, David 1988. *Prehispanic Settlement Patterns in the Lower Santa Valley, Peru: A Regional Perspective on the Origins and Development of Complex North Coast Society*. Smithsonian Institution Press, Washington, DC.

    1992. Research summary. *Willay* 37/38: 24–26.

Wilson, Peter 1988. *The Domestication of the Human Species*. Yale University Press, New Haven.

Wissler, Clark 1914. Material cultures of the North American Indians. *American Anthropologist* 16: 447–505.

Wobst, H. Martin 1974. Boundary conditions for Paleolithic social systems: a simulation approach. *American Antiquity* 39: 147–178.

    1977. Stylistic behavior and information exchange. In *Papers for the Director: Research Essays in Honor of James B. Griffin*, edited by C. Cleland. Anthropology Papers, Museum of Anthropology, University of Michigan 61: 317–342.

Wright, Henry and Gregory Johnson 1975. Population, exchange, and early state formation in southwestern Iran. *American Anthropologist* 77: 267–289.

Zevi, Bruno 1957. *Architecture As Space: How to Look at Architecture*, trans. Milton Gendel. Horizon Press, New York.

Zuesse, Evan 1987. Ritual. In *The Encyclopedia of Religions*, edited by M. Eliade, vol. 12, pp. 405–422. Macmillan Publishing Co., New York.

Zuidema, R. T. 1964. *The Ceque System of Cuzco: The Social Organization of the Capital of the Inca*. E.J. Brill, Leiden

    1973. Kinship and ancestor cult in three Peruvian communities: Hernandez Principe's account of 1622. *Bulletin de l'Institut Français d'Etudes Andines* 2: 16–33.

    1990a. *Inca Civilization in Cuzco*. University of Texas Press, Austin.

    1990b. Dynastic structures in Andean cultures. In *The Northern Dynasties: Kingship and Statecraft in Chimor*, edited by M. Moseley and A. Cordy-Collins, pp. 489–505. Dumbarton Oaks Research Library and Collection, Washington, DC.

INDEX

NEW STUDIES IN ARCHAEOLOGY

Series editors

Clive Gamble, *University of Southampton*
Colin Renfrew, *University of Cambridge*
Jeremy Sabloff, *University of Pennsylvania Museum of Anthropology and Archaeology*

Ian Hodder and Clive Orton: *Spatial analysis in archaeology*
Keith Muckelroy: *Maritime archaeology*
R. Gould: *Living archaeology*
Stephen Plog: *Stylistic variation in prehistoric ceramics*
Patrick Vinton Kirch: *Evolution of the Polynesian chiefdoms*
Dean Arnold: *Ceramic theory and cultural process*
Geoffrey W. Conrad and Arthur A. Demarest: *Religion and empire: the dynamics of Aztec and Inca expansionism*
Graeme Barker: *Prehistoric farming in Europe*
Daniel Miller: *Artefacts as categories*
Rosalind Hunter-Anderson: *Prehistoric adaptation in the American Southwest*
Robin Torrence: *Production and exchange of stone tools*
Bo Gräslund: *The birth of prehistoric chronology*
Ian Morris: *Burial and ancient society: the rise of the Greek city state*
Joseph Tainter: *The collapse of complex societies*
John Fox: *Maya postclassic state formation*
Alasdair Whittle: *Problems in Neolithic archaeology*
Peter Bogucki: *Forest farmers and stock herders*
Olivier de Montmollin: *The archaeology of political structure: settlement analysis in a classic Maya polity*
Robert Chapman: *Emerging complexity: the later prehistory of south-east Spain, Iberia and the west Mediterranean*
Steven Mithen: *Thoughtful foragers: a study of prehistoric decision making*
Roger Cribb: *Nomads in archaeology*
James Whitley: *Style and society in Dark Age Greece: the changing face of a pre-literate society 1100–700 BC*
Philip Arnold: *Domestic ceramic production and spatial organization*
Julian Thomas: *Rethinking the Neolithic*
E. N. Chernykh: *Ancient metallurgy in the USSR: the early Metal Age*, translated by Sarah Wright
Lynne Sebastian: *The Chaco Anasazi: sociopolitical evolution in the prehistoric Southwest*
Anna Maria Bietti Sestieri: *The Iron Age community of Osteria del'Osa: a study of socio-political development in central Tyrrhenian Italy*
Christine A. Hastorf: *Agriculture and the onset of political inequality before the Inka*
Richard E. Blanton, Stephen A. Kowalewski, Gary Feinman and Laura Finsten: *Ancient Mesoamerica: a comparison of change in three regions, second edition*
Richard Bradley and Mark Edmonds: *Interpreting the axe trade: production and exchange in Neolithic Britain*